Thinking Northern

Spatial Practices
An Interdisciplinary Series in Cultural History, Geography and Literature

2

General Editors:
Robert Burden (University of Teesside)
Stephan Kohl (Universität Würzburg)

Editorial Board:
Christine Berberich
Christoph Ehland
Catrin Gersdorf
Jan Hewitt
Ralph Pordzik
Chris Thurgar-Dawson
Merle Tönnies

Thinking Northern
Textures of Identity in the North of England

Edited by
Christoph Ehland

Amsterdam - New York, NY 2007

Cover Design: Pier Post

The paper on which this book is printed meets the requirements of "ISO 9706:1994, Information and documentation - Paper for documents - Requirements for permanence".

ISSN: 1871-689X
ISBN: 978-90-420-2281-2
©Editions Rodopi B.V., Amsterdam - New York, NY 2007
Printed in the Netherlands

The *Spatial Practices* Series

The series *Spatial Practices* belongs to the topographical turn in cultural studies and aims to publish new work in the study of spaces and places which have been appropriated for cultural meanings: symbolic landscapes and urban places which have specific cultural meanings that construct, maintain, and circulate myths of a unified national or regional culture and their histories, or whose visible ironies deconstruct those myths. Taking up the lessons of the new cultural geography, papers are invited which attempt to build bridges between the disciplines of cultural history, literary and cultural studies, and geography.

Spatial Practices aims to promote a new interdisciplinary kind of cultural history drawing on constructivist approaches to questions of culture and identity that insist that cultural "realities" are the effect of discourses, but also that cultural objects and their histories and geographies are read as texts, with formal and generic rules, tropes and topographies.

Robert Burden
Stephan Kohl

CONTENTS

Acknowledgements 11

Notes on Contributors 13

1 *Christoph Ehland*
  Introduction: Northern England and the Spaces of Identity 15

Chapter I
Infrastructures of Identity

2 *Thomas Leuerer*
  Rethinking Northern Politics: Northern England and Devolution 33

3 *Christoph Schubert*
  Identity and Dialects in the North of England 73

Chapter II
Politics of the Imagination

4 *Stephan Kohl*
  The 'North' of 'England': A Paradox? 93

5 *Jan Hewitt*
  "Such girls as you would hardly see anywhere else in England…": The Regional Feminine in Mary Linskill's Fiction 117

6 *Annisa Suliman*
  Diamonds or Beasts? Re-mapping English Conceptions of Northernness in the Late Victorian Periodical 139

7 *Amir Saeed*
  Northern Racism: A Pilot Study of Racism in Sunderland 163

Chapter III
Landscaping

8 *Marc Crinson*
  Manchester and the "Hypocritical Plan": Architecture,
  Shopping and Identity in the Industrial City — 193

9 *John Belchem*
  The New Livercool: History, Culture and Identity on
  Merseyside — 217

10 *Ian D. Whyte*
  The Lake District and Yorkshire Dales: Refuges from the
  Real World? — 239

11 *Richard Stinshoff*
  Beyond the Industrial Revolution: The Transformation of
  Britain's Canals and their Cultural Meaning — 257

12 *Konrad Schliephake and Keith Sutton*
  Speed, Steam and Nostalgia: The Heritage Railways of
  Northern England — 279

Chapter IV
Mediascapes

13 *Merle Tönnies*
  Constructing an Emblematic Northern Space under
  Thatcherism: The New Brigthon Photographs of Martin Parr
  and Tom Wood — 305

14 *Ralph Pordzik*
  Of Popular Spaces: Northern Heterotopias, Morrissey and
  the Manchester Britpop Scene — 325

15 *Susanne Schmid*
  Between L.S. Lowry and Coronation Street: Salford
  Cultural Identities — 347

16 *Christoph Ehland*
  Classy Northerners: Class, Space and the Wonderful
  Illusion — 363

Appendix

17 *Christoph Singer*
   The Image of the North in Facts and Figures   407

Tables   416

Index   435

Acknowledgements

The initial idea for this volume of essays was conceived during an excursion with a group of students to the North of England in 2003. In this context I want to thank Konrad Schliephake who was both an enthusiastic organiser as well as a knowledgeable guide on this tour.

No book of this kind could come into being without the encouragement and inspiration of a vibrant academic community. The idea for *Thinking Northern* owes much to a cycle of conferences jointly organised by Robert Burden and Stephan Kohl. I am grateful for the opportunity these occasions have given for academic exchange between British and German scholars in the field of cultural history. Furthermore I appreciate the fact that this collection is being published in Rodopi's *Spatial Practices* series of which Robert Burden and Stephan Kohl are the general editors.

The final version of this collection of essays is indebted to the unfailing scholarship and linguistic expertise of Roy Pinkerton. Throughout the birth pangs of this volume his support and friendship has been crucial and his patience with me was matched only by his perspicacity.

Moreover, I must express my gratitude to Elke Demant whose assistance has been invaluable in preparing the typescript and in solving the countless difficulties which had to be dealt with as the book moved towards completion. In this context I also want to thank Yvonne Humm, Angelika Schreiber and Christoph Singer. They have been of constant help in compiling the appendix and the index to this volume and theirs were the friendly faces I needed when things became hectic.

Many thanks must also go to my colleagues at Würzburg University: Guido Fackler, Robert Fajen, Pascal Fischer, Thomas Leuerer and Ralph Pordzik. They have left their imprint on this book through their critical comments, helpful suggestions and ongoing conversations, and in several cases through their own work.

Finally, I want to thank the contributors to this book: without their scholarly expertise and enthusiasm none of this would have been possible.

Würzburg, February 2007   C.E.

Notes on Contributors

JOHN BELCHEM teaches History at the University of Liverpool.

MARK CRINSON teaches History of Art at the University of Manchester.

CHRISTOPH EHLAND teaches English Literature and Cultural Studies at the University of Würzburg.

JAN HEWITT teaches English Literature at the University of Teesside.

STEPHAN KOHL teaches English Literature and Cultural Studies at the University of Würzburg.

THOMAS LEUERER teaches Political Science at the University of Würzburg.

RALPH PORDZIK teaches English Literature and Cultural Studies at the University of Würzburg.

AMIR SAEED teaches Media and Cultural Studies at the University of Sunderland.

KONRAD SCHLIEPHAKE teaches Economic Geography at the University of Würzburg.

SUSANNE SCHMID teaches English Literature and Cultural Studies at the University of Regensburg.

CHRISTOPH SCHUBERT teaches English Linguistics at the University of Augsburg.

Notes on Contributors

CHRISTOPH SINGER teaches German at the State University of New York College at Oneonta.

RICHARD STINSHOFF teaches British Studies at the University of Oldenburg.

ANNISA SULIMAN teaches Journalism and Media Studies at the University of Teesside.

KEITH SUTTON used to teach Geography at the University of Manchester.

MERLE TÖNNIES teaches English Literature and Cultural Studies at the University of Paderborn.

IAN D. WHYTE teaches Historical Geography at the University of Lancaster.

Introduction:
Northern England and the Spaces of Identity

Christoph Ehland

1. This England. What is it?

When in *Richard II* Shakespeare imagined England as "this scept'red isle" which, like a "precious stone set in the silver sea," was a "fortress built by Nature for herself" he not only conveniently forgot about the existence of Scotland and Wales on the same island but he also implied a unity of English identity based upon a geographical demarcation which has never withstood close scrutiny: the vision of unity Shakespeare puts into the mouth of the dying John of Gaunt is part of the propaganda of the Tudor state, artful but still propagandistic. How effective the myth of the "precious stone" has been for England during the last four centuries is still a subject of academic discussion. More important is the fact that already in Shakespeare's time it represented an attempt to paste over the deep fractures which the Wars of the Roses had left in the psychological constitution of England. Although it is more usually mentioned in the context of constitutional reform in the United Kingdom, 'The English Question' is partly an expression of the fact that this powerful myth has more recently become inherently doubtful.

Although the modern roots of regional identities within England reach at least as far back as the hegemonic struggles of the fourteenth century, many aspects of the complex system of regional differentiation which one is confronted with today developed alongside the rapid socio-economic transformation of English society since the eighteenth century: the programmatic title of Elizabeth Gaskell's novel *North and South* alludes to the North-South divide in England. The harsh economic prioritising of the Thatcher years has made this old gulf more visible than it ever was. In part, the recent debate on the identity of England tries to come to terms with this division. Whether they campaign for an English Parliament (see http://www.thecep.org.uk) or discuss their understanding of Englishness (see http://www.theenglandproject.net) those who abjure English unity and thus inevitably turn themselves into prophets of disintegration are many in number. English identity is indeed a difficult topic:

> Some people argue there is no such thing as a shared English culture. They say all those invasions by the Normans and Romans simply left us with a 'hotch potch' of other people's cultures. Paradoxically, this melting pot is what makes England unique. And today's multicultural communities make this mix even more vibrant and interesting. [www.icons.org.uk/introduction]

The Icons Project was designed to find ways of representing the characteristic features of English culture: everyone was invited to write to the organisers and suggest new icons to be added to the existing list. The final choice was made by an advisory board which met four times in 2005 and 2006 and chose from 998 nominations the 74 icons which are now included in an 'iconic' map of England.

Figure 1: The Icons Project: Map of England

However, even if this democratic approach is taken into consideration, one can see that the result clearly reflects the views of the specific group of people who have become involved in the project: the icons they have chosen bespeak their vision of an English identity as one safely rooted in a cultural history stretching from Stonehenge to Ironbridge, from the Lindisfarne Gospels to the Spitfire and from Jane Austen to Sherlock Holmes.

The Icons Project: A selection of 64 of the official 74 icons of Englishness

In many cases one must ask whether these icons depict Britain rather than England. The conflation between these two frames of reference points to the constitutional paradox which represents the root of the problem of an indigenous English identity: how can one demarcate Englishness from Britishness? The Scots have the bagpipes, the kilt, tartan and Nessie all to themselves. But what about the English? Isn't tea also consumed in Scotland and Wales? Doesn't the average Scotsman eat even more fish and chips than his English neighbour? Isn't rugby also played in Scotland and Wales? Isn't the red phone box an iconic feature in landscapes and cityscapes all over the British Isles? How English is a pint of beer? Isn't the Mini a British car rather than an English one? The same may be said about the Rolls Royce, only with the ironic twist that it has recently become German. But that is beside the point.

Recognising the difficulties of giving a clear image to England may help in understanding why regional identities are sometimes considered to be a similarly problematic issue. The icons project is a case in point: it uses iconic features of Englishness which may refer to a particular region but it integrates them into the wider context of a "portrait of England" as a whole. Inevitably, the regional perspective is of secondary significance.

2. The North of England

When Labour's attempt to devolve the regions of Northern England failed in November 2004 for some critics the rejection confirmed their doubt in the existence of separate regional identities in England as a tangible political concept. For these critics devolution means an artificial fragmentation of England's identity. Even for those who speak in favour of devolution there is evidence that the four official electoral regions of Northern England, the North East, the North West, Yorkshire, and Humberside, do not adequately represent the regional affiliations of the people living in the North. Of course, most of the debate is motivated and fostered by England's search for its own identity within the changing setup of the British state.

The proposed political adjustments noted above are the constitutional repercussions of a prolonged period of economic prosperity and dynamic change within British society. The whole country is in a process of political and cultural change and just as Scotland, Wales and Northern Ireland are re-defining their place in the United Kingdom so too are England's regions seeking for their individual identities. It is true that the administrative demarcations of the nine English regions do not necessarily represent a shared sense of cultural identity. Nevertheless, in this context the regional debate may represent the essential way out: if national campaigns for Englishness and England often carry hidden chauvinistic sentiments, focusing on regional patterns ideally emphasises the pluralistic and varied textures of identity in English society.

With the days of Tony Blair in Downing Street coming slowly to their end it seems time to revisit the sites of English identity. For the North of England the long and bitter process of de-industrialisation is slowly drawing to an end. After decades of economic decline, after a time when the heavy industries withered away and coalmining, shipbuilding and textile industry lost their significance, a new air of self-confidence is perceptible in the northern regions. Warehouses and mills are being converted into fashionable apartment buildings or sleek office blocks. The docks and canals, once the arteries of industrialisation, are being integrated into a landscape designed for the leisure-orientated urban classes. Finance and the culture industries are taking over where the grim sweat mills of the North once meant wealth for a few and a hard working life for the masses. Anyone coming to Leeds, Manchester or Newcastle will find a region in transition.

Changing economic patterns are changing the face of Northern England. They will alter the relationship between urban and rural areas. They will transform the social make-up of communities. Will they also change the texture of their identities? And if so, what is identity in the new global cultural economy? Clearly, the idea of fixed and stable identities has been thoroughly dismantled by postcolonial and poststructuralist studies and no longer provides a sensible point of orientation. In the light of this qualification, however, the idea of identities may still serve as a helpful way of indicating the socio-cultural production of a collective sense of belonging. It represents a way of thinking about a particular community which provides at specific moment in time a set of affiliations to relate to in a shifting world. Thinking about regions in transition ideally suits a concept which reflects the discursive, the coincidental, the transitional, the provisional, the fragmented and the imagined nature of postmodern identities. In this sense speaking about 'postmodern identity' is not a contradiction in terms but a chance to emphasise the open and pluralistic discourse about identity that recognises the manifold consciousnesses of transcultural communities.

Thinking Northern looks at the individual tesseras of identity in the North of England which are part of the great mosaic of English culture. With regard to the historical origin and the current transitional state of northern identities it is clear that the idea of the 'North' of England is still a fragmented vision, somewhere along the lines of Wordsworth's daffodils, Manchester Capitalism and Beatlemania. It seems that the perception of what the region is like remains safely locked into traditional views. Often these carry the sediment of decades or even centuries.

3. Perspective of *Thinking Northern*

The aim of the essays collected in this volume is to provide a reality check. What is out there? How do people live and imagine their lives in the North of England? What are the stories that their lives narrate? Do they communicate a collective identity which is particularly northern? In this context the title *Thinking Northern* signals a programmatic understanding of the discourses on identity in the diverse fields of cultural, economic and social activity in the North of England. The essays discuss the changing physiognomy of Northern England and provide a mosaic of recent thoughts on and new critical approaches to regional identity in Britain. Contributors from a wide range of subject areas look at the past, present and future of the people and their environment in the North of England. Their essays discuss how the received mental images of the North are constantly re-deployed, re-used and re-contained in the discourses on identity in Northern England.

The book develops its theme in a variety of ways, from articles that provide a general overview of the present state of affairs in and for the northern regions of England to essays on specific areas of the cultural and social life in the North. The spectrum of the essays covers such diverse topics as the music scene, the heritage industries and new architecture, as well as the representation of northern identity in the arts, literature and film. Four chapters allow for a wide variety of interdisciplinary discussions of the topic.

The first chapter, Infrastructures of Identity, deals with the fundamental societal predispositions which influence and facilitate the discourses on identity in the North of England. In his contribution Thomas Leuerer maps the constitutional territory of regional self-government in England and places the issue in the context of the current debate on devolution. The failure to devolve the North East was a decisive – and possibly calculated – political defeat for the devolution project for England. When in 1997 the Scots, the Welsh and the Northern Irish were offered political representation outside Westminster they embraced the chance to gain more control over their own affairs. In the North of England, however, 78% of the voters did not want this kind of devolution at that particular time. For the time being the official deadlock in the devolution process remains a fact, but the reasons given for its failure are as manifold as they are controversial. Although Leuerer acknowledges that the establishment of the Scottish Parliament and the Welsh Assembly has created a constitutional asymmetry he points out that this kind of anomaly is neither new in the setup of the UK nor should one uncritically associate it with a crucial crisis in UK constitutional affairs. In fact, asymmetry has been a constant characteristic of the British state as it has evolved. With regard to the North of England Leuerer points out that the failure of the referendum on an assembly in the North East ended plans to devolve England into nine self-governing regions. This failure has more to do with the political than the constitutional system of the UK because the referendum on regional self-government was conflated from the beginning with other issues. After all, whether England will be devolved in the same way as Scotland and Wales is of secondary importance because regionalisation in England began long ago and is surely inevitable.

It has been argued that one reason for the failure of the proposals for devolution for the North East was the lack of a sense of shared regional characteristics. The debate on English devolution emphasises the fact that any form of regional autonomy must presuppose a sense of a shared regional identity. Christoph Schubert turns in his essay to language as such a source of identity. As he discusses the linguistic varieties of the northern regions and delineates their particular characteristics it becomes evident how far the notion of northern English is a sociocultural construct. Drawing his examples from literature and film, he illustrates how dialect patterns serve as highly adaptable representational strategies. Seen from this perspective the vernacular is a functional tool for defining identities in the North of England. Particularly when northerners are represented in the popular media is dialect used to convey a sense of identity which not only demarcates an imagined community but also regulates the target group of consumers.

The second chapter of this book, Politics of the Imagination, contains essays which look at the construction of particular images for the North of England. In his essay Stephan Kohl examines the picture of the North as painted by travel writers from the 1920s to the present day and shows how Northern England has persistently been seen and judged from a point of view that takes the Home Counties as its standard of Englishness. Taking into consideration not only the topographical differences of the North but also the socio-economic variety of the region it is clear that its image must deviate from this basic model of perception. Dealing with the imagined North-South divide it is astounding to notice that this perspective not only reveals a predominantly negative picture of the North but far more importantly tends to add a moral dimension to it: the North's failure to impress the literary traveller as being truly English is interpreted not so much as an aesthetic disappointment but as an ideal that is tainted by the connotations of a 'fallen' region. This stigmatising vision of a 'sinful' and thus morally inferior England arises from the contrast between natural beauty and the industrial landscapes in the North. The impact of this kind of thinking is not limited to the strictly aesthetic realm: adjectives like 'rude' and 'simple' are frequently encountered in the travelogues and show that the North is often perceived as being only on the periphery of English civilisation. Of course, an identity constructed from such stereotypes is a shallow yet suggestive grave of metaphors.

How important the perspective of the traveller is for the construction of regional identity also shines through in Janet Hewitt's essay, which offers a glimpse of the intersection between landscape and gender construction in the work of the late-Victorian novelist Mary Linskill. Set on the Yorkshire coast Linskill's novels operate on the borderline between masculine features of northern topography and feminine counter-images of 'home' and 'haven'. Hewitt does not interpret these discourses as an isolated literary phenomenon but shows how Linskill's writing fits into a regional cultural industry that reacts to the transformation of Whitby into a tourist destination during the 1880s. As tourism projects its images onto a region and tends to see its people as part of the landscape Linskill responds in her writing to the dominance of the outsider's preconceived images of the typical northerner. Her fiction is deployed in the discourse arenas in which regional identity is not only produced but also negotiated, reshaped and transformed. Hewitt's understanding of literature is as an integral element in the cultural economy of a region.

A similar awareness of the cultural exchanges of identity is shown by Annisa Suliman. Using examples taken from Victorian periodicals Suliman discusses the societal forces which influence the construction of regional identities. In these publications the popular genre of travel writing presented the North of England alongside the exotic settings of Britain's imperial possessions and thus cast the North as the terra incognita for quasi-imperial exploration. In the elevated yet detached position of the imperial observer one looks at the North and its inhabitants as curiosities which seem as exotic as they appear foreign. Set in the landscapes of the colonial imagination the northerner is turned into a passive object of the imperial gaze and becomes a stock figure loaded with cultural meaning in the mythologies of society. The gaze, however, is that of the London-centred elites and those who belong to the cultural economy of the centralist British state who – from their vantage point of the capital and the South – define what is perceived as provincial and foreign. Suliman shows that a dialectical reading of the commodities of identity construction reveals the figure of the northerner essentially as a vehicle for Victorian anxieties about national unity, class and industry.

The example of the periodicals of the later nineteenth century makes it evident that the media presentation of Northern England calibrates the discourses on the region and provides an instrument for asserting and maintaining the ideological orientation of the societal superstructure of thought. In his study of racism in Sunderland Amir Saeed explores the extent to which the more recent production of media images of Englishness has created conflicts with the postcolonial reality of a multi-cultural and multi-racial society in the North of England. There can be no doubt that the occurrences of 9/11 have deepened the rift between ethnic groups in Britain. The Muslim population in particular feels increasingly alienated. Drawing on empirical data from a survey undertaken among non-white students at the University of Sunderland, Saeed makes clear the extent and effect of racial abuse in the city. He argues that the root of the problem of racism lies in the tendency to think of and define the nation as a culturally unified community: the presentation of northern identity as white, Christian and English-speaking echoes a nostalgic vision of England and builds upon patterns of identity which necessarily exclude minority groups within society.

The essays assembled in the third chapter of the book look at the intersection between identity and space and deal with the cultural practices which the creation of landscapes in the North of England involves. The economic prosperity of recent years in Britain has also started to transform the formerly deprived industrial cities of the North. Cities like Leeds, Newcastle, Manchester and Liverpool are once more marketing themselves as the commercial centres in Northern England. Mark Crinson turns in his essay to Manchester as the prototypical city of the industrial sublime: slums and industry on the one hand and prosperity and consumption on the other. With this polarised vision in mind Crinson discusses the strategies by which Manchester's image as a "fearful industrial city" is being countered and an alternative view constructed. In this context it becomes evident that the proclaimed renaissance of Manchester as a flourishing commercial metropolis is in fact an image which has arisen periodically in the history of the city. By his analysis of architectural displays and developments taken from three distinct historical periods since the 1880s Crinson not only puts into perspective the recent campaigns to improve the city's image but also demonstrates how the city has repeatedly turned to images and settings that create a pre-industrial vision of Manchester. There is a curious continuity in tone and representational strategy running through the Victorian image of 'Old Manchester and Salford' presented at the 1887 Royal Jubilee Exhibition, modern museological reconstructions such as Lark Hill Place at Salford Museum and the newly designed urban space of Exchange Square in Manchester's shopping centre: all tend to eliminate traces of the industrial city from their displays. In its attempt to identify itself as a city of commerce mock-ups of historic localities serve to fit the urban sprawl of Manchester and Salford into the expectations of a tradition of Englishness which essentially spurns the industrial as un-English. Thus integrated into the "hypocritical plan" of the economic arrangements in the city the identity on offer is as arbitrary as it is unauthentic. It plays with a form of nostalgia that aims to make consumers long to retrieve something they had actually never lost.

Similar critical undertones are to be detected in John Belchem's essay, which discusses the changing self-identification of Liverpool from Victorian city-state through the deprived urban sprawl of the 1970s and 80s to its recently announced rebirth as a cosmopolitan city. Within the socio-economic setting of the North of England Liverpool was inclined to define itself with reference to its industrial neighbours such as Manchester and Salford. Built by people who displayed a strong mercenary attitude Victorian Liverpool aspired to be the "second city of the empire", competing with London rather than the cities of the North. The vision of a 'Liverpolis' – a city of commerce, culture and civilisation – found its most pronounced expression in the architectural reinvention of the city during the later Victorian and Edwardian period. The dramatic triad of commercial buildings at the Pier Head gave material substance to the claim of the city's greatness. Ironically, the grand gesture of the buildings facing the Mersey also marked a climactic turning point: Belchem shows how Liverpool's 'otherness' changed from being a source of local pride to being a symptom of its problems and its steep economic decline during most of the twentieth century. Liverpool's self-proclaimed elevated position in Britain made it vulnerable to being picked out as the epitome of what had gone wrong in postwar Britain. More recently, however, Liverpool is being rediscovered as a cultural city; but it remains doubtful whether the polished surfaces of the centre and the water front, the reinvented cosmopolitanism of the city, are simply smoke screens for the tourist imagination rather than a real rebirth of the kind of urban identity which characterised Liverpool in the past as a distinct locale in the North of England.

Like Liverpool the Lake District is often characterised as being in the North but not of it. In his essay Ian Whyte discusses how certain parts of Northern England have developed the image of being refuges from the real world. He traces the impact this designation has on the environment and shows by the example of the Lake District that the protected nature reserve is not a true wilderness area: in fact its functioning as a landscape depends upon a close interaction between the physical environment and human society. Historically, the perception of this part of the region was shaped and categorised by aesthetic landscape concepts that range from Edmund Burke's theory of the sublime and the beautiful to the vision of nature entertained by romantic poets such as William Wordsworth. Along the lines of their prescriptive aesthetics there developed the models of regional geography which still govern the perception of the northern landscapes to the present day. The existence of nature reserves and national parks highlights the deep-rooted dialectics of aesthetic sensibilities in Northern England. Whyte shows how in the Lake District tourism and landscape preservation have become mutually dependent on each other.

It is difficult to ignore the potentially escapist and anachronistic tendencies in the preservation of these landscapes. In his essay Richard Stinshoff looks at the canals and waterways as features of the northern landscape which are closely connected with the region's industrial past. Built as the arteries of industrialisation and once serving the complex logistical needs of the economy of the North of England these old waterways are today being rediscovered and reused in a way that stands in stark contrast to their original purpose. Stinshoff discusses the historical origin of the waterways and their long decline before dealing in detail with the modern initiative to restore these formerly industrial infrastructures. In fact, the reinterpretation of the canal system as part of contemporary leisure culture started in earnest only after the Second World War when Britain began to look back to the nineteenth century as a better time. The nostalgic appeal of the canals and their potential for a wide variety of leisure activities define their place in the collective memory of northern society. The refurbished and reinterpreted canals are becoming part of the regional heritage and represent a staged version of the past: a tame and romanticised narrative of meta-history.

A related aspect of the industrial landscapes of the North is the railway network. Konrad Schliephake and Keith Sutton give a comprehensive account of the reuse of decommissioned railway lines in Northern England. As with the waterways, railway lines are being rediscovered and integrated into the ever-increasing landscape of heritage sites. Schliephake and Sutton point to the economic and social impact of the heritage railways in the North of England. Beyond the petty economic realities of turnover and invested money, however, the restored railway lines play a significant role in the exchanges of the cultural economy of the North of England. The railway enthusiast involved in his local heritage railway line and the tourist who experiences the delights of an old-fashioned steam engine may derive from each of these activities the same sense of regional identity. With regard to the process of appropriation of the formerly industrial landscapes as tourist attractions, however, one may come to ask with Odo Marquard whether this form of remembering the past is rather a systematised way of forgetting about it.[1] What remain are nostalgia and the economic opportunities granted by the tourist industries.

The fourth chapter of *Thinking Northern* contains essays that are concerned with different aspects of the varied mediascape which reflects and communicates the discourses on northern English identity. In her essay Merle Tönnies looks at the representation of the northern seaside town of New Brighton in the work of the photographers Martin Parr and Tom Wood. Discussing the strategies by which each of them creates a representational space that overlays its geographical location she places the images firmly in the context of the ideological conflicts of the Thatcher years. In terms of northern English identity Tönnies points out that even the name of *New* Brighton itself contrasts the northern place with the fashionable Southern seaside resort and thus implicitly revives the deep-rooted emotions of England's North-South divide. If the adjective 'new' once expressed the hopes and prospects of the region Parr and Wood depict the northern town as being caught in the deadlock of economic and social decline. Parr's photography, while described as documentary, constructs emblematic spaces: the common features and activities of the seaside resort are turned into a parody of Thatcherite ideology. The human buzz is alienated and alienating and presented as social criticism. Itself only a derivative of the real Brighton in the South the decline of New Brighton becomes a symbol for the northern crises of identity during the Thatcher years. Although both artists utilise the symbolic quality of New Brighton the message communicated by their work differs: Parr generalises where Wood tries to be specific and where Parr is concerned with presenting a sociogram of the industrial North Wood reveals his concern with his subjects' essential human dignity and raises them above the otherwise degrading and depressing circumstances of their environment. One cannot fail to notice in the photographic art of Parr and Wood a form of silent yet radical resistance against stigmatising images of northern identity. In this context the implied independence of the photographer's lens is crucially important for the con-

---

[1] See Marquard's essay "Homo compensator: Zur anthropologischen Karriere eines metaphysischen Begriffs", 52-53 (in: Odo Marquard (2000): Philosophie des Stattdessen. Stuttgart: Reclam).

struction of the vantage point of the critical but not uninterested observer – this is for example stressed by Wood in his recent book *Photie Man*.

Another cultural space in which the discourses on northern English identity are questioned, countered and realigned is explored by Ralph Pordzik in his essay on Manchester's music scene. Largely focusing on the songs and lyrics of the former Smiths front man Morrissey (Stephen Patrick) he interprets the idea of Northern England in Morrissey's songs as providing a dialogic cultural space and musical community for discussing the divergent fantasies of Englishness. Born in the atmosphere of the devastating economic recession of the late 1970s and 1980s the Manchester music scene represented a form of resistance against domination by the London-based music industry and contributed its own version and vision of its particular sociocultural environment. As a pointedly northern phenomenon Britpop claimed an imaginative terrain on which national and regional values were tested. Seizing upon the available imagery of the national media and contrasting it with local values Morrissey's intent is not so much to separate the various strands of the English tradition as to rearrange them as a hybrid reconfiguration of contemporary culture.

In her essay Susanne Schmid approaches the media production of the cultural identity of Salford and shows that the idea of the North does not rely on geographical demarcations but on 'imagined communities'. Since Robert Roberts's academic study *The Classic Slum* identified Salford as the epitome of working-class communal identity the city has remained, as it were, a screen on to which the fabrications of this ideal are projected. Schmid explores the development of this image and its impact on the understanding of Salford as a particularly northern city by discussing the lyrics of Ewan MacColl, the art of L.S. Lowry and the popular soap opera *Coronation Street*. It seems important to note that Roberts's persuasive account of Salford's working-class life is written in retrospect and thus ties into a generally nostalgic vision of northern Englishness. This perspective is paradigmatic for the media reception and production of the lost spaces and communities of northern working-class culture. There is a marked tendency to depoliticise the imagery of the industrial North and its communities as these are popularised in a nostalgic vision of northern identity.

In the final essay in this section of *Thinking Northern* Christoph Ehland partly returns to the Lake District and discusses the class-specific production and consumption of the conception of the northern landscape in the region. Looking at the deep-rooted dialectics of rural and urban spaces in the image of the North of England Ehland explores the strategies by which literary institutions such as writers' houses and literary museums play their part in the construction of northern identity. In this context the bio-literary space is defined by its otherworldly qualities which effectively turn the geographical space into a cultural reflector of class identity. The interdependencies among class, landscape and cultural institutions constructs a commemorative catch-22 situation: a way out of this only becomes tangible if the cultural practices of the literary site react to the demands of the broad mass-tourist audience and adapt their message to new media requirements. In fact, mass tourism, often blamed for depoliticising and trivialising cultural spaces, may foster a democratisation of landscape conception and thus may also serve to redefine the access to the imagined territories of the collective memory in the North of England.

Finally, the volume is completed by an appendix of statistical material on the North of England which has been compiled and introduced by Christoph Singer. It is clear that all empirical data must be approached carefully. Facts seem to speak for themselves. Singer tries to put them into perspective and highlights their contexts and backgrounds. It is astounding to see that the statistical data still seem to confirm the image of the deprived and predominantly working-class North of England. But do these figures represent a way of thinking northern?

Chapter I
Infrastructures of Identity

Re-thinking Northern Politics?
Northern England and Devolution

Thomas Leuerer

Abstract: Devolution is central to the current process of constitutional change in the UK, especially in Scotland and Wales. Despite the wide constitutional frame, however, England so far has been largely exempt from that process. An attempt to introduce an elected assembly in the North East of England failed in a referendum in 2004. This failure does however not indicate a fundamentally negative approach to regionalism in England.

Key names and concepts: Tony Blair - Gordon Brown; Devolution - North East England - Regionalism - Referendum - English Question - Regional Development Agencies - Nostalgia.

1. Introduction

> *That meeting was a total triumph for Sir Humphrey's strategy. All along he had been seeking to remove the Employment Secretary from the Cabinet, because he saw this as the only way to save thousands of senior officers and MOD officials from exile in the Siberia north of Birmingham.* (Lynn and Jay 1989, 260)

The officers who have to be saved from the threat of an "*exile in the Siberia north of Birmingham*" serve in the British armed forces, and in one episode of the BBC's famous political satire "*Yes Prime Minister*" they are afraid of a cabinet plan which aims at a major relocation of military bases from the South to Northern England, as there were "virtually no troops north of the Wash". For the senior military and departmental civil service staff such a plan is, however, entirely out of the question, because, in short, "civilisation generally would be completely remote" (269).

The metaphor "*Siberia*", a well known derogatory label standing for the periphery in many centralist states, indeed indicates the absence of civilisation: a wilderness where no one from London or the South with any self-esteem would care to live. Unemployment, dreary living conditions, declining industries like mining, shipbuilding or steel have given the North a bad reputation for decades. Not surprisingly, a hierarchical regionalisation of England maps the North Country at the lower end of England while London and the Home Counties mark the seat of influence and wealth (Taylor 1991: 150).

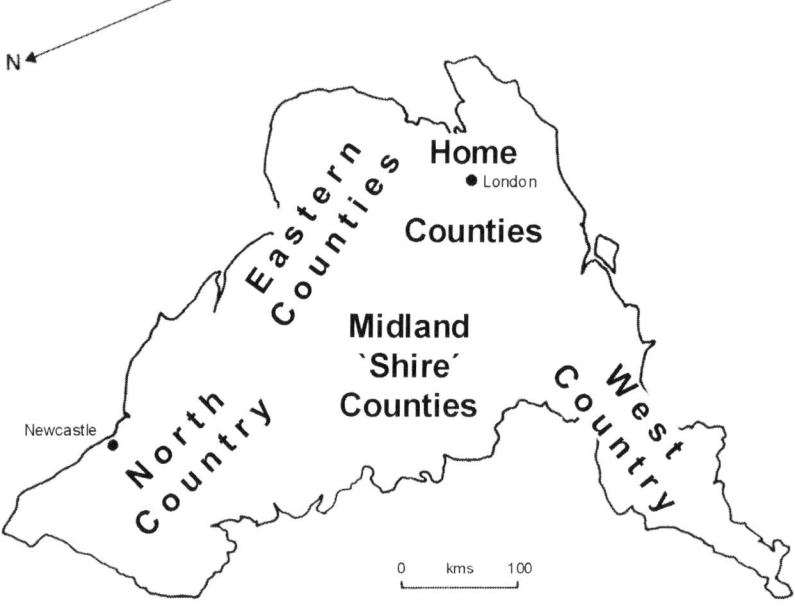

Experiences of decline and deprivation certainly form part of the collective memory in the North: "Here, plainly, were two separate worlds, two different philosophies of life. This was a place beyond the London-Birmingham axis of prosperity, a place with a keen sense of its own identity and its own unique heritage: a place, too, where the hurts of history still had a sting in them."[1] As this volume documents, however, northern identity consists of many different factors, cultural, religious, literary and political. Nostalgia for the days of industrial decline is surely not among them. In addition, the recent economic

---

[1] Graham Turner, *The North Country* (Eyre and Spottiswoode 1967) as quoted in Osmond 1988: 55.

growth and the highly dynamic revitalisation of the region, where "graduates and high-flyers no longer believe that they have to head to the capital if they're going to make a name for themselves", show a fundamentally different picture (Nseir 2004).

The most important change in this respect, however, is the devolution project initiated by the Labour government of Prime Minister Blair immediately following its rise to power in 1997. Regional parliaments for Scotland, Wales and Northern Ireland (though the last of these is still suspended due to the sectarian violence in the six counties) have changed the setup of the United Kingdom considerably. Even ardent opponents of devolution concede today that it has created a new political identity in the devolved areas. The idea of the Scottish Parliament as a 'good thing' has permeated not only official Scottish thinking, but has been readily accepted by much of the Scottish public, so that devolution and 'the Parliament' are now the status quo, as Alan Cochrane admits in Bill Jamieson's critical survey of devolution in Scotland (Cochrane 2006: 110). For a political party in Scotland to ignore this simple fact means a descent into acrimony, as can be seen in the case of the Scottish Conservatives, whose deputy chairman has suggested that devolution might be abolished and the Holyrood parliament scrapped.[2] In an ICM/Scotsman poll in October 2006 the Conservative Party consequently attracted the potential future votes of only 14% of those polled, less than half of the share promised to Labour and the SNP and behind even the Liberal Democrats (see Macdonell 2006).

The example set in Scotland and Wales might initiate similar developments in the English regions, England as a whole still not being devolved. Increasing alienation with Whitehall and strong feelings of regionalism in Scotland and Wales led Peter Taylor in his Maconochie Lecture in 1992 to describe the potential scenario of the break-up of the unity of England, and in consequence possibly even of the United Kingdom, when the North would follow the Scottish example and break away from London (Taylor 1993: 151ff.). The only serious attempt to start devolution in England failed, however, with the "humiliating rejection" in the referendum on the establishment of an elected regional assembly for the North East on 4 November 2004 (*The Guardian* 8 November 2004). While devolution roars powerfully

---

[2] See *The Sunday Times*, 22 October 2006.

in Scotland and, a little less fervently, in Wales, it seems as if Christopher Harvie's aphorism on English regionalism is still as appropriate as ever: *the dog that never barked* (Harvie 1991).

Is "somewhere up north" therefore still the metaphor for an invalid attempt at devolution, failed regionalism, both denied by and denying its own institutional infrastructure and devoid of socio-cultural markers of separateness like the religious or linguistic differentiations that can be found in Wales and Scotland?[3] Was the roaring sound of devolution north of the Tweed echoed only by whingeing in England as the referendum in the North East ended in complete failure? The obviously ambivalent relationship between the English regions and devolution as seen through the example of the "North Country" will be the focus of this paper. Premature conclusions about the failure of Northern English devolution should be treated with care, bearing in mind the 1978 referendum in Scotland and the entire political, cultural and social development which followed that bitter defeat. The result of the 2004 referendum indicates that there are grave problems in implementing devolution in England; it does not, however, provide sufficient proof either that the North suffers from a substantial lack of regional identity or that it would indeed be the "*Siberia north of Birmingham*". The focus lies on the questions why and how the regional identity of the North did not actualise within the framework of devolution and specifically at the referendum of 2004. This requires a closer look at the setup of devolution as a whole as well as a consideration of England's difficult position in that process.

2. Focus: Region, Regionalism, Regionalisation

The wider context for our considerations about the place of Northern England in the devolution project is provided by the debates on regionalism and regionalisation. Regions in this context are territorial units of a nation-state, intermediate between a larger supra-national unit (the United Kingdom) and including smaller sub-regional units (e.g. counties). These territories are subject to changes and eventually

---

[3] Harvie argues though, that instead of linguistic, religious or ethnic markers it has been social status which for most of the time has defined the character of Scotland in relation to England, see Harvie and Jones 2000: 7f.

may even disappear. Their existence depends on the actions of regional players, who constitute a region not as a natural unit but rather as the result of permanent political, administrative, socio-economic and cultural processes. Regions may refer to patterns of identity, based on cultural protagonists (cultural regions), or may also be defined administratively (federal states or regional governments) or functionally (economic or social criteria, etc.). In the process of devolution and decentralisation a supra-regional institution (such as Westminster) implements administrative units without necessarily creating a regional program. The latter depends on the existence or creation of collective regional partners which form part of the definition and implementation of the regional program. Regionalisation therefore creates regional actors in a top-down process, possibly by integrating sub-regional units as well as constituting a collective regional actor to represent the region in the nation-state. Regionalism on the contrary is characterised by the existence of players already in existence within the region. These actors aim to integrate and maintain a regional system and also to provide a collective actor to represent regional autonomy. Regionalisation can therefore be both a prerequisite for as well as the result of regionalism (Schmitt-Egner 2005: 55ff.). Finally, regional planning is the unilateral attempt of the supra regional actor to implement external control over a regional program without regionalisation. *Region* and *Regionalism* have not been invented by revolting autonomists, either in Scotland or in the Basque Country, but are administrative innovations meant to make the territorial dimension more suitable for profitable and effective growth (Krosigk 1986: 174). In its modern connotation, however, we understand regionalism rather as the political mobilisation of a sub-national territorial identity competing against the nation state, especially attacking centralism.

Regionalism as a phenomenon has been widely regarded as being a historical relict of tradition, bound to disappear in the course of modernisation. Nostalgia as an irrational foundation of regionalism should indeed not lead very far. Resistance against amalgamation within a national state is such a traditional source of regionalism, a concept which can be used only very carefully in the British case. Likewise a historical-ethnic regionalism is not applicable in Northern England as most of the respective markers are missing. The view that the North of England is a victim of a form of "internal colonisation", as Michael Hechter has stated with regard to the Celtic periphery, may seem a historically well-founded approach, though one which possibly fails to take full account of the wide range of factors involved (Hechter 1975). Regionalism in a wider perspective is therefore a form of opposition to centralising processes, be they cultural, economic or political.

John Tomaney has pointed out the need to adapt theoretical frames to the English reality, for England would still be "an anomaly in relation to the 'new regionalism'", remaining unfriendly to the charms of regionalism (Tomaney 2001b: 12ff.). Rather than defining England as a distinctive exception he prefers to see it as simply another case that needs to be explained in the context of its own historical and contingent circumstances. Regions and their distinctive markers of separateness and identity have indeed to be regarded in the light of whichever criterion, be it historical, climatic, linguistic, cultural, ethnic, economic or of any other kind, seems to be relevant for the actual question (Esterbauer 1978: 18). Neither a political ideology or a program such as devolution nor a regionalist movement *per se* produces regional identification, for the latter only comes about if the experienced reality is sufficiently interpreted and an appropriate attitude is provided. Regional identities exist as forms of social and cultural practice, discourse and action, not as abstract slogans (Paasi 2003: 478). Modern European regionalisms are, in the words of the political scientist Hermann Lübbe, movements declaring their political demands to be special and unique in their own right, each according to its own individual language and ethnicity, landscape and culture, origin and collective memory without the requirement of any additional justification (Lübbe 1985: 196). One might argue at this early stage that, if a suggested Northern English regionalism were to make its appearance only in the government's White Paper on the Regions, failure was part of the program. Regional pressure for devolution requires both the demand and the political actors willing to keep it on the political agenda and translate it into an actual policy.

The fact that the Northern region, England as a whole and the structure that derives from the Union are three interdependent variables leads to a discussion in three parts: (i) devolution as an attempt on the part of Westminster to meet and pacify regionalist challenges from Scotland and Wales and as part of Labour's concept of constitutional change in the United Kingdom; (ii) the consequences of this process for England, in relation both to its place within a devolved

United Kingdom as well as to its internal governance, and especially the question of the regionalisation of England itself; (iii) the question of regionalism in Northern England, especially the 2004 referendum for an elected assembly in the North East.

3. Devolution in the United Kingdom

Modern regionalism can be traced back to the French Revolution, when it was effectively a movement to preserve the regions which had evolved historically and to abandon the revolutionary departments, especially in Burgundy and the Gironde. French supporters of regionalism claimed that political unity meant strength, whereas administrative unity meant despotism (Esterbauer 1978: 25). In the heydays of the regionalist "rebellions" during the late 1960s and 1970s, the Welsh author John Osmond applied this philosophy to the British situation, urging that the movement towards imposing a centralised and regimented way of life "not yet experienced outside the Communist countries and totalitarian regimes" should be abandoned. Wales was for him the ideal home for a new, decentralised way of politics and business: "If it is not done here, there is little hope for the rest of the world" (Osmond 1974: 161).

Britain, however, looks back on a long tradition of regionalist challenges. The relations between the political and administrative centre of the UK and the regional periphery,[4] as it were, have evolved historically and are therefore of a distinctively individual character. The special status of Scotland deriving from the Treaty of Union (Northern Ireland and Wales later gained similar though not equal status) urged the British state at an early date to offer administrative, cultural and economic concessions toward decentralisation. Jim Bulpitt's study on the territorial dimension of British politics speaks of an "informal empire", which had characterised the pre-union relationship between England and Scotland and which at least during times of peaceful co-

---

[4] In the interdisciplinary context of this volume of essays it is necessary to point out that although the differentiation between centre and periphery – for understandable reasons – has become an embattled concept in postcolonial studies, political science tends to use it to describe the inevitable constitutional imbalances within the political and organisational system of the modern nation state.

existence had to a large extent been continued after the union (Bulpitt 1983: 2, 83). The dichotomy of centre and periphery has always been a characteristic of Great Britain; it is part of the grain of the state, whether it be called England, Great Britain or the United Kingdom (Steed 1986: 102). Debates about "devolution" have a long tradition in Britain, and its history seems to conjure up an almost endless procession of ghosts at the feast (Forman 2002: 38). The term "Devolution" found its way into British political language during the Westminster debates on home rule for Ireland in the nineteenth century (Krosigk 1986: 194). However, devolution as we know it since 1997/98 comes as the climax of a long period of evolution. Two features of substantial importance shall be the focus of the following discussion: pacification as the supreme achievement of devolution and asymmetry as its main characteristic.

3.1 Pacification

Pacification of regional demands has been a traditional feature of British decentralisation, and it still is. Even if it forms a constituent part of a wider concept of constitutional change initiated by the Labour government on gaining power in Westminster in 1997, the devolution project still does not aim at a fully comprehensive program of constitutional and administrative reform. It would be highly questionable to see the reform of the House of Lords and other Labour reforms as part of a single process together with devolution. Instead, devolution is the – so far – successful answer of the core institutions to regional challenges from Scotland and Wales. On the other hand it would be dramatically underestimating the political consequences of the Scotland and Wales Acts from 1997 to reduce them to their *de iure* function of simply devolving competences from the core to the periphery, even if Westminster strictly insists upon its parliamentary sovereignty and has the right to revoke devolution entirely.

> Constitutionally, devolution is a mere delegation of power from a superior political body to an inferior. Politically, however, devolution places a powerful weapon in the hands of the Scots and the Welsh; and, just as one cannot be sure that a weapon will always be used only for the specified purposes for which it may have been intended, so

also one cannot predict the use which the Scots and Welsh will make of devolution. [...]

Constitutionally, the Scottish Parliament will clearly be subordinate. Politically, however, it will be anything but subordinate. For the Scotland Act creates a new locus of political power. Its most important power will be one not mentioned in the Act at all, that of representing the people of Scotland. The basic premise of devolution, after all, is that there is a separate political will in Scotland. [...]

It will thus not be easy to bring into play the constitutional restraints in the Scotland Act. For it would be difficult to imagine an issue more likely to unite Scottish opinion than a conflict between the Scottish Parliament and a remote, London-based government. Even if London were to get its way in the end, this would probably be at the cost of considerable political disaffection and loss of support. In practice, therefore, Westminster will find it extremely difficult to exercise its much-vaunted supremacy. (Bogdanor 2001: 288f.)

Quoting Bogdanor's characterisation of devolution at length is well worth while. It provides us with the fundamental ambiguity of Blair's devolution project. In theory, the constitutional restraints put the entire process of devolution at the mercy of the core-state's institutions. Practically, however, devolution produced results which may not have been intended by Tony Blair and created political realities which Westminster can only change at an unreasonably high political cost.[5] An independent political will in Scotland and Wales cannot be ignored in Westminster. Even the national parties no longer present an effective means of disciplining the periphery. Unlike many politicians in German state parliaments, members of parliament in Scotland or Wales do not see themselves as aiming for a career in central government. MPs with seats in London and Edinburgh/Cardiff have even chosen to regard their regional representation as a matter of greater importance to them (Sturm 2002: 57).

Any model for the spatial division of power must include a statement about the respective forms of government and society. Democracies necessarily divide power between central and non-central elements of government, but as Lijphart has shown, different types of democracies may vary considerably in this regard. In a majoritarian

---

[5] Michael Howard, then chairman of the Conservative Party, acknowledged this fact at his party's convention in Dundee in May 2004: "We Conservatives will make devolution work for Scotland. That is my pledge here to you today, The Scottish parliament is here to stay", *Edinburgh Evening News*, 14 May 2004.

democracy like Britain, central government in theory must control both the central apparatus as well as the non-central, potentially competing governments such as the devolved governments in Wales and Scotland. Federalism and decentralisation are inspired by the opposite aim (Lijphart 1999: 186). One might argue that in terms of Lijphart's classification of different degrees of federalism and decentralisation the UK has moved from being unitary and decentralised to being semi-federal. The centre granted some of its component regional units extensive autonomy, as had been done before in Spain in the case of Catalonia, the Basque Country, Galicia and other regions, without becoming formally a federal state. Differences between federal systems and devolution, important as they may be in terms of constitutional law and political theory, tend to vanish in practice. Bogdanor suggests that the categories merge, especially with the Scottish Parliament operating vis-à-vis Westminster in a quasi-federal system of government (Bogdanor 2005: 85). There are certainly strong reasons to think so, but the ultimate proof has not been presented yet. The UK may be semi-federal, but it is still – at least – also semi-unitary. Federalism is the fundamental distribution of powers among multiple centres, not a mere devolution of powers from a single centre down (Elazar 1997: 239). Non-centralisation *per se* is not equivalent to federalism; it takes a distinctive will to decentralise power, a substantial part of which is being exercised at regional levels. Even if we credit Prime Minister Blair with aiming at a type of devolution in the UK which applies those standards, the fundamental principle of parliamentary sovereignty theoretically gives a Conservative government the power to recall devolution. This ought to be possible, as Bogdanor rightly expects, only at an unreasonably high political cost, which will, however, depend on the regional political identity of the devolved regions. Historically, constitutional traditionalists like Dicey had always been ardent critics of any form of federalism, but even the Scots and the Welsh during the nineteenth century had no strong notion for a federal idea. The furthest one could think was "home rule all round" (Kendle 1997: 61). The national consciousness and political identity of modern Scots are of course very different from this. The modern approach to devolution and the growing difference in political culture between England and Scotland, as *The Guardian* diagnosed ("There is no longer such a thing as British political life" (*The Guardian* 8 November 2001), suggest that a possible conflict between Westminster and Holyrood would indeed prove the semi-federal character of the UK.

A possible answer to this question might reflect the ability of the British state to withstand even such significant shocks as devolution, something Alan Trench considers a phenomenon which is itself worth further consideration and investigation (Trench 2005: 17). "The more things change the more they stay the same" is his characterisation of intergovernmental relations within the devolved UK (Trench 2004: 165ff.). There was no urgent need for fundamental changes, especially regarding Scotland, whose special status had always been respected to an extent many Scots could accept. At least the Lowlands had not been among the regions troubling Whitehall most:

> The way in which Scotland was now governed gave them room to do so. N. T. Phillipson characterises its position as being, like that of the American colonies, one of 'semi independence'. Draft legislation about Scottish affairs was generally vetted by Scottish lawyers in Scotland. Though Walpole brought Scottish patronage firmly under the British Treasury, the few Englishmen given posts north of the Border were greatly outnumbered by Scots preferred to positions in England. (Calder 1981: 535)

Preserving a unified civil service is one of the checks and balances of devolution. The Home Civil Service, always a pillar of the British state, has been affected by devolution but has not been entirely devolved itself. The Civil Service Code needed only some adjustments, not a fundamental reform. Thus, the importance of a homogeneous service and of Britain as a uniform administrative space could be respected and at the same time the administration made available for the devolved institutions. Within the areas of devolved competences, the Home Civil Service in Scotland or Wales reports to the respective member of the Scottish/Welsh government, not to Whitehall (Parry 2002). Under conditions of favourable Labour governments or coalitions in London, Edinburgh and Cardiff this system has so far produced a climate of informality and loose conventions. Devolution as a whole, however, has only been possible by relying on Britain's long-standing administrative tradition and it will face its acid test if the political climate should change. The ultimate question still needs to be answered and the clarification of the blurred lines of responsibilities might well end in a redefining of devolution (Trench 2004: 190).

There is, however, a second dimension to the basic process of the administration of the devolved UK. The treaty of 1707 was not a document so perfect in legal terms that it left nothing open to interpretation. Rather, it left many legal problems unanswered. The union created failed to reach its full potential and resulted in a union state much more than a unitary state (Bogdanor 2001: 14f.). Day-to-day business was and still is the realm of the Civil Service. This state of affairs is now under revision, but most probably without any intention on the part of the Labour government to destroy it. This may be a first hint towards explaining why the government has more problems devolving England as the core state of the UK: if England and Britain blended into one another, this would mean a much more fundamental alteration of the UK whereas concessions to the periphery can still leave the continuity of the whole unaffected. It should also help one to understand Whitehall's attitude towards preserving as much of the unitary – or unified – administration as is needed. The Civil Service is at the heart of the devolution project, juggling its various loyalties and facing new challenges hitherto unknown. Civil Services anywhere tend to react in such situations with caution and as devolution is an evolutionary project, civil servants cannot react to what they do not yet know. So far the Home Civil Service has resisted attempts to create territorially separate services, and it remains to be seen whether it can continue to do so in the future (McMillan and Massey 2004: 247).

3.2 Asymmetry

A compelling aspect of the devolution project is its asymmetrical character. While executive devolution can rely on a longstanding tradition which needs adoption rather than fundamental change, its asymmetric character affects more the parliamentary dimension of the devolution project. Since 1707, there has only been a UK Parliament replacing both the Scottish Parliament in Edinburgh and the English Parliament at Westminster (which was also responsible for Wales). Only Stormont in Belfast, the regional assembly for Northern Ireland, represents a regional parliamentary tradition, one which has been suspended since 1972 because of the civil war in Northern Ireland. The new quasi-federalist design gave Scotland a new or reconvened parliament, depending respectively on one's point of view, with primary legislative powers over a number of devolved affairs. The same provisions have been made for Northern Ireland, but the failure of both parties involved in the civil war to function in a cooperative way in the Northern Ireland Assembly led to suspensions, the last of which in 2002 still results in direct government from London. Recent Anglo-Irish talks in St. Andrews provided for the joint direct rule of Northern Ireland from London and Dublin in the event of any further suspension. Much to the disappointment of Welsh regionalists, the Welsh Assembly in Cardiff has only been provided with secondary legislation such as statutory instruments and orders, leaving the Assembly the weakest of the three regional parliaments so far, bearing in mind, of course, that England is still "the odd one out", the only non-devolved part of the UK. Even if the referendum in the North East had been successful, the proposed regional assemblies in England would have had no legislative powers at all and only very restricted functions.[6] The powers outlined in the White Paper are described as being "disparate, with a paucity of responsibility in key areas" (Hopkins 2004: 255).

In detail this means for Scotland a parliament acting largely independently within the restraints of the Scotland Act 1997, creating a distinctively Scottish system of government and, as can be seen after eight years of devolution, a distinctively Scottish political culture, e.g. concerning the voting system which introduces elements of proportional representation as opposed to the Westminster model of first-past-the-post. Scotland is also provided with a Scottish Executive under a Scottish First Minister and his Cabinet. The First Minister is not, as is usually the case in parliamentary democracies, elected by the parliament but is appointed by the Queen, just like the Prime Minister of the UK.[7] The most striking difference from the (abortive) Scotland Act 1978 lies in the question of privilege. The government had learned the lesson Prime Minister Callaghan had suffered in 1979, when the referendum on Scottish devolution failed not least because of the question of responsibilities for the proposed Scottish Parliament. So the Scotland Act 1998 lists the *reserved* matters, not the *devolved*.

---

[6] Cabinet Office and Department for Transport, Local Government and the Regions: *Your Region, Your Choice: Revitalising English Regions*, Cm 5511 (London: Stationery Office 2002).

[7] For these details see Bogdanor 2001 and Bradley 1997.

This means that anything not specifically reserved for the central government lies automatically within the legislative powers of the Scottish Parliament. This includes mainly questions of domestic policy, home affairs, and legal, cultural, health, social and environmental policies. Reserved matters include most of the classic functions which must be preserved at national level, such as foreign policy, defence, constitutional matters and others. The Scottish Parliament also has a direct relationship with the Crown, so that no additional approval of the passing of legislative acts by the Secretary of State for Scotland is needed. On the other hand provisions have also been taken to ensure that the Scottish Parliament does not abuse its powers. Westminster preserved its right to make laws for Scotland and could thus continue to legislate even on devolved matters (Bogdanor 2001: 202ff.). This possibility is of course largely hypothetical: "In England, the sovereignty of Parliament continues to correspond to a genuine supremacy over 'all persons, matters and things'. In Scotland, by contrast, it is becoming to mean little more than a vague right of supervision over the Scottish Parliament, together perhaps with the power in a pathological situation, such as afflicted Northern Ireland in 1972, to abolish that Parliament." The formal assertion then is empty, so long as it is unaccompanied by political supremacy. The term 'devolution' may be misleading as Bogdanor remarks, implying not just a mere delegation of powers but creating a quasi-federal relationship between devolved Scotland and Westminster (Bogdanor 2005: 84).

Wales on the contrary enjoys a far less advanced degree of devolution. This may be seen in relation to the much longer history of Wales being incorporated into England. The National Assembly for Wales – Cardiff does not have a parliament like Edinburgh – has only executive legislative functions and no primary legislative powers as is the case with the Scottish Parliament. This is, of course, a permanent deprivation and humiliation for Welsh nationalists and is not likely to be continued. The Welsh Assembly cannot be content with subordinate legislation transferred from UK ministers within narrow areas of competence. In other respects, the Welsh Assembly follows the example of the Scottish Parliament with its members elected in single-member constituencies as well as by proportional representation. Likewise, there is a Welsh Executive Committee with a First Secretary leading it. In both devolved regions there is no separate Civil Service, as has been mentioned before.

What role remains then for the centre? Michael Keating uses the dichotomy of the UK being a union state rather than a unitary state, the harbinger of a new type of union of nations and regions (Keating 2004). He sees the United Kingdom as an asymmetrical federation, reflecting the asymmetrical political and social realities in a necessarily asymmetrical constitution. Objections focussing on the disadvantaged status of the English and the Welsh compared to the Scots can be countered with the argument of "devolution on demand", leaving it to the respective regions to decide whether or how far they want to be devolved. Devolution on demand precludes enforced regional parliaments for regions if there is no such demand, but necessarily includes the asymmetries mentioned above. These may be fitting and widely accepted, but there has to be scrutiny by a corrective central government to avoid unwanted competition between the regions (Wilks-Heeg 2002: 10). The centre in that respect has to fulfil the function of a mediator and arbitrator to solve such potential conflicts, provided of course that the centre is interested in playing such a role. The traditional separate *high* and *low* politics in Britain seem to be counterproductive in that respect. Members of the Welsh Assembly complain bitterly about the slow and disinterested way Westminster is treating their resolutions for proposed legislation by the UK Parliament. It can take up to 18 months until Westminster finally places a Welsh resolution on its agenda. This atmosphere of humiliating asymmetry only culminates in competition between Wales and Scotland – a *"devo war"* (*The Scotsman* 16 January 2004). On the other hand, asymmetrical devolution has a supportive effect on the regional consciousness of the individually distinct devolved regions, in contrast to symmetrical devolution as found in France (Cole 2004).

While devolution-on-demand proved very successful in Scotland and Wales, it becomes clear why the English question is as crucial as it is painful for any UK government, especially one formed by the Labour Party. First, Scotland regained elements of sovereignty never surrendered entirely in 1707 and formally affirmed by an act of self-determination in the referendum of 1997. At its opening session, Winifred Ewing carefully declared the Scottish parliament, adjourned in 1707, to be reconvened.[8] Secondly, the English regions have so far

---

[8] Which is debatable since in 1707 the Scottish Parliament was not adjourned but was dissolved.

not reacted in a way similar to Scotland and Wales to the promise of devolution and therefore may rightfully be granted less strong assemblies – a question we need to investigate further in the following sections of this paper. Thirdly, the centre has not undergone any substantial transformation in the process of devolution and refuses to countenance reform, leading to what Keating sees as a new form of union (Keating 2004: 331).

Another cause for a certain amount of unease in the Labour party regarding devolution and home rule lies in its socialist heritage. Socialists stress class, not regional heritage. Devolution might even damage national solidarity by sharing benefits and burdens. Furthermore Labour had to make socialism "English" in order to reach wider parts of the electorate. Of course there have always been dedicated Scottish and Welsh nationalists in the party. Labour, however, has been from the beginning one of the important institutions fostering national unity. In this concept, "England" and "Britain" blended into one (Ward 1998). Blair has never been able to solve this dilemma: his superficial euphoria stands in a strange contrast to the failed decentralisation of his own party, for example in failing to give more independence and weight to Welsh Labour (McAllister 2001: 158). The Labour Party itself is still organised along devolutionary lines; although there exists a Scottish Labour Party, the national party reserves certain powers in the same way as the Westminster Parliament. In addition, a Scottish Policy Forum is meant to develop Scottish Labour policies. Whether the Scottish Labour Party would be prepared to risk an open confrontation with the national party can hardly be predicted until some conflict of interest should occur to break up the harmony between Scottish and British Labour (Shaw 2003).

Devolution is a process still full of dynamic and unpredictable outcomes. So far it has not led to final steps either to a federal UK or to independence for the fringe nations. The latter is still an option at least for Scotland, as can be seen by the numerous contributions to the publicity marking the 300th anniversary of the Union with England which focus on independence. A common feeling of Britishness, however, might some day be dearly missed, as Lord Lang of Monkton fears:

> People no longer see themselves as British; they think of themselves first as Scottish or English, and the idea of being British is gradually

disappearing. [...] Now that may not seem to matter very much, but when the crunch comes, when issues get difficult, when times are hard, my feeling is that is when it will become apparent just how much the United Kingdom has fragmented. (Kahn 2002)[9]

Clearly, there is an implicit imperative to solve the anomalies, especially those concerning the asymmetries in the devolution setup. In Lijphart's terms, the UK today is less centralist and unitary than it was, but still far from being truly federal or decentralised (Gamble 2006: 33). Despite the characterisation of the UK as being "quasi-federal", Jeffery and Wincott complain with good reason that the post-devolution UK lacks a clear normative underpinning (Jeffery and Wincott 2006: 10). What is the UK for since devolution and what public patterns are going to develop? To a large extent this is due to the unsolved English question.

4. Devolution for England – Devolution in England

More than half of the respondents in the British Social Attitudes survey (2003) in England preferred their country to be governed as it has been for centuries, with legislation passed by the UK Parliament; only a minority of 24% expressed the wish for regional assemblies, this desire being strongest in the North East and weakest in the South East (Curtice 2006: 121ff.). This suggests that the English, while being remarkably tolerant towards the developments in Scotland and Wales, are more or less uninterested in devolution for themselves. The question of how England can fit into devolution, however, cannot be solved by simply not asking it. So far, England has opted out of devolution, but the dynamics of the process of constitutional change will eventually require arrangements to be made for England as well (Hazell 2007: 7). Until it becomes inescapable, England's role in the UK "may well remain bound by the same virtual conspiracy of silence as for most of the twentieth century" (Sandford 2002: 790).

The longstanding tradition of England being identical with the centre and the fact that its sheer size and weight make it the core state

---

[9] Also critical is Marwick: "Veteran class warriors, trendy postmodernists and exuberant celtic nationalists declared that the very notion of there being a unified nation state called 'Britain' was now disintegrating." (2003: 419)

of the UK renders its situation far more complex than that of the nations on the periphery. Constitutionally, England does not even exist: there has not been an English Parliament since 1536 and there is no administrative institution like an "English Office" (Bogdanor 2001: 266). There are two dimensions which have to be considered: firstly, a proper place has to be found for England in the Union and secondly a decision has to be made as to whether England should be treated as a whole or whether the English regions should enjoy devolution as well. The latter leads us to the case study of the North East, so the question of England and the Union will be considered first.

4.1 England in a Devolved UK

The United Kingdom is described as a union of four nations working in practice, but not in theory. A comparison of its quasi-federalism with other federalist systems would suggest that the UK must be quite unstable (Hazell 2006b: 37). This is, however, not the case. The "anomaly" (Tomaney 2001b: 12ff.) of England's situation is widely accepted and, as the surveys suggest, this anomaly is in England's interests. If one accepts asymmetry as one of the major – positive – characteristics of devolution in the UK, would asymmetry then not include the right of the English to preserve their status quo, as it has been of such good use to them for such a long time? Since the question of devolution for England threatens neither the status of any of the other British nations nor UK politics *per se*, there would be no grave consequences for the stability of the United Kingdom if the English were to continue to opt out of devolution. Asymmetry after all has a far older tradition in Britain than the idea of home rule all round and England is part of that tradition: "The English can live with untidiness, so long as it works" (Hazell 2006b: 53). The ultimate answer to that lies in the hands of the English themselves.

There are a number of further options for defining England's role in the Union more clearly and for giving it a stronger voice:

(a) *English votes on English Laws*. A possible solution to the West Lothian Question, the anomaly that Scottish MPs in Westminster can decide on laws concerning purely English matters while English MPs can no longer debate matters devolved to the Scottish Parliament, would be that only English MPs should have the right to vote on English laws in Westminster. As the table below shows, this idea enjoys widespread public support. At first sight, it seems to be convincing as well. There are, however, serious questions attached to this option.

Parliamentary rules and such an 'in and out' solution do not correspond, as Bogdanor has shown. Which would be exclusively *English* matters and who would decide on that question? The West Lothian Question cannot be answered by special parliamentary arrangements for one part of the country (Bogdanor 2001: 228ff.). Also, there is no exclusively *English* party in Westminster and the Conservative and Unionist Party in particular must realise that it is very much in its interests not to produce such a public image of itself.

(b) *An English Parliament.* With devolved parliaments working in Edinburgh, Cardiff and Belfast, what would be more logical than to create one for England, presumably in London? This would mean that the United Kingdom would finally emerge as a federation of the four nations living within the British Isles, each enjoying a parliament with asymmetrically devolved competences.

The major argument against this solution is England's sheer size: like it or not, England is the dominant nation comprising more than 80% of the population and with superior economic capacity. Since most English domestic matters would be clearly more important than UK matters, what role would be left for Westminster? A national parliament that is inferior to one of the sub-national parliaments is simply unthinkable. A federation with one of its parts being so predominant cannot work properly, as can be seen by the example of Germany, where Prussia presented a major problem of a similar type (Hazell 2006a: 224). Because of its dominance Prussia created a disturbing situation for German federalism. Throughout the era of the German Empire and especially during the initial phase of the Republic in 1919, there were numerous attempts to partition Prussia into several federal states comparable in size and importance with the other German states. Arnold Brecht, a German political scientist, advised the Allied powers in a research project on Germany's position in European postwar reconstruction to divide Prussia into several federal states in order to create a stable federal system (Brecht 1945). To follow this pattern would mean dividing England as well into several regions, each with its own regional assembly.

Though the idea of an English Parliament is strongly advertised by the "Campaign for an English Parliament" (CEP), a non-partisan organisation voicing English nationalism, it does not appear on the political agenda, lacking the support both of the population and of the political elites. However, a recent poll carried out for the BBC's Newsnight, where 61% of voters in England would support the claim for their own parliament, indicates that this might change. Still, both Labour and the Conservatives stand united in their rejection of an English Parliament (see Mulholland 2007).

(c) *English independence*. Probably in reaction to the established nationalisms of the Scots, Welsh and Irish, some voices demand that England follow suit and consequently accept the break-up of Britain or, even more strongly, want to declare England itself an independent state. Among these, Simon Heffer's book *Nor Shall my Sword. The Reinvention of England* (Heffer 1999) is one of the powerful statements of English self-consciousness:

> The strong sense of identity, both cultural and national, that the Irish, Scots and Welsh have developed, has helped fuel the political movements of separatists in those countries. It has made them believe not just that they could face, but that they actively want a future apart from England. Now, the English must do the same, if they are to cope with the realities of a disunion that may be forced upon them. […]
>
> If it helps all sides to come to terms with these developments, there should be a general recognition that the English are doing this because the Scots, by gesturing that they may break the Union, effectively leave the English with no option but to reinvent themselves. The alternative […] is for England to cease to be a nation altogether, but instead to take its place in a Europe of the regions. (Heffer 1999: 36f.)

Voices like this, however, find no public resonance at all: support on all levels is negligible and despite the existence of an "English Independence Party", independence is not a political option worth discussing (Hazell 2006a: 228). Interestingly enough, though, the *Neue Zürcher Zeitung* from Switzerland expects an independent Scotland to play a vital role in the European Union, thanks to its claims to 90% of the North Sea oil and gas resources, whereas England, despite its dominant status within the British Isles, would lose influence on the international stage (Waser 2007).

Among the options described above it becomes pretty clear that only two have sufficient feasibility to provide England with a workable way ahead: to preserve the status quo, a political decision by non-deciding, or, if it proves capable of giving an acceptable answer, to allow English regionalisms to actualise on the institutional level in a democratic way.

4.2 Devolution in England

The English may be tolerant toward the claims of the other nations and indifferent toward the status of England in the Union, but they nonetheless have of course a huge interest in good governance for England. Might decentralising the government of England and regionalism be the answer to the English question, not a complete one, as Hazell observed, but the best at hand now? (Hazell 2006a: 236)

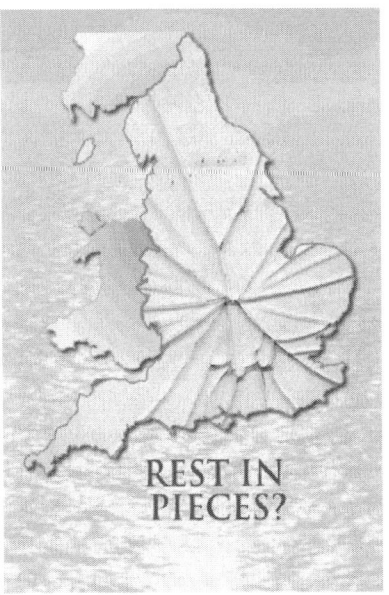

The first argument to be dismissed in that respect is that regionalism would ostensibly be unknown or even strange to the English. This is the main argument behind the illustration above, arguing in favour of *one* English parliament rather than a number of regional assemblies.[10] However, even if support for regionalism is not equally strong throughout the English regions, the suggested homogeneity is only a chimera. "The North is in England, but never quite of it", claimed Austin Mitchell, then Labour MP for Grimsby in a study on the English question published by the Fabian Society (Mitchell 2000: 46). Likewise it is not impossible that because of its economic strength the South East of England might develop a more positive attitude towards regionalism, though there is up to now little support for regional government there (John et al. 2002). The anti-European notion behind Heffer's quote ("The alternative [...] is for England to cease to be a nation altogether, but instead to take its place in a Europe of the regions", Heffer 1999: 36) may be popular, but not realistic. Exponents of a pro-European ideology rather see a chance for a new democratisation of England within the European project, free of the "dead weight of 'Britain' and 'Britishness'" (Preston 2004: 207).

There are, however, some reasonable suggestions for solving the problem of English governance:

(a) *Elected regional assemblies.* Dividing England into nine regions would create units comparable in size to Scotland and Wales, which, however, would not be balanced since those regions would differ in terms of economic capacity. The regional assemblies as they had been designed before 2004 'died' with the North East referendum. This may be largely due to a substantial lack of competence for the regional governments, which have been criticised as inadequate "talking shops" (Hazell 2006a: 232). The plan laid out in the White Paper on the regions[11] needs to be amended with stronger competences for the regions in the same way as had been done with the Scotland and Wales Bills in 1979 and 1997. Regional assemblies though are entirely feasible.

(b) *Modified administrative devolution.* Despite the defeat in the North East referendum, or maybe precisely for that reason, implementing functional regionalism seems to have made substantial pro-

---

[10] <http://www.thecep.org.uk>, 31 January 2007. CEP stands for "Campaign for an English Parliament".

[11] Cabinet Office and Department for Transport, Local Government and the Regions: *Your Region, Your Choice: Revitalising English Regions*, Cm 5511 (London: Stationery Office 2002).

gress. Government Offices, Regional Development Agencies and regional assemblies are the focus of an emerging new set of policy actors and are gaining a momentum of their own (Sandford 2006b). This may well fit into a top-down regionalism preferred by Whitehall and seemingly by the business community as well (Lodge and Mitchell 2006). However, for any policy actor *really* interested in regionalism and in trying to give the respective region its own voice in the political system, functional regionalism, alas, cannot offer any satisfactory perspective. Its main achievement would be just a stronger, more far-reaching and better-organised presence of central government in the regions (Jeffery and Mawson 2002: 717). No exponent of political regionalism can accept this and it is argued that at a certain point functional regionalism eventually turns into political regionalism. Yet the multinational constitutional questions of the UK do not correspond with the English Question, as the relationship between England and her regions is replicated elsewhere among European unitary states with the need for new meso levels (Keating 2006). Interestingly, Robert Hazell expects this as a "safer prediction" for England, lasting for some while and, possibly, for ever (Hazell 2006a: 233). The same can be said about the mistrust of stronger local government and elected mayors. Hazell summarises the potential answers to the "English Question" (Hazell 2006b: 41):[12]

	Elite support	Mass support	Comments
Strengthen England's place in the Union			
English parliament	Low	Low: 16-19 % (Hazell 2006c)	English parliament would risk being as overburdened and remote as Westminster
English votes on English laws	Conservative Party policy (2001 and 2005)	60% support in England, 50 %. support in Scotland	Major issue if UK government has a small majority. Unlikely to be implemented by a Conservative government.
English independence	Negligible	Negligible	

---

[12]   Chart slightly changed here.

Decentralise government of England

Elected regional assemblies	Labour Party (1997 and 2001) and Liberal Democrat Policy; opposed by Conservatives	24 % in 2003, highest in North, lowest in South and East	Little likelihood in near future, following defeat in November 2004 referendum in North East.
Administrative regionalism	Labour Party policy	Little public knowledge or interest	Regional chambers exist, and powers and functions slowly growing.
City regions	Low	Minimal	Need not cover whole of England.
Revive local government	No party with stringent proposals	Public seem to share some of national politicians' mistrust of local government competence[13]	High standards and national targets for public services militate against local autonomy.
Elected mayors	Low	High in opinion polls, less when tested in local referenda	Might also be linked to city regions.

5. Regionalism in Northern England and the North East Referendum

A conclusion at this point might indicate that England is indeed opting out of the devolution process and is doing so because the English do not care about devolution. Truly, regionalism is the dog that never barks. By a majority of almost four to one the voters in the North East defeated the proposed regional government: 77.9% "No" vs. 22.1% "Yes". Is the idea of "Thinking Northern" simply not strong enough to prevail in the political arena? After all, most English people want to continue to be governed by a UK Parliament and their support for re-

---

[13] Opposition to regional government from a different angle may also originate from Whitehall, where centralism is taken as a mean of protection for inherited values such as culture or civilisation in general – or to put it once more in the words of Sir Humphrey from *Yes Prime Minister*: regional government would mean that the Civil Service has less power, which would not be wrong per se, but lead to the unfortunate corollary that the wrong people get more power, see Lynn and Jay 1989: 392f.

gional assemblies is not nearly as extensive as it was in Scotland. It would still, however, be too easy to judge English regionalism as both powerless and hopeless. A closer look at the example of the North East should enable us to see things clearer. Three steps should help us to do so. First, there has to be found a cleavage which could find its expression in the political arena, secondly, this division needs actors and content to make its way on to the political agenda and thirdly, aspects of the referendum already carried out in the North East should be carefully studied.

5.1 A North-South Cleavage in England

Cleavages are social ruptures dividing a society along certain lines of conflict. Among the four major cleavages identified by scholars, two are specifically interesting in our context. The conflict between core and periphery has already been defined as being one of major importance for the UK. Is it, however, relevant within England as well? After all, the other predominant division in Great Britain has been and still is class, and the conflict between capital and labour and the social deprivation of the North may well fall under that cleavage. Church-state and city-country oppositions do not seem to be of major importance here and will be ignored.

This is not the place for literary excursions on the North, but the social stability of the North-South divide can hardly be better demonstrated than by Elizabeth Gaskell's *North and South* (1855). At that time, the class division was still less important than what has been described as a "division – part geographical, part economic, part psychological [...]. From this perspective, the vertically integrated community or economic interest, not its internal stratifications of class, was the central component of what, in emblematic shorthand, came to be known as the 'North-South' divide" (Powell 2002: 39). This divide lasted until the present day, as Austin Mitchell proves in his strongly worded 'Manifesto for the North':

> The North is in England, but never quite of it. There is a northern identity, a northern difference and little solidarity with 'Englishness' – a Home Counties, R.P. speaking, service-centred, rentier-ruled, elitist identity focussing on, and dominated by the Great Wen. The North

> feels itself different but defines itself by more than just reacting against the South [...]. (Mitchell 2000: 46)

The North is not a nation like Scotland or Wales and the North-South divide is not a nationalist issue. The North, though, differs from the rest of the English regions in its greater sense of identity and stronger regional feelings. More than for any other region, this can be said about the North East; as a matter of fact, Tomaney constructs the idea of English regionalism mostly around developments there (Tomaney 2006). Is it, however, justified to speak of a regional identity strong enough to constitute a fourth nation in Britain along with Southern England, Scotland and Wales? Osmond expected in the 1980s that the old North-South cultural and economic rift would widen to the point of the birth of a second English nation (Osmond 1988: 18). The "orgy of prosperity" did indeed create a deep North-South divide in this period (Weight 2002: 591). Still, the North did not exhibit the kind of politically attuned regional consciousness typical of other European countries. The deeply felt cleavage, though, remains:

> While ultimately accepting both the standard placing of northern identity within the hierarchy of English allegiances and its limitations as an intellectual construct, it remains vitally important to acknowledge the undoubted power and potential that it has possessed. The sheer extent and continuity of hostility to 'London', the 'South', the 'southeast', or whatever label its opponents chose has been apparent in every cultural form [...] and at every point in time, and with the strong likelihood that it has intensified over the course of the twentieth century as the provincial-metropolitan relationship has become ever more imbalanced. (Russell 2004: 275)

This distinctively anti-Southern, anti-Thatcherite attempt to create or strengthen regional political identity is orientated towards the regional community, but there is in addition another, more business-orientated, more top-down approach towards promoting the private economic sector and the regeneration of the region (Lanigan 2001: 105f.). It is rather evident that the former is supported by a neo-Thatcherite business community aiming at socio-economic self-reliance in the North East as much as at Victorian industrial prosperity. The latter approach is of course aligned more with the political left and with academic circles, strongly anti-Thatcherite but due to its central planning also anti-Blairite. As many Scots have lost faith in 'Britain', in the same way many northerners who think like this have lost faith in 'England', and are maybe even dreaming of achieving a form of regional socialism (Lanigan 2001: 116). The agony of de-industrialisation, which at the beginning of this essay stood for the bad reputation of the North is currently being reinterpreted as a means of revitalisation by investing in iconic cultural projects promoting a sense of identity with, e.g. the Newcastle/Gateshead area. Clearly a culture-led regeneration is being set against a business-led one (Miles 2005).

The question which remains open is why northern regional consciousness has not been, or has not sufficiently been, politically attuned. A core-periphery conflict is fundamentally a cultural conflict and as the last quote in particular demonstrates, it is one that extends over generations. In order to gain political impact, a social cleavage has to make its way to an organisational level, where interest groups, especially political parties, represent the respective segments of society and push their claims on to the political agenda. This is quite easily demonstrated by the examples of Scotland and Wales, where non-partisan pressure groups like the Scottish Constitutional Convention as well as nationalist parties like the SNP and Plaid Cymru have continuously been representing the regionalist cause and have fought for it on all levels, regional as well as national. It is considerably more difficult to find counterparts for Plaid Cymru and the SNP in Northern England. Since the North cannot provide a 'nationalist' party, the burden of promoting the regional identity lies on the shoulders of the regional levels within the national parties and other interest groups.

Since the Labour Party is the predominant political force in the North – the Conservatives being in any case opposed to the idea of regionalism and devolution – one should expect that at national level the party would promote regionalism in order to support the Labour government, which after all, at least in public, supported devolution for the English regions. However, as we have seen before, the Labour Party is facing problems in devolving its party structures and while one may be willing to accept *Scottish* Labour, a 'Northern' Labour does not seem to be within the limits of organisational constraint for Labour. Austin Mitchell's 'Manifesto for the North' includes a rather angry attack on his own party's policies:

> To change metaphors, the North is the spectre at the devolution 'feast' only to be served an anorexic's diet. The three regions of 'True North'

> are the vanguard of the campaign for regional devolution and elected assemblies. [...] Yet they are denied the same treatment that Scotland received. Labour dominates the North even more than Scotland or Wales and no nationalist party or other competitor threatens its electoral hegemony there. This explains why the North got no consideration and led angry North Eastern MPs to disrupt the first devolution proposals and eventually forced government to buy them off by the establishment of regional development agencies with 'regional chambers' to represent wider opinion. This isn't enough. (Mitchell 2000: 46)

The unfortunate fate of the first Scottish referendum on devolution and the role of Labour at that time indicate the risk of undertaking such an enterprise in the North East, should the Labour party be divided on that issue. In fact, in the North East especially Labour has a long tradition of regionalist debates. In no other region have Labour MPs been more attached to their claims and debates have not always been friendly.[14] In 2004, despite the strong support of Chancellor Gordon Brown, the Labour Party did not support unanimously the 'Yes'-campaign in the referendum. Blair hardly did good service to the cause of devolution admitting to the *Northern Echo* during the campaign that he had once been a devolution sceptic (Sandford 2005: 97). He committed himself rather late to the referendum in the North East (Tickell et al. 2005: 492). Opposition, however, was diverse and not just at the national level but at the regional level as well; it should also be remembered that only one in four Labour Party supporters voted 'Yes' (Rallings and Thrasher 2005).

This does not imply, however, that without euphoric support from Labour the cause of English regionalism would have been lost from the start. Especially in the North East, the debate left the confines of the Labour Party discourse and took place mainly within cross-party organisations like the "Campaign for a Northern Assembly" (1992) and the "North-East Constitutional Convention" (1999) (Tomaney 2006: 172). The latter especially, chaired by the Bishop of Durham, showed parallels to the Scottish example – but without the same success. The NECC specifically worked on the case for a de-

---

[14] Tomaney 2006: 168ff. See also Tomaney 1999. There are similar problems between the Northern Trade Union Congress (NTUC), which is willing to participate in devolution, and the centralised structures of the national Trade Union Congress (TUC), see O'Brien et al. 2004.

mocratic renewal in government at sub-national level. Central government does not give sufficient attention to the problems of Northern England. The structure which comprises the Government Office for the North East, the Regional Development Agency (RDA) and the regional chamber (the would-be assembly) has been criticised as not being transparent and as speaking with a divided voice rather than with a single regional one. The rather complex and difficult governance for the North East was to be replaced by a structure centred on the assembly. Learning from the Scottish experience, the NECC proposed the introduction of a "Civic Forum" to focus on civil society, while RDA and One North East are rather administrative in character (Tomaney 2000: 387, 392). One North East is a classical quango, with the regional tier of politics as installed by the government lacking local accountability and transparency (not to mention any representation of the population's diversity) (Robinson and Shaw 2001: 478).

Interestingly, at present it is the RDAs which are offering the best chance of progress towards regionalism, though it has turned out that northern identity tends not to be easily recognisable at an institutional level, the potential growth of regionalism still lies within the capacity of nascent regional organisations (Bond and McCrone 2004). So the failure of the North East referendum does not necessarily mean the end of regionalism in the North of England; if this should, however develop in a more administrative direction, some important initiatives from the NECC might be lost.

Supporters and opponents of an elected regional assembly for the North East finally organised themselves into two major and a number of smaller campaign groups. Campaigning in favour of devolution was "Yes4theNorthEast" (Y4NE), while the opponents were "North East Says No Ltd." (NESNO). NESNO was supported by elements of the landed establishment as well as leading businessmen, the Conservative Party and the UK Independence Party; their main campaigning argument, a mere soundbite, was "vote no to more politicians", the projected assembly being represented by a huge inflatable white elephant. The campaign organisation lay in the hands of professionals from the London-based "New Frontiers Foundation", a Eurosceptical interest group using the North East referendum as a dry-run for a possible referendum on the endorsement of a European Union constitution. As if to prove that the campaign was split along business-led and culture-led lines, Y4NE enjoyed public support mainly from the social and cultural spheres, such as a Manchester pop band or the President of Newcastle FC (Sandford and Hetherington 2005: 96).

Given that a BBC North poll from March 2002 indicated that 72% of respondents supported an assembly, while only 19% opposed it, and that in a MORI poll in August 2004 the support had diminished to 39% but the opposition had risen to only 22%, the swing against an elected assembly for the North must have been considerable (Sandford and Hetherington 2005: 99). The question is, how could that happen?

5.2 The Referendum

To understand the functioning and outcome of a referendum it is advisable to abstract it from questions of regional identity or democratisation. Katy Knock analysed the North East referendum, not by considering the policy questions at stake but simply by looking at the way it functioned, as one referendum among others (Knock 2006). British experiences with referenda are rather limited: apart from the 1975 referendum on the Common Market and the failed Scotland and Wales referenda of 1979, there were no other such occasions until the series of sub-national referenda in Scotland, Wales, Northern Ireland and London was implemented by the Labour government. The North East referendum had been preceded by legal action in the White Paper "Your Region, Your Choice", the Regional Assemblies (Preparation) Act 2003 and the Draft Regional Assemblies Bill in July 2004. It was also the first, and only, regional referendum and the first run by the Electoral Commission under the terms of the Political Parties, Elections and Referendums Act 2000 (PPERA). Knock concludes that the referendum should be seen as a considerable achievement, given the extent to which all the parties concerned operated under a new and untested legal and regulatory framework (Knock 2006: 682f.).

In the case of a referendum, however, the campaign is of crucial importance and the voters, unlike the legal framework, are extremely volatile. So it is not unknown in referenda that apparently solid majorities can turn into defeat – as we have seen in the North East. 70% of the 'No' voters and an astonishing 63% of the 'Yes' voters believed that the 'No'campaign was *very* or *fairly* effective, while a mere 34% of the 'Yes' voters could say that about their own campaign (Rallings and Thrasher 2005: 5). Campaigning in the North East referendum depended also on the all-postal ballot, where voters could cast their vote at any time between 20 October and 4 November 2004. Normally campaigns aim at a specific voting day, which was not the case here. The 'Yes' campaign for example was designed to peak at the beginning of the ballot period, while the 'No' campaign reached its maximum momentum towards the end. Some observers noted that this had not been the only tactical mistake of the 'Yes' camp. In short, their strategy was too intellectual, focussing too much on history, culture and identity while not involving the people of the region.[15] Their message was elite-orientated and media-delivered (Tickell et al. 2005: 491). Likewise, their attack against the 'No' campaign being 'Rats' – Rather Arrogant Toff Southerners – did more to cause alienation among the voters than it did to collect their support. Of course, it is much more difficult to campaign for a fundamental change like an elected assembly than to defend the status quo. Consequently, leading national Conservatives, though deeply opposed to the scheme, did not appear in support of the 'No' campaign, which could easily concentrate on a strategy of 'No votes for more politicians' or warn of higher taxes accompanying the assembly. The inflatable white elephant that toured the North for the 'No' campaign even gained iconic status and Alan Milburn conceded in frustration that the devolutionists were about to lose the race, because they had failed to deliver a coherent message (Tickell et al. 2005: 493).

The simplicity of the 'No' campaign resounded with the electorate. By a majority of almost four to one, the voters rejected the establishment of an elected assembly for the North East, with 77.9% voting against it and only 22.1% in favour. With a turnout of 47.1% this means that just one out of ten members of the electorate actually supported devolution at the ballot, a humiliating rejection indeed. The fault, however, did not lie with the Y4NE campaign alone. First, the referendum might well have provided some voters with the opportunity of casting a protest vote against Labour, since the mistrust of the Blair government even in the traditional Labour heartlands in the North had grown considerably (Knock 2006: 691). Yet this phenomenon is not unknown and is part of an electoral cycle, when sub-state

---

[15] *The Economist* (27 March 1999: "A Geordie Nation?") suspected from the start that the North East might be the first English region with an elected assembly, based, however on its academics and the political class.

elections suffer deeply from the impact of national affairs and are used by the voters to punish the government and by campaigners to present national issues; it has to be remembered that the 'No' campaign was engineered by a Euro-sceptical group as a training ground for a much harder battle on a proposed EU constitution. In federal systems, these cycles are well known and can damage state elections considerably. The result is also interpreted as a general sign of political mistrust in Britain, as a natural reaction of the voters against a political class which seems to act in its own interest alone (Tickell et al. 2005: 493). The blame, therefore, lies more on the centre than within the region, as the *Northern Echo* from Darlington put it:

> The government must not take the view that the north-east has had its chance and blown it. [...] The north-east didn't blow it – the government blew it by taking the region for granted, giving the proposed assembly inadequate powers, and assuming a Yes vote was assured [...] The No landslide should serve as a sharp warning that people do not trust politicians. It should not be seen as a signal that the region is content with a status quo that so blatantly discriminates against it. [...] The government should be very wary indeed of misjudging the region's mood a second time. (6 November 2004)

The *Northern Echo* seems to summarise the question of northern identity and the referendum perfectly in these few lines. It has indeed turned out that northern identity tends not to be easily observable at an institutional level, especially if it is not responded to in an appropriate way. It has been mentioned before that a true regionalist could hardly live with the government's proposal for elected regional assemblies in England – and the voters in the North East could not. This does not mean that there would be no regionalism at all. The referendum was chosen at a potentially maladroit point of time, burdened with a serious breakdown in Labour internal intelligence (be it national or national-regional); moreover, political elites who attempt to reform the constitution – however noble their case may be – should never take the public for granted, even if they are operating within a Labour heartland. There is a need to match the professional campaign trail with the actual regional identity, yet on the other hand a mere historical argument does not provide sufficient support either (Tickell et al. 2005: 495f.).

In the aftermath of the referendum and as a consequence of it, the referenda in the North West and Yorkshire & Humber were cancelled, a reasonable decision, given the size of the defeat in the North East. For the time being, elected regional assemblies for England have been declared dead by most academic and political observers. Inactivity seems at this point, however, not to be an option as the effect of the failed referendum had been foreseen by researchers:

> Those living in the more underprivileged English regions, such as the north-east or the north-west, may already regard themselves as second-class, because they have no territorial ministers able to argue their case in Cabinet. After devolution, they may come to believe that they are third-class, since they have no assemblies either. (Bogdanor 2001: 265)

To appoint a Minister for the North East, as well as other regional ministers of course, is one of the proposals for solving the regional dilemma the government is facing. Others include the introduction of regional select committees, unitary local authorities, elected mayors or city-regions (Sandford and Hetherington 2005: 102ff.). Any final assessment must be incomplete and sobering at this point, since the dynamic of devolution has not come to an end yet and this includes Northern England: "The future of sub-national government and governance in England has rarely been at such a point of uncertainty. But, the existing regional institutions are continuing to develop, to occasionally make new suggestions and try interventions in new areas" (Sandford 2006a: 9). Strangely, the Conservative Party sharply attacked the growth in competence for these regional unelected assemblies. Their shadow spokesman for local government attacked deputy prime minister John Prescott: "Mr. Prescott's disregard for the voice of the people bears the hallmark of East European dictators like Nicolae Ceausescu, and risks creating a 'regional tyranny' of governance with no legitimacy or accountability." (Mulholland 2005)

6. Conclusion

An interesting approach to this field of studies has been provided by Michael Münter from Erlangen University. He used the multiple-stream approach (MSA), originally designed for the American political system, to explain the first wave of devolution in Scotland and Wales in 1997 (Münter 2005). Three streams, problems, policy and politics, have to be coordinated in order to generate a "window of opportunity", which then gives a chance of successfully implementing constitutional change. The first stream, problems, in general puts its focus on the ways in which conditions become defined as problems; in our case, when does the English question present a problem, be it in order to pacify regional claims from the North, or because the English question has to be solved in a quasi-federal United Kingdom? The policy stream provides the primeval soup of concepts and ideas flowing in from the policy communities or networks: the NECC, the government, and so on. Finally, the politics stream includes a wide range of factors, from a vaguely defined political mood and a large number of people thinking along certain common lines to the decision-making process within the central government. According to the MSA, coupling these three essential streams is only possible in certain windows of opportunity. These windows open mostly under the pressure of external impulses, such as a crisis – or a fresh political mandate. Labour's landslide victory in 1997 did open such a window of opportunity and consequently created a unique chance to accomplish constitutional change, such as devolution for Scotland and Wales.

Such a window of opportunity, however, does not last forever. During the seven years between the referenda in Scotland and Wales on the one hand and the English North East on the other, the environment for the Labour government changed considerably. A parliament for Scotland, exciting as it may have been, proved to be a parliament with all the scandals and disappointments that parliaments usually suffer from. This is not surprising, as any political thinker from the Scottish enlightenment would have said, but nevertheless the "reality of the parliament disappointed many who had hoped for great things and who had talked enthusiastically of the vibrant and vigorously creative New Scotland that would emerge" (Massie 2006: 25). Labour, though triumphantly re-elected in 2001, moved into a deep crisis over Prime Minister Blair's policy concerning the War in Iraq in 2003, causing widespread protest. In brief, when the elected assembly for the North East was brought to referendum in 2004, most probably the window of opportunity that had opened at the time of Labour's honeymoon period in government was now shut. Political observers inside the North East were not surprised by the defeat, because the government presented its poor proposals at the wrong point of time in the political cycle.

In no way, however, does this imply that there cannot be another opportunity of constitutional reform. The Scots and the Welsh missed one in 1979, due to certain misconceptions and another set of poor proposals, but found a better chance than ever before in 1997. Why shouldn't this be possible for Northern England as well? The time-line for territorial politics in Britain is rather lengthy and within the confines of the present devolution settlement, its asymmetry is able to cover a multitude of solutions, from elected assemblies for the English regions to a continuing status quo. Even in the event of full Scottish independence, the English "elephant" would still be there. After all, geography, relative size and power may perhaps be more influential than constitutional status (Devine 2007: 9). It is up to the English people to push the English question back on to the political agenda and feed the streams that combine to create a new window of opportunity and then hopefully a better set of proposals. The demand for a regional parliament in Northern England will most certainly not be stifled. In the end most arguments, administrative, cultural and political, lead to the conclusion that regional assemblies as a matter of fact would suit England best. The slow regionalisation of England since 1997 and the fractured character of regional structures led to growing frustration among regional actors. There is a need for an overarching regional vision, integrating economic, cultural and political issues. This might be accomplished even by an improved RDA. *Democratic government* for the English regions, however, will be best achieved through elected assemblies (Tomaney 2002: 236f.).

After 1921, a constitutional expert found that 'home rule' was dead as soon as the English understood what it meant and that there had never been even a possibility of the abandonment of England's ancient institutions and the adoption of such a complicated, unfamiliar and un-English form of government (Coupland 1954, 330f.). I close by returning to Sir Humphrey's opening remark: even in the late twentieth century, outsiders were frightened of the region and desperately reluctant to go there, with phrases like 'emigration' being not unknown and with spouses learning of the move reacting "Oh God!" (Russell 2004: 31). Neither of these attitudes should be true any longer for twenty-first century England.

Works Cited

Research Literature

Bogdanor, Vernon (2001): *Devolution in the United Kingdom*. Oxford: Oxford University Press.
— (2005): "Constitutional Reform in Britain: The Quiet Revolution", *Annual. Review of Political Science* 8, 73-98.
Bond, Ross and David McCrone (2004): "The growth of English regionalism? Institutions and identity", *Regional & Federal Studies* 14, 1-25.
Bradley, A.W. and K.D. Ewing (1997): *Constitutional and Administrative Law*. London: Longman.
Brecht, Arnold (1945/1971): *Federalism and Regionalism in Germany. The Division of Prussia*. New York: Cornell UP; reissued New York: Russell & Russell.
Bulpitt, Jim (1983): *Territory and Power in the United Kingdom. An interpretation*. Manchester: Manchester UP.
Cabinet Office and Department for Transport, Local Government and the Regions (2002): *Your Region, Your Choice: Revitalising English Regions*, Cm 5511. London: Stationery Office.
Calder, Angus (1981): *Revolutionary Empire. The Rise of the English-Speaking Empires from the Fifteenth Century to the 1780s*. New York: Dutton.
Chen, Selina and Tony Wright (eds.) (2000): *The English Question*. London: Fabian Society.
Cochrane, Alan (2006): "Looking to a new political alignment", in: Bill Jamieson (ed.): *Scotland's Ten Tomorrows. The devolution crisis – and how to fix it*. London: Continuum, 109-124.
Cole, Alistair (2004): "What's Distinctive About Wales? Findings from a Comparison of Wales with Brittany", in: *Findings from the Economic and Research Council's Research Programme on Devolution and Constitutional Change*, No. 10 June.
Colls, Robert (2002): *Identity of England*. Oxford: Oxford UP.
Coupland, Reginald (1954): *Welsh and Scottish Nationalism*. London: Collins.
Crick, Bernard (ed.) (1991): *National Identities. The Constitution of the United Kingdom*. Oxford: Blackwell.
Curtice, John (2006): "What the people say – if anything", in: Robert Hazell (ed.): *The English Question*. Manchester: Manchester UP, 119-140.
Elazar, Daniel (1997): "Contrasting Unitary and Federal Systems", *International Political Science Review* 18, 237-251.
Esterbauer, Fried (1978): *Regionalismus. Phänomen, Planungsmittel, Herausforderung für Europa*. München: Bayerische Landeszentrale für politische Bildungsarbeit.
Forman, Nigel (2002): *Constitutional Change in the United Kingdom*. London: Routledge.
Fry, Michael (2006): "Scotland alone", *Prospect*, December 2006, 24-27.
Gamble, Andrew (2006): "The Constitutional Revolution in the United Kingdom", *Publius: The Journal of Federalism* 36, 19-35.

Harvie, Christopher (1991): "English Regionalism: the Dog that never Barked", in: Bernard Crick (ed.): *National Identities. The Constitution of the United Kingdom*. Oxford: Blackwell, 105-118.
— and Peter Jones (2000): *The Road to Home Rule. Images of Scotland's Cause*. Polygon: Edinburgh.
Hazell, Robert (ed.) (2006a): *The English Question*. Manchester: Manchester UP.
— (2006b): "The English Question", *Publius. The Journal of Federalism* 36, 37-56.
— (2007): "The Continuing Dynamics of Constitutional Reform", *Parliamentary Affairs* 60, 3-25.
Hechter, Michael (1975): *Internal Colonialism. The Celtic fringe in British national development*. London: Routledge.
Heffer, Simon (1999): *Nor Shall My Sword. The Reinvention of England*. London: Phoenix.
Hopkins, John W. (2004): "An England of Regions? The UK Government's Proposals for English Regional Devolution", *European Public Law* 10, 245-260.
Jamieson, Bill (ed.) (2006): *Scotland's Ten Tomorrows. The devolution crisis – and how to fix it*. London: Continuum.
Jeffery, Charlie and John Mawson (2002): "Beyond the White Paper on the English Regions", *Regional Studies* 36, 715-720.
— and Daniel Wincott (2006): "Devolution in the United Kingdom: Statehood and Citizenship in Transition", *Publius: The Journal of Federalism* 36, 3-18.
John, Peter, Steven Musson and Adam Tickell (2002): "England's Problem Region. Regionalism in the South East", *Regional Studies* 36, 733-741.
Keating, Michael (2004): "The United Kingdom as a post-sovereign polity", in: Michael O'Neill (ed.): *Devolution and British Politics*. Harlow: Pearson Education, 319-332.
— (2006): "From functional to political regionalism: England in comparative perspective", in: Robert Hazell (ed.): *The English Question*. Manchester: Manchester UP, 142-157.
Kendle, John (1997): *Federal Britain* (London: Routledge).
Knock, Katy (2006): "The North East Referendum: Lessons Learnt?", *Parliamentary Affairs* 59, 682–693.
Krosigk, Friedrich von (1986): "Regionaler Protest und staatlicher Wandel", *Der Staat* 25, 173-205.
Lanigan, Chris (2001): "Region-Building in the North East: Regional Identity and Regionalist Politics", in: John Tomaney and Neil Ward (eds.): *A Region in Transition. North East England at the millennium*. Aldershot: Ashgate, 104-119.
Lijphart, Arend (1999): *Patterns of Democracy. Government Forms and Performance in Thirty-Six Countries*. New Haven: Yale UP.
Lodge, Guy and James Mitchell (2006): "Whitehall and the government of England", in: Robert Hazell (ed.): *The English Question*. Manchester: Manchester UP, 96-118.
Lübbe, Hermann (1985): "Die große und die kleine Welt. Regionalismus als europäische Bewegung", in: Werner Weidenfeld (ed.): *Die Identität Europas*. München: Beck, 191-205.
Lynn, Jonathan and Anthony Jay (1989): *The Complete Yes Prime Minister*. London: BBC Books.

Marwick, Arthur (1982/2003): *British Society since 1945*. London: Penguin.
Massie, Allan (2006): "Change is the best option for the status quo", in: Bill Jamieson (ed.): *Scotland's Ten Tomorrows. The devolution crisis – and how to fix it*. London: Continuum, 25-36.
McAllister, Laura (2001): "Wales. Labour's Devolution Dilemma", *Parliamentary Affairs* 54, 156-159.
McMillan, Janice and Andrew Massey (2004): "Central government and devolution", in: Michael O'Neill (ed.), *Devolution and British Politics*. Harlow: Pearson Education, 231-250.
Miles, Steven (2005): "'Our Tyne': Iconic Regeneration and the Revitalisation of Identity in NewcastleGateshead", *Urban Studies* 42, 913–926.
Mitchell, Austin (2000): "Manifesto for the North", in: Selina Chen and Tony Wright (eds.): *The English Question*. London: Fabian Society, 45-62.
Münter, Michael (2005): *Verfassungsreform im Einheitsstaat. Die Politik der Dezentralisierung in Großbritannien*. Wiesbaden: VS Verlag für Sozialwissenschaften.
Nseir, Tarek (2004): "Is the balance of power finally shifting from South to North?", *New Media Age*, November 4.
O'Brien, Peter, Andy Pike and John Tomaney (2004): "Devolution, the governance of regional development and the Trade Union Congress in the North East region of England", *Geoforum* 35, 59-68.
O'Neill, Michael (ed.) (2004): *Devolution and British Politics*. Harlow: Pearson Education.
Osmond, John (1974): *The Centralist Enemy*. Llandybie: Christopher Davies.
— (1988): *The Divided Kingdom*. London: Constable.
Paasi, Anssi (2003): "Region and place: regional identity in question", *Progress in Human Geography* 27.4, 475-485.
Parry, Richard (2002): *The Home Civil Service after Devolution*. Edinburgh: The Devolution Papers, Economic and Research Council's Research Programme on Devolution and Constitutional Change.
Powell, David (2002): *Nationhood & Identity. The British State since 1800*. London: I.B.Tauris.
Preston, P.W. (2004): *Relocating England*. Manchester: Manchester UP.
Rallings, Colin and Michael Thrasher (2005): "Why the North East said 'No': the 2004 referendum on an elected Regional Assembly", *Devolution Briefings* No. 19 (Edinburgh: ESRC Devolution and Constitutional Change Programme), [http://www.devolution.ac.uk].
Robinson, Fred and Keith Shaw (2001): "Governing a Region: Structures and Processes of Governance in North East England", *Regional Studies* 35, 473-478.
Russell, Dave (2004): *Looking North. Northern England and the national imagination*. Manchester: Manchester UP.
Sandford, Mark (2002): "What Place for England in an Asymmetrically Devolved UK?", *Regional Studies* 36, 789-796.
— and Peter Hetherington (2005): "The Regions at the Crossroads. The Future for Sub-National Government in England", in: Alan Trench (ed.): *The Dynamics of Devolution*. Charlotteville, Virginia and Exeter: Imprint Academic, 91-113.
— (2006a): "The Only Certainty is Uncertainty: Monitoring the English Regions", in: The Constitution Unit: *English Regions Devolution Monitoring Report*, May

2006. 5 February 2007 [http://www.ucl.ac.uk/constitution-unit/ research/devolution].
— (2006b): "Facts on the ground: the growth of institutional answers to the English Question in the regions", in: Robert Hazell (ed.): *The English Question*. Manchester: Manchester UP, 174-193.
Schmitt-Egner, Peter (2005): *Handbuch zur Europäischen Regionalismusforschung. Theoretisch-methodische Grundlagen, empirische Erscheinungsformen und strategische Optionen des Transnationalen Regionalismus in 21. Jahrhundert* Wiesbaden: VS Verlag für Sozialwissenschaften.
Shaw, Eric (2003): *The Scottish Labour Party Under Devolution*. Cardiff: ESRC Devolution and Constitutional Change Programme.
Steed, Michael (1986): "The core-periphery dimension of British politics", *Political Geography Quarterly* 5, 91-103.
Sturm, Roland (2002): "Devolutions- und Verfassungsreformprozesse in Großbritannien", in: Udo Margeant (ed.): *Föderalismusreform: Föderalismus in Europa II. Zukunftsforum Politik, Nr. 51* (Sankt Augustin: Konrad-Adenauer-Stiftung), 48-63.
Taylor, Peter J. (1991): "The English and their Englishness: 'a curiously mysterious, elusive and little understood people'", *Scottish Geographical Magazine* 107, 146-161.
— (1993): "The meaning of the North: England's 'foreign country' within? (Political geography debates No. 5: The break-up of England?)", *Political Geography* 12, 136-155.
Tickell, Adam, Peter John and Steven Musson (2005): "The North East Region Referendum Campaign of 2004: Issues and Turning Points", *Political Quarterly* 76, 489-496.
Tomaney, John (1999): "New Labour and the English question", *Political Quarterly* 70, 74-82.
— (2000): "Democratically elected regional government in England: The work of the North East Constitutional Convention", *Regional Studies* 34, 383-399.
— and Neil Ward (eds.) (2001a): *A Region in Transition. North East England at the millennium*. Aldershot: Ashgate.
— and Neil Ward (2001b): "Locating the Region: An introduction", in: Id. and Neil Ward (eds.): *A Region in Transition. North East England at the millennium*. Aldershot: Ashgate, 1-22.
— (2002): "In What Sense a Regional Problem? Sub-national Governance in England", *Local Economy* 17, 226-238.
— (2006): "The idea of English regionalism", in: Robert Hazell (ed.): *The English Question*. Manchester: Manchester UP, 158-173.
Trench, Alan (2004): "The More Things Change The More They Stay The Same. Intergovernmental Relations Four Years On", in: Id. (ed.): *Has Devolution Made a Difference? The State of the Nations 2004*. Exeter: Imprint Academic.
— (2005): "The dynamics of devolution", in: Id. (ed.): *The Dynamics of Devolution. The State of the Nations 2005*. Exeter: Imprint Academic.
Ward, Paul (1998): *Red Flag and Union Jack. Englishness, Patriotism and the British Left, 1881-1924*. Woodbridge: Boydell Press.
Weight, Richard (2002): *Patriots. National Identity in Britain 1940-2000*. London: Pan Macmillan.

Wilks-Heeg, Stuart and Alan Harding (2002): Devolution for England? International Lessons (The Devolution Papers, Economic and Research Council's Research Programme on Devolution and Constitutional Change), Birmingham.

Newspaper Articles

Anon. (1999): "A Geordie Nation?", *The Economist* 27 March.
Anon. (2001): "Not such a united kingdom", *The Guardian* 8 November.
Anon. (2004): "Devo wars: It's Wales versus Scotland", *The Scotsman* 16 January.
Anon. (2004): "A humiliating rejection", Editorial, *The Guardian* 8 November.
Devine, Tom (2007): "The Elephant we can't forget", *The Scotsman, 1707-2007: 300 Years of the Union. Commemorative Supplement* 16 January, 6-9.
Hazell, Robert (2006c): "The English Question", *The Guardian* 29 March.
Kahn, Stephen (2002): "Devolution hits at Britishness", *The Observer* 21 October.
Macdonell, Hamish (2006): "Vital gains forecast for SNP in swing from Labour", *The Scotsman* 1 November.
Mulholland, Hélène (2005): "Tories turn fire on 'dictator' Prescott", *The Guardian* 11 March.
— (2007): "Blair rejects calls for English parliament", *The Guardian* 16 January.
Waser, Georges (2007): "Ein 'balkanisiertes' Großbritannien? Schottlands Unabhängigkeit ist einmal mehr ein Thema ", *Neue Zürcher Zeitung* 2 February.

Dialect and Regional Identity in Northern England

Christoph Schubert

Abstract: This article investigates the role of Northern English in the construction of a regional identity, taking into account popular images and stereotypes. To achieve this aim, it first provides an overview of distinctive linguistic features of Northern dialects on the levels of phonology, morphology, syntax, and vocabulary. On this basis, representations of the local varieties of English are examined in the nineteenth-century novels *Wuthering Heights* and *North and South* as well as in the contemporary films *Brassed Off*, *The Full Monty*, and *Billy Elliot*. It is demonstrated that the vernacular, which is usually contrasted with Standard British English, can either present the North as foreign and uncivilised or create the image of straightforward and good-hearted people with a harsh verbal behaviour. Generally, Northern English itself may – to a certain degree – be called a sociocultural construct as well, since it comprises numerous dialects with partly deviating features.

Key names and concepts: Peter Trudgill - Emily Brontë - Elizabeth Gaskell - Peter Cattaneo - Lee Hall - Mark Herman; Dialect - Non-Standard Varieties - Phonology - Morphology - Syntax - Vocabulary - Spelling Anomalies - Milieu.

1. Introduction

It is a well-known fact that language not only fulfils the function of communicating referential meaning, but also gives sociolinguistic information about the speaker or writer. Correspondingly, speakers of non-standard varieties of English in Britain often have to face linguistic prejudice, since "language as a social phenomenon is closely tied up with the social structure and value systems of society" (Trudgill 2000: 8). This applies particularly to the North of England, which is commonly associated with images of heavy industrialisation, an economically and socially underprivileged population, and a barren landscape.[1] For instance, the accent spoken in Liverpool, named 'Scouse'

---

[1] Along these lines, the American travel writer Bill Bryson, who lived in North Yorkshire for several years, gives his subjective impression of the region:

after the typical sailor's dish lobscouse,[2] is sometimes connected to regional characteristics:

> The weather, and the mists from the Irish Sea, are popularly believed to account for the adenoidal quality of the Scouse accent. The climate is matched by harsh and bleak scenery; and a harsh language: the granite and grit of the mountains of the Pennines and Lake District up to 350 million years old matched by the hard(y) or 'gritty' Northerners with their 'hard' consonants, [...] trying to graft a hard living sheep-farming from the infertile soil, or digging out the coal and lead. (Wales 2006: 25)

Of course, impressionistic notions like these are by no means restricted to Merseyside, but can be found with respect to various urban and rural regions of Northern England. However, a dialect may not only be subject to bias from the outside, but can also create a distinct regional identity, resulting in internal social coherence. Accordingly, the following remarks pursue two aims. The first is to give an outline of the language spoken in the North of England on the levels of phonology, grammar, and vocabulary. Second, the article investigates the role of dialect in the construction of a regional identity, based on representations of Northern speech in popular novels and films.

2. Linguistic Features of Northern English

For a description of the linguistic features of Northern English, it is first necessary to present a definition of its geographical boundaries. Trudgill (see 1999: 65) divides the English dialects into North and South, as indicated by the bold black line running from the Welsh

---

"[o]ne of the great surprises to me upon moving North was discovering the extent to which it felt like another country. [...] Mostly what differentiated the North from the South [...] was the exceptional sense of economic loss, of greatness passed, when you drove through places like Preston or Blackburn" (1995: 212).

[2] As for its history, Scouse is "believed to have come into existence in the nineteenth century, when large numbers of Irish immigrants, as well as a fair number of Welsh, settled in this corner of the north of England" (Wells 1982: 371). Other terms for urban dialects are 'Geordie' in Newcastle upon Tyne and 'Brum' or 'Brummie' in Birmingham (see McArthur 1992: 130-131 and 437).

border to the Wash on the map (see fig. 1),[3] so that the North from a linguistic perspective does not match the region popularly referred to as the 'North' (see Beal 2004a: 113).

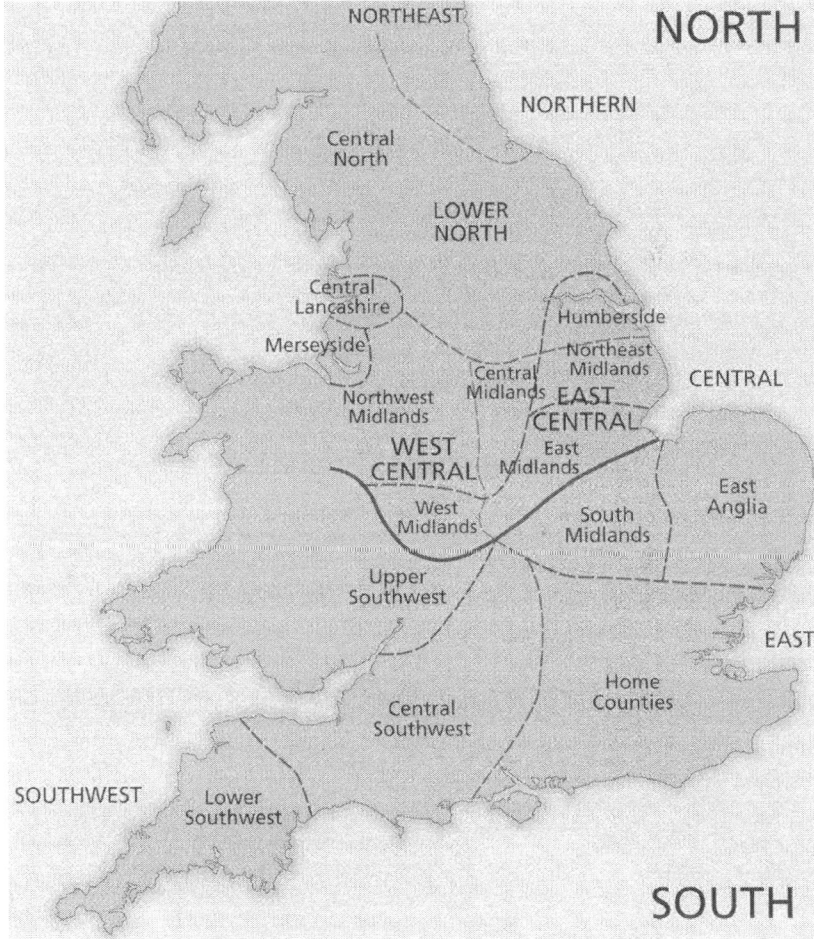

Figure 1: Map of modern dialect areas in England (see Trudgill 1999: 65)

---

[3] It should be noted that the modern dialect areas are different from the traditional ones, as modern dialects are today used by the majority of non-standard speakers, whereas traditional dialects are spoken only by a minority (see Trudgill 1999: 5-6, 34, and 52).

In other words, the linguistic North not only covers a region north of a line from the Mersey to the Humber, but also comprises most of the Midlands, including cities such as Birmingham and Leicester (see Wells 1982: 349).[4] However, Trudgill draws further distinctions on the basis of overlapping isoglosses, dividing the North into the areas of Northern and Central. The Northern region 'proper' is once again split up into the Northeast and the Lower North, which consists of the Central North, Central Lancashire, and Humberside (see fig. 2).[5]

Northern			Northeast	Newcastle, Durham, Sunderland, Middlesbrough
		Lower North	Central North	Carlisle, Lancaster, Leeds, Bradford, York, Sheffield
			Central Lancashire	Blackburn, Burnley, Accrington
			Humberside	Hull, Scunthorpe, Grimsby
NORTH	**Central**	West Central	Merseyside	Liverpool, Birkenhead
			Northwest Midlands	Derby, Stoke-on-Trent, Chester, Manchester
			West Midlands	Birmingham, Wolverhampton, Walsall
		East Central	Central Midlands	Nottingham, Leicester
			Northeast Midlands	Lincoln, Louth
			East Midlands	Grantham, Peterborough

Figure 2: Typology of modern dialects in the linguistic North of England (see Trudgill 1999: 66-67)

---

[4] Moreover, the modern dialect area of the North is different from the Old English region of Northumbria (see Wells 1982: 350); see the map in Baugh and Cable (2002: 54) and the short history of Northern English in Beal (2004a: 115-120).

[5] The Northern English richness in regional variation corresponds to the fact that the groundbreaking *Survey of English Dialects (SED)*, published between 1962 and 1971, was a project of the University of Leeds (see Barnickel 1982: 148).

Errata

Spatial Practices Vol. 2

Correct phonetic symbols:

Page 77:

Hence, the monophthong /ʌ/ of Received Pronunciation (RP) is substituted by /ʊ/ in lexemes like *but, up, gull, some*, or *country*, so that *putt* and *put* are homophones. Northerners intending to adopt RP are therefore in danger of producing hypercorrect forms (see Gimson 2001: 89), pronouncing /ʌ/ in words like *put* or *butcher* as well.

The second crucial feature is the substitution of RP /ɑ:/ by [a] when this vowel immediately precedes voiceless fricatives such as /f/, /s/ and /θ/ in *laugh, grass*, and *path*, or nasals in words like *dance*.

There are many educated northerners who would not be caught dead doing something so vulgar as to pronounce STRUT words with [ʊ], but who would feel it to be a denial of their identity as northerners to say BATH words with anything other than short [a].

As the RP vowel /æ/ in *trap, cap*, or *man* is also realised as [a] in the North, *gas* typically rhymes with *glass*.

Page 78:

For instance, the lexical sets represented by the words GOAT and FACE have the monophthongs [o:] and [e:] instead of the RP diphthongs /əʊ/ and /eɪ/ exclusively in Northern dialects 'proper', which are linguistically more conservative than the Central ones in this respect.

The Northeast stands out within the Northern region in its substitution of RP /ɜ:/ in *shirt* by /ɔ:/ as in *short*, and words with the spelling *al* such as *walk* are pronounced with the vowel /ɑ:/. This circumstance is reflected in the Geordie joke about "the non-Geordie doctor who asks his patient if he is able to *walk*, which his patient interprets as a query about *work* and replies 'Wawk [/ɔ:/]! I cannot even wahk [/ɑ:/] yet!'".

2.1 Phonology

Generally, the linguistic North of England as a whole can be separated from the South by means of two major phonological features. The first is the Northern absence of the "FOOT-STRUT Split" (Wells 1982: 349), which means that the North has retained the Middle English vowel quality. Hence, the monophthong /ɒ/ of Received Pronunciation (RP) is substituted by /Y/ in lexemes like *but, up, gull, some,* or *country,* so that *putt* and *put* are homophones. Northerners intending to adopt RP are therefore in danger of producing hypercorrect forms (see Gimson 2001: 89), pronouncing /ɒ/ in words like *put* or *butcher* as well. The isogloss of this prominent feature corresponds to the bold line on the map (see fig. 1), extending from the Welsh border in the West via an area south of Birmingham to the Wash in the East (see Trudgill 1999: 53-54). The absence of this phonemic opposition, which is "popular in linguistic stereotyping" (Wales 2006: 20), has also given rise to anecdotal humour: "[a] traveller asking at an inn for a double room was given a large glass of Jamaica rum" (Brook 1963: 32).[6]

The second crucial feature is the substitution of RP /A:/ by [a] when this vowel immediately precedes voiceless fricatives such as /f/, /s/ and /T/ in *laugh, grass,* and *path,* or nasals in words like *dance*.[7] The isogloss of this "flat" BATH vowel or "BATH Broadening" (Wells 1982: 354) is similar to the FOOT-STRUT line in the East, but in the West of England it reaches further south to the Severn estuary (see Wales 2006: 21). This second characteristic is less socially stigmatised than the first, which already hints at the identity-forming function of regional pronunciation:

> There are many educated northerners who would not be caught dead doing something so vulgar as to pronounce STRUT words with [Y], but who would feel it to be a denial of their identity as northerners to say BATH words with anything other than short [a]. (Wells 1982: 354)

---

[6]   Leisi and Mair (see 1999: 178) point out that early representations of dialect in English literature particularly serve humorous purposes, as, for instance, Chaucer already ridicules Northern English.

[7]   As the RP vowel /Θ/ in *trap, cap,* or *man* is also realised as [a] in the North, *gas* typically rhymes with *glass* (see Wells 1982: 349).

Additionally, there are several phonological features which can only be detected in special areas of the North. For instance, the lexical sets represented by the words GOAT and FACE have the monophthongs [o:] and [e:] instead of the RP diphthongs /↔Y/ and /eI/ exclusively in Northern dialects 'proper', which are linguistically more conservative than the Central ones in this respect (see Beal 2004a: 123 and Hansen, Carls and Lucko 1996: 46). As far as the non-prevocalic /r/ in words like *far* and *arm* is concerned, the North including the Central area is non-rhotic, with the exception of rhotic Central Lancashire (see Trudgill 1999: 55-56). The Northeast stands out within the Northern region in its substitution of RP /∈:/ in *shirt* by / :/ as in *short*, and words with the spelling *al* such as *walk* are pronounced with the vowel /A:/. This circumstance is reflected in the Geordie joke about "the non-Geordie doctor who asks his patient if he is able to *walk*, which his patient interprets as a query about *work* and replies 'Wawk [/ :/]! I cannot even wahk [/A:/] yet!'" (Trudgill 1999: 70).[8]

2.2 Morphology and Syntax

Although the pronunciation comprises the most salient features of Northern English, there are also several grammatical characteristics regarding morphology and syntax. Beal points out the "Northern Subject Rule", which is typical of the entire Northern area. It refers to the fact that verbs take the inflectional morpheme *-s* in the plural if the subject of the sentence is "a noun or noun phrase, but not when it is a pronoun" (Beal 2004b: 121-122), resulting in forms like *Our young one's mates talks something like you.*[9] In addition, Northern dialects are characterised by frequent past participle forms in *-en*, as in *getten* for Standard English *got* or *putten* for *put* (see Beal 2004b: 115). Another inflectional feature is the usage of *I is* in the Lower North (see Trudgill 1999: 107), as opposed to *I am* in Central varieties and Standard English.

---

[8] Beal investigates the use of the term "Geordie Nation", arguing that "[t]he word 'Nation' is used in its Native American sense here, suggesting that the Geordies are a tribe with a unique language and culture, threatened and exploited by the colonial power in the Southeast" (1999: 33).

[9] See the corresponding maps in the atlas by Viereck, Viereck and Ramisch (2002: 84).

Moreover, Northern English function words deviate from their Standard English equivalents in various ways. For instance, the subordinator *while* has the meaning of 'until' in Yorkshire, which is the basis for another anecdote at the expense of the Northerners:

> In 1967 the Ministry of Transport decided to change the wording on new level-crossing warning-boards because their use in Yorkshire was causing misunderstanding that might have had fatal results. The notices read 'Stop while lights are flashing'. (Brook 1963: 36)

Reflexive pronouns in the Northern area are generally regularised, so that forms such as *hisself* and *theirselves* take the place of *himself* and *themselves* (see Beal 2004b: 119). A very common feature of Northern dialects, particularly of Yorkshire and Lancashire, is the reduction of the definite article, which therefore frequently occurs in stereotypical representations. Depending on the region and the phonetic context, this determiner can appear in the form of a glottal stop, /t/, /T/, or even zero (see Beal 2004b: 120).

With regard to sentence structure, Northern English dialects show special forms of right-dislocation, in which the dislocated element is coreferential with a noun or pronoun in the preceding sentence. Hence, a characteristic Northeastern construction is *I'm a Geordie, me, like*, where *like* has the function of emphasis, while a typical Yorkshire utterance includes an additional auxiliary verb, as in the sentence *He's got his head screwed on, has Dave* (see Beal 2004b: 135-136).

2.3 Vocabulary

Lexical Northernisms typically have their origins in the fact that the greater part of the North of England was part of the medieval Danelaw, which can roughly be located north and east of a line from Chester to London (see Beal 2004b: 137-139 and Trudgill 1999: 119-121). Hence, examples of words going back to Old Norse are *beck* 'stream', *gate* 'path', *kist* 'chest', *lake* 'play', *bairn* 'child',[10] and *lass* 'girl',[11]

---

[10] For the distribution of *lake* and *bairn*, see the maps in the linguistic atlas by Upton and Widdowson (see 1996: 74 and 158).

and *happen* has the function of the Standard English adverb 'perhaps'. Obviously, such lexical items are not as frequent as phonological features of Northern speech, but the particles *aye* and *nay* for 'yes' and 'no' are rather noticeable. Apart from the Scandinavian influence, there are also a few Anglo-Saxon items which are used differently in Northern English, as, for instance, the noun *night* covers the meanings of both 'evening' and 'night' (see Viereck, Viereck and Ramisch 2002: 88-89). Moreover, terms of endearment, particularly *love*, are very frequent in service encounters and are used both by women and men in the Northern area. Finally, there are special discourse markers employed to get someone's attention (see Beal 2004b: 139), such as *ey up* in Yorkshire and Lancashire or *howay* in the Northeast.

3. Representations of Northern English

The stereotypes associated with a particular region and its dialect are strongly influenced by its representation in popular novels and films. In written texts, the dialect manifests itself mainly in orthographic alterations indicating phonological features, while grammatical and lexical features play a minor role. In the spoken medium, the characteristic pronunciation can be realised directly, so that it has a more immediate effect. Usually, the linguistic difference between the speakers of the regional variety and Standard English is reflected by extralinguistic circumstances concerning social class or economic situation.

3.1 Nineteenth-Century Novels

An outstanding and well-known example of Yorkshire dialect representation in nineteenth-century literature is Emily Brontë's *Wuthering Heights* (1847). The character marked by non-standard speech in this

---

[11] Discussing the process of vocabulary loss, Trudgill (see 1999: 123) investigates the example of Standard English *girl*. Equivalents in modern dialects are *girl* and *lass*, whereas traditional dialects show the possibilities of *girl, lass, mawther, maiden,* and *wench*. For the future, Trudgill expects a further decrease in dialect words on the one hand but more differences in pronunciation on the other (see 1999: 132-133).

novel is the old servant Joseph, a minor figure,[12] whose utterances abound with spelling anomalies. The following extract contains Joseph's answer to Hindley's question asking what he was doing out in the rain.

> 'Running after t' lads, as usuald!' croaked Joseph, catching an opportunity, from our hesitation, to thrust in his evil tongue.
> 'If Aw wur yah, maister, Aw'd just slam t' boards i' their faces all on 'em, gentle and simple! Never a day ut yah're off, but yon cat uh Linton comes sneaking hither – and Miss Nelly, shoo's a fine lass! shoo sits watching for ye i' t' kitchen; and as yah're in at one door, he's aht at t' other – und, then, wer grand lady goes a coorting uf hor side! It's bonny behaviour, lurking amang t' fields, after twelve ut' night, wi' that fahl, flaysome divil uf a gipsy, Heathcliff! [...]'
> (Brontë 1985: 126-127)

First of all, it is striking that the dialect speaker "croaked", since this verb metalinguistically implies harsh and unpleasant sounds, as they are popularly expected from Yorkshiremen. Moreover, the narrator employs the ambiguous term of Joseph's "evil tongue", by which the aggressive and malicious contents of his utterance are transferred to the linguistic forms as well.[13] At the same time, the character himself is shown in a negative light, appearing as a "grotesque and uncouth figure" (Page 1973: 67). Regarding punctuation marks, Joseph's speech contains a lot of apostrophes indicating the omission of phonemes, by which an impression of linguistic deficiency is evoked. Numerous exclamation marks have the function of underlining the excitement and forcefulness connected with the utterances.

Generally, this excerpt demonstrates that the dialect representation in this novel is rather dense, so that it creates an extraordinarily vivid image, but at the same time it makes the text difficult to read and understand (see O'Donnell and Todd 1991: 134). A typical grammatical feature frequently used in Joseph's speech is the reduction of the definite article to "t'", characteristic Northern words are "lads", "lass",

---

[12] This corresponds with the observation that "English writers have seldom felt able to take the risk of depicting a hero or heroine as a dialect speaker. [...] Of course, if the intention was to portray a character as ignorant and comical the use of dialect would serve very well" (O'Donnell and Todd 1991: 133).

[13] Hence, Joseph's "dialect is used to suggest coarseness and a latent evil" (Blake 1981: 151).

and "bonny", and a phonological peculiarity is represented by the vowel in "amang" (see Upton and Widdowson 1996: 12). There are also a few general markers of colloquial speech, such as the reduction of *them* to "'em" and the use of the adjectives "gentle" and "simple" instead of the corresponding adverbs.

It can be concluded that the servant's dialect has the function of isolating him from the other characters, whose language is not marked by regional features. Therefore, the vernacular creates distance between its speaker and its recipients (see Mace 1987: 71-72), who are unlikely to identify with the Yorkshireman. Northern English here serves as a "marker of inferior status" (Page 1973: 53), concerning ethical as well as social parameters.

> Dialect [in *Wuthering Heights*] is still the language of the poor. Naturally this is the working poor of the North, because with the Industrial Revolution it was there that most poor people were congregated and it was there that violence erupted most frequently in the nineteenth century. (Blake 1981: 151)

Correspondingly, the North of England appeared as wild, foreign, and uncivilised to many Southern English travellers in the eighteenth and nineteenth centuries, so that *Wuthering Heights* "epitomised the untamed nature of the moorland and its inhabitants with their unintelligible vernacular" (Wales 2006: 26).[14]

Another nineteenth-century novel representing Northern English is Elizabeth Gaskell's *North and South* (1855). Its title already alludes to the basic dichotomy between the industrialised North and the wealthier agricultural South.[15] In this text, it is the Lancashire dialect

---

[14] Other examples of literary Yorkshire are an anonymous poem of the seventeenth century entitled "A Yorkshire Dialogue between an Awd Wife, a Lass and a Butcher", nineteenth-century *Almanacks*, and the poetry of Stanley Umpleby and Fred Brown in the twentieth century (see McArthur 1992: 1143-1144). Brook names John Hartley (1839-1915) as the "most prolific and versatile of all Yorkshire dialect writers", who produced poems with the characteristic ingredients of dialect poetry, i.e. "sentiment, strong affection, a winter setting, and interest in the doings of very poor people" (1963: 195).

[15] Accordingly, it may be asserted that "[d]uring the nineteenth century dialect literature flourished in the North of England because it satisfied the needs of the new industrial communities that were then coming into existence" (Brook 1963: 193-194). This is confirmed by a list of English regional novelists (see Bentley 1941: 48), most of whom come from Yorkshire.

that is used particularly by the mill worker Nicholas Higgins, so that his regional dialect again has the function of a "class marker", although its representation is not as dense as in *Wuthering Heights* (see Blake 1981: 152).[16] After Higgins's application for a job has been rudely rejected – "[t]h' o'erlooker bid me go and be d——d" –, he declares that communicative behaviour of such a kind is customary in the North: "As to th' language, I'm welly used to it; it dunnot matter to me. I'm not nesh mysel' when I'm put out" (Gaskell 1973: 307). Hence, this utterance strengthens the image of Northerners as outspoken and straightforward people who do not beat about the bush.[17] Moreover, regional forms like "nesh" with the meaning of 'fastidious, squeamish' help the speakers to dissociate themselves from the South and to shape their own Northern identity (see Mace 1987: 92), which is here based on the in-group of the underprivileged working class.[18]

3.2 Recent British Films

The milieu of working-class families and their economic problems in England's North is taken up again in recent British films like *Brassed Off* (Herman 1996), *The Full Monty* (Cattaneo 1997), and *Billy Elliot* (Daldry 2000).[19] The titles of the first two of these films are already colloquial and idiomatic, hinting at the fact that the characters use a slangy, dialectal and partly even vulgar language. *Brassed Off* is set in

---

[16] The Lancashire dialect is also portrayed in literary works by John Collier in the eighteenth and Edwin Waugh in the nineteenth centuries (see McArthur 1992: 570-571).

[17] Of course, the vernacular may function as a linguistic mitigation, since "[t]he deliberate use of dialect, like that of slang, can tone down the severity of a rebuke" (Brook 1963: 30).

[18] In contrast, "the accents of many middle-class Northerners continue to appear to be drawn towards RP" (Wales 2006: 167).

[19] Besides these films, Wales names further representations of Northern English in popular culture, such as the very successful television soap opera *Coronation Street* "set in the working-class area of a fictional Northern town called Weatherfield" (2006: 160), the strip cartoon of *Andy Capp* (2006: 9), and the "animated films starring Wallace and his dog Gromit, created by Preston-born Nick Park" (2006: 28), in which the Lancashire accent adds to the comic effect.

the South Yorkshire coal-mining town of Grimley,[20] located in the Barnsley area, and tells the story of Grimley Colliery Brass Band. This group of musicians, whose future is as uncertain as that of the local pit, finally manages to win the National Brass Band Championship in London. Besides their common profession and hometown, the miners' vernacular serves as a vital bond among them, constituting a local identity. The following extract, in which flugelhorn player Gloria asks the bandleader Danny whether she may join the all-male brass band, shows this function of the local variety.

> DANNY. I know it might sound like we need all 'help we can get, but I'm sorry, love, as a rule we don't usually allow ... you know ... outsiders ...
> GLORIA. Aye, I understand, except ... I'm not strictly an outsider. I were born in Grimley.
> *Andy looks even closer.*
> DANNY. Is that right, love? What's your name? (Herman 2003: 27-28)

Gloria, first rejected as an "outsider" on grounds of her sex and her presumably non-regional origin, is eventually accepted as a member of the band when she reveals that she is a local, which she accentuates by means of the regional expression "[a]ye" as well as the nonstandard plural form of the verb in "I were". As a result, the vernacular here – in contrast to *Wuthering Heights* – does not create distance, but evokes familiarity. However, Gloria's role in the film is ambiguous, since she is in love with the miner Andy, played by Ewan McGregor, and at the same time works for the management intending to close the pit. Correspondingly, she is capable of code-switching, using Standard English in conversations with her superior but regional forms when she talks to her fellow musicians. The contrast between the desperate miners and their determined adversaries is also emphasised by a television report on the pit closures, in which Standard British English can be heard. Hence, in addition to the authentic location, the dialect provides local colour and creates a lively and credible atmosphere.

---

[20] For a description of the occupational variety of coal-mining see Wakelin (see 1977: 143-146).

The action of *The Full Monty* takes place in Sheffield, South Yorkshire, which also belongs to the dialect area of the Central North. It relates the story of six unemployed steel workers who are inspired by the male strip group named 'The Chippendales' and finally perform a successful strip show. The film begins with a television commercial dated twenty-five years before the action of the film, glorifying Sheffield as England's "beating heart of the industrial North" (Beaufoy 1997: 3). The variety of Standard English in this ostentatious programme already creates an ironic and humorous contrast to the vernacular of the unemployed workers. Their non-standard language manifests itself in features such as the attention-getter "[e]y up" (Beaufoy 1997: 10), in forms of right-dislocation as "[y]ou're in trouble, you" (Beaufoy 1997: 21), and in lexical items like "lasses" (Beaufoy 1997: 26). Hence, the standard language of the media and the government appears as the language of hypocrisy and pretension, while the workers' dialect is a symbol of their candid and down-to-earth character.[21] This corresponds to the fact that dialect words often have strong connotations which make them appear more lively and friendly (see Barnickel 1982: 168).

Thus, dialect speakers like the protagonist Gaz are presented as simple, likeable and authentic people with a pronounced sense of humour, so that they can be certain of the viewers' sympathy. Like the terraced houses and the cloudy sky, the regional variety is a basic constituent of the film, creating an affective bond between the characters. Furthermore, their *non-standard* language reflects the fact that the physical appearance of the Sheffield workers does not meet the *standards* of professional strippers, so that their success relies on their originality and unique entertainment qualities.[22] Consequently, the film corroborates the positive stereotype of "the resilient Northerners, hard-working and humorous in the face of adversity, blunt speaking

---

[21] In the dubbed German version of the film, the steel workers speak in a colloquial and informal style without regional characteristics, so that the effect of local identification largely disappears.

[22] Similarly, Scouse gained a higher prestige in the 1960s because it was the native dialect of the Beatles and other 'Mersey Sound' pop groups (see Wales 2006: 162).

and straight-forward, friendly to strangers, their working flat caps matching their 'flat' vowels" (Wales 2006: 28).[23]

The film *Billy Elliot* is set in the fictional town of Everington in Durham, so that the characters speak the dialect of the Northeast. As in *Brassed Off*, the main plot develops in the milieu of coal workers who are on strike in order to prevent the closure of their pit. It is the story of the eleven year-old boy Billy Elliot who by chance discovers his exceptional talent for ballet dancing and eventually manages to be admitted to the Royal Ballet School in London. A striking contrast is created between the grim and ordinary life of the miners on the one hand and the artistic world of ballet and music on the other. This is linguistically mirrored by the opposition between the regional working-class vernacular and the rather affected standard language – including French terminology – used by the tutors at the ballet school. In the following extract, for instance, Billy is intimidated by the first tutor's question in the audition, which almost renders him speechless.

> TUTOR I. You realise that we shall have to consider this [*i.e. Billy shoving another pupil*] very seriously and it will be bound to affect our final decision. Yes, well, just a few questions then. Billy, could you tell us why you first became interested in ballet? *Long pause.*
> BILLY. Dunno. *Dad looks at him.*
> Just was. (Hall 2000: 87)

As the stage direction implies and his facial expression in the film shows, Billy's father is so overwhelmed by the linguistic and situational circumstances in the capital city that he is hardly able to support his son verbally. This lack of education and cultural interest among the miners in the film also manifests itself in the fact that Durham County Library is represented only by a bus in the working class neighbourhood. It is noteworthy that *Billy Elliot* resembles the other two films in the fact that a TV report – in this case on the politics of Margaret Thatcher – conveys the impression of RP as the language of the 'enemy'.

---

[23] Along these lines, Bryson states that Northernness "was to do with the accents, the different words, the refreshing if sometimes startling frankness of speech" (1995: 212).

Ultimately, all three films show the artistic achievements of dialect speakers who are more successful than popular opinion might have expected them to be. They turn out to be rough diamonds who eventually manage to reach the required standards of dancing and music despite their non-standard language. Hence, the Northern vernacular has the function of a *pars pro toto*,[24] symbolising an alleged inferiority which is finally discarded. Additionally, the Northern dialect serves a sociolinguistic purpose involving "the identification and self-identity of the local community and its social boundaries" (Mace 1987: 303). In particular, Northern English in these films helps to construct the image of tough but friendly locals who have a soft core beneath their hard shell,[25] while the latter manifests itself in their dialect and frequent use of four-letter words.

4. Conclusion

As the examples have demonstrated, representations of Northern English may shape both the external perception and the internal self-image of the region. Stereotypes can vary between the alien and rude Northerner on the one hand and the sympathetic and amiable one on the other. Accordingly, the vernacular may either be regarded as foreign, unintelligible, ridiculous, and sub-standard, or as quaint, familiar, original, and sincere. In both cases, though, the use of the Northern dialect in novels and films provides local colour, shows that the characters belong to the underprivileged working class, and supports the emotional involvement of the reader or viewer, which can lead to entertainment or compassion.

The use of the Northern dialects in the three films exemplifies the fact that in contrast to the overt prestige of Standard English,[26] fea-

---

[24] Wales rightly comments that "[l]inguistic features, like cultural artefacts such as caps and braces, leeks and whippets, serve [...] as metonyms or synecdoche" (2006: 29).

[25] As Brook points out, "[a] speaker may use dialect to cover up the embarrassment that he feels on being praised. A fairly common North Country reply to praise for lavish hospitality is 'Aye, we're short o' nowt we 'ave'" (1963: 30-31).

[26] Generally, local varieties of English face the problem of acceptance, as "[i]t is true that, in our not entirely egalitarian society, it is unfortunately still consid-

tures of Non-Standard English may have the positive connotations of a "covert prestige [which] bestows status on their users as being members of their local community and as having desirable qualities such as friendliness and loyalty" (Trudgill 2003: 30). In the case of these films, this covert prestige not only operates within the in-group of the main characters, but is transferred to the viewers' perception as well, confirming the aesthetic and literary legitimacy of Northern English.

Finally, it is not only regional identity that is a sociocultural construct, but to a certain extent, Northern English itself is a construct as well (see Wales 2006: 24). This is due to the linguistic heterogeneity of the dialects in this area and the fact that some places can hardly be allocated to a specific regional variety of English (see Trudgill 1999: 67). Moreover, isoglosses are not necessarily identical with county boundaries, and there are smaller dialect areas within counties, so that terms like 'the Lancashire dialect' are simplifications.[27] Nevertheless, as was pointed out before, there are linguistic features uniting the North of England, and in connection with characteristic socioeconomic circumstances, they strongly contribute to the general notion of Northernness.

---

ered to be acceptable to discriminate against people, especially young people, on the grounds of their dialect, in a way that would now be unthinkable on the grounds of their race or their sex" (Trudgill 1999: 134).

[27] Similarly, the accent of Liverpool is distinctly different from that of the surrounding region (see Hughes, Trudgill and Watt 2005: 97).

Works Cited

Primary References

Beaufoy, Simon (1997): *The Full Monty*. Suffolk: ScreenPress Books.
Brontë, Emily (1985): *Wuthering Heights* [1847] (ed. David Daiches). London: Penguin.
Bryson, Bill (1995): *Notes from a Small Island*. London: Black Swan.
Cattaneo, Peter (dir.) (1997): *The Full Monty*. Twentieth Century Fox Home Entertainment.
Daldry, Stephen (dir.) (2000): *Billy Elliot*. Universal Studios.
Gaskell, Elizabeth (1973): *North and South* [1855] (ed. Angus Easson). London: Oxford UP.
Hall, Lee (2000): *Billy Elliot*. London: Faber and Faber.
Herman, Mark (dir.) (1996): *Brassed Off*. London: Channel Four Television Corporation.
— (2003): *Brassed Off: A Film Script* (ed. Herbert Geisen). Stuttgart: Reclam.

Research Literature

Barnickel, Klaus-Dieter (1982): *Sprachliche Varianten des Englischen*, vol. 1: *Nationale, soziale und regionale Varianten*. München: Hueber.
Baugh, Albert C. and Thomas Cable (2002): *A History of the English Language*. 5th ed. London: Routledge.
Beal, Joan C. (1999): "'Geordie Nation': Language and Regional Identity in the Northeast of England", *Lore and Language* 17, 33-48.
— (2004a): "English Dialects in the North of England: Phonology", in: Edgar W. Schneider et al. (eds): *A Handbook of Varieties of English*, vol. 1: *Phonology*. Berlin: Mouton de Gruyter: 113-133.
— (2004b): "English Dialects in the North of England: Morphology and Syntax", in: Bernd Kortmann et al. (eds.): *A Handbook of Varieties of English*, vol. 2: *Morphology and Syntax*. Berlin: Mouton de Gruyter: 114-141.
Bentley, Phyllis (1941): *The English Regional Novel*. London: George Allen & Unwin Ltd.
Blake, Norman F. (1981): *Non-Standard Language in English Literature*. London: André Deutsch.
Brook, George Lesley (1963): *English Dialects*. London: André Deutsch.
— (1973): *Varieties of English*. London: Macmillan.
Gimson, Alfred C. (1995/2001): *Gimson's Pronunciation of English* (revised by Alan Cruttenden). London: Arnold.
Hansen, Klaus, Uwe Carls and Peter Lucko (1996): *Die Differenzierung des Englischen in nationale Varianten: Eine Einführung*. Berlin: Erich Schmidt.
Hughes, Arthur, Peter Trudgill and Dominic Watt (1979/2005): *English Accents and Dialects: An Introduction to Social and Regional Varieties of English in the British Isles*. London: Hodder Arnold.

Leisi, Ernst and Christian Mair (1999): *Das heutige Englisch: Wesenszüge und Probleme.* Heidelberg: Winter.
Mace, Renate (1987): *Funktionen des Dialekts im regionalen Roman von Gaskell bis Lawrence.* Tübingen: Narr.
McArthur, Tom (ed.) (1992): *The Oxford Companion to the English Language.* Oxford: Oxford UP.
O'Donnell, W. R. and Loreto Todd (1991): *Variety in Contemporary English.* 2nd ed. London: HarperCollins*Academic*.
Page, Norman (1973): *Speech in the English Novel.* London: Longman.
Trudgill, Peter (1990/1999): *The Dialects of England.* Oxford: Blackwell.
— (2000): *Sociolinguistics: An Introduction to Language and Society.* 4th ed. London: Penguin.
— (2003): *A Glossary of Sociolinguistics.* New York: Oxford UP.
Upton, Clive and J. D. A. Widdowson (1996): *An Atlas of English Dialects.* Oxford: Oxford UP.
Viereck, Wolfgang, Karin Viereck and Heinrich Ramisch (2002): *Dtv-Atlas Englische Sprache.* München: Deutscher Taschenbuch Verlag.
Wakelin, Martyn F. (1977): *English Dialects: An Introduction.* London: The Athlone P.
Wales, Katie (2006): *Northern English: A Cultural and Social History.* Cambridge: Cambridge UP.
Wells, John C. (1982): *Accents of English,* vol. 2: *The British Isles.* Cambridge: Cambridge UP.

CHAPTER II
POLITICS OF THE IMAGINATION

The 'North' of 'England': A Paradox?

Stephan Kohl

Abstract: Literary tours of England, from the inter-war years until present times, have used a 'Southern' perspective to emphasise the difference of the 'North'; occasionally, 'Northern England' seems to be used as an oxymoron. A few well tried rhetorical strategies of making the 'North' a 'fallen' version of England can be identified.

Key names and concepts: Bainbridge, Beryl - Bryson, Bill - Burke, Thomas - Campbell, Beatrix - Chesshyre, Robert - Dimbleby, David - Fairfax-Blakeborough, J. - Hillaby, John - Hillier, Caroline - Mais, S.P.B. - Morton, H.V. - Orwell, George - Priestley, J.B. - Theroux, Paul; Rural England - Englishness - Moral Landscapes - North-South Divide - The North of England - Paradise - Tours of England - Fallen World.

1. Introduction

The purpose of this article is to examine representations of the 'North' of England (as a region different from the 'South' of England) in a number of twentieth-century popular literary tours of England in order to establish the textually-produced dubious Englishness of the English 'North'. Admittedly, 'Englishness' itself is a concept that remains vague: "Englishness is experienced, but not explained." (Sutton 2000) More thoughtful discussions of what it means to be English suggest the replacement of the concept with 'Englishnesses', thus stressing the ethnic and regional diversities of the English experience. And yet, with the centres of power and almost all mass media concentrated in London, and politicians, journalists and producers mostly spending their lives in the South, discussions of 'Englishness' almost invariably apply Home Counties standards.

That the 'South' indeed provides the basis for an understanding of England and Englishness will be apparent from the texts selected for this article. They cover a long period, from the late 1920s to the present day, and were chosen for no other reason than their popularity.

There is good reason for this catholic choice: it is intended to show that the prevailing representational patterns for the landscapes of the 'North', as popularised by H.V. Morton in 1927 and 1928, proved so powerful as to shape even today's literary tours of the 'North'. One can indeed define these texts, with their insistence on characterising 'Northern' landscapes as manifestations of a fallen England, as one 'collective text' (see Easthope 1991: 166-67). These literary tours all propagate the idea of a morally inferior England in the 'North', by commenting again and again on those features of these landscapes which are un-English.

The popular literary tours of England are seen, then, as essential texts for the production of meaning which define the discursive practice in relation to the 'North'. Analysing this collective text, hardly any distinction between texts from the inter-war years and texts published in more recent times can be observed: they show the persistence of a literary convention. When, for instance, Beryl Bainbridge, in her *English Journey* of 1984, states: "I had thought that North and South had long since merged, and discovered they were separate countries" (1985: 8) the term 'discovery' seems to imply a description of conditions in Northern England based on empirical field work. It will be seen, though, that perceptions of the 'North' by (nearly) contemporary writers are still shaped by powerful long-established discursive practices relating to the 'North' and that travelogues incorporating Northern England should be seen as parts of a discourse which continues the creation of a morally negative image of the 'North'.

2. The 'South' *vs* The 'North'

The 'Rural England' of poetry and guidebooks, of novels, films and advertisements is usually located somewhere in the South of England. Whereas the elements of these rural English scenes – hedges, brooks, byroads, fields, small forests, thatched cottages, the occasional manor house etc. – are well defined, precise information on their actual place on the map is the exception: it is important only that this imagined 'Rural England' exists as a place of true Englishness, and consequently it does not matter where exactly it can be found – as one should be able to find it everywhere in England. Significantly, H.V. Morton's *In Search of England*, arguably the most influential book for the propagation of the idea of 'Rural England' as the real England, develops his last climactic scene in the churchyard of an unnamed, and therefore untraceable, village:

> 'Well,' smiled the vicar, as he walked towards me between the yew trees, 'that, I am afraid, is all we have.'
> 'You have England,' I said. (1933: 280)

The distinctively southern quality of real England provokes at least two questions: (1) does the North of England as the 'other' not qualify as the real England, and (2) is this emphasis on a southern Rural England just one of many strategies of contrasting a "barbarous" (Rawnsley 2000: 5) region with a more civilised 'South', thus re-enforcing the North-South divide? If it is true that "there is an unshakeable conviction [...] that civilization ends at St Albans, or some point a little farther north" (Hillier 1978: 15) then the real England, and with it 'Rural England', cannot be found in the 'North'. Only one writer disagrees with this conclusion (see Campbell 1984: 4-5); for all the others the concept of the 'North' of England constitutes, strictly speaking, a paradox.

The long history of the construction and perception of the North-South divide is amply documented (see Jewell 1994), and Stuart Rawnsley (2000) points out that all developments and institutions which, in the past two centuries, should have fostered the development of a unified and standardised England – such as Received Pronunciation, the railway network, a nation-wide broadcasting corporation – did in fact intensify the perception of the 'North' as a region different from the 'South'. In fact, in the words of John Osmond, "[t]he fault line of England remains, as it has always been, a boundary drawn between the Severn and the Wash. Somewhere here 'The North' begins." (1988: 12) This statement is repeated in most travelogues down to the present day.

As this quotation, ranging undecidedly between confident geographical information and a resigned "somewhere", reveals it is not at all clear where exactly the 'North' begins – although everyone in England seems to be aware only too clearly of the North-South divide (see Shields 1991: 207). Morton notes a "startling" "change of country" "at the Cheshire-Lancashire border" (1933: 185), and in his companion book *The Call of England* the 'North' begins in Hull (see 1949: 16);

Priestley crosses the border to the 'North' somewhere on a bus "between Coventry and Birmingham" (1997: 79), whereas Orwell notes differences only "beyond Birmingham" (1962: 94). John Hillaby sees "the beginning of the Pennine Way" as the border to "the North of England" (1970: 129) whereas Caroline Hillier passes the same frontier more conventionally at "that old watershed of Watford" (1978: 8) and, although not venturing farther north than Birmingham, feels she is writing about 'the North' whereas Burke uses the 'North' as a synonym for Yorkshire and Lancashire (see 1933: 176ff.). Further examples of dissonant geographical identification could be given just to prove the point that examining literary tours of England for a topographical definition of the border between the 'South' and the 'North' is a futile business.

And yet there is a border between the 'South' and the 'North': all writers insist on a "complete contrast" (Mais: 1937: 21), "a real difference between North and South" (Orwell 1962: 102). And as this border can not be found on a map but is defined on an individual basis, the 'North' is obviously a discursively constructed space, forming part of the writers' "'imaginary geographies'" (Shields 1991: 29).

3. Postlapsarian Spaces
3.1 Devaluations

It is at the moment of crossing the border into what they feel to be the 'North' that writers feel obliged to explain their perception of this non-southern space. Usually, the imagined border provokes them to establish some sort of typology of 'the South' *vs.* 'the North', and the purpose of this chapter is to survey the various attempts at structuring England in two different spaces.

Travellers to the 'North' of England have always realised that the region would provide them with aesthetically different impressions from what they were offered in the 'South'. However, what started as a perception of difference was immediately referred back to the traditional artistic convention of linking 'deformity' (see Morton 1933: 186) and 'ugliness' (see, for instance, Priestley 1997: 216) with moral depravity. Consequently, all writers discuss the landscapes of the 'North' as moral landscapes, and it depends only on their political affiliations whether that moral ugliness is ascribed to the inhabitants of the 'North' or whether the exploitation of the 'North' by the 'South' is held responsible for that 'hellish' (see Priestley 1997: 135) condition of the 'North'.

In any case, beautiful 'Rural England', which stands, after all, for the true England, cannot be found in the 'North' – at best it might exist as a poor imitation in some places. Thus, the North-South divide is interpreted as a borderline between Englishness and a lack of Englishness – an opposition which in turn stabilises the negative image of the 'North'. In order to emphasise this 'essential' distinction between the 'South' and the 'North', travellers create literary northern landscapes with features which render the 'North' as alien and difficult-to-visit for the average English person.

Not surprisingly, then, Morton's *In Search of England* contrasts "a green England" with "Industrial England" (1933: 185). However, his traveller-narrator disturbs this simple static typology by introducing an element of time into his definitions: the 'North' is "New England" (186) whereas "beautiful Old England" (186) "might never have known the Industrial Revolution" (186). This awareness of change in the 'North' is contrasted with the traveller-narrator's refusal to acknowledge the impact of the 'new' on his rural 'South' when he insists – against all evidence ("round Bristol, it is true, I saw factories" [186]) – on its invulnerable rural beauty. This opposition of a 'North' which is subject to time and which – judging by the "ominous grey haze in the sky which meant Manchester" (185) – is, perhaps, nearing its end, and a perennial 'South' evokes ideas of the contrast between the fallen world and Paradise.

The moral element in this opposition is enhanced by suggestions that it is the 'North's' lack of resolve to remain truly English which can explain its careless concession to the demands of an industrialised age. In a passage characterised by highly emotionalised imagery, Morton's traveller-narrator makes it quite clear that the 'killing' of "Old England" must have been a prolonged act of brutality and carelessness:

> Yet how difficult it is to kill an English field, to stamp out the English grass, and to deform an English lane! Even here, within sixteen miles of the two great giants of the north [i.e. Liverpool and Manchester], men were raking hay in a field within a gunshot of factory chimneys. (186)

The factory is compared to a hunter allowed to proceed with the destruction of English rural life, and – according to the logic of this imagery – the hay-raking scenery stands for a wounded character possibly facing death. Wounded England is still alive; and, rhetorically, the 'North' is given all the negative connotations of cruelty, danger, lack of concern – of being deprived of elementary civilised decency. Against the background of a pastoral, Eden-like southern 'Rural England', the 'North' is fallen, 'deformed' (Morton 1949: vii) and 'monstrous' (see Morton 1933: 186). In short, Morton's traveller-narrator creates the 'North' as a morally negative space.

In spite of these serious qualifications, only one year later, Morton published a book, *The Call of England*, which was meant to do justice to the 'North' by no longer 'shirking realities' (see 1949: vii) and in which he consequently sends his intrepid traveller to that deplorable space. Testing his moral resolution and physical courage might only be avoided, so it seems, if this traveller-narrator restricted his visit to "the real north, which, apart from these areas of dense populations, remains, as it always has been, one of the most historically romantic and naturally beautiful divisions of England" (207). Obviously, the typological definition of the 'North' in *The Call of England* is not supposed to pursue the moral argument of the earlier book.

Instead, Morton's traveller-narrator distinguishes between two types of reality: the 'essential' reality of an imagined ideal, and the empirically observable reality of contemporary industrialised England. As the two quotations given in the preceding paragraph reveal, the reader of Morton's *The Call of England* has to distinguish carefully between the two meanings of the book's 'reality'. If, in the second quotation, the 'North' is said to be 'real', the reader would have to conclude that the imagined ideal of a real England can also be found in the 'North', created, as in so many cases, as an "inevitable consequence of the urban-industrial revolution" (Bunce 1994: 10). The first quotation's "realities", though, refer to the un-English realities of urban and industrial contemporary scenes, and in that sense "England is an incredible jumble of romance and reality" (Morton 1949: vii).

No doubt, it is the book's purpose to draw attention to the eternally English qualities of the 'North'; "two-thirds of the book have gone before the narrator pays close attention to an industrial city"

(Bartholomew 2004: 114). Curiously enough, *The Call of England* is only partially successful in this attempt. Again and again, it is made clear that the northern version of real England is but an imperfect copy of the 'South': "Yorkshire can imitate the best of Devon and Cornwall" (Morton 1949: 82), "the York moors are the Dartmoor of the North of England" (88), Robin Hood's Bay is "a Yorkshire Clovelly" (88) etc. Obviously, the standards set by ideal England remain too high for the 'North' to have any chance of meeting them: "there is no 'prettiest' village in Yorkshire" (87). Even if real England can be found in the 'North', it is, at best, a well done imitation, inferior and second-rate.

Not all travellers agree with this verdict. For S.P.B. Mais, for instance, the 'North' "is very English" (1937: 130), even quintessentially English: "If the English character is to be sensed anywhere, it is in this cross-section from the North Sea to St. George's Channel, from the blast-furnaces to the cotton-mills" (132). But Mais's traveller-narrator fails to make a convincing case for the 'North's' Englishness by imitating Morton's literary strategy of refusing things 'Northern' the complete fulfilment of all expectations that are derived from the 'South': "At Preston I remember a tall spire almost as lovely as that of Salisbury" (130/1). This is echoed by Thomas Burke, in his *The Beauty of England*: "There are parts of Lancashire [...] where lovers may walk in groves, not, perhaps, as fair as the groves of Somerset and Devon, but surprisingly fair when found in Lancashire." (1933: 328) In spite of Mais's rhetorical claims, when it comes to actual evaluations the 'North' fails to be truly English.

Burke presents the 'North' in ambiguous terms throughout. Repeatedly, he grants the 'North' the ideal 'dream-like' (see 1933: 176 and 326) quality of true Englishness: in Nidderdale, for example, "you will feel rushing upon you here the whole beauty and power of England" (319) – yet he will qualify this assessment by reminding his readers of the inevitable coexistence, in the 'North', of beauty and ugliness. Yorkshire 'offers' "extreme beauty sorted with drabness" (176), its Whitby is "shadowy and odorous" (183), and "Durham County is not without its beauties, but they do not grace its eastern half" (186). Significantly, even some of its historical monuments fail to carry the inspiration of English history. Lastingham's Saxon church, for example,

> presents itself as a well of darkness, cold and still and silent. From the damp walls and the massive piers [...] presses the stillness that follows centuries of sound, the coldness that follows the end of religious fire. [...] only dank air, and stones that do not even sigh. (181)

Thus hovering between ideal and bleak reality, the 'North', though occasionally "a benediction to the eyes" (311), is not always pleasant to the senses, and for Burke the lack of untainted beauty corresponds to a lack of proper religious life. It is still England, as Burke's remark, just a few miles before crossing the border to Scotland, reveals – "we are now [...] aware of a change from purely English scenery" (187) – but it is again a fallen England.

Although making no attempt to avoid the industrialised parts of Northern England, Priestley, in his *English Journey* of 1934, arrives at a similar definition of the 'North'. In its "ugliness" (1997: 216) and sadness it offers too many "depressing" (84) journeys, and entering an industrial town suggests the imagined experience of a descent into Hell: Sheffield's "smoke was so thick that it made a foggy twilight in the descending streets, which appeared as if they would end in the steaming bowels of the earth" (135).

At a more analytical level, the horror of a similar scene unfolds its drama as it must be acknowledged that towns of the English 'North' provide the experience of "our urban and industrial civilisation" (85) generally. Introducing a temporal dimension into his survey, Priestley's narrator points out that before this infernal civilisation of the 'North' was created, paradise with its ideal conditions of living in happiness and peace could be found – even along the river at Tyneside:

> I asked myself [...] whether the whole Tyneside had not taken a wrong turning. There was a time when this must have been one of the prettiest of our green estuaries. With a clear sky above him and clear water below, a man could have been happy here in the old days, content to live in peace. (263)

The moral dimension of this "wrong turning" is explained at more than one point in *English Journey*: "past greed" (255) left us with a "cynically devastated countryside" (322). Industrialisation "had done more harm than good to the real enduring England" (323). Thus, the deformed landscape of the industrialised 'North' turns into an emblem of the sinful state of mankind: "What you see looks like a debauchery of cynical greed." (323)

Even the open country of the 'North' is "deeply scarred" (134) by man's activities, and the untouched parts of the moors are seen mainly as a temporal respite from the suffocating conditions of living an unhappy life in an industrial town: "if you can use your legs [...] you need never be unhappy long in Bradford" (151). As a consequence, J. Fairfax-Blakeborough sees beauty in the natural features of the 'North' only because they offer "relief [...] from the industrial towns they shelter" (1946/47: 125). Fallen man is, by definition, caught between two worlds.

In more recent times, the tradition of linking the 'North' with hell was continued by the popular walker and writer John Hillaby and by Beryl Bainbridge in her ill-tempered retracing of Priestley's journey through the 'North'. Summing up her impression of Stockton she states: "My impression is that I have landed in hell" (1985: 136; similarly 92). The sins committed are listed, as if selected from a confession manual: "greed", "lack of confidence", "naivety" and "murder" (104). Again, the people are blamed for their lot, and the landscape of the 'North' is discussed in moral terms.

Hillaby even extends, in his *Journey Through Britain* of 1968, the negative 'hellish' space to the open countryside. Announcing to his readers that they will now encounter "all that is usually meant by the North of England" (1970: 129) this traveller-narrator steps, at the southern beginning of the Pennine Way, into a "depressing" (135), "cheerless" (143) world, reminding him only of faeces: "Manure is the analogy that comes most readily to mind" (134). Botanical explanations for this analogy are given, but cut short by the narrator's apocalyptic verdict: this is "land at the end of its tether" (135), a statement made all the more urgent by the rhetorically motivated, but otherwise incoherent, insertion of an observation involving the destruction of man-made machinery :

> Looking down on the Snake road I saw what from that height appeared to be a beetle lying on its back, surrounded by ant-like figures. A car had crashed and turned over [...] and disintegrated. (135)

Man is an endangered species in this bleak land, one has to conclude, and the reader is well advised to follow the narrator's example: "I don't suppose I shall ever go there again." (136) In fact he makes it quite clear that he has to endure in the 'North' a situation which is "the very worst you can encounter" (138).

For Hillaby's narrator, then, entering the 'North' is presented as a descent into the land of death. And again, as with Priestley, there is a moral dimension to this: "fertility has almost reached the point of no return" (137) as the result of an age-long exploitation of the earth by "burning, tree-felling, and overgrazing" (135). The northerners' activities have inevitably left them in an environment which is as far away from Paradise as one can imagine. Their incorrigible stupidity is depressing when, at the beginning of his journey in the 'North', the traveller observers further abuse of the exhausted land: "it swarmed with hikers, bikers, nudists, naturalists, motorists, coach and train parties, day-trippers, week-enders [...]" (130).

Although he chose a Yorkshire village as his British home, Bill Bryson shares in the negative view of the 'North' – basically because it is not the 'South': "it felt like another country" (1996: 212). When he defines the difference as an "exceptional sense [...] of greatness past" (212) he agrees with Hillaby's verdict that this region is moving towards its end in history – in spite of some "pockets of immense prosperity" (219). Although desperately looking for rhetorically effective ways of being amusing, there is definitely an apocalyptic note, too, in his observation that a place like Bradford has arrived at the bottom line of a hierarchy of places where one would like to live: "Bradford's role in life is to make every place else in the world look better in comparison" (196). *Notes from a Small Island* does its best to confirm the 'North's' reputation as being on the brink of leaving history.

Theroux's notoriously ill-tempered traveller finds, as soon as he enters the 'North', only unemployment which in turn produces "hopelessness and depression" (1984: 207) everywhere. "Ugliness" (315) prevails, and the landscape of the North between its "horror cities" (212) is characterised as "dark brown and depressed and enfeebled" (316). Apocalyptic notes are introduced by referring – against all evidence – to "the great silence" (209). Somehow, the narrator seems to imply that, in moral terms, this silence was a just retribution for previous complaints:

> Industry had come and gone. It was as if a wicked witch had heard Orwell's carping ('factory whistles ... smoke and filth') and said, 'Then you shall have nothing!' and swept it all away. (209)

Robert Chesshyre's *The Return of a Native Reporter* of 1987 continues the tradition of this argument when he notes the unchecked 'despoliation' of northern landscapes by industry (see 1988: 37) and backs his apocalyptic impression by quoting figures concerning "the worst health in Britain" (45) and the high mortality rate in the 'North' (see 39). The end of the world can be inspected by studying the landscapes of the 'North':

> The Don Valley between Sheffied and Rotherham, which once contained more smoke than Hades, is a desert, like Hiroshima after the firestorm had subsided [...]. Beowulf and the monster Grendel might have been out there somewhere (48).

In contrast to other writers, though, Chesshyre places the moral responsibility for the punishment of being damned to live in the 'North' on people living in the 'South' of England who had exploited Northern England (see 45), thus taking the guilt from the inhabitants of the 'North'. Nevertheless, his version of the 'North' remains a moral landscape, too.

3.2 Inverted Standards

It is George Orwell's *The Road to Wigan Pier*, which argues, in the inter-war years, most strongly against this moral devaluation of the 'North'. For Orwell, the 'South' is peopled by "the parasitic dividend-drawing class" (1962: 102), and "Southern England" is reduced to "one enormous Brighton inhabited by lounge-lizards" (102). Consequently, this traveller-narrator, preferring the morals of the 'North', characterises an unspoilt rural scenery as "strange, almost unnatural" (17) and takes the "ugliness of industrialism" (94) as something one can "come to terms with" (94). Through this inversion of a common pattern, Orwell's traveller makes an end with the traditional parallelism of ugliness and infernal qualities, but he remains true to the argumentative pattern that the differing scenes in the 'North' and the 'South' constitute moral landscapes.

This inversion of what had become, by the late thirties, a conventional way of representing the 'North' is important enough for Orwell to insert, in his travelogue, an extended meditation on the scenery north of Birmingham (see 94) Admittedly, one encounters in the 'North' "the real ugliness of industrialism" (94), and rhetorically, Orwell's traveller-narrator fully exploits the infernal dimensions of industrialised environs: Sheffield, for instance, suffers from "drifts of smoke rosy with sulphur" in "foundries you see fiery serpents of iron" and in this context of fire and burning,"the scream of the iron under the blow" (all 96) evokes images of torture. But, according to this traveller-narrator, "the beauty or ugliness of industrialism hardly matters" (98) compared with the unjustifiable gross social differences an economy organised along capitalist lines will inevitably produce. Under this system of production, "clean and orderly" (98) factories in the 'South' are equally evil. The morally negative landscape is found wherever "the parasitic dividend-drawing class" (102) likes to live.

Whenever the moral evaluation is inverted, and the South seen as "complacent" (Hillier 1978: 8), "bloodless" (17) and marked by "more cynicism" (17) than one would find beyond the Watford Gap, the 'North' is perceived – some factories notwithstanding – to be 'rural' and "its green border-land characteristically beautiful" (8), presenting the traveller with a landscape "as it must have looked in George Eliot's day" (26). The impact of industrialism is there, but for Caroline Hillier, writing in the mid-seventies, its effects can easily be accommodated within that 'rural' environment: just like any traveller in southern 'Rural England', Hillier's narrator exclaims in the 'North': "I began to breathe more freely", continuing in the same happy mood: "lorries thundered up the road" (19). Ridiculous as this may read, one has to see it as an abstraction and idealisation of observed reality in no way different from the corresponding efforts of all those writers praising the 'South'.

4. Estranging the 'North'

All tours of England, from the inter-war years until present times, have used a 'Southern' perspective to emphasise the difference of the 'North'; occasionally, 'Northern England' seems to be used as an oxymoron. The general paradox of a 'Northern England' is conveyed, in these texts, by a few well tried rhetorical strategies of making the 'North' a strange country indeed.

4.1 Climate

It might come as a surprise that, as part of this rhetoric of paradox, rain and wetness are used, by English writers, as one of the features to convey the message of the un-English 'North'. But if one remembers that the construction of 'Rural England' follows the artistic conventions of devising pastoral landscapes, with their everlasting benign climes, it makes sense to underline the negative qualities of the 'North' by inverting just these conventions and evoking an inhospitable northern space of rain (see Hillaby 1970: 143), mist (see 136), cold winds or wintry conditions. "The weather was still fine but colder" (Priestley 1997: 79) is one of the milder qualifications of the pleasant pastoral climate connected, through literature, with the 'South'.

For Theroux and Bainbridge, both given to stronger language, rain seems to pour continually on the built-up areas of the 'North' (see Theroux 1984: 206, 210, 317; Bainbridge 1985: 77 and 129), and the effects of the wet weather are duly emphasised by using rhetorically charged language: "Our journey to Hubberholme was a wet affair, through blinding rain under a slate-grey sky." (Bainbridge 1985: 118) For Robert Chesshyre's narrator, too, "a heavy drizzle [...] reduced visibility to the width of the street" (1988: 43), and a "wet Sunday night" (48) is followed next morning by a "ferocious wind" (48). And Bryson's traveller-narrator links Bradford, predictably enough, inseparably with drizzle and even creates a new generic meteorological term in the process, "the drizzly twilit bleakness of Bradford" (1996: 203). This list of examples could be continued *ad nauseam*.

If meteorological 'realities' fail to live up to these literary expectations, some deft imaginative creation will have to do, as this example from Priestley's *English Journey* demonstrates:

> I find it impossible to imagine what the city [i.e. Liverpool] looks like in clear bright sunshine. I think of it existing in a shortened year, only running from November to February, with all its citizens forever wearing thick overcoats. (1997: 194)

Obviously, one should not read this information on weather conditions as a descriptive passage, but as a rhetorical device. The 'North' is given a literary 'reputation' of bad weather, and some writers even exploit this tradition with some degree of self-conscious irony:

> Leeds lived up to Manchester's reputation that day in providing a fine drizzle [...]. It was the right weather for those slag-heaps, refuse dumps, and warehouses that line the western exit from Leeds. (Mais 1937: 128)

In travelogues, a northern town under a warm sun is impossible. This literary strategy of meteorological debunking is ignored only when the 'North' is claimed as a truly English space. Thus, Thomas Burke, patriotically intent on presenting his readers with the beauties of England in all its regions, discovers "a pastoral country" (1933: 177) even in various parts of the 'North' and praises Nidderdale as "a plate of happy England" (318). Consequently, the weather in those parts is not too bad – but even Burke tends to interrupt his brave attempt at claiming true Englishness for the 'North' with the odd demonstration of "the weather's ferocity" (317) in the northern parts of the country:

> Their [i.e. the moors' and dales'] dreaming beauty then becomes terrible. The great basin of sky is a wrath of cloud, the valleys are turmoils of conflicting rains, and the wind rips across them with the fury of a coast hurricane. Mists close upon you and retreat. Under the veil of rain the landscape shivers. The moor is a grey blanket of wetness. (317)

One notices how this writer struggles to combine his ambition to extend true 'Rural England' into the 'North' with an obviously powerful convention of producing negative northern landscapes. There is indeed a good view to be had from the hills around Huddersfield, but the potential experience of a truly English scene is spoilt by a typically northern "razor wind [which] met us with open blade." (338) The juxtapositions of praise and meteorologically phrased qualifications give an indication of the contested nature of the 'North' as an English region. Only Hillier, who fails to see moral corruption in the 'North' paints, with some artistic logic, a picture of a climatically favourable 'North': "The sky was unclouded, and it was spring." (1978: 19)

4.2 Exoticism

A more powerful literary strategy of turning the 'North' into a foreign, un-English country consists in simply taking literally the idea of strangeness and depicting the 'North' as an exotic country. This device is used by Morton in both of his books. In *The Call of England* exoticism is created by placing the 'North' in a romantic distant past – "Newcastle [...] stands on its hill like a knight in sable armour" (1949: 99) – or comparing it with the moods of an enigmatic woman – a Tyne bridge "has as many moods as a woman" (99). *In Search of England* manages to turn the few textual passages about the 'North' into sketches of an exotic Orient. In a rhetorically powerful passage, he first points out that the aesthetic experience provided by the 'strange' Lancashire landscape must not be discussed in terms of the Beautiful:

> With the beautiful Old England that I love so fresh in mind, I stood ready to be horrified by the Black Belt; yet strangely, I stood impressed and thrilled by the grim power of these ugly chimneys rising in groups. (1933: 186)

The distinction between "beautiful" and "ugly" is obvious, yet ugliness exerts some fascination on the traveller-narrator. Even in the Black Belt, so the reader is informed, some appeal to the senses can be found, although the exact nature of this aesthetic experience is not yet defined. With his intention of giving the 'North' at least some aesthetic quality without granting 'beauty' to this part of the country, Morton then manages to change the bleak view of bored and hopeless miners into an exotic sight:

> On Sundays, in all the grey villages of Lancashire, the miners sit on their haunches against the walls, their hands between their knees. They are the only Englishmen who squat like Arabs. (1933: 186/7)[1]

"Englishmen" with the habits of Arabs: the 'North' presents us with definitely un-English views which the average reader expects from exotic countries. Really, Northern England seems to be located worlds apart from the 'South'. Morton's strategy of aestheticising the 'North' is also a strategy of estranging the 'North'. Indeed, "sites are never simply locations" (Shields 1991: 6).

---

[1] This passage is also discussed in Bartholomew (2004: 96).

Interestingly enough it is J.B. Priestley's middle-class voice of Englishness in the inter-war years which most consistently turns the 'North' into an exotic country, composed of all the different images of a foreign country his readers might have in mind. A slag-heap is presented as "an ebony pyramid" (1997: 136), the hills near Huddersfield seem "nearly as wild and cold as Greenland" (137), the Yorkshire moors are "Tibetan" in their "emptiness" (155), Halifax excels in "Siberian bleakness" (162) etc. Stuart Rawnsley who collected these and many other examples of making the 'North' exotic rightly states: "When Priestley reaches the North of England he takes the reader through a very un-English terrain." (2000: 16) This tradition continues as a conventional way of emphasising the non-English quality of the 'North': "With the spray and the wind it might have been somewhere in the middle of Finland" (Hillaby 1970: 138). The process of exoticising the 'North' has been so successful that Beatrix Campbell sums up her experience of Southerners discussing the 'North' by remarking that "London experiences the 'provinces' as if they were up the Amazon" (1984: 33). And there, as is well known, true England cannot be found.

4.3 People

The majority of the countries used in these comparisons are characterised by their desert-like landscapes and they are, in the common imagination, inhabited by people whose civilisation is considered to be radically different from, if not inferior to, English standards. This racist element is indeed exploited in the literary presentation of the 'simple' people living in the 'North', and with this strategy, the process of distancing the southern traveller from the 'North' reaches its most powerful expression.

The tone is set, again, by H.V. Morton whose *In Search of England* introduces the "sturdy and rather tough Lancashire folk" (1933: 187) by sketching a short conversation with a man from Wigan. Suddenly, Morton's oily journalistic style is rudely interrupted by the representation of dialect speech ("'I'm reet glad to hear thee say that!'" – 188), something hardly ever found in this text when it depicts corresponding encounters in the 'South' (see 58). Thus, his refined exploratory attitude is threatened by an idea of shared activities he will not tolerate. Conversely, it is impossible for the man from Wigan to understand the traveller's insistence on individual exploration:

> He beamed on me. He offered to show me the chief glories of Wigan. I told him that I wanted to find them for myself. Still he beamed on me! They all do this in Wigan if you go up and say frankly that the town has a certain attraction. (188)

Obviously, two worlds meet at this moment: the knowledgeable *flâneur*, and a native eager to please someone he considers to be some sort of master whom one should be eager to please – though in a spirit of uncomplicated cooperation. And this passage by Morton sets the native's child-like identification with his possessions against the sophisticated traveller-narrator's cool assessment of Wigan's attractions. No wonder that the traveller mutters, in an aside: "rather pathetic!" (188) This verdict contrasts significantly with the characterisations he reserves for simple people living in the 'South', as just one quotation illustrates. Near Beaulieu, "the people are slow Saxon, well-mannered, deferential people, with their wits about them and their tongues padlocked" (33-4).

No doubt, it is only in the 'North' that Morton's, Hillaby's and other travellers feel superior: they come from a realm of civilisation to meet people of comparatively rude and simple emotions and "offensively blunt" (Hillaby 1970: 142) ways of acting. These travellers exemplify how, in the inter-war and post-war years, the 'South' constructed the 'North' as a space peopled by human beings certainly not meeting the standards of English civilisation. The polemical thrust of this devaluation of the 'North', as expressed in *In Search of England*, is all the more apparent if one compares its presentation of 'Northern' people with passages from the more 'empirical' *The Call of England*. In this later book, literary versions of dialect speech are rare, and the local language is even praised for having preserved its rich historical vocabulary (see 1949: 89); moreover, people in the 'North' are good at jobs no person from the 'South' could do equally well (see, for example, 77).

In Search of England, then, sets the pattern for a long tradition of cultural production of 'Northern' people as un-English in the sense that they do not live up to the standards of English civilisation. Inevitably, the subject of "Yorkshire humour" (Burke 1933: 336) is made to serve the same purpose. Burke, for instance, rather hesitantly, grants that this humour might be "Yorkshire common sense" (336), but immediately destroys any positive connotations by singling out one particular joke – "or what seemed to us a joke" (337) – as a rather unlikely case of "the honest operation of a literal mind" (337). Similarly, Hillaby links this humour with deprivation: his traveller-narrator develops the theory that it is "a long history of poverty" (1970: 140) which has produced that reduced form of humour. A strong suspicion remains, then, that Yorkshire's population is uncivilised to such a degree that they have to rely on their "macabre humour" (Hillaby 1970: 140) where people in the 'South' would use their knowledge and common sense.

It emerges, then, that the fundamental separation between the 'South' and the 'North' is based on two main distinctions: the morally evaluated Fall, manifesting itself in an expulsion from an Arcadian paradise, still preserved in representations of the 'South' but only occasionally visible in the 'North', and the degree of civilised Englishness, only achieved in perfection in the 'South', and hardly ever present in the 'North'. The efficacy of the cultural construction of an inferior 'North' can be gathered from the very writers who are not interested in the continuity of this tradition. A telling example is given in Mais's *England's Character* when its traveller-narrator meets an efficient and polite bus conductor in Stockton: with all the (unconscious) patronising which only a person from the 'South' would be capable of in circumstances where a clash with non-civilised people is expected, this traveller comments with 'surprise' on his bus conductor's cleverness and sensitivity:

> He [...] wrestled with a window that refused to stay shut, jammed pieces of paper into another that rattled, and volunteered information about every passing object of interest. I was surprised to find how extensive was his knowledge, and even more surprised to find him so sensitive to rattling windows. (1937: 123-4)

5. The Creation of a Northern Identity

Predictably, the constant debunking, during the inter-war years, of the population living in the 'North' of England, produced oppositional voices which would praise the virtues of the 'Northern' character.

What is essential in this process of rewriting cultural history is that it also creates the North-South divide by ascribing distinct identities to each part of the population. In a very clear-sighted passage, George Orwell comments on this process and its results:

> The North-South antithesis [...] has been rubbed into us for such a long time past. There exists in England a curious cult of Northernness, sort of Northern snobbishness. A Yorkshireman in the South will always take care to let you know that he regards you as an inferior. (1962: 98)

By an inversion of the existing pattern of authority according to which the 'South' was able to define the 'North', people from the 'North' now assume the power to define themselves against the 'South'. "The Northener has 'grit', he is grim, 'dour', plucky, warm-hearted, and democratic" (98) whereas a Southern person would be lacking in all these desirable points. For this definition of a 'Northern' identity to succeed, though, it is necessary to construct a 'Southern' identity against which non-Southern qualities shine all the more brilliantly. The consequences are dramatic: in the inter-war years, England and Englishness develop into contested categories, based on "a reinscription of identity as inevitable alterity" (Ebbatson 2005: 3). Thus, social identities are created by difference, dialectically derived from place, and formed according to a strategy of polarisation. The North-South divide as a cultural construct seems cemented for a long time.

Thus, people from the 'North' can now, in a blunt, reductionist manner, blame the 'South' for the decay of northern towns (see Bainbridge 1985: 97-8). But how effective the continued construction of the 'North' as the space of the fallen world has been, is demonstrated by the absence of any self-assertive oppositional stance in the concluding section of the speech of Bainbridge's representative 'Northern' voice:

> London and Maggie said what was right and proper and if the people of Liverpool didn't behave like good little children they were punished for it. That was the reason for the riots. More and more punishment, more and more police. The inhabitants must be taught obedience at all costs. (98)

The same ambivalence can be detected in most voices praising the qualities of the 'North'. "The spirit is still alive", claims Caroline Hillier's traveller-narrator (1978: 9) in what is no doubt intended as a paean to the 'North', but the examples given for that spirit are all taken from that storeroom of not-yet civilised behaviour: 'Northern' people are "ready with smiles or a straight answer, still walking briskly without overcoats on a bright winter day" (1978: 8). And Robert Chesshyre explicitly states that the "'northern' qualities friendliness and bluntness" (1988: 47) necessarily go together. Elaborate civilised codes of social communication or dress, implied here, have not yet arrived in the 'North', and this traveller's journey turns into an exercise in primitivism. A positive 'Northern' identity is postulated, yet an inferior otherness is observed.

The reason for these ambivalent definitions of a 'Northern' identity is easy to find: the 'North' is perceived primarily as the region of a working-class living in sprawling industrial conurbations. Therefore it cannot possibly be constructed in terms of an Arcadia which provides the idea of 'Rural England' in the 'South'. The descriptive elements which constructions of space have to use as a starting point are too dissimilar to fuse the 'North' and the 'South' of England into one coherent space. And as the decision about which of the two parts is 'English' had long been taken, the 'North', even in contemporary travelogues, will lack in real 'Englishness'. The 'North' and its people remain on the periphery of English culture. Obviously, this is to be expected as 'Rural England' was invented to counter the realities of industrialism and its urban forms of settlement in the first place (see Bunce 1994: 20; Ebbatson 2005: 3).

However, the few writers who have argued the case for the 'North' have not been at work without some success. Orwell's negative comments on the exploiter's culture prevalent in the 'South' have also impaired the 'South's' ability to persist in its tradition of a self-confident self-definition. One detects, in recent books on the condition of England, a new 'Southern' sense of inferiority in its relationship with the 'North':

> Those of us who live south of the Trent [...] produce none of life's necessities, nothing as tangible as a chair you can sit on, coal you can burn, a car you can drive, a steel beam with which you can open up the ground floor of your bijou Victorian cottage. (Chesshyre 1988: 47)

In sum, then, the few alternative constructions of the 'North' have not led to the establishment of a 'Northern' identity which could be said to be free of an apprehension of inferiority. What they achieved, though, is an awareness both of 'Northern' qualities and of the effects of 'Northern' propaganda: "As a southerner […] I have always been slightly in awe of northerners, accepting the image they cultivate of themselves as tougher, blunter, less effete than the soft southerner." (Dimbleby 2005: 23) This confession of a television celebrity might accelerate the development of an unquestioned 'Northern' identity; it might also indicate that, within England, two problematic identities coexist – at a time when the definition of 'Englishness' seems to be an urgent issue.

Works Cited

Primary References

Bainbridge, Beryl (1984/1985): *English Journey, or The Road to Milton Keynes*. London: Fontana.

Bryson, Bill (1995/1996): *Notes From a Small Island*. London: Black Swan.

Burke, Thomas (1933): *The Beauty of England*. London: Harrap.

Campbell, Beatrix (1984): *Wigan Pier Revisited: Poverty and Politics in the Eighties*. London: Virago.

Chesshyre, Robert (1987/1988): *The Return of a Native Reporter*. London: Penguin.

Dimbleby, David (2005): *A Picture of Britain*. London: Tate Publishing.

Fairfax-Blakeborough, J. (1939/1946-47): "Moors and Fells", in: H.J. Massingham (ed.): *The English Countryside: A Survey of Its Chief Features* (The Pilgrims' Library). London: Batsford.

Hillaby, John (1968/1970): *Journey through Britain*. London: Paladin.

Hillier, Caroline (1976/1978): *A Journey to the Heart of England*. London: Paladin.

Mais, S. P. B. (1937): *England's Character*. London: Hutchinson.

Morton, H. V. (1927/1933): *In Search of England*. London: Methuen.

— (1928/1949): *The Call of England*. London: Methuen.

Orwell, George (1937/1962): *The Road to Wigan Pier*. Harmondsworth: Penguin.

Priestley, J. B. (1934/1997): *English Journey: Being a Rambling but Truthful Account of What One Man Saw and Heard and Felt and Thought during a Journey Through England During the Autumn of the Year 1933*. London: Folio Society.

Theroux, Paul (1983/1984): *The Kingdom by the Sea: A Journey Around the Coast of Great Britain*. Harmondsworth: Penguin.

Research Literature

Allen, J., D. Massey and A. Cochrane (1998): *Rethinking the Region*. London: Routledge.

Baker, Alan R.H. and Mark Billinge (2004) (eds.): *Geographies of England: The North-South Divide, Material and Imagined*. Cambridge: Cambridge UP.

Banks, Mark (2001): "Representing Regional Life: The Place Discourses of *Granada Tonight*", *North West Geography* 1(1), 2-10.

Bartholomew, Michael (2004): *In Search of H.V. Morton*. London: Methuen.

Bell, Ian A. (1995): "To See Ourselves: Travel Narratives and National Identity in Contemporary Britain", in: Ian A. Bell (ed.). *Peripheral Visions: Images of*

Nationhood in Contemporary British Fiction. Cardiff: University of Wales Press, 6-26.

Bunce, Michael (1994): *The Countryside Ideal: Anglo-American Images of Landscape.* London: Routledge.

Duncan, Simon (1989): "What Is Locality?", in: Richard Peet and Nigel Thrift (eds.): *New Models in Geography: The Political-Economy Perspective.* London: Unwin Hyman, 221-252.

Easthope, Antony (1991): *Literary Into Cultural Studies.* London: Longman.

Ebbatson, Roger (2005): *An Imaginary England: Nation, Landscape and Literature, 1840-1920.* Aldershot: Ashgate.

Gebhardt, Hans, Paul Reuber und Günter Wolkersdorfer (2003): "Kulturgeographie: Leitlinien und Perspektiven", in: Hans Gebhardt, Paul Reuber and Günter Wolkersdorfer (eds.): *Kulturgeographie: Aktuelle Ansätze und Entwicklungen.* Heidelberg: Spektrum Akademischer Verlag, 1-27.

Jewell, Helen M. (1994): *The North-South Divide: The Origins of Northern Consciousness in England.* Manchester: Manchester UP.

Matless, David and Chris Philo (1991): "Nature's Geographies: Social and Cultural Perspectives", in: Chris Philo (ed.): *New Words, New Worlds: Reconceptualising Social and Cultural Geography.* Aberystwyth: Cambrian Printers, 39-48.

Osmond, John (1988): *The Divided Kingdom.* London: Constable.

Rawnsley, Stuart (2000): "Constructing 'The North': Space and a Sense of Place", in: Neville Kirk (ed.): *Northern Identities: Historical Interpretations of 'The North' and 'Northernness'.* Aldershot: Ashgate, 3-22.

Shields, Rob (1991): *Places on the Margin: Alternative Geographies of Modernity.* London: Routledge.

Sutton, Mike (2000): "England, whose England? Class, Gender and National Identity in the 20th-century Folklore Revival", [http://www.mustrad.org.uk/articles/-england.htm].

"Such girls as you would hardly see anywhere else in England...": the 'regional feminine' of Mary Linskill's fiction

Jan Hewitt

Abstract: This essay will explore female contributions towards constructions of regional identities in the late nineteenth century through the work of Mary Linskill, a writer from Whitby, North Yorkshire in the North of England. It argues that her work demonstrates a 'regional feminine', signalling the presence of significant female constituencies in the cultural industries that transformed Whitby, not least in the production and consumption of the regional novel and linking them to the strong anthropological tradition newly concerned to identify and categorise 'indigenous cultures' of specific environments, landscapes and regions. It further suggests how ongoing power relationships are negotiated discursively between north and south, region and metropolis, working not simply as a one-way imposition of dominant images but as a more dynamic site of exchange and interactivity.

Key names and concepts: Mary Linskill - George Du Maurier - Michel Foucault - Mary Louise Pratt - John Urry - *Punch*; Encounter - Transculturation - Tourist Gaze - Representation - Regional Feminine - Whitby - Englishness - North and Northernness - Tourism - Landscape - Environment.

1. Introduction

Complex and contradictory readings of the North lie behind the opening action and dialogue of *Between the Heather and the Northern Sea* (first published 1884) where its heroine Genevieve Bartholomew and her artist father travel from London to live on the North Yorkshire moors. As they cross the moors, Genevieve articulates a contemporary perception of urban crisis by anticipating they will find there "peace, freedom from anxiety and deliverance from the pressure of modern ideas" that are only too prevalent in the metropolis with its "three or four millions of unquiet souls" (Linskill 1991: 9). Genevieve is an *outsider* to this northern landscape; consequently their journey across it highlights her perceptions of its difference to the one she already knows. It is also clear that this is an intelligent and independent young woman who will make her own judgements notwithstanding her father's occasionally jaundiced remarks. For him a typical Yorkshirewoman is "a thing to be found more frequently on the stage and in third-rate novels than in any of the three Ridings of Yorkshire" yet Genevieve persists in her belief that not only does such a figure exist, but that she will be personified by "hardness, keenness and shrewdness" and, if "not quite free from the suspicion of sarcasm", will have "a certain dignity about her." Genevieve further hopes that this imminent encounter between herself and Dorothy Craven, the projected embodiment of such virtues, will be one where she is "able to hold my own" (Linskill 1991a: 8). Happily, the London girl makes a favourable impression on the dour Yorkshirewoman from whom she will learn much in return – not least that the region "between the heather and the Northern sea" is a harsh one. She will have to come to terms with tragedy and loss in an environment where tenant farming is rendered all but impossible for such families as the Cravens, where the sea dictates life and death for the fisherfolk of nearby Soulsgrif Bight, and where her own father will be mortally stricken. Yet when father and daughter take the letting of a simple moorland cottage from Dorothy, and Genevieve wistfully observes how easily the breezy lanes with their profusion of ripe brambles could offer physical and mental sustenance to "a hundred little gutter children from the London slums" (Linskill 1991: 19), we also see that same landscape offering a potentially nurturing and regenerative space for a wider population.

It is this contradiction between the harsh northern environment and its potentially regenerative 'feminine' spaces that prompts my concerns in this chapter. In the late nineteenth and early twentieth centuries rural and nostalgic constructions of England marked a widespread cultural reaction to the disruptive effects of industrialisation. Whether or not this has been responsible for a more general decline of a British industrial spirit is open to debate but it is clear that a general perception of crisis in urban society in the 1880s stimulated a response across a wide spectrum of the arts in general, and an antidote was found in the recourse to a rural vision. It culminated in the cultural vision of a 'real' England imagined as rural yet, increasingly, as located in the south (Howkins 1986: 207-212; Weiner 2004: xiii-xviii). In this context my discussion will concentrate on three novels of the 1880s with specifically northern settings, written by a northern writer, which played their own part in wider responses to crisis and change. I will argue that Mary Linskill's *Between the Heather and the Northern Sea* (1884), *The Haven under the Hill* (1886) and *In Exchange for a Soul* (1887) participate in a mode I have come to describe as the "regional feminine", which highlights a set of stances, discourses, and concerns where female interests predominate to link them closely to region and place.

2. Female Encounters and Female Cultures

The titles of *Between the Heather and the Northern Sea* and *The Haven under the Hill* locate their North at a point where topographies meet and boundaries blur, where the 'masculine' geographical features of hill and sea elide with the more empathetic 'feminine' attributes of 'home' and 'haven'. Nineteenth-century women writers frequently adopted regional settings or stances in their work yet consideration of specifically gendered constructions has had relatively little place generally in the discussion of regional fiction (see Dodd 1998: 120-122). This would be especially so when contained in domestic fiction seen as predominantly having a female readership. However, the encounter between female characters, like Genevieve and Dorothy is an important device, not simply because its construction within a "contact-zone" mirrored Whitby's wider 'discovery' by outsiders such as tourists and artists but because Linskill's constructions of it are part of a range of local responses to dominant constructions of the North as 'other'. Reading her work with this in mind suggests a process of 'transculturation' that Mary Louise Pratt has argued interrupts the 'totalising momentum' of metropolitan assumptions (Pratt 1992: 5-6) and suggests how perceptions from *inside* were implicated in wider constructions of region. Linskill's writing, and its dissemination, indicates how local communities also defined *themselves* through a process of encounter as part of an area that, in its supposed simplicity, honesty and ruggedness, held something of value for the modern world (see also Burke 1997: 201-206).

Mary Linskill (1840-1891) was a native of the fishing, whaling, alum-making and trading port of Whitby. Her novels of the 1880s are geographically located in areas around the town, thinly disguised under the name 'Hild's Haven,' or sometimes 'Port St Hilda'. Their plots and characters reproduce conventional narratives of women's romances where moral strength and purity of intent win out: in the love triangles where male heroes are competed for by contrasting female characters, or in the tangles of a cross-class love match where a working woman is socially elevated. Though frequently melodramatic, Linskill is no idle sensationalist. Hers are Christian narratives where redemption comes through suffering and is articulated through sentimental tropes; they are part of a huge body of minor fiction that existed with the aspirations and expectations of nineteenth-century women in mind. With their evangelical precepts and copious literary allusions, reading them now requires some persistence; however Linskill's novels of the 1880s enjoyed a popular circulation throughout Britain and its empire and were still in print well into the 1920s.[1] Much of this circulation is due to the appeal of her romantic plots to a 'respectable' readership, but Linskill was also clearly noted for her capacity to construct compelling accounts of region. One reviewer described her as "the novelist of the North" whose characters were "portraits of Northern folk, as they who have lived among them will recognise, and her scenery is precisely what one recalls", another praised her "shifting scenes of a great sea storm", its "aspects of wild, high moorland; ...lonely, desolate and reedy marshes; ...rare bits of cornland, [and] sheltered orchard", and yet another in an obituary further opined that "what Mr Hardy is to the West Country, Mary Linskill might have been to the North Riding of Yorkshire" (Quinlan and Humble 1969: 13).

This area itself clearly offered a distinctively northern space for rural escape; by the 1880s Whitby's representation as a picturesque landscape, generated from a broadly metropolitan base, played an important part in shaping its desirability for middle-class families seeking leisure and escape from urban industrial centres. Yet the perception was a relatively recent one. Here was a commercial and industrial community that had experienced severe economic decline in the years following the Napoleonic Wars, with the 1820s and 1830s a period of

---

[1] Linskill's novels were distributed widely throughout the British Empire (and are still to be found in library holdings) where their regional attributes would no doubt have appealed to exiled subjects. See e.g. 'Cheap Literature' in the Kingston, Jamaica *Daily Gleaner*, 29 June 1885; Popular Fiction Collection of Launceston Reference Library, Tasmania.

acute anxiety for its commercial elites who despaired of its rank harbour and stinking quayside and looked towards the new industrial centres of nearby Teesside, Durham and Newcastle with considerable envy (Hugill 1830: 1-43). However, desires to be part of a new northern industrial culture were never satisfied partly because of the town's geographical isolation and also because, by redefining itself as a leisure landscape based on the growing popularity of the Victorian seaside holiday, Whitby started to see in itself a new kind of redemption. Historians of the town have accounted for the transformation mainly in economic and structural terms; the arrival of the railway and new speculative developments from the 1840s and 50s saw rapid changes in visitor patterns, with the decline of local industries of whaling, shipbuilding, alum and jet working counterbalanced by a burgeoning tourist growth; George Hudson, "the Railway King" invested heavily in the West Cliff estate, prompting others to build hotels, villas and lodging houses to cater for better-off visitors staying for the traditional month in the summer (White 1998: 78-93). Yet such accounts can underestimate the cultural underpinnings of Whitby's transformation: most visitors were not coming just for the plush railway carriages, sunny promenades and comfortable hotels, but to see for themselves what the cultural industries of mid-Victorian Britain in their exhibitions, journalism and literature were chronicling as a landscape and way of life far enough away from the centre to be preserved from the encroaches of modern industrialism and urbanisation. Once seen as stagnant and provincial Whitby was increasingly hailed as wonderfully unspoilt; its cramped alleys and dilapidated houses turned out to be delightfully picturesque; the vulgar and coarse was reframed as simple and unaffected.

Redefinition as a tourist location relied on new ways of seeing people within its landscapes. Visitors came to Whitby not only to find a picturesque seaside town and dramatic surrounding landscapes but also to experience a place with an indigenous population of native fisherfolk who came to represent an idealised community. It was their 'tourist gaze' (Urry 2002) that made class encounters an inevitable element for Whitby's leisure trade. Whilst it would be an exaggeration to say that all visitors were from middle or upper-class backgrounds, those evidenced in the *Whitby Gazette's* annual visitor lists – introduced to facilitate social interaction between individuals within visiting elites and to promote commercial transactions with local traders –

were clearly comfortably off. Whitby prided itself on the social status of the visitors it attracted, measuring success against neighbouring Scarborough, which had a much longer tradition as a watering place. The *Gazette* lists[2] indicate the elite nature and social scope of visitors in the later nineteenth century and show Whitby to be particularly popular with families from the gentry, the professions and the clergy. In 1886, for example, they include a number of major landowners, Skipton's first medical officer, the secretary of the Youth Hostels Association and Ramblers Association and clerical visitors of various denominations and positions drawn no doubt by its Abbey and status as a key site of British Christianity. What is notable though is just how many of these visitors are women. It is not unusual to find family parties formed mainly or entirely of women and children with groups of sisters and in-laws, or aunts, grandmothers, mothers and daughters in various combination. Wealthier families also included nurses and maids in their parties. Cross-referenced with the 1891 census, the 1886 lists also indicate, from a different perspective, just how female that holiday industry could be. Almost half of the 104 residences listed in Whitby's main residential area are lodging houses and of these 50, an overwhelming 43 are represented as having women either as heads of household or working in combinations with sisters, mothers or daughters. It indicates a summer population with a significantly female profile comprising both indigenous and visiting populations.

It was not the existence of a *local* middle-class culture though that drew its visitors primarily to the town. In fact, in this new tourist dynamic middle-class residents could perceive themselves somewhat awkwardly placed: however much they might feel themselves central to the town's commercial and cultural concerns they were nevertheless more or less invisible in terms of its imagined character. Moreover, local elites actively involved in promoting images and ideas of an apparently unspoilt indigenous community also lived in close enough proximity to know its shortcomings. They thus occupied an ambivalent position between visitors and natives especially when they contributed to or colluded with myths of Whitby's indigenous 'fisherfolk'. However much they might facilitate encounters with it, whether through the contact-zone practicalities of hotel keeping, municipal

---

[2] *Whitby Gazette*. July-September 1886 passim. (I am indebted to Emma Taylor for access to her research into the *Whitby Gazette* visitor lists).

management or novel writing, at the same time they also held a sincere desire to improve, change and 'civilise' it.[3]

3. Landscape and the Feminine

The regional feminine of Mary Linskill's Whitby novels addresses a mixed female culture of both locals and visitors in a newly feminised landscape where women played a central role in economic, social and cultural activities. Whitby promised the dramatic wildness of its surrounding moors, towering cliffs and most importantly the sea itself. This was a northern landscape with the romantic power to inspire its urban visitors by the very nature of its difference to their own working lives, and also to provide the spaces for imagined encounters, in art and literature, which constructed and sustained their anticipations of place (Urry 2002: 3). In *Between the Heather and the Northern Sea* Genevieve witnesses an event that occurred near Whitby just three years prior to the novel's publication, when the local lifeboat was hauled overland through a hostile winter landscape to save the crew of a boat wrecked on the rocky coastline:

> [T]he day and the deed will live, as brave deeds have lived in England always. The children of children yet unborn will tell of the cutting of the frozen and deeply drifted snow over hills and through hollows for six long miles; the painful dragging step by step, of the massively built boat, mounted on her own carriage, by men who wrought in silence, in utter obedience, in splendid willingness, with desperate resolve. (Linskill 1991a: 37)

The narrative makes national history from this local event where "brave deeds have lived in England always". Through a heroic register that transforms the "brave sea-soldiers", with their "buoyant armour" and "pale blue lances" into knights battling with the stormy sea (Linskill 1991: 38), its Victorian medievalism heightens the myth of the heroic fisherman to interpellate a nation that prided itself on its history of naval supremacy and maritime disposition in images and

---

[3] See e.g. Webster, 2004, on the heated debates over whether to adopt the Libraries Acts in Whitby, which would have provided a free provision of library services across its whole community.

accounts of sea rescues and lifeboat bravery from all around Britain's coasts (Lübbren 2002: 41-42). Yet alongside such conventionally heroic narratives, 'feminine' romantic and melodramatic plots are also closely aligned with landscape in Linskill's novels.

'The Landslip at Whitby', *Graphic*, Jan 21, 1871.

Erosion along this northern coastline had a strong popular appeal and its effects were widely documented throughout the period in newspapers and illustrated magazines. Such dramatic land- and sea-scapes submit Linskill's *female* characters to extreme and intense experiences too, by simultaneously dramatising their emotional turmoil, framing and facilitating romantic narratives, heightening moral sympathies and ultimately participating in bringing about resolution. They intervene in key scenes, as when a landslip threatens the delicately balanced admission of love between Genevieve and the local landowner:

> It seemed as if the very stones and the stems of the trees were cracking and rending asunder... Genevieve... only heard the riving, snapping, craunching sounds; ... only felt... the shiver of earth, then, even while a strong arm was clasping her, almost flinging her outward from the path, there came the thunderous thud of falling rock. (Linskill 1991a: 92)

Here the picturesque woodland setting is rendered terrifyingly – but thrillingly – sublime, implicitly encouraging its reader's participation in the thrill of female romantic surrender. It suggests how female readerly pleasures, constructed through the commercially produced mass-market romance (Radway 1991: 582-583), may also be projected onto specific topographies of place.

Elsewhere in Linskill's novels and stories, the landscape regularly swallows up characters from the traditional industries of fishing, mining and jet working, yet newer social actors like tourists, artists and teachers thrive. This emphasis on the ground that constantly moves, changes and literally falls away from beneath the feet suggests also a landscape that metaphorically dramatises the doubts and anxieties of modernity, especially those challenges to the gender ideals that underpinned Victorian life. Along with the social concerns that afflicted the metropolis, the 1880s saw demands for female independence bearing fruit across a spectrum of legal, economic, social and cultural issues. Legislation for women's improved position within marriage and ownership of property had been taking place since mid-century and the period also saw growing female access to the professions, to wider employment and to education. By the 1880s the appearance of the 'new woman' in a literature that highlighted her sexual and intellectual parity with men also indicated new and, to some, disturbing advances in gender debates (Ledger 1997; Pykett 1995: 54; Jalland 1986: 59). In this context, Linskill's female protagonists participate in wider debates by demonstrating their own intelligence and independence. It is ultimately their displays of moral courage, based on Christian ideals, that demonstrates their agency in their own lives.

The moral framework of *The Haven under the Hill* is triggered through the landslip motif when its alum-master hero rescues the heroine, Dorigen, to realise the full nature of his feelings towards her: "'My darling! My darling! You must live, for I love you, I love you passionately.'" (Linskill 1991b: 130). However its wider function and effect is to realign and reconcile class and gender boundaries. Here the conventional romantic trope shows how Linskill's northern landscape also adjudicates between contrasting modes of female independence: here the landslip episode proleptically foreshadows another also based on a local event: the 1829 disaster when alum workings at Kettleness, north of Whitby, slipped into the sea.[4] This dramatic climax kills the

---

[4] Another local event that clearly had had wider recognition. An article in the *Illustrated London News* discusses another destruction, by landslip, of the Victoria Iron and Cement Works at nearby Wreckhills (24 April 1858: 415-416) and cites this earlier Kettleness disaster, where "Warehouses, offices, dwelling-houses, and cottages, together with mine-heaps, machinery &c, to a large amount, were completely swallowed up". It comments that along "the whole

alum-master's wife on the night she leaves him to become an actress in London (Linskill 1991b: 456-457), confirming her actions as those of a 'bad' woman, who abandons her children to be punished by a terrain she despises but cannot escape. Dorigen's quiet self-containment as a writer, having fulfilled her moral obligations by the end of the novel and chosen finally to lodge simply in a cottage by the sea, offers a strong contrast to that of the tormented child-abandoning wife with her unrequited 'metropolitan' yearnings.

In prioritising moral obligations in order to maintain local and familial loyalties along with her wider literary ambitions Dorigen, the woman writer protagonist of *The Haven under the Hill*, also highlights the dilemma of a writer like Mary Linskill herself. As an 'insider', very consciously representing her native area and people in her novels, she was nevertheless dependent on the approbation of an outside readership which, though it might selectively code the 'primitive' and 'simple' in positive terms, might also and all too easily see through that construction to locate it as 'uncivilised' and even 'vulgar'. At the same time, being a *female* writer within late nineteenth-century provincial society made her, and in a very real sense, an 'outsider' to her neighbours as well. Any woman writer drawing on her home region as subject material could find these positions awkward to balance.

3. Environment and Female Representation

Mary Linskill's 'regional feminine' engages with that strong anthropological tradition newly concerned in the nineteenth century to identify and categorise 'indigenous cultures' and link them to specific environments, landscapes and regions. This tradition operated at any number of levels from theoretical debates about race, through new scientific methods of collecting, interpreting and classifying artefacts and rituals, to folklore studies, local histories, popular magazines and indeed, the popularity of the regional novel itself (Snell 1998: 5-14). The idea that certain regions had their own distinctive folk cultures, was deeply entrenched in intellectual and popular debate, and is well illustrated in the popularity of images of fisherfolk from Linskill's

---

line of coast… these landslips have been of such frequent occurrence as to excite but little notice."

home town. Images of fisherfolk were routinely offered as picturesque representations of working-class life and widely disseminated in the later nineteenth century, forming an aesthetic category linked to critiques of European industrialised urban life. Metropolitan artists came to the area from the 1840s onward in an intellectual vanguard that disseminated images for an educated middle-class, which increasingly had the means to come and see for itself. By exhibiting their paintings in London galleries they created new audiences for Whitby's old world charms; such paintings stimulated a huge amount of popular seaside imagery in magazines like the *Illustrated London News*, *Graphic* and *Punch,* where Whitby is a recurrent location with its writers and artists.

'The Viqueens of Whitby', *Punch,* September 29, 1883.

George Du Maurier's illustrations for *Punch* were a particular favourite in middle-class drawing rooms. "The Viqueens of Whitby" (1883), follows an earlier grouping of fishermen and boys, "The Vikings of Whitby", to suggest the particular fascination with such representations of the female working classes. These are strong, hardy-looking women. Standing apart from and foregrounded against the crowds of holidaymakers on the pier a central fisherwoman stares confidently back at the viewer, another glances sideways out of the picture while a third tends to a toddler sitting on the harbour wall that visually segregates locals from visitors. Their bare arms and rolled up sleeves indicate a capacity for hard work; their headscarves distinguish them from the leisured, parasol carrying ladies in the distance. Yet, with their ample bosoms, nipped-in waists and voluminous skirts, they are by no means unfeminine; indeed the presence of children acts as a visual signifier of the health and fertility of the group as a whole.

It has been argued that specifically northern constructions of fishing communities can resist the values of the dominant Southern metaphor (Newton and Gerdts 2003: 11-39). Most local interpretations of Whitby's fisherfolk community, despite individual divergences, tended to show it in a positive light: it is difficult, for example, to read into Frank Meadow Sutcliffe's photographs of lifeboatmen, gossiping wives, bonny 'flither-pickers' or wading children any critical stance towards them. Yet while Linskill's novels can share this place-myth construction of a timelessly naturalistic and picturesque fishing community, they also locate it historically and even highlight the processes of representation involved. *In Exchange for a Soul* (1887) has two local characters from different social backgrounds – Barbara, a fishergirl and Thorhilda, the novel's genteel protagonist – brought together amid rivalries and malicious violence among fishing families exacerbated by the recent impact of steam trawling on their livelihood. Steam fishing, much deplored by Sutcliffe (Hiley 2005: 117-122), is conspicuous by its absence from his compositions of Whitby.

Like Du Maurier's "Viqueens", *In Exchange for a Soul* (1887) also suggests the regenerative potential of fisherwomen in its description of:

> [...] a group of tall, handsome fisher-girls who were down by the edge of the tide – such girls as you would hardly see anywhere else in England for strength and straightness, for roundness of form and bright, fresh healthfulness of countenance. (Linskill 1887: 5)

The fishergirls are natural, healthy, products of their environment and landscape, as indigenous as its flora and fauna. Their grouping here is more distinctively localised than that of du Maurier, though, whose sense of place comes not from his figures but from the recognisable outline of Whitby's West Pier: as composite fisherwomen they might be found in any number of seaside settings. Linskill's characters are more specific: "such girls as you would hardly see *anywhere else* in England" [my emphasis] suggests that the evolutionary attributes of health, strength and fitness are integral to the North and metonymically extended towards the nation. They are portrayed both as working women and – in an unusually explicit aside – simultaneously part of a wider visual economy:

> They wore blue flannel petticoats, and rough, dark-blue masculine-looking guernseys of their own knitting. Their heads were either bare, or covered with picturesque hoods of cotton – blue, pink, lilac, buff, pale blue. One of the tallest of them, and decidedly the handsomest, had no bonnet at all, and her rich chestnut hair blew about in the breeze in shining rings and curls in a way that attracted Thorhilda's attention, and even her admiration, though as a rule she had slight sympathy with the 'admired disorder' school of aesthetics. (Linskill 1887: 5)

This scene is focalised through the consciousness of the novel's genteel heroine and has two perspectives: a dominant one of colourful bonnets and shining curls that renders the fisher-girls the more or less passive recipients of an elite tourist gaze, and another that counteracts it with the naturalistic "masculine-looking guernseys" to suggest the realities of working life. The broadly picturesque image is further undercut by broad dialect and asides of tittering disdain: "Wheä telled ya her neäme?" [...] "Mebbe she kenned it of her oän sharpness" (Linskill 1887: 7). It registers a tension between the artist's image and his subject's perceptions, developed later when Barbara turns up in her best clothes to sit for a gentleman artist, rather than the working dress he had assumed she would wear.

The three novels all have mediating artist characters that work *en plein air*, which allows them key insights into and interactions with fisherfolk and gentry, natives and visitors alike. *In Exchange for a Soul* highlights the representation of fisherfolk in a way that is quite different from those of both Sutcliffe and Du Maurier. Sutcliffe's naturalistic photographs both exclude middle-class tourists and efface the photographer and Du Maurier sidesteps the assertive and reciprocal gaze of his central "Viqueen" by placing himself, in a signature motif, as the unnoticed onlooker with his dog at the left of the picture. Both construct their fisherwomen through an elite, male gaze. Yet the novel's fishergirls, reinforced by its accompanying illustration, are shown as actively involved in and engaged with the exchange. Linskill's own illustrator, Albert Morrow, gives them local bonnets and depicts the girls standing over the artist's work as they engage in discussion with him. Though the other girls taunt her to make a bargain with him, Barbara shrinks from attempt at payment, but the point is made that artists and their fisherwomen models generally have an economic relationship, the assumed naturalism of their pictures is entirely artificial and that power comes from both sides in the exchange.

'With the last words they stopped by the easel'
Sunday Magazine, 1887, 147.

Indeed Barbara is portrayed in *In Exchange for a Soul* as a fisherwoman who will never be merely a passive picturesque figure, either of the gentleman artist or of dominant metropolitan desires. Her dignity and composure is at least equal to that of the genteel Thorhilda. Though still representing a deferential moral culture, she is also an admirably resourceful figure whose maternal qualities are determined by the melodramatic narrative of a terrifying ordeal when trapped with three small children in a capsised schooner, where all but one die around her: "'Standing there with the cold sea-water up to my throat, and three children clinging to my hair, *I* knew…! I'll feel those hands in my hair till I die!…'" (Linskill 1887: 284). A further dramatic subplot sees Barbara rowing out into a storm to rescue Thorhilda's brother who has been bound and cast adrift by a group of jealous and hot headed fishermen. This stoicism and bravery, exposed by the two extreme sea stories, not only reconfigures the heroic conventions of the lifeboat rescue for the female, they also underline Barbara's worthiness for marriage to Thorhilda's brother and (though this remains implicit) her social elevation.

'The bow of the boat as it grated upon the bed of gravel' *Sunday Magazine*, 1887, 366.

4. The Wider Exchange

This particular encounter between a fishergirl and a gentry daughter suggests the heady possibilities for women, whether insiders or outsiders, both of class mobility *and* the regenerative potential of the regional stereotype. Though class boundaries have not been overtly breached, *In Exchange for a Soul* shows not only the earnest middle-class female character who awakens the fishergirl to her 'finer' sensibilities, an underlying myth in itself of female social concern, but it also manages to suggest that this can also work the other way – that the qualities of heroism and endurance displayed by the fishergirl form a point of connection between women of both classes.

'Advancing rapidly towards them was her brother Hartas.' *Sunday Magazine,* 1887, 6.

It suggests a further and wider point concerning the 'regional feminine'. Like many artists a century later Mary Linskill was working at the interface between the local and the metropolitan as she and her work became part of the town's self-representations for tourist purposes. In 1888 an article by her entitled "In and about Whitby" appeared in the *Whitby Gazette* with the holiday visitor firmly in mind. Her overview of Whitby through the ages is liberally sprinkled with accounts of old fishermen's tales, local traditions and superstitions. Read alongside a "London Correspondence" column that describes the capital's 'mammoth and costly hotels", "crammed" with American tourists, which are like "convict establishment[s]", or the extortionate lodging house charges in Henley (Whitby Gazette 1886), Whitby's visitors and locals alike could easily count themselves as fortunate to avoid the stresses of a systematised and commodified mass tourism.

Here Linskill discusses George Du Maurier's illustration "At the Fountain Head" (called by her "The Fish Sale"), "one of the most amusing drawings [...] ever provided for the pages of *Punch*".

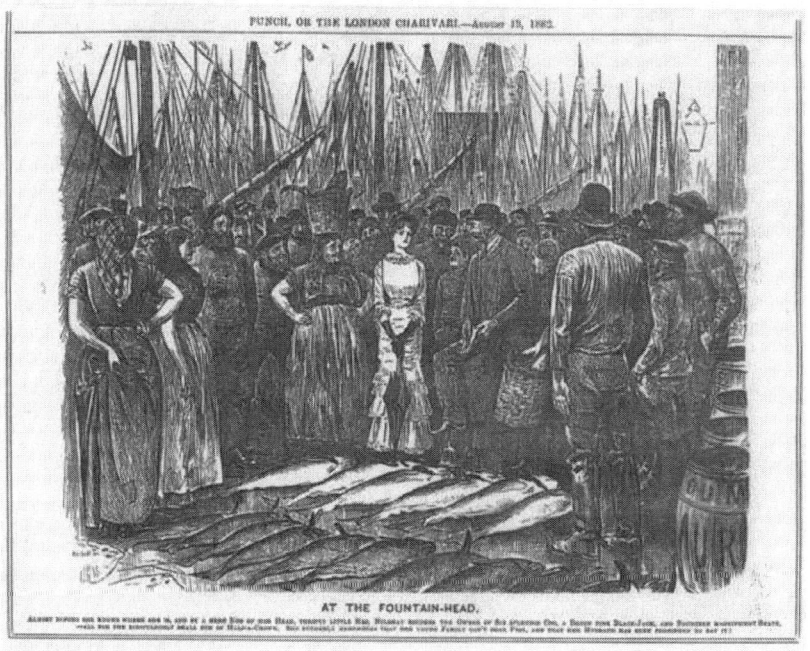

'At the Fountain-Head' *Punch,* August 19, 1882.

Du Maurier's own joke is on Mrs Mildmay, the "graceful and dainty" lady visitor to the fish sale, who has unwittingly just bought a bargain lot of fish her family cannot eat and his illustration extends it by juxtaposing her somewhat dim-witted gentility against the group of "grinning fisherfolk" behind her.

The inclusion of "At the Fountain Head" disrupts Linskill's rather lengthy account of local tales, traditions and superstitions despite its light-hearted metropolitan version of the encounter between Whitby's well-heeled visitors and their indigenous hosts. In choice of words her text colludes with Du Maurier's elite 'othering' of local fisherfolk – grinning because, of course, it is not they who are out of place in this environment – yet she also steers the emphasis away from the hapless woman's predicament to a wider discussion of the pier where the fish sale is held. As another insider, Linskill avoids too close an identification of her own voice with that of the somewhat threatening 'grinning' mass by supplementing the illustration with an "echo of the noise, the fun, the confusion, the perpetual tinkle of the auctioneer's bell", and volunteers what the picture "happily" cannot betray: "that indescribable combined odour of fish and fishy humanity" (Linskill 1888: 4). In its awkward suggestion of evolutionary classification we perceive a carefully balanced alignment and exchange in process with the metropolitan image selected and re-presented, rather than simply and superficially described, to maintain a stance on both sides of the exchange.

As 'insiders', local writers like Linskill were key mediators in the wider encounters between local and national print culture. Though they might well (and profitably) collude in the construction of narratives and images of dominant aspirations and beliefs they were, at the same time, also in a position to qualify or reinterpret them. Linskill's re-presentation of 'At the Fountain-Head' mirrors a routine scouring of national periodicals by the local press for images to reproduce under headings such as "Whitby as Strangers See It"[5] for discussion by visitors and locals alike. Such a process also suggests the self-scrutiny and self-presentation on the part of regional constituencies as they picked up or rejected aspects, nuances and perspectives for their own purposes.

4. Conclusion

Seen as part of this wider interchange of print and visual culture Mary Linskill's novels highlight how growing interests in the emergence of Whitby as a tourist destination could both participate in and diverge from dominant representations as an 'innocent' romantic and picturesque landscape. Her 'regional feminine' therefore exists within the wider context of complex power relationships operating between north and south, metropolis and region, high and low cultures. It also highlights 'feminised' assumptions of regional writing and representations,

---

[5] n.d. This appears in a nineteenth-century scrapbook found in the archives of the Whitby Literary and Philosophical Society, and comes from a local newspaper, possibly the *Whitby Gazette*.

and their relative subordination to the requirements of the metropolitan centre where the high profile writers, the main ideas and most powerful publishing houses and galleries were situated. Linskill's work shows how local writers and artists were well aware they worked within that wider interchange of print and visual culture where texts and intentions could be picked up, scrutinised and responded to in any number of ways. Whilst cultural, political and economic power often would be concentrated in the metropolitan centre, it is not enough to see power purely in terms of a dominant player on one side and a subordinate on the other. Power, as Foucault has pointed out, is more mercurial and febrile than this (Foucault 1990; 1980) and flows in any number of directions. Nowhere is this more apparent than in the complex and nuanced gender relationships of men and women, or in the cultural exchanges facilitated by print culture in the nineteenth century that took place between the north and south, between region and metropolis.

The new cultural industries of the late nineteenth century were fuelled by women as well as men, offering opportunities for them to shape public and proactive roles in shaping and disseminating identities, whether as writers of regional fiction like Linskill, as providers of visitor amenities in the tourist industry, or as tourist consumers of the 'new' leisure landscapes. Linskill's 'regional feminine' highlights a northern landscape that offered a direct challenge to identities bound up with 'traditional' images of masculine-dominated work while at the same time rejecting the more worrying implications offered by the independent 'new woman'. It invites us to recognise that northern towns have regularly had to redefine themselves through time and on many levels, and have often used cultural frameworks to do so. Lest we be tempted to assume 'the North' has any fixed and stable entity, let alone any straightforwardly masculine one, prior to the current "long and bitter process of de-industrialisation" this collection of essays explores, the parallels given by Mary Linskill's 'regional feminine' suggest that, on the contrary, ideas of 'Northernness' are always mobile and open to contestation on any number of levels.

Similarly to nineteenth-century Whitby, a significant feature of the post-industrial North has been the redefinition of its urban landscapes and communities. In our own late capitalist economy landscapes associated with manufacturing and commerce are increasingly having to position themselves within a new service sector as earlier markets – for West Riding and Lancashire textiles, Tyneside coal, shipbuilding and maritime commerce – respond to changing global forces. With primary and secondary sector economies no longer competitive, the communities that have grown up round them must seek new sources of wealth creation. In this context we see such centres as Manchester, Liverpool, Newcastle and Bradford recasting themselves, as Manchester warehouses become desirable city apartments, Liverpool's dockside warehouses are transformed into museums and art galleries, and the Baltic flour mill in Newcastle, a quayside industrial building, has become a prestigious contemporary art gallery. The list could go on, but what all of these transformations have in common is their strong reliance on cultural industries. Art galleries, museums, photography, film, civic sculptures and architecture are all deployed in an effort to change the visual face and meanings of the north of England. Whatever the future of 'the North' as a political identity, what remains crucial will be our sensitivity to the nuanced dimensions of its many *cultural* representations and the wider spectrum of voices that speak for it.

Works Cited

Primary References

Anon, (1871): "The Landslip at Whitby", *Graphic*, January 21.
Advertisement (1885): "Cheap Literature", *The Daily Gleaner*, June 29, (Kingston, Jamaica).
Du Maurier, George (1882): "At the Fountainhead", *Punch,* August 19.
— (1883): "The Viqueens of Whitby", *Punch*, September 29.
Hugill, John (1830): "An address to the inhabitants of Whitby and its Vicinity shewing the recent declining state of the town", *Whitby Tracts*, 1-43.
Linskill, Mary (1884): *Between the Heather and the Northern Sea,* serialised in *Good Words*.
— (1887): *In Exchange for a Soul*, serialised in *Sunday Magazine*.
— (1888): "In and About Whitby", *Whitby Gazette*, July 13, 4.
— (1900): *In Exchange for a Soul* [1887] London: Macmillan.
— (1991a): *Between the Heather and the Northern Sea* [1884] Republication of serialisation in *Good Words*, 1884. Privately published. Whitby: Cordelia Stamp.
— (1991b): *The Haven under the Hill* [1886] Republication of Whitby: Horne and Son, 1928 edition. Privately published Whitby: Cordelia Stamp.
Whitby Gazette (1888): "London Correspondence", July 6.
Whitby Gazette (1886): July-September passim.

Research Literature

Burke, Peter (1997): *Varieties of Cultural History*. Oxford: Polity Press.
Dodd, Philip (1998): "Gender and Cornwall", in: K.D.M. Snell (ed.): *The Regional Novel in Britain and Ireland 1800-1990*. Cambridge: Cambridge UP, 119-135.
Foucault, Michel (1978/1990): *The History of Sexuality: Volume 1*. Harmondsworth: Penguin.
— (1980): "Prison Talk", in: C. Gordon (ed.): *Power/Knowledge*. Brighton: Harvester, 37-52.
Hiley, Michael (1974/2005): *Frank Sutcliffe: Photographer of Whitby*. Chichester: Phillimore and Co.
Howkins, Alan (1986): "The Discovery of Rural England", in: Robert Colls and Philip Dodd (eds.): *Englishness: Politics and Culture 1880-1920*. London: Croom Helm, 62-88.
Jalland, Pat (1986): *Women, Marriage and Politics 1860-1914*. Oxford: Clarendon Press.

Ledger, Sally (1997): *The New Woman: Fiction and Feminism at the Fin de Siecle*. Manchester: Manchester UP.

Lübbren, Nina (2002): "'Toilers of the Sea': Fisherfolk and the Geographies of Tourism in England, 1880-1900", in: David P. Corbett, Ysanne Holt and Fiona Russell (eds.): *The Geographies of Englishness: Landscape and the National Past 1880-1940*. New Haven and London: Yale UP, 29-64.

Newton, Laura with Abigail Gerdts (2003): *Cullercoats: A North-East Colony of Artists*. Bristol: Samson (in association with Tyne and Wear Museums).

Pratt, Mary Louise (1992): *Imperial Eyes: Travel Writing and Transculturation*. London: Routledge.

Pykett, Lyn (1995): *Engendering Fictions: The English Novel in the Early Twentieth Century*. London: Edward Arnold.

Quinlan, David A. and Arthur F. Humble (1969): *Mary Linskill: The Whitby Novelist*. Whitby: Horne and Sons.

Radway, Janice (1991): "The Readers and their Romances", from: *Reading the Romance: Women, Patriarchy and Popular Literature* [1984]. In: Robyn R. Warhol and Diane Price Herndl (eds.): *Feminisms*. New Brunswick: Rutgers UP, 551-585.

Snell, K.D.M. (1998): "The Regional Novel: Themes for Interdisciplinary Research", in: Id. (ed.): *The Regional Novel in Britain and Ireland 1800-1990*. Cambridge: Cambridge UP, 1-53.

Urry, John (1990/2002): *The Tourist Gaze*. London: Sage.

Webster, Jon (2004): "'Don't have a library rate thrust upon you': the Libraries Act debate in Whitby, 1878", *Library History* 20, 117-135.

Weiner, Martin J. (1981/2004): *English Culture and the Decline of the Industrial Spirit, 1850-1980*. Cambridge: Cambridge UP.

White, Andrew (1998): "The Victorian Development of Whitby as a Seaside Resort", *The Local Historian* 28 (2), 78-93.

State Library of Tasmania: Launceston Reference Library Popular Fiction Collection. http://www.statelibrary.tas.gov.au/whathave/collections/researchandref/vande

Diamonds or Beasts? Re-mapping English Conceptions of Northernness in the Late Victorian Periodical

Annisa Suliman

Abstract: Establishing boundaries and marginalising difference were key strategies for a Victorian ruling group that was inherent on forging a stable national identity. Often, in the pages of the popular periodical press, the figure of the northerner is used to foreground anxieties regarding the fragmentation and degeneration of a society characterised by massive economic, physical and ideological upheaval. But, towards the end of the century, there's a move towards re-mapping conceptions of otherness and belonging. Using nineteenth-century periodical narratives, this essay will show how the northerner functions as a vehicle that explodes the myths of regional difference and encourages readers to enter into a negotiation of what it means to be British in a modern age.

Key names and concepts: Thomas Burt - John Arthur Roebuck - John Cassel - Matthew Arnold - Richard Hoggart - Roland Barthes - William Cobbett; Victorian Periodicals - Northerner - Stereotypes - Literary Market - Mass Media - London-centeredness.

1. Locating the Northerner

The highly paid North-country mechanic is [...] little better than a beast. His whole life is passed in mere sensual enjoyment; getting drunk is his chief business; and once he has got drunk, his necessary business is to get sober.[1]

Colliers are a hard, resolute, strong, rough lot. Their lives being in continual danger, they often lose them from want of precaution.[2]

---

[1] These remarks by John Arthur Roebuck appeared in *The Times* on 20 January 1862 and were included in an article criticising Roebuck's ideas, "Gentlemen", (anon.) *The Cornhill Magazine* 5 (1862): 327-342 (328). Roebuck was one of two MP's representing the Borough of Sheffield in the 1860s.

[2] *Cassell's* 1872: 103.

In 1883, *Cassell's Family Magazine*[3] published a series of articles about the North[4] entitled *Under the Crust*. Written in the popular travel writing genre, the objective was to delve beneath a hard exterior to expose the softer, undiscovered aspects of northern British life. Though anthropological explorations that sought to enlighten readers about the habits and habitats of Queen Victoria's colonial subjects are common at this period, these essays explore the underbelly of life within Britain's own shores. In particular, they use the figure of the northerner as a vehicle for exposing late Victorian anxieties concerning identity and place.

Focussing on the *Cassell's* series, this study will explore representations of northerners in the popular periodical press, in particular the way that, during the closing years of the century, their portrayal begins to highlight the fear of fragmentation brought about by wide-scale industrialisation and colonisation. All three articles are written by 'north country-men' (see Burt 1883), one based in Lancashire and two in Tyneside. This study deals with the 'Tyneside Collier' essays that detail the lives and practices of people living in mining communities around Durham and Newcastle.

From the outset, the writer foregrounds the issue of location. The reader is very much placed in the role of outsider far removed from any real knowledge of the northern pit community, and the series title carries the assumption that the landscapes soon to be uncovered are unknown to the mass of readers. But whilst readers may be deficient in terms of knowledge, their status is anything but lowly. The title, *Under the Crust*, metaphorically locates readers above the surface of the earth, immediately placing them in an elevated position, setting them apart from the subterranean subjects of the articles, and indeed the author (who we later learn is himself a Tynesider). Though they may inhabit a different world, readers can achieve proximity of a sort, whilst maintaining their elevated status, through the act of reading. Reading enables readers to peek underneath the surface, and actively

---

[3] This periodical was founded in 1853 by John Cassell. It went through various titles, including *Cassell's Illustrated Family Paper*, and *Cassell's Family Magazine*, until its demise in 1932; therefore this article will use the title *Cassell's* when referring to this family of publications.

[4] According to Donald Read the North is defined as the area lying north of the River Trent and running up to the Scottish border (see Read 1964: 276).

advance their knowledge of the northern man or woman without having to get their hands dirty.

It is important that the writer establishes boundaries between reader and subject here, because the northern pit communities have a reputation for being intemperate and violent. Aware that the reader may approach the text with pre-conceptions, the writer stimulates interest by immediately defining the subjects by their similarity to hard-working Victorians and by their difference from them: "this hardy and illustrious population have a character and individuality of their own – different from anything else to be found in other parts of the world" (Burt 1883: 245). And their difference is not just an everyday one – it is one worth reading about because it is a difference on a global scale.

Casting the Tynesider within a global framework serves two purposes: it moves the potentially undesirable character further away from the reader whilst also presenting him as a unique curiosity.

Locating northerners within a global community is hardly surprising given Britain's colonial expansion and the fascination of newspapers and periodicals for stories with a foreign focus. The writer is tapping into a popular consciousness fascinated by the exotic, and the periodical itself is operating on the level of an exhibition space at a time when examining and collecting foreign curiosities was almost an obsession among the intellectual classes (see Hall 2003: 186-199). Here the reader is placed in the position of explorer:

> To the stranger from a distance – especially to the man of education and refinement – there is much that will appear rough and unattractive, if not absolutely repulsive, in the demeanour of the Northern pitman; but he will soon find that under this somewhat coarse exterior are sterling qualities, which will reveal and approve themselves on closer inspection and better acquaintance (Burt 1883: 245).

The ideal reader then is male, refined, educated and inquiring – traits in combination that would attract approbation in Victorian ideology. Once confident that the reader is comfortable with this evaluation, the writer begins to refute common assumptions:

> To judge from the sketches which occasionally appear in the London newspapers, one would suppose that the pitman is always either drinking champagne or going about with an ugly bulldog at his heels! [...] among miners, as among other men, tastes differ – some are very deli-

> cate, others coarser and more commonplace in their choice of their hobbies.
>
> To nearly every house a garden is attached, and some of the colliers cultivate flowers, as well as more substantial products, with great success – often carrying off the best prizes at the annual floral and horticultural exhibitions (Burt 1883: 269).

Here, as in the title, the focus is on proximity, the distance that exists both physically and metaphorically between North and South, between the 'acquaintance' and the 'stranger', the 'delicate' and the 'coarse'. This use of binaries relies on dominant discourses surrounding identity and behaviour. But, as the writer attests, these binaries are not absolute when it comes to Tynesiders and those dwelling outside the region.

This writer goes out of his way to represent the typical northerner as someone who defies the stereotypical intemperate, barbaric, improvident brute depicted by many contemporary periodical narratives. It could be argued that it is hardly surprising the *Cassell's* articles are sympathetic given a large northern readership, and especially since they are penned by "north countrymen". But, these articles are worthy of exploration because, rather than attempting to re-configure notions of northernness by offering only positive representations of the North, they acknowledge that some of the stereotypes have a basis in reality.

The pen behind the Tyneside articles belongs to "pitman philosopher" (Waller 2006: 23) Thomas Burt, MP for Morpeth, a trade unionist and one of the first working-class members of Parliament. A temperance advocate, Burt was a self-educated miner, who rose through the ranks to become a respected political figure and inspector of mines. Revered for his intelligence and persuasive oratorical style, in this series of articles Burt remains true to his reputation. Shrewd in his approach, he works to draw his readers in, by promising a glimpse into an unknown and fascinating world. Though he is well-known as the miners' champion, he is careful not to alienate readers, and his narrative never stretches their credulity. He is quick to praise the northern men and women for their bravery, determination, thrift, and zeal for self-help, and he lists as admirable the growth of Mechanics Institutes, the building of churches, education, music, cricket and reading; yet he strives, as ever, for balance:

> I need hardly say that there is another side to the picture I have given. The miners are not all thoughtful, studious, and thrifty. There is a good deal of drinking and gambling, though less than formerly [...]
>
> One of the saddest sights to be witnessed in the colliery districts on holiday occasions, is to see groups of fine young fellows wasting their money, and their time in ... pitch and toss [*a game*]. This however, I believe may be said for the gamblers – that they love honesty and straightforwardness, and give no quarter to those who try to cheat their fellow. (Burt 1883: 270)

Coming from a Tynesider and former miner, such criticism of his countrymen cannot fail to impress the reader into accepting Burt's account as true. Immediately after this revelation, Burt chooses to lay bare his real intention:

> When such qualities are exhibited by these men, surrounded as they are by such temptations and associations, one may indulge the hope that with improved education, and the opening out of new and purer resources, much of the time now worse than wasted in gambling and drinking will be devoted to pursuits of a nobler and a more elevating character (Burt 1883: 270).

These men are victims of circumstance and environment, but given the opportunity they can become "a blessing and a source of well-being to the community among whom they dwell" (271).

So, whilst Burt is at pains to champion the virtues of the northern pitman and to present him as a man with infinite capacity for development, he is not averse to repeating the less than attractive qualities more commonly listed in periodical literature of the day. It is a useful tactic, because by drawing as he does on representations of northern men familiar to Victorian readers, he is offering a reality they are comfortable with. Once they are comfortable, he can begin dismantling the northerner as he or she exists in the recognised, if fabricated, landscapes of common understanding.

Burt's miners are, in the main, 'hospitable', 'intelligent', 'reliable', 'calm, self-contained, modest and unpretentious', 'a blessing and a source of well-being to the community among whom they dwell'. He reconstructs them to fit the mould of the archetypal hero, stoic, brave and willing to die for the good of their community. Northern pit men are:

> heroes [...] unconscious of their heroism – it is really so much a part of their every-day life – and, in truth, they share this courage with their fellow-countrymen, who never shrink from danger or death whether on a battle-field or in the peaceful walks of industry (245).

Burt's narrative offers what Du Gay and Hall call a "negotiated code" – though dominant tropes regarding northern representations are prevalent in his articles, also contained is a world view that rebuts those common assumptions (see Du Gay and Hall 1997: 10). Employment of this code creates a dialectic that offers readers the opportunity to enter into a negotiation of meaning around the construction of northern identities. It is in this way that this series of articles can be read as an attempt to re-configure the "conceptual maps" (Hall 2003: 22) that govern the representation of northern figures in periodicals towards the end of the nineteenth century. This is an effective strategy as a dialogue can only be sustained between reader and writer if there is a shared recognition of cultural codes. As Stuart Hall attests, "power circulates through knowledge, but codes only work if they are to some extent shared" (Du Gay and Hall 1997: 11).

Burt's intention to change perceptions would have accorded well with the ethos of John Cassell, who founded *Cassell's Illustrated Family Paper* in 1853. A Lancastrian by birth, he made his fortune by selling tea and coffee. A fervent Christian, temperance advocate and evangelical educator, he used this money to produce literature that sought to "supply an interesting series of comments on passing events, tending to rectify the public judgement of men and measures, and to promote a rational and beneficial management of public affairs" (Nowell-Smith 1958: 20). Priced at one penny, it was aimed at the lower end of the market. *Cassell's* is important because it was one of the first weekly family papers to reach and maintain sales of 285,000.[5]

Cassell's working-class background and the magazine's use of fiction to woo lower-class readers earned both criticism and praise. This comment from the *Edinburgh Guardian* sums up the dominant mood surrounding *Cassell's* cheap fiction-based publication:

---

[5] For comparison the more upmarket *Household Words* (priced 2d) at its height achieved sales of 100,000 copies, and *The Cornhill* (priced 1 shilling) averaged monthly sales of 84,000 (see Altick 1957: 351).

This magazine, for such it is, is another of the marvels wrought by the benevolent enterprise of its publisher...it contains eight folio pages of interesting and instructive matter, crowded with illustrations, in many cases of wonderful merit...Among the benefactors of this country, Mr Cassell, by the singular versatility and vigour of his efforts in the elevation of the popular taste, must undoubtedly rank. We have heard disparaging allusions to the unusual connection of *Literature* and *Coffee*. The more honour, we say, to the man who, sprung from the lower ranks of the people, is not content with a flourishing business as a coffee-merchant, but steps out of his way to lend a hand in the great work of popular education. (Nowell-Smith 1958: 40)

Though by 1882 Cassell's was owned by Petter and Galpin, the original ideals of educating and entertaining the working and lower middleclass reader remained largely intact. Though the new owners did share Cassell's moral and religious leanings, it was felt that the paper's success was largely due to its mix of fiction and educational material. It would have been foolish to abandon this format, especially at a time when the mortality rate of periodicals was "shocking" (Altick 1957: 391). With such a large readership, *Cassell's* was in an influential position with regard to promoting particular messages.

2. The Periodical and the Evolution of Urban Society

It has been argued that the periodical genre more than any other print form played a central part in the formation of mass culture. Despite its ephemeral nature over the past three hundred years the genre has proved pivotal to the evolution of urban societies, driven the evolution of print technology and communication networks, and "occupied a crucial place" in the dissemination of information and ideologies. As such, Margaret Beetham asserts, it represents "*the* characteristic modern form of print" (Beetham 1990: 19).

During the 1850s the unprecedented production and consumption stimulated by advances in technology and a newly literate mass readership turned the genre into a phenomenon. By the 1890s what began as an experimental form had become an essential part of the nation's reading ritual.

The "annus mirabilis of the British press" (Chalaby 1998: 35) happened at a time when Britain was in a state of flux. Industrial towns were developing at an incredible rate, particularly in the North.

Revolution in Europe, the Manchester-led Anti-Corn Law League campaign[6] and the Chartist uprising of 1848 had left Victorian society with a fear of the unruly mob. Commentators such as Frederic Harrison believed "there never was an age when the need was so urgent for synthetic habits of thought, systematic education and a common moral and religious faith." (Harrison 1882: 11) He saw the explosion of the periodical market as an opportunity for the dominant patriarchy to make what Marxists regard as "cultural capital" (Balibar and Macherey 1996: 52) out of literary production. In the hands of the ruling classes, language, a tool deemed "dangerous in the hands of the multitude" (Dickens 1994: 166)[7], could be used to ensure that all referential information was filtered through the same ideological machine. As Raymond Williams suggests, writers and publishers were in an ideal position to act as "agents of transmission"[8], imbued as they were with the power to provide a medium of expression for the world-view. Though it would be wrong to suggest that the literary elite overtly sought to create something along the lines of George Orwell's "Newspeak" (Orwell 1948: 214), their literature is coded with the messages of the ruling group and as such has the power to promote dominant ideologies.

Matthew Arnold saw literature as this and more. For him, it was a means of embracing the plurality of the classes and creating a culture that would provide the antidote to the threat of anarchy (see Arnold 1867: 136). At the start of the nineteenth century, the power of the press lay with the "Barbarians" (or aristocracy) but, increasingly, as the century wore on ownership of the publishing houses and periodicals fell into "Philistine" (bourgeois) hands.[9] Arnold felt that the "Philistines" had a duty to act as social, intellectual and moral guides for both the "Barbarians" and the "Populace" (mass public). He recognised that "the voice which makes a permanent impression on each

---

[6] The Anti-Corn Law League, inaugurated September 1838, succeeded in getting the Peel government to overturn the Corn Law in the summer of 1846, see Read 1964: 4.

[7] Charles Dickens's *Hard Times* was serialised in *Household Words* during 1854.

[8] Raymond Williams uses this term for writers in *Culture and Society: 1780-1959* (Williams 1963: 292).

[9] For a fuller account of Arnold's definitions of the aristocratic ("Barbarian"), middle ("Philistine") and working ("Populace") classes, see ibid.: 136-187.

of our classes is the voice of its friends, and this is [...] a comforting voice" (ibid.: 175). But while the voice that came from the periodical writer may have been "comforting" to the "Philistines", ideologically, intellectually and socially it was at odds with the growing millions of poorly educated readers.

Research suggests that the literary world was essentially a bourgeois one.[10] Studies of authorship, though not based upon the regional origins of writers, indicate a predominantly southern influence. Richard Altick's statistics reveal the extent to which writers shared the same cultural and ideological backgrounds. Large numbers of nineteenth-century writers attended southern-based grammar schools. This is of significance when considering how these writers represent the North. Altick's statistics are as follows:[11]

PERIOD	1	2	3	4
Grammar schools				
The nine "ancient" ones:				
Eton	11	18	9	19
Harrow	9	6	7	6
Rugby	2	5	2	9
Shrewsbury	—	2	2	3
Winchester	2	3	1	5
Westminster	7	3	—	3
Charterhouse	3	4	—	5
St. Paul's	2	—	2	6
Mechant Taylors	—	3	2	2
Total	36	44	25	58
Nineteenth-century foundations				
King's College School (1829)	—	4	3	—
University College School (1833)	1	2	2	—
Cheltenham (1841)	—	1	4	2
Marlborough (1843)	—	1	3	6
Edinburgh High School	3	6	—	—
Other (local) grammar schools	36	41	37	95
Total of all Grammar Schools	76	99	74	161
Dissenting academies	10	7	12	3
Edinburgh Academy	—	2	2	2
Private venture schools	58	61	45	8

---

[10] See Altick 1989: 96.
[11] Table reproduced from Altick 1989: 96.

	1	2	3	4
"Privately educated" (by tutor)	9	23	12	15
Catholic schools (especially Stonyhurst)	4	2	8	8
Foreign schools	5	9	9	6
Miscellaneous (teacher training schools, Birkbeck Instiute, etc.)	—	—	—	12

(Period 1, 1800-30; period 2, 1830-70; period 3, 1870-1900; period 4, 1900-35.)

Again, most authors attended university and more than half of these were educated at Oxford and Cambridge (ibid.: 104):

PERIOD	1	2	3	4	Total 1/4
Oxford	33	40	58	78	209
Cambridge	22	45	25	51	143
London (i.e., King's College, University College)	—	14	7	8	29
Edinburgh	8	18	9	4	39
Trinity College, Dublin	13	10	6	5	34
Glasgow	9	5	8	3	25
Other universities	2	1	1	13	17
Art schools (especially Slade)	3	11	6	10	30
Miscellaneous (including Woolwich, Sandhurst, medical college)	3	3	2	19	27

Altick's research, which is supported by Diana Laurenson,[12] also suggests that the majority of authors were upper or middle class. According to Laurenson, "only a minority of working-class writers in [Altick's] sample were able to supersede meagre education and poverty, limited access to books, leisure and contacts, restricted verbal codes and the middle-class bias of audiences and publishers." (Laurenson 1969: 317)

Not even the emergence of a mass reading public – millions of whom came from the lower orders – could shift the "middle-class bias" that marginalises the impoverished, poorly connected working-class writers. Even though increasing wealth and educational opportunities led to more movement between the classes (in particular between the working and the middle class), there were still relatively few opportunities for lower-class and northern-based writers. As

---

[12] In this context Diana Laurenson's research into 170 authors shows that nearly half of male writers went to independent public schools, with Eton being the most popular, and 47% attended Oxbridge (Laurenson 1969: 317).

Raymond Williams later attests, from 1830-1900 a "highly organised upper-middle class", consisting of the gentry, merchant and professional families, made the largest contribution to the literary market (see Williams 1961: 217; Waller 2006: 96-97). Given these statistics, it would be surprising if the producers of periodical literature did not favour southern or middle-class attitudes.

But, whilst "the author class remained relatively constant in its make-up [...] the reader–class did not." (Waller 2006: 97) Improved education for the lower orders, particularly following the 1870 Education Act, in conjunction with less expensive reading material, created a growing market of readers. Malcolm Bradbury argues that this caused a "literary lag" to develop between the audience and the artist, whose "traditional recourse to the leisured middle-class audience was disturbed by the influx" of readers from a different "social sector" (Bradbury 1971: xxxiii). Writers had to deal with the fact that in the rapidly expanding urban centres it was the middle-class industrialist and the factory hand and their families that formed a large part of their audience. Readers were no longer predominantly "Philistine". As a result, the successful bourgeois man or woman of letters had to write for both the merchant and for the barely literate labourer, or as Wilkie Collins put it for "the Unknown Public" (*Household Words* 1858: 217). With the first free library opening in Manchester in 1852, quickly followed by libraries in Sheffield and Liverpool, it was during the latter half of the nineteenth century that reading became "genuinely democratised" (Waller 2006: 143).

The key to the success of the periodical was market appeal, and the use of stereotypes was the stock in trade of a press intent on creating literary landscapes that had instant access to the psyche of a nation. In order to succeed in a highly competitive market where the lifespan of a periodical was often short, a publication's readership had to be large and stable. As Richard Hoggart has pointed out, by its very nature a mass audience is a diverse and therefore unstable series of audiences and to ensure success "the job of a mass media is to weld the [...] series of audiences into one very much larger group." (Hoggart in Ford 1984: 512) Aware of this, Victorian publishers battled to create a homogeneous family of readers that would secure their financial viability. One of the approaches relied upon offering representations of culture with which readers identified. This culture proffered stock situations, peopled by constructions of men and women that represented standard types. Hoggart argues that this strategy reinforced the "given life of the time" and helped the "new or emerging mass audience accept the 'reality'"(Hoggart in Ford 1984: 512) they were being offered. In other words, literature reinforced what its readers already believed to be true.

3. The North-South Divide and the Fear of Fragmentation

Depictions of the North offered to Victorian readers, though manufactured, were comforting because it was a landscape inhabited by easily recognisable types – the taciturn but talented businessman, the drunken mechanic, the poor factory worker, the fallen woman. In this way, periodicals became the producers of what Roland Barthes terms "mythologies" (Barthes 1972: 155). These stock figures are loaded with cultural meaning: not only do they present versions of reality but they often mirror and thus reaffirm the mythology of the dominant group. As Barthes points out, "myths tend towards proverbs. Bourgeois ideology invests in this [stereotypical] figure interests which are bound to its very essence: universalism, the refusal of any explanation, an unalterable hierarchy of the world." (Barthes 1972: 154-155) Barthes takes the idea of cultural manipulation a stage further than Hoggart, suggesting that stereotypes work by inoculating readers. For him mythologies are effective because they present a myriad of stereotypical images that, seen frequently, will anaesthetise the reader (see Balibar and Macherey 1996: 67). Once they become used to standard representations, readers eventually fail to challenge those constructions, and thus come to accept a spurious reality.

But the use of stereotypes in Victorian literature may indicate other preoccupations. With the rapid growth of the market, writers finding themselves struggling to come to terms with a mass and widely dispersed readership often sought refuge in middle-class and historical notions of region and race, especially when it came to the North and South. From a southern perspective, the northern figure was traditionally just that – an outsider. An historical prejudice between North and South had existed since the time of King John (indeed, the term "northerner" dates from the thirteenth century[13]) but it was during the Wars of the Roses when northern troops were used to fight battles in the South, that the idea became firmly planted in the national consciousness (see Jewell 1994: 45). In this period, London reacted by gathering all things to itself, further strengthening a "centralist tradition" (Royle 1998: 9), a tradition that still affects many aspects of British political and cultural life. In the Victorian era, London, "the great emporium for books," was the unrivalled literary centre of Britain. "Peculiar historical circumstances" had contributed to its "predominance"[14] and writers, publishers and booksellers all felt the effects of London's "centrifugal pull" [*sic*] (Royle 1998: 14). The expansion of the mass media in the 1850s further increased the capital's kudos. A move there not only provided unique networking opportunities for the would-be novelist, but offered alternative employment in the fields of journalism and publishing, and placed writers in ideological touch with the majority of readers who, pre-1850, were drawn from the upper echelons of society and for whom London was the cultural capital (see Altick 1957: 147).

However, the dynamics of the literary marketplace underwent major changes in the middle of the century. Because of its accessibility, literature was now a commodity increasingly consumed by the poorly educated millions. Furthermore, many of those readers lived in cities that were geographically and ideologically miles from London. In 1850 six out of the seven most densely populated areas in Britain – Glasgow, Sheffield, Birmingham, Manchester, Leeds and Liverpool – were situated in the North of England and lay between 120 and 409 miles from London.[15] Until the 1840s and the emergence of a reliable rail network, difficulties with transport would have made these centres essentially "foreign"[16] to southerners, and those who lived in close

---

[13] The north country barons who forced the Magna Carta on the king in 1215, were named "Northerners". (Read 1964: 276)

[14] Before 1696 the printing of books was allowed only in London, Oxford and Cambridge, see Laurenson 1969: 312-313.

[15] All these centres were designated cities in the Victorian period, see Parker 1994: 206.

[16] Jewell describes how Beau Brummell (1778-1840) learning that his regiment was to go from Brighton to Manchester joked about being sent on "foreign service" (Jewell 1994: 3).

proximity to London – one of Europe's most important centres of commerce – regarded northerners as provincial and subordinate.

In the face of a wide ideological lag, one recourse for the southern-based writer was to evaluate the region and its inhabitants through their own understanding. Evidence suggests that some writers resorted to condemnation, condescension or humour, and in story after story northern men and women are objects of ridicule, pity or criticism. A recurrent motif is the northern man emasculated by the demands of industrialisation, who, lacking emotional restraint, cries, flies into rages, fights, gambles and drinks. These excesses force them to abandon and mistreat their families – as in the case of David Dunster, the anti-hero of the *Household Words* story "The Miner's Daughters" whose drunken rages threaten and impoverish the lives of his wife and children (*Household Words* 1850: 126).

By necessity, periodicals also had at their heart topicality and, at mid-century, the northern figure became a commodity in terms of news and interest. In the early Victorian era, the North and its inhabitants had become a locus of concern. The Chartist uprising, which was centred on Manchester, and the success of the Anti-Corn Law League were still fresh in the minds of the public. Furthermore, for the first time, Manchester had outstripped London in terms of economic wealth and population, and reliable productivity in the North was vital to the commercial health of the nation. Hence, the threat of revolt from this quarter brought real concerns for national stability. Added causes for anxiety were the masses pouring into industrial centres, and the unsanitary and overcrowded conditions in which they lived. The North, then, presented a paradox. It was the backbone of the economy of England, but it was also constantly under threat of moral and physical degeneration.

The representation of northern figures reflects this dichotomy. Northerners are portrayed as physically "strong" and "powerful" (*Cassell's* 1872: 103) miners and manufacturers bravely struggling against adversity to supply a burgeoning consumer society. But their strength is more physical than moral. The men are intemperate wife-beaters, their wives victims, harridans or "slatterns" (Anon. 1862: 327). John Arthur Roebuck, one of the two MPs for the Borough of Sheffield in the 1860s, believed that any money spent on education in the northern cities would be wasted because the northern working man's nature made him incapable of being educated and attaining the status of gentleman. He believed:

> The highly paid North-country mechanic is [...] little better than a beast. His whole life is passed in mere sensual enjoyment; getting drunk is his chief business; and once he has got drunk, his necessary business is to get sober.[17]

By contrast, the Hampshire labourer whilst he may never attain the status of gentleman is, nevertheless "a clever fellow" (ibid.) and is more worthy than the bestial Sheffield steel worker – a product of high wages and low moral fibre (ibid.: 328) (incidentally, Roebuck was from Salisbury, Hampshire). This view is far from rare in the pages of the ephemeral press.

Given that Cassell was a Lancastrian, did his periodical offer a different perspective? Despite Cassell's background, the publication reveals a decided London-centeredness, perhaps because, in common with the majority of high circulation periodicals, *Cassell's* was based in the capital. The title page of its December 1882 edition proudly proclaims in large font "Cassell and Co. Ltd, London, Paris and New York". The word 'London' is pre-eminent. This is not for alphabetical reasons – the rest of the list does not adhere to that criterion – but underlines the pre-eminence of London as a centre of world-wide commerce and literary culture. Furthermore, the foregrounding of London's importance and *Cassell's* association with it imbues the publication with literary and economic status. In addition, by establishing a London focus, the periodical is able to draw upon historical associations of power and government.

Again, despite its founder's northern pedigree, *Cassell's* relied upon a pool of southern-based, freelance writers to fill its pages, the same writers who supplied material for a host of other periodicals. This means there was a shared culture. So even in *Cassell's* we find articles that present northerners as somehow lacking and that show writers employing "flexible *positional* superiority" (Said 1995: 336), repeatedly presenting a series of encounters with northerners or the North that always give the southerner or the South the upper hand.

---

[17] John Arthur Roebuck's comments appeared in *The Times* on 20 January (1862) and were quoted in an article critical of his point of view in "Gentlemen", (anon.) *The Cornhill* 5 (1862), 327-342 (328).

Just as Orientalists seek to define their own status by defining their difference from and superiority over all things Oriental, the southern-based writer uses the northerner as his or her 'other'. So, "by making statements about it [the North], authoring views of it, describing it, by teaching it, settling it, ruling over it" (Said 1995: 3) the writer or producer of literature is attempting to dominate and control the North.

Just as Orientalists often define the Orient as stereotypically weak, feminised, other, and conquerable, so it is that those living at a distance from the South are often cast as exotic others. Northerners are referred to as "natives". In articles, often presented as travelogues, the linguistic register is also redolent of imperialism, encouraging the reader to draw comparisons between northerners and colonial subjects. Northerners are represented as strange curiosities, objects existing outside of the dominant culture and thus fitting subjects for scrutiny and cataloguing. Writers treat visits "down"[18] to the North as field trips, with details of landscape, rivers, history and dialects dominating. (The use of the word 'down' is worthy of note here. As the North is higher cartographically than the South, ought travel from south to north be referred to as 'up' rather than 'down'?) Figuratively the word 'down' implies that the writer is going down among the natives; it suggests danger – the unknown; it indicates a fall, or a return to the uncivilised. The implication of a descent into primitivism is reinforced by the use of epithets that were normally reserved for people living in deepest, darkest Africa. In the two *Cornhill* articles already cited, northerners are "primitive" (*Cornhill* 1864: 96), "brute[s]" and "beast[s]" (Roebuck 1862: 327).

Again, *Cassell's* is not exempt from this. The title of an 1872 article on coalmining in Yorkshire is "Seeking Black Diamonds". This gives the area an exotic tinge that far removes it from the grim reality. The 'natives' of this piece are "very black" colliers "attired almost like that celebrated Indian chief of historical fame" (*Cassell's* 1872: 100). In an encounter with a Leeds mine owner the anonymous writer casts himself in the role of the big game hunter "lying in wait" to outwit his prey. In an account of a public dinner, he writes:

---

[18] Dickens writes that he travels "down to Preston" in "On Strike", *Household Words* 8 (1854): 553-576 (555). It is also used by the anonymous writer of "Seeking Black Diamonds", *Cassell's* (1872): 100.

> The burly Yorkshireman [...] appeared to be brusque and taciturn; but believing as I did that every man can converse on some subject, I sat as it were in a state of ambushment, lying in wait for the shortest monosyllable that might fall from his lips. For some time all conversation proved futile. (ibid.)

The tone, coupled with the plentiful use of the pronoun "I" throughout the article, impresses it with the writer's arrogance.

Another anonymous *Cassell's* article "Two Famous Yorkshire Towns: Harrogate and Knaresborough" (*Cassell's* 1882: 655-657) provides further illustration. Here the actual words of the northerners are translated because, says the writer, "**we** have difficulty in following [...] the peculiar *lingo* of the Yorkshire" (ibid.: 655) people. The term 'lingo' here is pejorative – a derogative, slang definition of a regional dialect. The use of the pronoun 'we' is socially divisive. The North is further cast in the role of foreign by the writer's suggestion that it is of interest merely as an oddity. The North is "a very amusing place for a visit of a few weeks", or indeed for a few minutes – the time it takes the reader to finish the article.

Throughout, the Yorkshire men and women lack agency and, indeed, most of the sentences are in the passive voice. At the market "the usual loud talking and chaffing, buying and selling, in simple fashion, were going on". Though the sentence has action in it, the actors are absent. The farmers' dealings are "simple", their speech "loud" and not worth reporting in detail or directly. In the whole narrative, the only sentence in which the farmers are active subjects is one detailing how they "hung about the inn doors, and filled the long low-roofed rooms" (ibid.). The verbs "hung" and "filled" imply limited action and suggest movement *en masse*. The farmers are not individuals but a herd-like collective. This tendency to construct northern groups *en masse* takes on a more sinister aspect when applied to large urban settings:

> There is undoubtedly something almost feminine in the excessive impressionableness of the natives of all large and crowded towns. They are subject to the influence of opinion as they are to the influence of miasma or typhus, and are accustomed to act collectively rather than individually [...]. (*Cornhill* 1864: 88)

Feminine, diseased, impressionable and herd-like – strong words reserved for the urbanised northern masses. This extract highlights the anxiety that Victorian industrial society was on the brink of chaos. As hundreds of thousands of people poured into urban areas, the city as a space became pathologised as dangerous, its inhabitants susceptible to disease and degeneration. Though the North was not alone in being affected by mass urbanisation, London differed because it had been a large urban centre for generations; its problems were seen as nothing new. Also as the seat of the most powerful ideological state apparatuses[19] – Monarchy, State and Church – London's reputation for governance and order helped dispel fears of disorder. This connection with the South imbues southerners – both writers and characters – with authority. If, as we suspect, some Victorian writers and readers accepted this power paradigm, then they, willingly or not, aligned themselves with the dominant group and thus appropriated status.

As already stated, the success of ephemeral literature brought great opportunities for writers, but this success was double-edged. The advent of the writer as professional was frowned upon by many in the cultural elite. With this in mind, the London-centeredness of producers of ephemeral literature may be a defence mechanism, a way of positioning themselves within the dominant group. Seen in this way, there are numerous examples of what Said terms "power using knowledge to advance itself" (Said 1995: 336). Writers advance themselves by composing a reality that is recognised and in many respects supported by the cultural elite.

So, even when a story is located in the North, the frame of reference is almost always London. Hence, a Leeds pit is described as being "twice as deep as St Paul's" (*Cassell's* 1872: 100). (The *Cassell's* writer assumes that readers share the knowledge that St Paul's is a large cathedral in London.) The same pit has "airways like the maze at Hampton Court" (ibid.: 102). In *Household Words,* James Lowe expresses surprise to find that in Preston "the atmosphere […] is as clear as the air upon Hampstead Heath" (*Household Words* 1853: 345). And, in *The Cornhill* "there is no place out of London so polite and elegant to live as the city of York" (*Cornhill* 1864: 84). (York attracts praise in this instance because it mirrors metropolitan attitudes.) Thus, through the symbolic reality of periodical narratives, writers seek to define their own subjectivity.

---

[19] Althusser uses these definitions in his essay "Ideology and the State" (see Rice and Waugh 1996: 52-53).

4. Re-mapping Conceptions of Northernness

Returning to Burt's essays we can see the danger of relying on symbolic representations and spurious knowledge. He suggests that by relying on information offered by others, we may come to be "grossly imposed upon". In *Under the Crust*, he cites William Cobbett's 1832 article "Tour in Scotland and the Four Northern Counties of England" as one of the culprits for propagating "curious" myths surrounding the region. Of his visit to Tyneside, Cobbett writes

> Here is the most surprising thing – thousands of horses continually living underground; children born there, and who sometimes, it is said, seldom see the surface at all, though they live to a considerable age (Burt 1883: 246).

Though polite, Burt's response to this is emphatic:

> With respect to the latter statement someone had, of course, grossly imposed upon the credulity of the sturdy Sussex yeoman. It need hardly be said that the allegation of children living underground, and living there for days without coming to the surface, is wholly mythical. (ibid.)

Here, Cobbett's blind acceptance of myth – which flies in the face of common sense – emphasises the vulnerability of the tourist, the observer who finds himself in unfamiliar territory. But not only does such an example highlight the dangers of blind acceptance, it also serves to elevate Burt's position as a reliable narrator. Whilst outsiders like Cobbett fall prey to spurious information, Burt's credentials as chronicler of the North are impeccable.

Burt's articles are an attempt to redraw the conceptual map of the North by offering us a snapshot of real life. Though he is mindful to effect change, his narrative differs from the meliorist narratives that from the 1840s to the 1870s represented the northerner as victim – victim of domestic violence, industrial accident or capitalist oppression – in a bid to evoke common understanding and stimulate change. His series appears at a time when the idea of the northerner as victim has lost its fascination – perhaps due to the passing of humanitarian legislation such as the advent of free education, and the Factory Acts.

Burt is keen to offer a portrayal of the northerner as a distinct, albeit sometimes flawed, entity, who has a place and a valuable part to play in a wider community. His narratives acknowledge a changing world and call for a changed attitude towards difference at a time of immense social change. By the late nineteenth century, the North, as well as the rest of the country, was made up of disparate groups – especially in the urban centres – drawn from distant communities, possessing different cultures and languages. In the provinces, poor urban conditions had created tensions that threw issues of "nationhood and regionality" (Royle 1998: 9) into sharp relief. But, as communities grew as a consequence of industrial expansion, the North began to acquire a distinct identity (ibid.: 8). Urban communities embraced those identities and developed fierce loyalties to their towns and cities. For Donald Read "the northern industrial districts gloried in being different and even a little barbarous because their difference and barbarism were symptoms of success." (Read 1964: 276) Burt's articles are an attempt to breech the widening gap generated by spurious information that the North is a foreign land populated by savage natives.

3. Towards the Fin de Siècle

By the end of the century, Britain had been involved in wars and skirmishes across the Empire for several decades. Anxiety was turning away from the regions and towards the rest of the world. These articles of *Cassell's* are symptomatic of a habit amongst periodical writers of foregrounding issues of regionality, culture and nationality at this particular period. Just as Britain's colonialist expansion was driven by a desire to shape and control a world away from its shores, the desire to forge a secure home base from which to operate strengthened. The key to this formation of a firm base was the construction of an ideal type of Briton, one that shared the same practices and values.

Though Burt's articles are in essence a defence of northern men and women, they also represent a shift away from the foregrounding of the North as different in a negative way. Towards the fin de siècle, there is a general trend within popular discourse to construct a homogeneous British identity. This desire to forge a stable cultural landscape had grown out of the tremendous geographic and cultural changes brought about by the Industrial Revolution, widespread colonisation, and the development of global media transmission. Indeed, Anthony Giddens sees the advent of mass media in the late nineteenth century as a pivotal moment in the creation of modern British society. With the advent of the electric telegraph cable (the transatlantic cable was laid in 1850 and the transcontinental system was complete by 1861), messages could be transmitted across the globe in a matter of minutes, and the print media was quick to exploit this in terms of news and information. These advances in print and communication technology served to 'uncouple' the relationship between place and time. This effective "'emptying' of time and space set in motion processes that established a single 'world' where none existed previously" (Giddens 1991: 27).

As the century draws to a close, the pages of periodicals reflect this compression of space which brings them into closer proximity with the rest of the world. With news travelling across continents in a matter of minutes, Victorian readers began to develop what John B. Thompson terms "mediated worldliness" (Thompson 1995: 34). They begin to move away from personal experience and towards a world in which meaning is experienced second hand. Though Thompson's discussion focuses on twenty-first century media, his concept of 'mediated worldliness' could just as usefully be applied to nineteenth-century audiences. Then, just as now, the media has created the feeling that "our sense of the world which lies beyond the sphere of our personal experience, and our sense of our place within this world, are increasingly shaped by mediated symbolic forms." (ibid.) As readers were able to "experience events, observe others and, in general, learn about a world which extends beyond the sphere of our day to day encounters" their "spatial horizons of […] understanding" were "greatly expanded" (ibid.). This had an impact on their sense of belonging:

> By altering their sense of place and of the past, the development of communication media also has some bearing on individuals' sense of belonging […] the sense of belonging derives, to some extent, from a feeling of sharing a common history and a common locale, and a common trajectory in time and space." (ibid.)

So, in a world of rapid change, the periodical press begins to play a large part in binding communities together. "The communication media provide a way of sustaining cultural community despite spatial dislocation" (Thompson 1995: 203). Readers are encouraged to see themselves as part of a wider community, and the British nation is constructed anew as a space "in which members of the nation have a strong bond with each other, a bond that triumphs whatever differences (of class, gender, or religion [...]) may divide people within" (Mitchell 2000: 269) it. Narratives such as Burt's proffer a vision of the world that celebrates difference – but only to a degree. His is a discourse that accepts individuality and difference, but only insofar as it does not interfere with the greater good of society. His proffered national landscape – though it may contain thorns and weeds, is as cultivated as the gardens of his enlightened, green-fingered pitmen; and the brute strength of the rough Tyneside collier is a blessing when pressed into service on behalf of a wider community.

Works Cited

Primary References

Anon. (1862): "Gentlemen", *The Cornhill Magazine* 5, 327-342.
— (1872): "Seeking Black Diamonds", *Cassell's Family Magazine*, 100-103.
— (1882): "Two Famous Yorkshire Towns: Harrogate and Knaresborough", *Cassell's Family Magazine*, 655-657.
— (1850): "The Miner's Daughters", *Household Words* 1, 271-273.
— (1864): "Yorkshire", *The Cornhill Magazine* 9, 84-96.
Arnold, Matthew (1867/1974): "Culture and Anarchy" (first published in *The Cornhill Magazine* 1867), in: Alan W. Bellringer and Christopher B. Jones (eds.): *Victorian Sages*. London: Dent, 136-187.
Burt, Thomas (1883): "Under the Crust: The Tyneside Collier", *Cassell's Family Magazine* 8, 245-247 and 269-271.
Collins, Wilkie (1858): "The Unknown Public", *Household Words*, 217-219.
Dickens, Charles (1854): "On Strike", *Household Words* 8, 553-576.
— (1854): "Hard Times', *Household Words* 8, 1 April – 12 August.
— (1994): *Hard Times*. London: Dent.
Lowe, James (1853): "The Preston Lock-Out", *Household Words* 8, 345-348.

Research Literature

Althusser, Louis (1969/1997): "Ideology and State", in: P. Rice and P. Waugh (eds.): *Modern Literary Theory*. London: Arnold.
Altick, Richard D. (1957): *The English Common Reader: A Social History of the Mass Reading Public 1800-1900*. Chicago: University of Chicago Press.
— (1989): *Writers, Readers and Occasions: Selected Essays on Victorian Literature and Life*. Columbus: Ohio State UP.
Balibar, E. and P. Macherey (1996): "Literature as an Ideological Form", in: P. Rice and P. Waugh (eds.): *Modern Literary Theory*. London: Arnold.
Barthes, Roland (1972): *Mythologies*. London: Vintage.
Beetham, Margaret, (1990): "Towards a Theory of the Periodical as Publishing Genre", in: L. Brake et al. (eds.): *Investigating Victorian Journalism*. Basingstoke: Macmillan, 18-31.
Bellringer, A.W. and C. B. Jones (eds.) (1975): *The Victorian Sages: An Anthology of Prose*. London: Dent.
Bradbury, Malcolm (1971): *The Social Context of Modern English Literature*. Oxford: Basil Blackwell.
Brake, L., A. Jones and L. Madden (eds.) (1990): *Investigating Victorian Journalism*. Basingstoke: Macmillan.

Chalaby, Jean K. (1998): *The Invention of Journalism*. Basingstoke: Macmillan.

Du Gay, Paul and Stuart Hall (eds.) (1997): *Questions of Cultural Identity*. London: Sage.

Ford, Boris (ed.) (1984): *From James to Eliot: The New Pelican Guide to English Literature*. London: Penguin.

— (ed.) (1982): *From Dickens to Hardy: The New Pelican Guide to English Literature*. London: Penguin.

Giddens, Anthony (1991): *Modernity and Self-Identity: Self and Society in the Late Modern Age*. Stanford, CA: Stanford UP.

Hall, Stuart (2003): *Representation: Cultural Representations and Signifying Practices*. London: Sage.

Harrison, Frederic (1882) "A Few Words About the Nineteenth Century", *Fortnightly Review* 4, 11-26.

Hoggart, Richard (1958): *The Uses of Literacy*. London: Penguin.

Jewell, Helen M. (1994): *The North-South Divide: the Origins of Northern Consciousness in England*. Manchester: Manchester UP.

Laurenson, Diana (1969): "Sociological Study of Authorship", *British Journal of Sociology* 20, 311-324.

Mitchell, Don (2000): *Cultural Geography*. Oxford: Blackwell.

Nowell-Smith, Simon (1958): *The House of Cassell 1848-1958*. London: Cassell.

Orwell, George (1948/1954): *1984*. London: Penguin.

Parker, Geoffrey (ed.) (1994): *The Times Atlas of World History*. London and New York, Sydney: BCA.

Pollard, Arthur (ed.) (1987): *The Victorians*. Suffolk: Sphere Books.

Read, Donald (1964): *The English Provinces 1760-1960: A Study in Influence*. London: Camelot Press.

Rice, Philip and Patricia Waugh (1996): *Modern Literary Theory*. London, New York and Sydney: Arnold.

Royle, Edward (1998): *Issues of Regional Identity*. Manchester: Manchester University Press.

Said, Edward (1995): *Orientalism*. London: Penguin.

Thompson, John B. (1995): *The Media and Modernity: A Social Theory of the Media*. Cambridge: Cambridge UP.

Waller, Philip (2006): *Writers, Readers and Reputations in Literary Life in Britain 1870-1918*. Oxford: Oxford UP.

Williams, Raymond (1961): *The Long Revolution*. London: Chatto & Windus.

— (1963): *Culture and Society: 1780-1959*. London: Penguin.

Northern Racism: A Pilot Study of Racism in Sunderland

Amir Saeed

Abstract: This essay examines how constructions of national identity are influenced by media representations. Raising the question of how British national identity can be understood in racialised media discourse the essay aims to illustrate how asylum seekers and non-white immigrants in the North East of England have been represented in the national media and what impact these representations have had on both the 'indigenous white community' and the various non-white communities that reside in the North East. To demonstrate this point the essay describes the results of empirical work carried out with non-white respondents relating to issues of national identity, sense of belonging and the experience of racism. This work seems to indicate that non-white communities feel misrepresented and 'not wanted' due to their skin colour.

Key names and concepts: Payman Bhamani - Enoch Powell - David Blunkett; Sunderland - Racism - Ethnicity - Minorities - English Identity - Immigration - Asylum Seekers - Muslim Community - Islamophobia - BNP

1. Introduction: Background to Research

In the summer of 2002 a young Iranian refugee, Payman Bhamani, was stabbed to death in Hendon, Sunderland. Many believed the attack was racially motivated and the tragedy brought Sunderland's record of race relations into the media spotlight, albeit briefly.[1]

Whilst most of the media coverage of the incident concentrated on racism directed towards asylum seekers it should be noted that this prejudice was also directed towards other minority groups. Local community groups have spoken out about the racial abuse suffered by non-white residents in the city. In addition, Kundnani (2001: 47) notes

---

[1] See [http://news.bbc.co.uk/1/hi/uk/2226218.stm] [http://news.bbc.co.uk/1/hi/-england/2222840.stm] [http://politics.guardian.co.uk/farright/story/0,11375,-890645,00.html]

that the hostility against asylum seekers can easily turn into abuse directed against anyone who looks different. This has meant an increase in abuse directed against anyone not white living in Sunderland. Statistically, Sunderland is still a large city with a relatively low Black and Minority Ethnic (BME) population. The 2001 census indicated that approximately 2% of the total population of some 280,000 belong to a minority ethnic group. Nonetheless, this represents a near doubling of the proportion belonging to these groups since the 1991 Census.[2] This situation has been exacerbated by the fact that there has recently been an increase in the number of international students and non-white students from other parts of the country moving into Sunderland.

Given this background, the purpose of this research is to examine the extent of overt racism suffered by non-white residents in Sunderland who are asylum seekers, students or permanent residents of this city.[3] In order to do this the article will examine how national identity is constructed in the British media to mean *white* and *Christian*. This is underpinned by theories of racial and media hostility towards migrant groups settling in Britain. Furthermore recent wider political developments encourage an increasingly widespread belief that the presence of non-white, non-Christian groups in the UK is basically a problem which potentially undermines the community, or in more specific terms, is a threat to the Englishness of the North of England, as will be explained later on.

These theoretical considerations will be discussed in relation to two pilot studies that examined the views of non-white groups in Sunderland. These pilot studies allow non-white minority groups to voice their concerns, feelings and expectations about living in Sunderland. In short it allows a group who is demographically small and politically disenfranchised an opportunity to express its opinion about living in a predominately 'white' city. Brief findings will be presented to enhance the aforementioned theoretical considerations.

---

[2] See [http://www.sunderland.gov.uk/public/editable/life-episodes/ancs/race-e-quality/default.asp]

[3] It must be noted that asylum seekers cannot be included as 'residents' because if their appeal fails they may be deported from the city or even the country.

2. National 'Identity' Concerns

Recent academic research into the British media's coverage of issues relating to immigration and asylum has drawn attention to the underlying themes of race and nation which dominate media reporting (Finney and Peach 2004). It may be added that Gilroy has claimed that in the past twenty years the 'new racism' has successfully distanced itself from crude notions of biological inferiority and instead forged links between race, nationhood, patriotism and nationalism. It has done so by defining the nation as a unified cultural community, a national culture ethnically pure and homogeneous in its whiteness (Gilroy 1992: 53). For example, Greenslade has claimed that the general response of the British press to asylum and immigration is typified in the following remark by Charles Moore, the distinguished former editor of *The Times* newspaper:

> Britain is basically English speaking, Christian and white, and if one starts to think it might become basically Urdu speaking and Muslim and brown, one gets frightened. (Greenslade 2005: 6)

Although Moore's comments were made in the context of *The Spectator*[4], a relatively small-circulation magazine noted for its outspoken and unashamedly right-wing views, Greenslade is nevertheless correct in claiming that such views are highly symptomatic of the British press's general approach to questions of asylum and immigration. From the journalistic treatment of these issues it becomes clear that there is a tendency in the British press to ignore the country's postcolonial reality and thus to avert the challenges which arise from the coexistence of groups of different ethnic and religious backgrounds in modern communities: close analysis of the attitudes that underlie media coverage of asylum and immigration issues have confirmed that these are commonly written and spoken about in a tone which suggests anxiety over the erosion of the perceived 'indigenous' national culture – in Moore's words: English-speaking, Christian and white. It echoes an inherently nostalgic vision of England and thus promotes a model of the nation's identity that reflects historical yearning rather

---

[4] Cf. "Time for a More Liberal and 'Racist' Immigration Policy", *The Spectator*, 19 October 1991.

than a pragmatic approach to the problems and challenges of the present.

Throughout the years Britain's black and other ethnic minorities have tended to be portrayed in terms of a limited repertoire of representations and within contexts characterised by conflict, controversy and deviance. In the 1960s and 1970s studies observed how immigrants were reported in relation to problems of 'numbers' and to the tensions caused by 'race relations' (Hartmann and Husband 1974). In the 1970s and 1980s representations tended to criminalise Britain's black population – ignoring social inequalities and growing anger at police tactics – and the 1990s have witnessed attacks on anti-racist groups, vilifications of black representatives and the seeming endorsement of 'new racism' by prominent politicians – actively disparaging attempts to further multicultural and anti-racist agendas (Van Dijk 1991). The current representation of asylum seekers and British Muslim communities appears to follow this trend of problematising non-white communities as un-British (Saeed 2004a).

Hall, Held and McGrew (1992: 298) have observed that in recent times biological notions of race have been replaced by cultural definitions which draw on discourses of national belonging and national identity. This has led to a new form of 'cultural racism' associated as much with ethnicity as with race. In this context Gandy (1998) has suggested that the concept of ethnicity was first employed by social scientists and policy makers as a way of shifting the definition of race away from the biological and towards the cultural. His views are supported in this respect by Mason (2000), who holds that ethnicity is a more appealing concept than race not merely because it is inherently social but also because ethnic categories are defined partly through the conscious efforts of those who belong to them. Following the same argument, Gilroy (1992: 53) has claimed that in the past twenty years a 'new racism' has successfully distanced itself from crude notions of biological inferiority and instead forged links between race, nationhood, patriotism and nationalism. It has done so by defining the nation as a unified cultural community, a national culture ethnically pure and homogeneous in its whiteness.

For example, Modood (1992) reminds us that the term 'British' is practically 'quasi-ethnic' in its close identification with whiteness. He goes on to claim that the right of individuals and communities to be culturally different in Britain is often neglected in favour of the expectation that they be absorbed or assimilated into the homogeneous host culture. Likewise Mason (2000: 15) has observed that the distinguishing criterion for belonging to a designated 'ethnic minority' group is normally skin colour. Thus the conflation of ethnic identity with skin colour can lead to the classification of second or third generation immigrants – who may be culturally indiscernible from their white neighbours – as 'ethnic minorities':

> the visibility of somatic characteristics is not inherent in the characteristics themselves, but arises from a process of signification by which meaning is attributed to certain of them. (Miles 1993: 87)

Thus people with non-white skin in Britain have habitually been designated as outsiders (or Other), as 'ethnic minorities' whose culture is alien and incompatible with that of the host nation. This occurs in a context where discourses of national belonging and national identity assume a key role. For the North of England with its relatively small non-white population it can be argued that it is assumed that to be British one needs to be white (Gilroy 1987).

3. Constructing the Nation

The exact nature of the relationships between concepts of race, racism and nationalism (or the nation) has been disputed by social scientists. Balibar and Wallerstein (1991: 40) have suggested that the national frontier, like race, is a fairly recent and formerly European phenomenon and can be seen as a 'prior criterion' to racism, adding that different strains of racism are constantly emerging from nationalism. For Balibar and Wallerstein (1991: 60) this is because race and nation both involve the classification, differentiation and exclusion of groups constructed as Other: "Collectivising features [...] will be set up as stigmata for exteriority and impurity, whether those relate to style of life, beliefs or ethnic origin."

Anderson (1991: 149), on the other hand, has argued that nationalism and racism are distinctly different and, to a certain extent, antithetical to one another – for while nationalism is concerned with 'historical destinies', racism is concerned with biological 'eternal contaminations.' Nevertheless, Anderson sees many parallels between race and nation, particularly in the way both categories draw on the presence of natural ties, such as skin colour, parentage or birthplace, over which people have little choice. Something of a compromise between these views is offered by Miles (1993), who asserts that while racism is not antithetical to nationalism, neither does it arise simply as a consequence of it. Rather, Miles contends that race and nation are best described as synonymous historical developments against the background of industrial capitalism. However, Miles utilises Anderson's theory of the nation as an 'imagined community' and applies this phrase equally to race, arguing that both can be seen as socially constructed categories of inclusion and exclusion.

Anderson's thoughts on the formation of nationhood and national consciousness were presented in his landmark work *Imagined Communities*, in which he observed that the boundaries assembled in the construction of nations were possible only in particular historical contexts, namely the emergence of print media and the onset of industrial capitalism. These facilitated the production of 'imagined communities' whereby people within man-made physical boundaries were compelled to rally around symbols which evoked feelings of solidarity, simultaneity and unison (Anderson 1991: 145). Although most people within such imagined communities have little or nothing in common with their fellow compatriots (and will never meet a vast majority of them), they remain connected by their shared recognition of constructed 'national' symbols such as a national anthem (Anderson 1991: 160).

Since racial boundaries are often constructed around phenotypical markers (i.e. skin colour), those markers may be used to signify a sense of fellowship and unity, sometimes bound up with the idea of the nation, while any visible differences are marked and defined as exterior or Other (Miles 1993: 57). Miles reminds us that racist ideologies are therefore relational – they imagine and construct a multiplicity of other racialised populations, defined by their shared or collective attributes, and place them in binary or hierarchical positions (1993: 60).

Billig (1995) has noted that the everyday reproduction of national identity and consciousness is pervasive and almost overwhelming. In *Banal Nationalism* he surveyed the ways in which 'we' are constantly reminded that we live in nations – to use his term, our national identity is constantly 'flagged'. Billig comments that even the use of small, seemingly innocuous words in everyday language and conversation offer unconscious reminders that 'we' share a common national identity, evoking a sense of fellowship in an imagined community. This is particularly pertinent in political and media discourse, and as Billig discovers, it is usually possible to open a newspaper or watch a news broadcast on any given day and find a cluster of stories replete with references to the nation. What must be remembered is the extent to which this can be a profoundly ideological process. Despite its apparent naturalness, the nation is a construct – it forms not only part of our own identity but also that of Others who lie outside the boundaries of our nation. As Hall (1992: 296) observes, the nation is a structure of cultural power, as can be seen in the media's treatment of post-war migrants to the UK.

In the light of these theories it becomes clear that the formation of a national identity needs the construction not only of an imagined community but also of the Other. Given the likelihood that chauvinistic tendencies will develop, the problem connected with national identities is made even worse when this Other is found within one and the same community: in that case the close association between race and nation becomes the focal point for the concepts of inclusion and exclusion that differentiate a heterogeneous group into a cultural core and marginalised others. These processes potentially undermine the community and prevent a shared sense of belonging.

4. Immigration in Post-war Britain

Although the presence of Asian and black communities in Britain is by no means a phenomenon unique to the latter half of the twentieth century, the appearance of large, permanently settled groups in British towns and cities is undoubtedly a recent historical development which arose as a consequence of the dissolution of the British Empire and thus as a number of post-war migrations from Britain's former colonies (Pilkington 2003: 33). During the 1960s and 1970s emigration exceeded immigration, but this fact failed to prevent the question of numbers from cropping up regularly in political and media discourse. Furthermore the furore which surrounded immigration throughout the post-war era was focused almost exclusively on the dangers associated with 'coloured' immigration, not the white Australians, South Africans, Canadians and New Zealanders who were received with barely the bat of an eyelid by both the state and the media. In stark contrast, blacks and Asians had to suffer a constant barrage of hostility and prejudice in which the media played a key role.

When Enoch Powell[5] made his infamous "rivers of blood" speech in April 1968, it was greeted with considerable public backing. Dockers in East London marched in his support, newspaper editors who criticised him were besieged by letters in his support and one opinion poll even suggested that as many as 75% of the population agreed with him (Greenslade 2005: 20). Given the popular stereotype of black people as lazy, unemployed and predisposed to criminality and sexual promiscuity, such hostility to 'coloured' immigration was hardly surprising. There is little doubt that the media played some role in cultivating the negative stereotypes which had such austere consequences for immigrants and minorities.

5. Media Representations of Minorities

In relation to race and ethnicity, the media provides information where public knowledge is fragmentary. Although there are some two million black people in Britain, they live mainly in a few major population centres and therefore the white majority's contact with them is often slight (Van Dijk 1991). Research into the media's treatment of race over the years has suggested that its reporting has been limited in its themes and negative in its content. Research into minority representation in the British context can be summarised in two distinct but complementary stages (Saeed 1999). Firstly, immigration issues have been formulated as a 'problem', or to use Thatcher's words a fear of 'swamping.' Secondly, minorities who were born in Britain have also been perceived to be 'problems.' From the "criminal mentality" of the Afro-Caribbeans (Hall 1978), to the "cheating Asians" (Sivanandan 1988 and the "Islamic fundamentalists" (Ahmed 1993) minority

---

[5] Enoch Powell was a right-wing politician, who held a seat in Parliament for the Conservative Party between 1950 and February 1974. In 1968 he made a notorious speech attacking immigration policies in the UK.

communities tend to be represented in negative ways. The most recent surveys of the media (Speers 2001) clearly show that the media is biased and at times overtly racist in its attitudes to asylum seekers:

> As soon as asylum seekers are described as 'illegal immigrants', it is a small step before the debate spills over to the issue of immigrants generally, and the very notion of Britain as a multiracial society is called into question. (Kundnani 2001: 50)

6. Religion, Refugees and Nation

During the 1990s interest in the Muslim community in the UK increased significantly. Beginning with national issues such as the Rushdie affair and international matters such as the 1991 Gulf War, a series of events brought Muslims into the media spotlight and adversely affected the Muslim population in the UK. New components within racist terminology appeared, and were used in a manner that could be argued were deliberately provocative to bait and ridicule Muslims and other ethnic minorities. Many social commentators have noted that media language has been fashioned in such a way as to cause many to talk about a 'criminal culture' (see Saeed et al. 1999; Modood 1997; Wahab 1989).

Since September 11, the loyalty of British Muslims to Britain has been further questioned with polls indicating that British-Muslims should make a special effort to emphasise their Britishness (*The Observer* 25 November 2001). The perceived support amongst British Muslims for Bin Laden, Palestinian suicide bombers and Kashmiri separatists has been further fuelled by recent events in the North of England, such as the incident referred to in the opening paragraph of this essay. The disturbances in the North of England have in some quarters been presented as a particular problem with the Muslim community and not with the British-Asian community as a whole. In a recent analysis of the situation Kundnani states that

> the popular press first blamed 'outside agitators', then blamed the community leaders who had failed in their allotted role: to control "their people." Then it was the inherent separatism of Islamic culture that was to blame - these people did not want to integrate: they were 'self-segregating'. (Kundnani 2001: 110)

Pakistani and Bangladeshi communities in particular have been represented as separatist, insular and unwilling to integrate with wider society. Furthermore the old stereotypical image of "Asian passivity" has been replaced by a more militant aggressive identity which is meant to be further at odds with 'British secular society' (Modood 1997). The concept of culture clash has been re-introduced to imply that British-Muslims are at odds with mainstream society. Recent comments by a variety of senior politicians appear to substantiate these populist beliefs. David Blunkett and Peter Hain have both lately made comments that have suggested that British-Muslims must make more of an effort to integrate into society, a position of course which in turn implies that the Muslim community is unwilling to integrate into British society. Blunkett has gone as far as to suggest 'oaths of allegiance' and 'not marrying spouses from the Indian subcontinent' and has spoken out in favour of the introduction of 'English Language Tests' for any one with a non-Anglo-British background (Saeed 2004b). However, it has been argued that some politicians are pandering to the right and are fuelling populist beliefs for their own political agenda. If, however, they were to look at recent research done in the area of national identity and ethnic minority communities many of their concerns would appear to be unsubstantiated. Saeed notes in this context:

> Post September 11 polls done by the British-Asian newspaper *Eastern Eye* (23 November 2001) show overwhelmingly that British-Muslims perceived themselves as loyal citizens despite opposing US/UK bombing of Afghanistan. This right to disobey is one of the cornerstones of democracy and one should consider that white Britons who may oppose government policy are not usually questioned about their loyalty. Indeed, the most recent survey on Muslim opinion (*The Guardian* 17 June 2002) show that the majority consider themselves British-Muslims. (Saeed 2004a: 14)

Furthermore it could be suggested that the issue of asylum seekers/refugees has been conflated with the issue of Islamic fundamentalist terrorism to create a new form of racism and thus, it may be argued, to create new criteria of exclusion. Fekete draws attention to the difficult situation which ensued after the passing of legislation against terrorism:

> What has finally set the seal on xeno-racism, legitimising even further its populist appeals and inflammatory expression in the press, is the

passing of the Terrorism Act 2000. This, the first permanent anti-terrorism law in twenty-five years, directly targets exile organisations. Even as Macpherson in his report into the death of Stephen Lawrence[6] warned of the danger of stereotyping black communities as criminal, the government gave legitimacy to a new set of stereotypes: asylum seekers are phonies and fraudsters; refugees are terrorists and the enemy within. (Fekete 2002: 38)

For example, the image of the "enemy within" featured prominently in the tabloid newspaper *The Sun* where it was noted that due to the lack of asylum laws "Britain is now a Trojan horse for terrorism." (*The Sun* 14 January 2003) This, Fekete notes, is systematic of how the mainstream press now conflates terrorism, asylum seekers and Islamophobia into another 'moral panic.' She shows that this form of stigmatisation of the Muslim community is not restricted to the level of the tabloid press: David Blunkett, home secretary of the Labour government, gives evidence of the extent to which Muslims have been placed under general suspicion. Fekete writes:

> In the UK, home secretary David Blunkett, announcing new reception arrangements and the introduction of identity cards for asylum seekers, has stated that, in future, all asylum seekers will be tracked from arrival to removal because, in the past terrorists have used the asylum system to gain entry to the UK. (Fekete 2002: 2)

At present this attitude may predominantly cause distress and irritation to minorities. In the long run, however, it may potentially undermine the fragile post-war, post-colonial arrangement of British society. For the North of England these developments may turn out even more disruptive: the economic pressure on the region may enhance processes of alienation within the community where the Other may not only be seen as different but may also be readily identified as the reason for one's own economic failure.[7]

---

[6] Stephen Lawrence was a black British teenager who was murdered in April 1993 at the age of 18. Such attacks had happened previously, but this time widespread publicity attracted national attention that threatened civil disturbances and severely damaged relations between Britain's non-white communities and the police. A Public Inquiry known as the Macpherson Report, or the Stephen Lawrence Report found police investigation had been incompetent and found that the police were institutionally racist (see Cottle 2004).

[7] See also: (http://www.ners-sunderland.org.uk/key.asp)

7. Methodology and Local Demographics
7.1 Local Concerns

As previously stated, Sunderland's Black ethnic minority population accounts for approximately 2% of the population: in December 2005 there were 3287 asylum seekers in the North East in NASS accommodation, a decrease of 4.58% from September 2005. The largest group, 1081 or 32.9%, is living in Newcastle. It is estimated that between 800 and 1,500 asylum seekers are currently living in Sunderland. These figures illustrate how marginal this group of people is compared to the overall population in the region. One might think therefore that racial problems should be an unpleasant exception. But the contrary is true: despite certain economic successes the region remains a hotbed of social and economic problems. According to official reports:

> Sunderland is still a relatively poor city and, in certain respects, its relative position has worsened. The Index of Multiple Deprivation (IMD) for 2000 indicates [...] six wards among the most deprived 5% of wards in England and eleven within the most deprived 10% [...]. The city has suffered from a legacy of poor health and a loss of population. Economic activity is low and despite recent improvements [...] high male and very long term unemployment are particular problems which along with other factors contribute to social exclusion" (Government Office North East website: www.go-ne.go.uk/corporate/europe/sund_p4_pdp.html)

It could be argued that it is likely that this socio-economic position fosters resentment toward 'outsiders' who could potentially be seen to be benefiting from jobs, health and housing provisions at the expense of local people. Similar circumstances have surrounded recent racial conflict in the North West of England and in Glasgow.

Chris Mullin, MP for Sunderland and chairman of the home affairs select committee, has 1,500 asylum seekers in his Sunderland constituency and he takes his constituents' protests seriously: "There is real anger, especially from those who are only just up the ladder from the asylum seekers. They do think resources are being diverted. They think asylum seekers are getting mobile phones and cars from the state, and certainly better benefits, when of course they get much less."[8]

---

[8] (http://society.guardian.co.uk/comment/column/0,7882,886196,00.html)

Moreover, the far right-wing British National Party (BNP) has begun campaigning in the North East of England, most notably in Sunderland, where their candidates acquired a significant proportion of the vote in local elections in 2000 and 2002. It is worthwhile looking at the furious mood documented by the following quotation at some length because it illustrates how media myths and local resentment can help to boost support for the far right:

> The government should be looking after their own. I work in a bar where the BNP meet every Thursday, and what they are saying is right. It's about time somebody stood up for us. "Get them out," she said to nods from the other women around the pub table. "They come in here - they are shoplifting, robbing people, stabbing people. Keep them out. Keep them out. Our government can't look after us. If the government looked after us there wouldn't be a problem. We've lived here all our lives. We don't get free mobile phones. They get free air flights. Sunderland city council are flying them out from wherever they come from." The other drinkers, in a pub in the rundown Southwick area of Sunderland, chime in with their own asylum seeker stories. It is a blend of embroidered fact and outrageous fiction; the refugees get houses "fully furnished", they push trolleys piled high with food, they wave their babies in your face as they beg for change. So why should foreigners get something for nothing?
>
> *One speaker drops a tabloid catchphrase into the argument:* 'Britain is a soft touch,' *said Derek, a retired labourer, picking up a phrase* The Sun *has repeated in 37 stories over the past year.*[9] (italics my emphasis, A.S.)

Seeing the opportunity, the far right has capitalised on such stories and at times fuelled the myths. In the local elections of 2006 the BNP managed to gain 13,500 votes in a city with fewer than 4,000 non-white residents. Asylum myths were clearly one of the main reasons for the BNP vote. A CRE (Commission for Racial Equality) analysis may explain why Sunderland voted in such large numbers for the BNP:

— the BNP now gets support from people who do not normally vote in local elections.

— Many of its new supporters are aged between 18 and 35. Most of them are male.

---

[9] (http://politics.guardian.co.uk/farright/story/0,11375,890645,00.html)

— Its support is moving up the social scale. It is gaining endorsements from the lower middle classes, many of whom were 'Thatcher's children' and now feel that their earlier support for Tony Blair was misplaced. (CRE 2004)[10]

The CRE study continues to point out that the BNP shows particular skill in picking promising battlegrounds. *The Guardian* summarises the report and writes that "experts say the most fertile wards appear to be those with a very small number of minority residents, or all-white areas that have minorities close by. This allows the party to peddle the myth that wards are about to be swamped and to play on fears of multi-culturalism." (http://www.politics.guardian.co.uk/farright/story/-0,,1043020,00.html).

7.2 Research Methodology

Given the relatively small non-white ethnic minority population of Sunderland it is suggested that the racism experienced by all non-white groups will be quite similar. This in some ways refutes the suggestion of Modood (1997) that different ethnic groups in Britain also have different experiences of daily life. Although this seems to hold true for such issues as housing, employment and health care, our study was based on the working hypothesis that in terms of actual racist abuse the experience of minority groups depends on locality rather than ethnicity. In order to support this hypothesis by empirical research the following field study was carried out:

In May 1995 six focus groups were conducted involving a total of 33 participants (seventeen male and sixteen female). Two of the focus groups were conducted in the office of a local youth organisation. Four were conducted at the University of Sunderland. All of the participants were volunteers. The participants included students, residents and asylum seekers resident in Sunderland. Two focus groups were conducted by a female researcher and four by a male researcher. The sample was achieved through contacting individuals and advertising for participants who then contacted friends etc. In short, a system of

---

[10] For full details see CRE (2004): *National Analytical Study on Racist Violence and Crime: RAXEN Focal Point for the UK*. (http://eumc.europa.eu/eumc/-material/pub/RAXEN/4/RV/CS-RV-NR-UK.pdf)

purposive sampling was employed. Besides demographic details such as age the participants were also asked to affirm their ethnic origin and to describe themselves in terms of their nationality. In addition to the focus groups, structured questionnaires were handed out in May 1997 to non-white students around the campus of the University of Sunderland to gather further data for the research. This was done through contacting the Muslim students association at the University and also using the snowball technique, where one participant acted as a gatekeeper for the research. A total of 120 questionnaires were handed out, of which 58 were returned, 24 by female participants and 34 by male participants. Academically the respondents' views were linked to previous research work and theoretical concepts. Although the survey is not representative it still offers qualitative insights into the issues relevant to non-white residents in Sunderland and allows a glance at the views and experiences of ordinary people.

7.3 Findings: The Questionnaires

Only a brief snapshot of the findings can be presented here due to the limited space available. Nevertheless these results do indicate how ideologies of race, ethnicity and racism are evident in the experiences of these participants. The participants were asked eleven questions with regard to their experience of racial abuse in Sunderland. The following gives a descriptive account of the main findings.

All of the students had lived for at least one year in Sunderland. Out of the 58 students 57 had noticed racial abuse in that time. All 57 had noticed abuse both on the campus and around the city. Of these 57, 48 had personally been the subject of overt racial abuse such as name-calling, spitting and physical attacks. Of the 48, 40 had experienced abuse on more than one occasion, with 14 describing themselves as being harassed on a regular basis. In response to questions on the frequency and nature of the racial abuse they had witnessed during their time in Sunderland the following statements give an indication of the findings. They responded to the following question: "Have you witnessed any racial abuse? Please, specify was this verbal or physical." Their answers are presented according to the following criteria: gender, age, ethnic self-description:

Female, aged 20, Black British:
"In the first year it was almost daily – called a 'Paki black bitch' and names like that. It hurt first, a shock but you still get hurt and angry."

Male, aged 22 Black African:
"Yes, many black bastard, black cunt…even called a Paki."

Male, aged 22 Indian:
"Called names a number of times especially if you were in a group of non-whites."

Male, aged 22, British Muslim:
"Yes my friends and I have been attacked and called names and also challenged physically. Twice I have been spat on and punched and kicked."

Male, aged 20, Indian:
"Some students in Manor Quay started calling a Sikh guy names."

Male, aged 21, Indian:
"Yes, on the University bus back from Manor Quay [the local student disco]. One guy started talking about refugees loudly whilst staring at me and my friend."

Female, aged 20 Black British:
"Yes, in Clanny House last year, next door neighbours rang up our house with racial abuse shouting about the BNP, niggers and Pakis."

Female, aged 21, British Pakistani:
"In Metro centre 2 guys tried to rip off my hijab whilst calling me a fucking Paki and shouting Bin Laden at my friend."

Male, aged 24, Chinese:
"Yes, they fight us."

If the above statements give an idea of how widespread the experience of racist abuse is among non-white residents in Sunderland another of the questions in the survey was concerned with reporting racist abuse and asking for suggestions as to what could be done about it ("Reporting Matters and What Can Be Done"). Out of the 58 participants in the survey who were subject or witness to racial abuse only 14 reported matters to the police, whilst 22 reported to University authorities. Unfortunately, all of the respondents said no action was taken by the University. Of those who reported to the police ten said that the police were sympathetic but could not proceed with the investigation of the incident due to lack of witnesses etc. Generally, the survey showed that there was a reluctance to report matters to the police. All of the respondents thought the University and the police should do more. Some suggested that more should be done in 'Freshers Week' or that police officers should give talks at the University in order to raise awareness. With regard to the specific situation in Sunderland 46 of the 58 participants thought Sunderland was more racist than other parts of the country, whilst 43 said they would not have come to the University if they had known the extent of racism in the city.

From the previous extracts it can be seen that non-white people in Sunderland experienced overt racism. This racism encompassed simplistic (almost primordial) belief about who was allowed or not allowed in the city. The abuse also seemed to combine xenophobia ("Pakis"), racism ("niggers") and Islamophobia. It could be argued that current wider political and social issues combined with economic concerns have helped create this animosity. To allow for clearer understanding of the issues involved, the results of the focus groups will now be examined and qualitative data from them presented.

7.4 The Focus Groups – "The Capital of Hate"?

The interviews were semi-structured thus allowing the respondents to explain issues of importance to them but at the same time an informal flow was maintained keeping in line with the aims of the research. The basic structure of the interview was split into two complementary parts: the first part enquired into reasons for coming to Sunderland, and the second part asked for experiences in Sunderland.

The reason why a semi-structured interview was favoured was that it was felt this would allow the respondents more scope to express themselves although it has to be noted that there are some disadvantages with semi-structured interviews and focus groups. The following are just quotes from the focus groups to give an indication of what the participants were saying. Participants in these groups were first asked about their reasons for coming to Sunderland and their initial reactions on arrival there. Due to the different backgrounds of the people who took part in the survey they reported different experiences when they came to the North East. The following three statements are typical:

> A 25-year-old, male, asylum seeker from Angola stated:
> "In London, a lot of people was complaining about the North-East. Yes, because they were saying that the people there are more racist than the people in London because they don't used to be with the black communities…Other asylum seeker people, guys from London, even white guys they said this. But we didn't scare because we faced

more than this is, that's why we didn't care about this. For me, myself... compared to living in Angola, because I was living also in South Africa for 5 years, and I faced a lot of racism there. For me, it's like I'm used to it that's why I don't care any more..."

A 25-year-old, female, Bangladeshi student said:
"When I was moving to Sunderland, I didn't know what it was like. All I knew was that it was going to be close to the sea... One particular friend came up to me and said, 'You're going to Sunderland?' 'I went, yeah, why, what's wrong with it?' 'You can't be going to Sunderland, you won't be able to live there'. 'Why?' 'Because there's so much racism there. You won't be able to live there. It's the bloody capital of the NF'... When I actually moved here and I started going to Uni in Newcastle, my friends up there were also saying, that's where the NF are based...My feelings here, to do with racism, were no different to back in Manchester. But, because everybody thought Sunderland was the capital of hate and racism I was a bit wary of coming here."

A 22-year-old student, male of British-Pakistani origin said:
"I came to Sunderland to go to the University did I not really know much about the place, but it was cheaper than London and Newcastle. Also the degree was reasonably good so I thought what the heck? However my initial reaction when I moved was of being scared. It was very white and very hostile."

As these cases illustrate, it was clear that for the respondents Sunderland appeared to be an ethnically homogeneous place. That is, the respondents felt Sunderland was 'white and hostile' (see final quote above). They observed a clear divide in the community, based on skin colour and biological notions of race (Mason 2000). From the participants' answers it becomes clear that in comparison to other parts of the UK the North East of England is perceived as unwelcoming. Furthermore the presence of actively racist groups in the area adds to this sense of unease. This picture is sustained by the participants' reports on their experiences as residents in Sunderland. A 25-year-old male asylum seeker from Angola summarises his experiences in the city as follows:

"In Sunderland, when I came in Sunderland first, in my place, I live in Redhouse, people talk to you and tell you 'you must move, we don't want you here, we don't like'. In my flat where I live, I've called the police more than 2 times because they came during the night to smash the window. I was scared. I was talking with our social worker to try to change my place because I was scared. They say they can do nothing because the HO will not change. That's why people come and then they go... I would like to change my area...sometimes we feel we are in a prison because we cannot move easily...that's why we moved from our place because you are not free to move, the land mines, conflict, bad things, we have to move. If these things will happen more and more in Sunderland I think we'll have to move again..."

This statement makes it clear that one result of the sustained racist attacks is a sense of claustrophobia among non-white residents in Sunderland. Similarly, a 25-year-old female Bangladeshi British citizen describes her experiences:

"I could be here all day going on about my experiences...A lot of people I know they would just ignore it, they won't stick up for themselves, their culture, colour, religion. I can't do it, I have to respond because I won't feel good about myself then. The biggest group in Sunderland is the Bangladeshi community and they get a lot of racist abuse, especially during the last election...I think asylum seekers are the scapegoats for the time being, but Bangladeshis...I know that some of them have had quite bad experiences when going to the mosque or just in the street, people try to take off their prayer caps because of their beards, or clothes that they've worn..."

How aggressive the otherness of non-white residents in Sunderland is sometimes regarded becomes clear from the statement of a 19-year-old male black British student:

"The vast majority of people here think you are a refugee or an asylum seeker just because you are not white. Going to the city centre is no-no at night especially the weekends unless you are in big group. You get stares and aggressive looks all the time. It is quite an intimidating place but then again most of my friends who are white say the same."

Once more what becomes clear from these replies is the overt racism felt and perceived by these different non-white groups. These quotes suggest that non-white groups experience various forms of racism. Its range is wide and combines anti-Muslim, anti-Black and anti-migrant sentiments. As the final quote shows, the participants seem to view the influence of the media in framing these events. A 21-year-old male student of British-Indian origin identifies the local press as one reason for the problems in Sunderland:

> "I really hate the local press here. It always has stuff from the BNP and people read that who don't know any black people, put 2 and 2 together and come up with 5. No wonder so many people hate us. I wish the Echo was bit more open minded."

8. Media and Public Hostility

In recent years a substantial amount of research has been carried out by various organisations in order to discover what the British public thinks about immigration and asylum. Most of this research has discovered that public opinion tends to be significantly hostile towards asylum seekers. For example, a MORI poll conducted in 2001 found that 44% of people agreed that Britain should not take any more asylum seekers. The same poll also estimated that 74% of people believed that refugees came to the country because they thought Britain was a 'soft touch' (http://www.icar.org.uk/?lid=5054).

Finney and Peach remind us that although polls and anecdotal accounts certainly indicate a great deal of public hostility and suspicion, the focus and wording of such surveys can often influence the responses which are given. Whilst this does not render the evidence completely invalid, it can be a little misleading. For this reason, academic-based research which utilises focus groups, in-depth interviews and local case studies (occasionally carried out in partnership with polling organisations such as MORI) is crucial for the development of a deeper understanding of public attitudes towards asylum and the influence of the media in forming them (Finney 2005: 21-2). In 2004 and 2005 a series of research studies commissioned in partnership with organisations such as the Commission for Racial Equality and the Institute for Public Policy Research set out to examine public attitudes to asylum and immigration in the UK. Each of the reports revealed evidence of widespread hostility towards asylum seekers and other migrants. Finney and Peach (2004: 23) observe that several of the studies discovered that when people actually encountered asylum seekers on a personal level, there was considerable tolerance and empathy. Yet there still existed "considerable confusion, ignorance and misinformation" about asylum seekers and refugees which could easily be full of myth and rumour. As I have claimed before, "In race and ethnic relations, the media provide information where knowledge is fragmentary." (Saeed 1999: 20) In a study of thirty-two localised focus groups from different parts of Britain, Lewis (2005) also found that hostility to asylum seekers was greatest where the respondents had least contact with asylum seekers, migrants and other ethnic minorities. In areas of high social deprivation there was a perception that asylum seekers were competing for resources like housing, healthcare and jobs. Older people (over 50) were likely to be the most hostile and the least well-informed, and were more likely to express fears over the loss of British identity, while some people from established ethnic minority communities were concerned that some people may confuse them with asylum seekers because of their appearance.

Although Greenslade notes that the term 'asylum seekers' is 'racially impartial' taken at face value, he acknowledges that this often leads to the use of inflammatory language against asylum seekers that few would find acceptable against other immigrants or blacks. (Greenslade 2005: 8). Nevertheless Finney confirms that in-depth public surveys have verified that racist language is commonly used to articulate concerns over asylum seekers, and that there is even a tendency in some places to conflate asylum seekers with anyone who is non-white or visibly 'non-British' (Finney 2005: 24). A study by ICAR (Information Centre about Asylum and Refugees) in 2004 used focus groups and in-depth interviews in order to ascertain the extent to which local and national media reporting had an impact on communities where asylum seekers and refugees settled. The report's findings supported the hypothesis that "some press coverage is unbalanced and lacking in accuracy in ways likely to increase tension." (Finney and Peach 2004: 98) Although the influence of the media was variable – i.e. amplified or modified according to specific circumstances – the nature of resentment and the type of language used in harassment was found to reflect the themes of press reporting. The study also concluded that hostile attitudes towards asylum seekers were more common when negative media images coincided with local experiences of deprivation and that they had a particularly strong effect on those whose racist prejudices were reinforced (2004: 99).

Furthermore, as previously noted, the erroneous substitution of words such as 'asylum seeker', 'refugee', 'immigrant', 'Muslim' etc. has had a wider implication in the public consciousness in relation to "race issues." Thus there is almost a re-racialisation of Islam/Muslims as meaning Pakistani, Bangladeshi or of South-Asian appearance.

Given the media treatment of the so-called "War on Terror" this itself has been open to much media mis-representation (Saeed 2004a, b).

9. Final Comments: The North East

This essay has examined media and political responses to immigration and asylum both historical and contemporary. In doing so it has demonstrated that the responses are invariably hostile and that the issue of immigration has been constantly racialised and constructed as a threat or a problem which 'the nation' must confront. The same themes arise time and again: a question of numbers and a question of threat to the indigenous national culture. The empirical research has suggested, in line with much of the previous literature that the influence of the media on the population's perception of asylum and immigration is predominantly negative. Although it is by no means a direct and one-way process, the media nevertheless promote an interpretative framework of meaning in which immigrants are seen as a problem, are particularly influential when people have little or no direct experiences of them personally, and can also create confusion and scope for misunderstanding and resentment with their constant misuse of terminology.

With regard to the results of the survey, it can be said that for the vast majority of the respondents racism and the issue of asylum have merged. This view is specifically sustained by the 33 participants of the focus group, all of whom agreed that if they were not white they were regarded as asylum seekers. In turn the experiences of the non-white participants in both studies show that Sunderland was perceived as an un-welcoming place to live, study and work. It must be noted with some despair that even the University of Sunderland was seen as no real sanctuary from racism. A relatively little known report known as PROUD (People Respecting Others Understand Difference) (PROUD 2002: 2) noted:

> PROUD believes it is essential to have a 'joined-up' strategic approach which locates racism within the wider environment. There is currently no coherent inclusive strategic plan that offers a comprehensive anti-racist response from the white-dominated institutions. (PROUD 2002: 13)

The recent spate of racist attacks has led to the opening of a new 24-hour telephone helpline to combat the problem. Sunderland Council has launched the service after a series of worrying incidents across the city. The new helpline will be run by the social services department. Pauline Blyth, assistant head of support services, summarises the task of the new service:

> The staff operating it also operates the community care alarm service, so are used to dealing sensitively with vulnerable people. We've produced the contact details in a number of different languages and they are available from various public buildings around the city. (http://www.monitoring-group.co.uk/News%20and%20Campaigns/-news-stories/2003/regions/north%20east/increase_in_racist_attacks_-in_sunderland.htm)

At the same time Northumbria Police Inspector Dave Goodchild, Sunderland's local authority liaison officer, formulates the new police directive:

> Racism and racist behaviour are not acceptable. They can make a victim's life a misery. By encouraging the reporting of individual incidents we can obtain a better understanding of the extent of the problem. We can then work together with all our partners to make sure people can enjoy a peaceful life. [...] a racial incident can mean anything perceived to be racist by the victim or any other person, such as verbal or physical abuse, damage to property, threatening behaviour or graffiti. (ibid.)

Political and social developments in the wider world help formulate theories of belonging such as national identity. These 'feelings' of inclusion/exclusion can filter down to populations in a local context. The media's focus on non-white immigration into the UK and other parts of Europe has re-awakened debates of 'otherness' and 'culture clash'. Too often these debates ignore the reality of the existence of the marginalised groups and concentrate on the 'fear of the outsider' rather than on the contribution immigrants can make. This homogenisation of 'otherness' and stereotyping, however, generates fear, contempt and hatred of the groups deemed the 'other': non-whites, Muslims, asylum seekers etc.

With this in mind, the words of Frantz Fanon seem particularly relevant even now: "hate is not inborn; it has to be cultivated, to be brought into being" (Fanon 1986: 53). There can be little doubt that through the detrimental representation of the 'other' in the press this 'hate' has almost demanded to come into existence.

Works Cited

Ahmed, Akbar S. (1993): *Living Islam.* London: BBC Books.

Anderson, Benedict Richard O'Gorman (1991): *Imagined communities: reflections on the origin and spread of nationalism* (revised edition). London: Verso.

Balibar, Etienne and Immanuel Wallerstein (1991): *Race, Nation, Class: Ambiguous Identities.* London: Verso.

Banton, Michael (1988): *Racial Consciousness.* London: Longman.

Billig, Michael (1995): *Banal Nationalism.* London: Sage.

Bowler, R. (2002): *PROUD (People Respecting Others Understand Difference) Report).* Hendon District Sunderland: Sunderland City Council.

Cottle, Simon (2002): "'Race', Racialization and the Media: A Review and Update of Research", *Sage Race Relations Abstracts* 17.2, 3-57.

— (2004): *The Racist Murder of Stephen Lawrence.* London: Praeger.

Fanon, Frantz (1986): *Black Skin, White Masks*: London: Pluto Press.

Fekete, Liz (2002): *Racism, the Hidden Cost of September 11.* London: Institute of Race Relations.

Finney, N. and E. Peach (2004): *Attitudes Towards Asylum Seekers, Refugees and Other Immigrants: A Literature Overview for the Commission for Racial Equality.* London: ICAR/CRE.

— (2005): *Key Issues: Public Opinion asylum and refugee issues.* London: ICAR.

Gandy, Oscar H. (1998): *Communication and Race: A Structural Perspective.* London: Arnold.

Gilroy, Paul (1987): *There Aint No Black In the Union Jack.* London: Hutchinson.

— (1992): "The End of Antiracism", in: J. Donald and A. Rattansi (eds.): *'Race', Culture and Difference.* London: Sage.

Greenslade, R. (2005): *Seeking Scapegoats: The Coverage of Asylum in the UK Press.* London: IPPR.

Hall, Stuart et al. (1978): *Policing the Crises.* London: Constable.

— D. Held and T. McGrew (eds.) (1992): *Modernity and its futures.* Cambridge: Polity Press/Open University.

Hartmann, Paul and Charles Husband (1974): *Racism and the Mass Media.* London: Dans-Poynter.

Kundnani, A. (2001): "In a foreign land: the popular racism", *Race and Class* 43.2, 41-60.

Lewis, M. (2005): *Asylum: Understanding Public Attitudes.* London: IPPR.

Mason, David (2000): *Race and Ethnicity in Modern Britain.* Oxford: Oxford UP.

May, T. (1995): *Social Science Research Methods.* London: Open UP.

Miles, R. (1993): *Racism after 'Race Relations'.* London: Routledge.

Modood, Tariq (1992): *Not Easy Being British: Colour, Culture and Citizenship.* London: Runnymede Trust.

— (1997): *Ethnic Minorities in Britain: Diversity and Disadvantage*. London: PSI.

Pilkington, Andrew (2003): *Racial disadvantage and ethnic diversity in Britain*. Basingstoke: Palgrave Macmillan.

Saeed, Amir (1999): "The Media and New Racisms", *Media Education Journal* 27, 19-22.

— et al. (1999): "New ethnic and national questions in Scotland: Post British identities among Glasgow-Pakistani teenagers", *Ethnic and Racial Studies* 22.5, 821-844.

— (2004a): "9/11 and the Consequences for British-Muslims", in: John Carter and Dave Morland (eds.): *Anti-Capitalist Britain*. London: New Clarion Press.

— (2004b): "My Jihad", *Soundings* 27, 57-65.

Sivanandan, A. (1988): "The New Racism", *New Statesman* 4 November, 8-9.

Speers, Tammy (2001): *Welcome or Over Reaction? Refugees and Asylum Seekers in the Welsh Media*. Cardiff: Wales Media Forum.

Van Dijk, Teun A. (1991): *Racism and the Press*. London: Sage.

Wahab, I. (1989): *Muslims in Britain*. London: Runnymede Trust.

Web Links

"Dignity and despair in Sunderland", *BBC News* 30 August 2002. 24 August 2006 [http://news.bbc.co.uk/1/hi/uk/2226218.stm].

"Fourth Arrest in 'race attack' stabbing", *BBC News* 30 August 2002. 24 August 2006 [http://news.bbc.co.uk/1/hi/england/2222840.stm].

"BNP fuels anger about people 'getting something for nothing': Scare stories inflame local hysteria", *Guardian Unlimited* 7 February 2003. 24 August 2006 [http://www.guardian.co.uk/uk_news/story/0,3604,890608,00.html]

Toynbee, Polly: "Poison pens of racism: Public fears over asylum seekers must be addressed – but not by pandering to a hysterical press", *Guardian Unlimited* 31 January 2003. 24 August 2006. [http://www.guardian.co.uk/comment/story/-0,3604,885938,00.html].

Muir, Hugh: "Racists cash in on asylum hysteria: Commission for racial equality shows how a newly sophisticated BNP has changed its image and tactics to win votes and seats", *Guardian Unlimited* 16 September 2003. 24 August 2006 [http://www.guardian.co.uk/guardianpolitics/story/0,,1042973,00.html].

"New Deal for Communities East End and Hendon", *Government Office for the North East*. 22 March 2005 [http://www.go-ne.gov.uk/gone/peopleandsustcomms/-neighbourhood_renewal/new_deal/east_end_hendon/].

"Racist Attack Sparks Hotline", *Monitoring Group* August 2003. 24 August 2006 [http://www.monitoring-group.co.uk/News%20and%20Campaigns/news-stories/2003/monthly%20news/june_2003.htm]

"Race Equality Monitoring - Social Services 2005/6: Black and Minority Ethnic (BME) Groups", *Sunderland City Council* 20 July 2006. 27 November 2006 [http://www.sunderland.gov.uk/public/editable/life-episodes/ancs/race-equality/default.asp] and

"Ethnicity Profiles: North East England", *Commission for Racial Equality – Diversity and integration* 14 November 2006. 27 November 2006 [http://www.cre.gov.uk/diversity/map/northeast/sunderland.html].

"Asylum Seeking Communities in the North East of England – Quarterly Statistics as at December", *North of England Refugee Services Sunderland* 2 July 2006. 9 December 2006 [http://www.ners-sunderland.org.uk/key.asp].

"Mori Poll: Genuineness of asylum seekers", *ICAR* 29 July 2005. 18 December 2006 [http://www.icar.org.uk/?lid=5054]

Finney, Nissa and Esme Peach: "Attitudes to Asylum Seekers, Refugees and Other Immigrants", *Commission for Racial Equality* 2004. 26 December 2006 [http://www.cre.gov.uk/downloads/asylum_icar_report.pdf].

Chapter III
Landscaping

Manchester and the "Hypocritical Plan": Architecture, Shopping and Identity in the Industrial City

Mark Crinson

Abstract: This essay traces how various attempts to identify Manchester as a city of commerce and consumption have been played out in terms of either the architecture of shopping or architectural reproductions of shops in Manchester. All the chosen examples, from three distinct periods in the city's history, projected an alternative view to that of the fearful industrial city, and sought to do this in part through resurrecting pre-industrial images of the city, particularly of shops and shopping.

Key names and concepts: Friedrich Engels - L.S. Lowry - Arjan Appadurai - Ford Madox Brown - Alfred Darbyshire - Frederic Leighton - W.G. Sebald; Commercialism - De-industrialisation - Scenography - Pre-industrial Past - Technoscape - Financescape - Imperialism - Authenticity - Museological Reconstruction.

1. Introduction

For more than a hundred and fifty years, it was Manchester's identity as an industrial city that usually received most attention from outside commentators, whether campaigning investigators or tourists of the industrial sublime. To many it seemed that the industrial city created in the late eighteenth and early nineteenth century was a force of nature, a city that seemed to have been produced unconsciously, but nevertheless one that was the prototype of many to come – "the classic type of modern industrial town" (Engels 1987: 83). In the historian Asa Briggs's famous phrase it was "the shock city of the age" (Briggs 1968: 96), an entity both unimaginable and fearful, apparently without history or precedent, destructive of fragile existing localisms, new in its urban forms and effects yet also a necessary product of the industrial revolution. Accordingly, when Manchester was hit by recession and de-industrialisation in the mid-twentieth century it was marked out as a type for urban decay and the imagery of blighted industrial landscapes. One might argue that Manchester's twentieth-century image as that of the stereotyped grim northern city of blackened and smoke-wreathed buildings, so ideally captured by the miserabilist paintings of L. S. Lowry, was simply an adaptation of the 'shock city' image for a time of economic retreat and decline. A closer reading, however, would show that even in its earlier industrial sublimity, Manchester's commentators were as much aware of its entropic decay as of its convulsive energies.[1] It would follow this epochal sequence, and certainly accord with the rhetoric of the city's current business and political elite, to claim that Manchester's contemporary post-industrial regeneration is the inverse of these earlier identities: upbeat, ostensibly – and ostentatiously – centred on culture and the knowledge economies, and, above all, a place of leisured consumption.

But in some ways this last identity rehashes an old story, and if it might currently depend on a post-industrial melancholy and post-industrial reversion to cultural fixes, it did not always. Although it is the industrial city that has hogged the attention of historians, in fact other versions of Manchester – particularly the civic and the commercial – have been tensely vying for dominance in the city's image battles since the early nineteenth century.

The image of a prosperous commercial city has arisen periodically in Manchester's history and might even be understood as the complementary opposite of the industrial city. Friedrich Engels's famous description of Manchester first brought together descriptions of the city of slums and industry and the city of shopping, and his argument that the latter should be treated with deep suspicion established the central dynamic in his account, the platform on which his descriptions of Manchester's slum areas could then work as a series of revelations. Engels saw that the city was a system of dissembling for the middle-classes. Suburban dwellers might go in and out of the city on a daily basis for their work in the inner commercial core centred on the Exchange and never see working-class areas, partly because these areas were separated from their own "by unconscious tacit agreement, as well as with outspoken conscious determination", but also because the poorer areas were, in Engels's cutting phrase, "concealed with the cloak of charity."[2] The radial roads that suburbanites travelled on were

---

[1] See for instance De Toqueville in Marcus 1974: 66.
[2] 'Charity', of course, to the middle-class viewer.

lined with "an almost unbroken series of shops... [that] suffice to conceal from the eyes of the wealthy men and women of strong stomachs and weak nerves the misery and grime which form the complement to their wealth" (ibid.: 86). Engels accepted that for reasons of commercial logic and land values such an arrangement was common in cities, but in Manchester this was taken to an extreme: "I have never seen so systematic a shutting out of the working class from the thoroughfares, so tender a concealment of everything which might affront the eye and the nerves of the bourgeoisie, as in Manchester" (ibid.: 87). This 'hypocritical plan' was not just a form of compensation for what was in almost all other respects an unplanned city, but also evidence of some deeper order of economic arrangement within the city in which the apparent nature of Manchester as 'an outgrowth of accident' was revealed as actually essential to its capitalist logic: for Engels the slums had, in Steven Marcus's words, "a negative existence that is paradoxically a positive fullness, the indispensable creative source of all that positive wealth that lies beyond it" (Marcus 1974: 174). We might say that the shop-lined streets in Engels's description act as much as an ideological as an actual barrier to, and a distraction away from, the slums and the poverty behind them. They function as mere scenography, the acceptable face of the city, the scene that covers over the obscene behind them.

This article will trace how various attempts to identify Manchester as a city of commerce and consumption – usually without the extra twist that Engels arrived at in his analysis – have been played out in terms of either the architecture of shopping or architectural reproductions of shops in Manchester. The examples are drawn from three distinct periods in the city's history: the 'Old Manchester and Salford' display at the 1887 Royal Jubilee Exhibition at the height of Manchester's industrial power; the Lark Hill Place display constructed in 1955 in the midst of rapid changes consequent on de-industrialisation; and, finally, the new urban space known as Exchange Square developed after 1996 as a manifestation of the new post-industrial city. All three examples were clearly positioned to project an alternative view to that of the fearful industrial city, and all three sought to do this in part through resurrecting pre-industrial images of the city, particularly of shops and shopping. First, though, before coming to these examples, some more needs to be said about the complex ways in which the civic and the commercial related to nineteenth-century Manchester's local, national and international standing.

2. Victorian Manchester – Commerce and Locality

There seems to have been widespread and extended efforts from the early mid-nineteenth century, related to its belatedly acquired municipal status (1838, though not officially becoming a city until 1853),[3] to wrest Manchester's image away from the chaotic city of industry and towards the image of a civic city, one both cultured and commercial, and to do this using Manchester's pre-industrial past as well as contemporary notions of what constituted urban civility. Slums began to be removed from the city centre. Attempts were made to present the city as sharing the outward forms of Renaissance city states or the contemporary swish of London or Paris. Portland Street, for instance, was developed in homage to several models: named to make London links, built with Italian palazzo-style warehouses, and inviting Parisian comparisons with its continuous cornice-lines. As well as a name again having links to London, when Piccadilly Gardens was laid out in 1854 it was ornamented with monuments to national figures. Architects like Edward Walters in buildings like the Free Trade Hall (1853-56) "used Italian architecture as the means of giving beauty appropriately to the great emporiums of merchant princes" (Darbyshire 1987: 22). The Manchester Art Treasures Exhibition in 1857 was promoted to display Manchester's importance as a centre for the fine arts. At the same time as the city was gentrified and made more orderly through street-widening schemes, demolition and new roads, so, as in many other cities in which locality seemed threatened, antiquarians proliferated, searching for traces of the city's only recently eradicated past,[4] recording what could not be saved, treating the city as a set of consoling memory-traces.

As the city began to aspire to the status of 'second city of the empire', so its central imperial building, the Manchester Exchange, was enlarged and rebuilt periodically throughout the nineteenth cen-

---

[3] Some have suggested that shopkeepers played an important role in Manchester's incorporation (see Briggs 1968: 108).

[4] See Crinson 2002.

tury, and rebuilt in ways that not only gave it the largest dealing space in Europe but also evoked an imperialism authorised by the forms of classical architecture. It came materially to represent not some identity bound up in regionalism but instead Manchester's position at the centre of the global cotton trade. Accordingly, and partly because no alternative topographic centre was obvious in this city, in many nineteenth-century maps the Exchange was placed either at the intersection of north-south lines or at the centre of a radiating series of concentric circles measuring distances from the city's symbolic heart and also, by implication, calibrating distances to its cotton empire beyond. Thus the Exchange represented a stable point within a globalised economy. To adapt Arjan Appadurai's formulation, it incarnated both the 'technoscape' of a global configuration of technology and a 'financescape' of a disposition of global capital, allowing capital flows through both.[5] The suffix 'scape' in this formulation usefully indicates how these were 'deeply perspectival constructs' (Appadurai 1996: 33), inflected in this case by their situatedness within empire, within Britain, within the North, and finally, within the locality that Manchester identified itself as being.

Just as the civic city attempted to re-brand Manchester as an imperial city related to a global space, so the city was also seen as having a deep regional history of independence complexly linked to the national story. This can best be epitomised by the murals that Ford Madox Brown painted for the Manchester Town Hall between 1878 and 1893.[6] Brown's murals showed a city where "economic materialism [was viewed] as the foundation of culture" (Codell 1998: 325) and where the harsh and socially divisive modern experiences of industrialism were softened by showing links back to a longer history of innovation and enterprise binding groups of people by shared ambitions and shared ideas of the local and the national. Ford Madox Brown's murals in the town hall largely cut Manchester's industrialism out of their optic, representing

> mercantile and commercial interests as the sources of art, philanthropy and science... Crabtree's laboratory over his draper shop allows science to thrive in the midst of commerce, Kay is bundled in a wool

---

[5]   See Appadurai 1996: 34-35.
[6]   See Brown 18??; Barlow 1996: 81-97; Codell 1998: 354-55.

sheet, Chetham the draper and money-lender creates a bequest that appreciates into the modern period, Bridgewater's canal funds a collection of Old Masters (ibid.: 354).

As Julie Codell has argued, "after mid-century Manchester citizens redefined their activities within the framework of romance and chivalry to revise commerce into social good" (ibid.: 326). Manchester's political leaders identified themselves with the Hanseatic League of the Middle Ages – cities whose prosperity was based on the trade and commerce of a powerful class of burghers and which stood for regional independence. All the major new civic buildings – the new assize courts (1859-64), the new town hall (1867-77), the new Owens College (1869-74), the new Reform Club (1870-71), as well as many new commercial buildings – were designed from the mid-century onwards in self-conscious emulation of medieval Gothic precedents. Antiquity became revalued and elevated into a salient part of the city's image "to mitigate the sense of rootlessness produced by abrupt expansion and the sense of inferiority fostered by the lack of respectable pedigrees".[7] In other words, like Brown's murals, there was a deliberate attempt to re-order and rehabilitate Manchester's image so that it fitted better with the aspirations of the urban middle class, adopting both established models of civic status and longer regional traditions.

As Appadurai has defined it, we need not think of Manchester's 'locality' as something static or even as something fundamentally opposed to the global: we can see

> locality as primarily relational and contextual rather than as scalar or spatial [...] a complex phenomenological quality constituted by a series of links between the sense of social immediacy, the technologies of interactivity and the relativity of contexts. (Appadurai 1996: 178)

I do not wish to suggest here that Manchester's turn to non-modern forms of urban architecture and culture and to regionally-specific forms was a sign of a neglect of industrialism and its rapid cycles of

---

[7] Charles Dellheim quoted in Codell (1998: 327). Although it is outside my concerns here, one should not ignore that this period also saw another, complementary architecture emerging that was concerned with controlling unruly social energies and unhealthy bodies. "Hospitals, courts and gaols... mental asylums and workhouses... formed a kind of institutional, disciplinary girdle around the centre" (Joyce 2003: 159).

change, rather that the two were being made to co-exist as necessary parts of a modern economy and a modern history-minded culture.[8] However, in its later incarnations, the projected city of civilised commercial relations was not just a balance to unfettered industrial development as a necessary accompaniment to it.

---

[8] In other words, what I am arguing here goes against the kind of thesis that Martin Weiner presented in *English Culture and the Decline of the Industrial Spirit 1850-1980* (Weiner 1985).

3. Dreamland of Shops

Figure 1: 'Old Manchester and Salford', 1

One of the most interesting examples of this retrofitting was the 'Old Manchester and Salford' display shown as part of the 1887 Royal Jubilee Exhibition in Manchester. Although somewhat forgotten now, despite the attention given by historians to other exhibitions of the nineteenth century, with four million visitors the Royal Jubilee Exhibition was as well visited as the 1855 international exposition in Paris and in fact the best-visited exhibition in Britain after the 1851 Great Exhibition.[9] Like those other exhibitions it was a piece of capitalist boosterism, propaganda for the city's economic power and, more specifically, for its planned Manchester Ship Canal, a major engineering project to run close by the exhibition's site, intended to diversify the city's economy. The exhibition's galleries were filled with examples of industrial design, the latest machinery, and the products of the region's chemical industries.

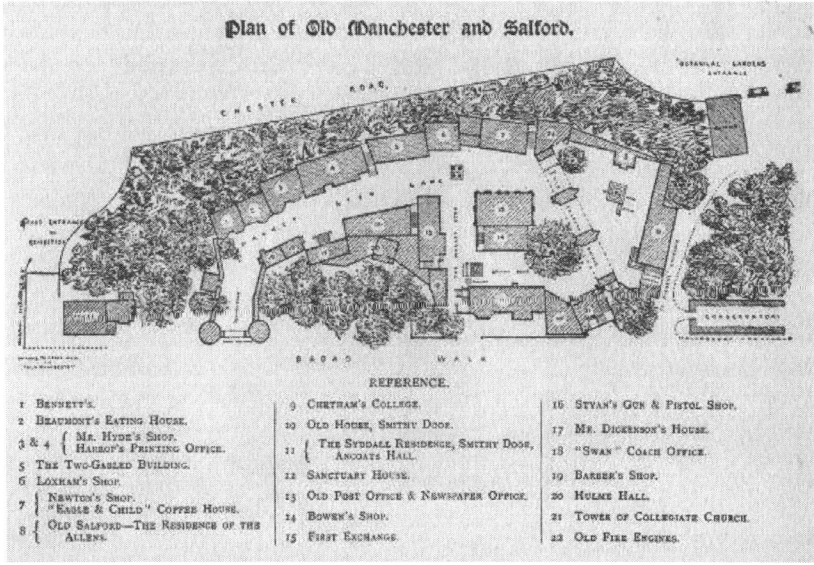

Figure 2: 'Old Manchester and Salford' – plan, Darbyshire 1887.

It might seem strange, then, that the most commented-upon and most popular part of the exhibition was the display known as 'Old Manchester and Salford', a representation of what the city was not known

---

[9] See Kidd 1993: 61. Following contemporary usage, I have referred to the larger urban conurbation as Manchester, and only when the historical examples I discuss have distinguished between the two intimately contiguous cities of Manchester and Salford have I used the names of both cities.

for by the outside world, a resuscitated image of pre-industrial locality.

The designer of the 'Old Manchester and Salford' display was the architect Alfred Darbyshire, who had already established his name as what he called an 'Architectural Showman' with several exhibition displays of reconstructed medieval towns.[10] Sited in the grounds of the Royal Botanical Society gardens outside the city centre on Chester Road and separated from the rest of the exhibition by the 'Fairy Fountain and Lake', 'Old Manchester and Salford' consisted of a set of slightly scaled-down reproductions of key buildings from Manchester and Salford's pre-industrial past, which were staffed by shopkeepers in period dress and craftsmen who were specifically working on and selling pre-industrial handicrafts such as handloom weaving, pottery and printing.[11] Paradoxically, the exhibition celebrated the pre-industrial city whose demise, so it was thought, was a necessary condition for the emergence of Manchester's commercial prosperity.[12] Mainly consisting of one street, 'Old Manchester and Salford' housed its fifty-nine exhibits in a collection of reproductions of shops, houses, the tower of a church, an Exchange, a Roman gateway, 'Old Salford Bridge and Oratory', Ancoats' Hall, the so-called Poets Corner, the Sun Inn, Wellington Inn and Chetham's College, only the last two of which were still extant. The exhibition did not attempt any topographical accuracy in its layout: Old Salford Bridge crossed the main street, while the Old Church Tower was jammed beside it; Chetham's Hospital was on the 'wrong', Salford side of the bridge; and the first Exchange building was placed beside Wellington Inn. The result was a "delightful jumble... a sort of dreamland where nothing happens but the unexpected" (*City News* 25 June 1887)[13]: a Roman gateway led to Tudor houses, a bridge spanned a river of cobblestones; a cathedral tower had no cathedral attached; there was a coach house from which no coaches started; a crockery shop sold jewellery, a bookshop sold

---

[10] See Darbyshire 1897: 174-177.
[11] See Alfred Brothers *Scrapbook*.
[12] See Harrison 1988: 67. Harrison was quoting A. A. Gillies's 1888 *Report of the Executive Committee*.
[13] See *City News* 25 June 1887. The incongruities could also be ignored: see *Manchester Guardian* 29 May 1887, which quotes Lord Leighton on the exhibition's 'artistic triumph'.

watches, and a barber's shop displayed fustian cutting; and, finally, medieval crossbowmen, ancient mariners and Georgian watchmen could all be seen wandering the streets.

Despite all this, there was a serious side to the exhibition, including even an interest in authenticity. Those buildings not based on still extant originals were mocked up by the architect Alfred Darbyshire from old drawings by J. Ralston as well as from marginal illustrations in old maps.[14] Darbyshire drew his authority for the Roman arch from a manuscript in the British Museum and reprinted theatre bills and original proclamations from boroughreeves.[15] 'Old Manchester and Salford' represented an easy relation via the city's religious institutions and monuments to a history of commercial life, a deep past of unalienated craft labour. But it was also intended as a complement to the rest of the exhibition which, by showing the industry and art of fifty years of Victoria's reign, was promoting the city's grand new project, the Manchester Ship Canal.[16] By reminding visitors of scenes and buildings from a pre-industrial past it would re-join Manchester to a national history, playing against the tendency to regard Manchester as outside accepted traditions of Englishness emanating from a feudal past.[17]

'Old Manchester and Salford' combined architecture and consumption as a means for a concentrated conspectus of stories about the city, for which each architectural form acted as an emblem for memory. For Louis Hayes, remembering the exhibition some twenty years later, memory compacted the already physically concertina-ed reconstruction: 'the Church was approached on the North side by natural formations in the old red sandstone on the crest of which the Old Church stood. I seem to have some recollection of this approach, or is it some old print that recalls the fact to my mind?' (Hayes 1905: 115) In a tale that marks an interesting shift in the place of culture in society, Alfred Darbyshire made much of being congratulated for the effectiveness of the exhibition by the painter Lord Leighton. On the same spot, at the Manchester Art Treasures Exhibition thirty years be-

---

[14] See Darbyshire 1887. Darbyshire had actually been involved in the restoration of Ordsall Hall, Salford.
[15] See Darbyshire 1897: 194.
[16] See Kidd 1993: 55.
[17] On this see also ibid.: 55-56.

fore, Darbyshire himself had admired Leighton's painting 'Cimabue's Madonna carried through the Streets of Florence' (1853-55).[18] One of the themes in Leighton's painting, a great success when it was exhibited at the Royal Academy before coming to Manchester, was the power of art to sustain religion at the centre of a society; the representation of Cimabue's paraded and adored painting offered implicit critique of the place of art in Victorian society. Another theme of Leighton's work, complementary with this, was the case for a revived form of history painting in which the cult function of art was replaced by the independent power of art as aesthetic object: asceticism replaced by aestheticism.[19] Taking its place on the same spot three decades later was a reconstruction of just such an idealised society, but now with commerce where religion and history painting would have been.

The exhibition might be described as a form of 'imagined nostalgia' for a commercial Merrie England not so much as an alternative to the harshness of industrial urbanism but as something that could be layered over it, obscuring it but also complementing it. It strategically evoked a sense of pastness, and sentiments about that past, for which its consumers could not possibly have had any memory. As Arjun Appadurai has argued, such nostalgia is a central feature of much modern merchandising, teaching consumers to miss things they have never lost: 'they create experiences of duration, passage, and loss that rewrite the lived histories of individuals, families, ethnic groups, and classes.'[20] But while 'Old Manchester and Salford' might be called an 'ethnoscape', a highly self-conscious and codified construction of local identity, it also acted as a kind of memory-training in values at the core of capitalist progress. These are not, then, archaicisms or ruined figures in Walter Benjamin's sense, which could recover their potential in moments of crisis, using memory to create a dream-figure legitimating the course of history if not the actual form of its results. As the *City News* commented, "one would like to live in this little town, and read Harrop's Mercury, and drink sack, and help Master Caxton to print, and do all the other wonderful things they did in those days" (*City News* 7 May 1887). The *Manchester Weekly Times* echoed these

---

[18] See Darbyshire 1897: 195.
[19] On this second theme see Prettejohn (1999: 92).
[20] I am paraphrasing Appadurai (1996: 77).

sentiments: "in wandering therein we lost touch of the nineteenth century, became absorbed in our surroundings and verily believed that this was our real life, and that the noisy, restless, modern world was merely a baleful dream" (*Manchester Weekly Times* 17 December 1887). The journal *Black and White* picked up on the contrast with the present: "At this time of day, when utilitarianism has removed many traces of the picturesque from our streets, when correspondents in the daily papers deplore the unloveliness of Manchester, it is well to retain something which will remind us of what our city was before the speculative builder and the necessity for gigantic premises took possession of it" (*Black and White* 21 September 1887: 199). And in similar vein, the official publication *Exhibition Sketches* accompanied its bird's-eye view with the comment that "modern structures [...] certainly cannot rival them in picturesque beauty, however much they may surpass them in sanitary arrangement or convenience." (*Royal Jubilee Exhibition* 1887)[21]

This last comment points to one of the sources for the exhibition. While 'Old Manchester and Salford' claimed to be regionally-specific, it was also heavily inspired by recent exhibitions in London. It was at the International Health Exhibition of 1884 – which was also reconstructed in the Colonial and Indian Exhibition of 1886 – that the 'Old London' street probably first established the idea of a reconstructed period street.[22] Sited proximate to actual surviving Elizabethan housing as well as the medieval Crosby Hall in the City of London, 'Old London' involved typification and recombination, including "a papier mâché life-size replica of the old 'Bishop's Gate', the eastern entrance to the old walled city; 'Whittington's House', built Elizabethan style with latticed windows; and the stocks and whipping post which one of the souvenir photographs of 1884 has complete with a bearded figure in place" (Samuel 1994: 182). But although both reconstructed streets involved a routinisation of the past, 'Old London' was presented as a bad example of an inflammable, cramped and dark city contrasted with the abundant displays of health-signifying foun-

---

[21] See Royal Jubilee Exhibition, Manchester, *Exhibition Sketches*, Manchester: Taylor, Garnett and Co, 1887.

[22] Darbyshire acknowledged this as the main inspiration for 'Old Manchester and Salford' (Darbyshire 1897: 192).

tains elsewhere in the exhibition,[23] whereas 'Old Manchester and Salford' was an expression of civic pride in commerce offsetting the powerful image of the contemporary industrial city as a place of sprawling chaos, pollution, and blighted lives. Effectively, 'Old Manchester and Salford' used shops to represent these two intimately neighbouring northern cities. Shops played the role of an interchange or buffer zone, cleaning commercial life of its industrial associations and dependencies, not just disciplining consumption but detaching it from any realistic sense of its necessary conditions of production, from any temporal connection with industrialism. At the same time, however, any dangerous evocation of a state of inertia, or any actual conjuring up of a powerful residual structure of feeling (that is, one that might threaten communal resistance to change), were safely distanced by the very theatricality, artificiality and ephemeral nature of the display.

4. Shopping in the Hollow City

I turn now to a later piece of museological reconstruction created within a museum, the permanent display 'Lark Hill Place' in which a group of streets from Salford in the 1860s were reconstructed at the Salford Museum and Art Gallery.

Although its abbreviated urban forms and slight changes of scale may recall the 1887 'Old Manchester and Salford' exhibition, 'Lark Hill Place' is also very much the product of a later era of de-industrialisation. After the Second World War many of Salford's Victorian by-law streets and terrace housing began to be cleared by the City Council and replaced by housing estates. At the same time these post-war decades witnessed the onset of huge changes in Manchester and Salford's economy, a restructuring that saw industrial decline and a shifting from manufacturing industries to the service sector. Long-term patterns of unemployment and inner-city decay set in.[24] This was the state of the city memorably described by W. G. Sebald in his novel *The Emigrants* (1993), on the basis of his experiences in the 1960s:

---

[23] See Adams 1994, 205-211.
[24] See Kidd, 1993, 189.

Figure 3: Lark Hill Place, City of Salford

> In Moss Side and Hulme there were whole blocks where the doors and windows were boarded up, and whole districts where everything had been demolished. Views opened up across the wasteland towards the still immense agglomeration of gigantic Victorian office blocks and warehouses, about a kilometre distant, that had once been the hub of one of the nineteenth century's miracle cities but, as I was soon to find out, was now almost hollow to the core... One might have supposed that the city had long since been deserted, and was left now as a necropolis or mausoleum. (Sebald 1997: 151)

In 1955 the Salford Art Gallery and Museum "decided to salvage features from houses and shops being demolished and re-create a small street within the museum which would help future visitors, living in modern houses or high-rise flats and shopping in chain stores and supermarkets, to re-capture past living conditions in Salford" (Salford Museum 1985: 7). Most interestingly, there was very little attempt to evoke the nineteenth-century industrial city in this display. To indicate a longer past, back to eighteenth-century Salford, the street was named after the Georgian mansion, Lark Hill, that used to stand on the site of the present-day museum. Lark Hill was the hillside mansion that James Ackers built for himself in the early 1790s, just as Ackers became boroughreeve of Manchester, and Ackers himself was commemorated at the museum by naming one of Lark Hill Place's streets after him. There is, then, a strong whiff of the pre-industrial in this supposedly Victorian street. The display imagined Salford on a winter's evening just after the lighting of the street lamps. The shops, stocked with a combination of authentic objects from the museum's collection and reproductions, represent the city as a tight-knit group of small-scale commercial concerns underwritten by contemporary sponsors (Terry's of York, Tate and Lyle), and giving glimpses into longer trade and craft histories (as in the music shop and the printer's shop). The reconstruction includes several buildings that assemble materials from different times and places, such as the Blue Lion, which was assembled from a number of local pubs. Further up the social scale, the William & Mary Room is an extraordinarily creative concatenation of diverse things. The building itself was reconstructed from the timber frames of a house known as 'The Rovers Return' in Shudehill, which was demolished in 1958. Sheathing the interior of this is seventeenth-century panelling from Kenyon Peel Hall, Little Hulton, and there is also a staircase from an old house in Gravel Lane, Salford.[25] Other displays show a toyshop, tobacconist, chemist, pawnbroker, a blacksmith and wheelwright, and a dressmaker and haberdasher, and for extra frisson, 'James Critchley, Clogger' and 'Mrs Driver, Bleeder with Leeches'. Only one house, the 'artisan's cottage', comes anywhere near to approaching Engels's nineteenth-century city: a one-up one-down house, with cast iron range and a water boiler.

In both 'Old Manchester and Salford' and 'Lark Hill Place' commercial and museological interests were associated with a pre-industrial image of Manchester. Commerce, to paraphrase Benedict Anderson, deployed 'antiquity' as the necessary consequence of 'modernity',[26] the veil or façade that would allow it to be dissembled. Importantly, in neither exhibition was the industrial heritage put on display: in one probably because the active industrial present was on display elsewhere in the grounds of the Royal Jubilee Exhibition; in

---

[25] Ibid.: 11.
[26] Anderson 1991: xiv.

the other, possibly, because the difficulties attendant on industrial downsizing were too real a contemporary presence. The making of Manchester and Salford's industrialism into an object of heritage would have to wait until the 1980s when such industrialism could be seen as something finished and past.[27] But one interesting aspect of these assemblages is also their denial of the patina of age; they have few of those signs of wear that would evoke 'the right sort of duration in the social life of things'; the 'right sort', that is, for those who would be able to spot the difference between the authentic and the fake.[28] Yet the semiotic handling of these displays was perhaps more subtle than this. It played to a knowing stylistic and historical allusiveness, much the same as had been acted out in the Victorian city itself through an eclectic urban architecture.

5. Ersatz Exchange

On the face of it, the new Exchange Square seems to be doing something rather different.

Triggered by the destruction caused by the 1996 IRA bomb and part of a wave of projects across the country driven by millennial celebrations ordained by government and local bodies, Exchange Square is principally a new focus for shopping in inner-city Manchester, an attempt to hold off the threat posed by the enticements of out-of-town shopping at Trafford Park, the vast shopping mall on the city's western outskirts.[29] The Square, and the linked developments of New Cathedral Street and the Corn Exchange, mixes a range of mid- and top-range shopping outlets with outdoor café areas and landscaped public space. Exchange Square itself is framed on one side by the Harvey Nicholls store and the new Marks & Spencer building, whose entirely glazed façade (on this side now occupied by Sel-

---

[27] Hence, for instance, the establishment in the 1980s of the Museum of Science and Industry, incorporating one of the world's oldest railway stations, and the flagship regeneration of the derelict Castlefield area around it, converting its mills into flats and bars and preserving other features as part of an industrial heritage park.

[28] See Appadurai 1996: 75.

[29] On rebuilding the city's shopping centre after 1996 see Holden (2002: 133-154).

fridges) would have provided an image of shopping as spectacle if the occupant had not inserted blinds to shield products from the glare. On the other sides are the renovated Corn Exchange, a big new Next store, and the largely rebuilt faces of the older and unpopular 1960s shopping megastructure, the Arndale Centre, a symbol for the style of containment or rejection of urban energies of an earlier period.[30] Exchange Square is, to all intents and purposes, then, like many contemporary shopping districts.

Figure 4: Exchange Square, © Mark Crinson

By contrast with the huge flooring capacities of the stores, the open space in Exchange Square is small, not to say cramped. It is articulated by a series of curved sloping terraces and a water feature in the form of a short curving stream with flat rocks enabling children easily to step over it. Further public decorations are the large metal windmills, vastly enlarged versions of the kind that were long sold to amuse children, which line up along the Selfridge's side, and the metal tracks and over-sized rolling stock – a reference to Manchester's importance in the development of railways – that serve as benches: together these act like leftovers from some Brobdingnagian play

---

[30] See Williams 2004: 206.

space. Added to these features in the last year, and cluttering the area even more, is a ferris wheel, a slightly smaller version of the highly successful London Eye. Inner-city shopping is thereby represented as a fun, child-friendly thing to do. And further, on the Corn Exchange side of the square a large screen has been placed, a kind of hopeful wish for public space as public sphere using both the means and the image of one of the media technologies that has most diminished it.

But the area can also be seen as a museological recreation of references, reproductions and renovations, a locale of memory directly in the local tradition of 'Lark Hill Place' and the 'Old Manchester and Salford' display. One might argue that Exchange Square is neither a museum display nor a temporary exhibition, but this is not a sustainable distinction given both the infiltration of the museological by the commercial and the use of historical and reconstructed forms within urban space. Instead it could be said that all three examples share an investment in the production of locality in a collapsed and compacted sense of space and temporality. Thus the stream, positioned as a transitional marker between new and old within the Square, acts as a kind of reminiscence of Hanging Ditch which, almost on the same spot, was one of Manchester's several inner city streams and in this case a defensive ditch for a long-disappeared medieval castle. These streams, in common with the utilitarian attitude to all Manchester's waterways, were treated as virtual sewers in the nineteenth century and long culverted over: in Exchange Square it is as if one has been revealed again, if now as a piece of landscaping. On one side of Exchange Square an ersatz cathedral close has been created with the cathedral tower visible over the ring of buildings. To one end of the cathedral (itself with ersatz history as a collegiate church upgraded to cathedral status in the mid-nineteenth century), creating a transition between it and the reshaped shopping area, there now stand two wooden-framed pre-industrial buildings, the Old Wellington pub and Sinclair's Oyster Bar, the first of which had been reconstructed for the 'Old Manchester and Salford' display. In 1998 these buildings, with sixteenth- and seventeenth-century origins and known together for a long time as the Shambles, were moved some five hundred yards to their new location, completing a length of older buildings that frame one side of the cathedral. Using computer records and elaborate systems of coding these wooden-framed buildings were painstakingly dismantled and reconstructed piece by piece in their new location, their original walls "rebuilt complete with the original uneven brickwork" (*Manchester Evening News* 18 Sept. 1998). They were also changed in their relationship by turning them at right angles to form an outdoor eating area facing the new shops and other distractions of Exchange Square. The two pre-industrial buildings thus serve several purposes: they help frame both the 'medieval quarter' of the cathedral and the 'shopping quarter' of Exchange Square; they point backwards to the pre-industrial city that has been such an important image of the city whenever it has had to encounter periods of change; and they also help to underline the leisured city of consumption that seems most likely to be resorted to whenever any of Britain's cities have tried to reorganise and redesign its public spaces in the last two decades.[31] Their usefulness for these purposes, as indeed their ubiquity for earlier purposes, is related to their adaptability as buildings. Unlike far more important buildings from the city's pre-industrial past, which have been demolished even in recent years, the unlisted Shambles buildings give developers the chance to evoke historical detail and to fetishise the contingency of the past in, for instance, their evidently old exposed wooden beams or their painstakingly reconstructed 'original uneven brick work', while at the same time changing the orientation of the buildings and adding extensions with stone cladding adopting the fake forms of timber framing.

Altogether, Exchange Square offers an interesting re-assertion and transformation of certain elements of Manchester's past together with the new aspirations of its urban elites and the policies of its city fathers. The IRA bomb gave a chance to change the area around the Arndale Centre from a largely working and lower-middle-class shopping district into a disinfected buffer zone, a precinct for the middle classes. Exchange Square has been conceived of as the renovated heart of a post-industrial Manchester, a neo-Haussmannised quarter of café-bars, designer shops and dressed pavements where the city's past takes the playground form of blown-up toytown amenities, a newly-created cathedral close, medieval watering holes and big-screen television. In all this, however, there is an expected sameness: despite its production of locality, Manchester could be Birmingham, Frankfurt or Dijon; possibly even Kuala Lumpur, Singapore or Melbourne. Local-

---

[31] On this see Williams 2004, particularly chapters 6 and 9.

ity as produced in this space is a marketing device, the result of global pressures and anxieties more than an emanation of regional forms.

Can we regard the new images of Manchester that have appeared in the last few years as having different effects from Engels's 'tender concealment' and 'hypocritical plan'? The collection of architectural representations of Manchester discussed in this article clearly show that at important periods in the city's history a compact has been worked out between its commercial interests and a non- or pre-industrial image of the city. But in the nineteenth and early twentieth centuries this compact was premised on the notion of a continuity between the values of ordered or civic-minded commerce and the energies and modernisation required by industry. Equally accepted and essential to this compact was Manchester's undoubted status as a global city, based in particular on its pre-eminent role in the business and manufacturing ends of the 'technoscape' that was the worldwide cotton industry, which was itself underpinned by the British Empire. Since the Second World War that pre-eminence is no more and Manchester has not recaptured its status as a global city. It is still more at the receiving end of globalisation than able to control its destiny in the world order. Despite its attempts to reach beyond the nation-state and not to be seen as a merely provincial city – now, as much as signs of industrial decline, the major concerns of its city fathers – despite its success in winning European money for cultural projects, and despite the fashion for devolution and regionalism, Manchester is still peripheral to the major European economic developments.[32] In this context the concentration of funding that has been directed in the last ten to fifteen years at Manchester's central areas to develop its shopping and cultural assets, and only slightly outside those areas to develop its sporting and knowledge economies, can be seen as another 'hypocritical plan'.[33] Manchester's problems have been shunted out but not solved. The benefits of its much-applauded cultural and urban renaissance are hardly evident in the arc of western, northern and eastern inner suburbs. Nor indeed in many of its ring of satellite towns, with which it had been symbiotically linked during its period of economic power. These are economically dislocated areas, still awaiting the

---

[32] See Dicken 2002: 28.

[33] For a similar argument concentrating on sociological material, see Mellor 2002: 214-235.

trickle-down effects of post-industrial regeneration, flashpoints for friction between right-wing groups and Asian communities. The 'tender concealment' hides such areas from the businessman, sports tourist or shopper who either lives in one of Manchester's many new central city apartments or arrives in Manchester via plane or its newly rebuilt Piccadilly Station. If there is a connection between the policies of regeneration and suburban car-jackings, student muggings, derelict housing, endemic low pay and the cash-and-crime economy, it is not one often made by those who most enjoy Manchester's commercial and cultural facilities.

Works Cited

Adams, Annmarie (1994): "The Healthy Victorian City – The Old London Street at the International Health Exhibition of 1884", in: Z. Celik et al. (eds.): *Streets: Critical Perspectives on Public Space*. Berkeley, Los Angeles and London: University of California Press, 205-211.

Alfred Brothers: *Scrapbook*. Manchester Central Library. No date.

Anderson, Benedict (1991): *Imagined Communities*. London and New York: Verso.

Appadurai, Arjun (1996): *Modernity at Large*. Minneapolis and London: University of Minnesota Press.

Barlow, Paul (1996): "Local disturbances: Ford Madox Brown and the problem of the Manchester Murals", in: E. Harding (ed.): *Reframing the Pre-Raphaelites*. Aldershot: Palgrave, 81-97.

Briggs, Asa (1968): *Victorian Cities*. London: Penguin.

Brown, F. M. (18??): *Interpretive Narratives for 12 Manchester Town Hall Frescoes*. Manchester: Manchester Town Hall.

Codell, Julie F. (1998): "Ford Madox Brown, Carlyle, Macaulay, Bakhtin: The Pratfalls and Penultimates of History", *Art History* 21:3 September, 354-355.

Crinson, Mark (2002): "Photography and the industrial city: Manchester and Salford, ancient and modern", *Word & Image* 18:4 (Oct-Dec), 303-305.

Darbyshire, Alfred (1887): *A Booke of Olde Manchester and Salford*. Manchester: Heywood.

— (1897): *An Architect's Experience: Professional, Artistic and Theatrical*. Manchester: Cornish.

Dicken, Peter (2002): "Global Manchester: from globaliser to globalised", in: Jamie Peck and Kevin Ward (eds.): *City of Revolution: Restructuring Manchester*. Manchester: Manchester UP.

Engels, Friedrich (1845/1987): *The Condition of the Working Class in England*. London: Penguin.

Harrison, M. F. (1988): *The Royal Jubilee Exhibition, Manchester, 1887*. MA thesis, Manchester Polytechnic (now Manchester Metropolitan University).

Holden, Adam (2002): "Bomb sites: the politics of opportunity", in: Jamie Peck and Kevin Ward (eds.): *City of Revolution: Restructuring Manchester*. Manchester: Manchester UP, 133-154.

Joyce, Patrick (2003): *The Rule of Freedom: Liberalism and the Modern City*. London: Verso.

Kidd, Alan (1993): *Manchester*. Keele: Keele UP.

— (1993): "The industrial city and its pre-industrial past: the Manchester Royal Jubilee Exhibition of 1887", *Transactions of the Lancashire and Cheshire Antiquarian Society* 89, 61.

Marcus, Steven (1974): *Engels, Manchester, and the Working Class*. London: Weidenfeld and Nicolson.

Mellor, Rosemary (2002): "Hypocritical city: cycles of urban exclusion", in: Jamie Peck and Kevin Ward (eds.): *City of Revolution: Restructuring Manchester.* Manchester: Manchester UP, 214-235.

Prettejohn, Elizabeth (1999): "Aestheticising History Painting", in: T. Barringer and E. Prettejohn (eds.): *Frederic Leighton: Antiquity, Renaissance, Modernity.* New Haven and London: Yale UP.

Samuel, Raphael (1994): *Theatres of Memory* — Volume 1: *Past and Present in Contemporary Culture.* London: Verso.

Sebald, W. G. (1993/1997): *The Emigrants.* London: Harvill.

Weiner, Martin (1985): *English Culture and the Decline of the Industrial Spirit 1850-1980.* London: Penguin.

Williams, Richard (2004): *The Anxious City.* London: Routledge.

Illustrations

Figure 1: 'Old Manchester and Salford' — view of oratory from Market Sted Lane. From Alfred Darbyshire: *A Book of Old Manchester and Salford.* Manchester: Heywood, 1887.

Figure 2: 'Old Manchester and Salford' — plan. From Alfred Darbyshire: *A Book of Old Manchester and Salford.* Manchester: Heywood, 1887.

Figure 3: Lark Hill Place, Salford Art Gallery and Museum. From Salford Museum and Art Gallery, *Lark Hill Place.* Salford: City of Salford Education and Leisure Department, 1985.

Figure 4: Exchange Square, Manchester. Photograph by Mark Crinson.

The New Livercool:
History, Culture and Identity on Merseyside

John Belchem

Abstract: Once the proud 'second city of empire', Liverpool fell rapidly down the urban hierarchy to become the 'shock city' of post-industrial Britain. Somewhat later than other northern cities, Liverpool is now undergoing remarkable regeneration. Looking back at previous exercises in urban re-branding and economic diversification, this essay casts critical historical reflections on the new vision of 'Livercool', a city seeking to secure its future on creative and cultural industries.

Key names and concepts: Ramsay Muir - Charles Reilly; Liverpool - Merseyside - Cosmopolitanism - Slave Trade - Emigration - City-state - Liverpolis - Irishness - UNESCO World Heritage - University of Liverpool - Unemployment - Nostalgia - European Capital of Culture - Regeneration Programme - Liverpool F.C. - Festival of Britain - Tourism - Multi-culturalism.

A city apart, Liverpool sits outside the narrative frameworks of British national history, a kind of other or outsider within Northern England. Once a source of local pride, this 'otherness' has proved more problematic in recent times. Indeed, this sense of difference has been perceived as a symptom of the Liverpool 'problem': Liverpudlians purportedly exhibit an un-English propensity for mawkish self-pity, indulging in a self-image of put-upon miserablist isolationism.[1] How different things were in the glory days of the nineteenth century. For the Victorian Liverpolitan, otherness was a register of prosperity and success, attesting to the superiority of commerce over industry, of the Liverpool gentleman over the mere Manchester man. The second city

---

[1] For the complex and contested ways in which Liverpool has projected itself and how it has been portrayed by others, see the new history commissioned by the City Council and the University of Liverpool to commemorate the 800th anniversary in 2007 of the granting of letters patent, John Belchem (ed.), *Liverpool 800: culture, character and history* (2006).

of empire, Victorian Liverpool acted like a kind of independent city state: it was the only British municipality with its own office in London, a form of embassy to safeguard and promote its interests as 'second metropolis' (see Henderson 1933: 473-479). Cosmopolitanism underscored the city's vaunted status. The most un-English of Victorian provincial cities, polyglot Liverpool transcended the national urban hierarchy, standing above the 'Coketown' monoculture of adjacent textile and industrial towns. Gateway to the west, it was hailed in the 1880s as "the New York of Europe, a world-city rather than merely British provincial" (*Illustrated London News* 15 May 1886). Having risen so high, however, the great world seaport had further to fall in the twentieth century. Studies of its remarkable trajectory have tended either to apply supra-national models, as in sociological deployment of globalisation theory to explain the collapse "from world city to pariah city" or to insist (not without self-pity) on its urban exceptionalism.[2]

The would-be 'Florence of the north', Victorian Liverpool defined itself against industrial Manchester and in rivalry with commercial London. In the North of England but not of it, Liverpool (and its 'sub-region' of Merseyside) was (and has continued to be) highly distinctive, differing sharply in socio-economic structure, cultural image and expression, political affiliation, health, diet and speech from the adjacent industrial districts. The industrial conurbations of the North grew out of conglomerations of small towns and villages, augmented by short-distance rural in-migration which tended to reinforce their culture, character and status as regional centres. By contrast, long distance in-migration – the multi-ethnic, mainly celtic inflow (Irish, Welsh, Scottish and Manx) – transformed Liverpool and its 'scouse' culture, setting it apart from its environs. Beyond the 'inland' Irish Sea, Liverpool's private celtic empire, the great seaport looked to the oceans, adding an external dimension to the city's cultural life and its migrant mix. The 'community' mentality of the Scottie-Road 'slummy' co-existed with a broader culture, a seafaring cosmopolitanism which made the diaspora space of Liverpool particularly receptive to (un-English) foreign ideas (syndicalism, for example) and to Ameri-

---

[2] See Wilks-Heeg (2003: 36-52) and Belchem (2006): The introduction to the second edition, "The new 'Livercool'", offers some historical and critical reflections on the city's current renaissance.

can popular music. Liverpool's distinctive cultural character is probably best captured through comparison with other 'edge' cities, decentred major ports like Naples and Marseille with similar 'second city' pretensions and picaresque reputations. In chronicling popular music from the Cavern to the Coral, Paul Du Noyer describes Liverpool (designated as the United Kingdom's number one music city in 2002 with 53 number one chart hits by 23 different bands and soloists over the previous 50 years) as 'a sort of sunless Marseille', defiantly non-provincial, the capital of itself:

> It's deeply insular, yet essentially outward-looking: it faces the sea but has its back turned on England. There were local men for whom Sierra Leone was a fact but London only a rumour. They knew every dive in Buenos Aires, but had no idea of the Cotswolds. And Liverpudlians speak with merry contempt for their Lancashire neighbours, displaying all the high indifference of a New Yorker for Kansas. (Du Noyer 2002: 5)

The most famous history of Liverpool written by Ramsay Muir to commemorate the 700th anniversary in 1907 of the granting of letters patent, divided Liverpool's past into two phases: the gradual removal of natural and other obstacles to its development within the region; and its subsequent exponential growth into a great world port with a dock system, seven and a quarter miles long, "as solid and enduring as the Pyramids, the most stupendous work of its kind that the will and power of man have ever created", quite without rival "anywhere in the world". Economic potential was unleashed by the integration of entrepreneurs and their assumption of political authority, by a potent combination of mercantile ambition and civic power. Council investment in an innovatory wet-docks system in the early eighteenth century, a risky undertaking which drew upon the security of the Corporation Estate, was soon followed by improvements in internal communication. Here were the beginnings of an effective transport infrastructure for the developing economic region of South Lancashire, Cheshire and North Staffordshire, facilitating an internal triangular trade carrying such vital commodities as salt and coal. Liverpool was thus well placed to reap the commercial dividends of a remarkable subsequent conjuncture: development of the Americas; British naval supremacy secured in the 'second hundred years' war; and industrial revolution in the adjacent 'manufacturing districts'. Having tamed the Mersey's thirty foot tidal range, commercial Liverpool exploited its hard won comparative advantage, establishing itself as the western emporium of Albion. With a pro-active (and comparatively youthful) risk-taking mercantile oligarchy at the helm, unrestricted by chartered companies or guilds, Liverpool's remarkable history had truly begun.

In charting commercial Liverpool's 'stupendous development', Muir did not minimise the contribution or horrors of the slave trade. Here too the propensity for risk-taking was to place Liverpool, whose sea captains were renowned for lower charges and faster speeds, ahead of rivals in this infamous triangular traffic. Through efficiency gains, market penetration, institutional knowledge and locational advantage (shipping lanes around the north of Ireland were relatively safe from enemy attack at time of war), Liverpool established itself (with unashamed commercial pride) as the "slaving capital of the world". In early guides to the town, the lucrative slave trade, assessed in the same quantitative terms as other traffic, exemplified Liverpudlian enterprise *par excellence*.[3] At the expense of any moderate or neutral position, the attitude hardened into what was perhaps the first expression of Liverpool's self-declared 'otherness', upholding local commercial acumen and success against the meddlesome moralism of 'outside' abolitionist opinion. Having cut itself off from the mainstream of changing British ideology, Liverpool, Seymour Drescher notes, "was faced with a threat not just to its economic base but to its cultural identity" (Drescher 1988: 128). As abolitionists claimed the high ground, materialist Liverpool stood condemned for barbarism, philistinism and lack of civilised culture, charges which Muir was to re-iterate with force (see Muir 1907: 270-284).

Muir took solace from the more laudable entrepreneurial flair with which Liverpool subsequently adjusted to abolition of the slave trade. Having previously deployed Corporation funds to defend the slave trade to the last, Liverpool placed itself at the very forefront of the subsequent campaign (which achieved success in 1833) to abolish slavery itself within the British colonies. Merchants quickly adjusted to the new circumstances, opening lucrative new markets and trade to Africa and elsewhere (in the process attracting significant numbers of Kru, Lascar, Chinese and other sea-faring communities within and be-

---

[3] See, for example, William Enfield, *An essay towards the history of Liverpool* (1773), ch.vi.

yond the 'black Atlantic' to the port). Faced with economic adversity, 'cosmopolitan' Liverpool had shown itself at its best, thereafter a recurrent (and reassuring) trope in the articulation of Merseypride.

The cosmopolitan complexion was enhanced by the development of the emigration trade (in which a number of migrants remained in Liverpool, some out of choice, most through hard luck, accident or poverty). By the mid-nineteenth century, Liverpool was already the premier European emigration port, the "flood-gate of the old world". Of the 5.5 million "moving Europeans" who crossed the Atlantic between 1860 and 1900, 4.75 million sailed from Liverpool (Read 1993: 31-47). Some groups, such as the Mormons from Scandinavia en route to Utah, kept themselves insulated and apart in their own mission and accommodation houses in Liverpool, while the less wary fell victim to the notorious 'sharpers' who practised various costly deceits upon unsuspecting emigrants awaiting trans-shipment.[4] Migrants to the Australasian colonies were kept in a form of quarantine in an Emigrant Depot across the Mersey in Birkenhead, safe from the 'sharpers' (see Hollett 1988). Gateway to the empire and the new world, waterfront Liverpool catered (as Charles Dickens discovered in the *Uncommercial Traveller*) for a vast floating, migrant and casual population.[5] Differing markedly from other British urban settings, sailortown Liverpool – with its pleasures, dangers and 'edge' – was more akin to Five Points, New York (also visited by Dickens) with its 'syncretic' cultural fusion. Here was a cultural contact zone between different ethnic groups with differing needs and intentions as transients, sojourners or settlers (categories, which as Linda Grant's grandparents attest, were by no means mutually exclusive).[6]

As an accompaniment to the new post-slave trade cosmopolitanism, Liverpool underwent its first major re-branding exercise, rewriting its recent history to find inspiration for a more worthy future.

---

[4] See the pages on Mormon emigration on the Norway Heritage website: [http://www.norwayheritage.com]. See also *Morning Chronicle* (15 July 1850).

[5] See chapter 5 in Charles Dickens's *The Uncommercial Traveller*.

[6] See Linda Grant's article. "History broke Liverpool, and it broke my heart", *Guardian* 5 June 2003, on how her grandparents, transients turned settlers, mistook Liverpool for their intended destination, New York; see also her novel, *Still Here* (2002).

Reviled at the time, those who had opposed the slave trade against the odds were rehabilitated and revered. In the process, radical abolitionists such as the blind poet Edward Rushton, a former sailor in the trade, tended to be passed over in favour of the more refined 'Humanity' men, most notably William Roscoe and his circle of merchant-scholars. Here were appropriate role models for the civilised city of commerce, the would be 'Florence of the north'. Through his studies of renaissance Florence, Roscoe, Muir noted approvingly, had "found refreshment from the brutal materialism of his native town, and inspiration for the attempt to breathe into it a new spirit". Roscoe's life-story – from humble, self-taught origins to mercantile success, distinguished scholarship and civic responsibility – provided the framework for the urban biography of Liverpool which Muir wished to write. Revered as the new Medici, the Roscoe circle were the inspiration for post slave-trade Liverpool, the new 'Liverpolis' of Victorian Britain, a kind of city-state imbued with classical references and renaissance embellishment, dedicated to commerce, culture and civilisation (see Muir 1906).

By the mid-nineteenth century, the new 'Liverpolis' was taking shape, given physical form in what C.H. Reilly (one of Muir's contemporaries at the new University of Liverpool) was to categorise as 'neo-Grec' architecture, combining Greek refinement and scale with Roman strength and magnificence (Reilly 1927: 29). A plethora of clubs, reading rooms and learned societies attended to the promotion of literature and the arts, supplemented by a number of voluntary associations specifically geared to the education and recreation of young clerks, 'Liverpool gentlemen' – not 'Manchester men' – in the making.[7] Following municipal reform in 1835, the new council, imbued with an 'improving' ethos of civic duty, initiated programmes of educational, sanitary and health reform, and was among the first to establish a public library and museum. Much applauded by Muir, the 'new spirit of civic pride' reached a high-point with the construction of St George's Hall, "that noble building, one of the noblest in the modern world, which is to-day the supreme architectural boast of the city" (Muir 1907: 313).[8] However, the cost of the building scandalised sanitary reformers who were concerned less about reversing Liverpool's

---

[7] See Wilson (1998: 55-80) and see also Stobart (2002: 471-85).
[8] See also White 1951.

philistine image than eradicating its reputation as 'the black spot on the Mersey', an early instance of a recurrent controversy in urban promotion between public display and basic infrastructure. Liverpool was the first to appoint a Medical Officer of Health, Dr Duncan, but his advocacy of heavy expenditure on sanitary works (which he believed the corporation could well afford with its vast income from dock dues) was accompanied less by materialist understanding of the poverty at the bottom of the local residential and social hierarchy with its vast casual labour market than by 'racist' condemnation of the Irish famine influx into Liverpool (see Kearns and Laxton 2002: 13-40). Such denigration was to persist, portraying the Liverpool Irish as a kind of under-class, unable, unwilling or unsuited to take advantage of opportunities elsewhere in Britain or the new world. Constructed in this pejorative manner, it was 'Irishness' of this order – immobile, inadequate and irresponsible – that purportedly set Liverpool and its notorious social problems apart.

Despite ongoing civic improvement and further pioneer exercises in public health reform, the Victorian city failed to sustain Roscoe's vision. Mercenary attitudes prevailed, a culture of capital oblivious of higher things: indeed, mercantile support for the Confederate South suggested that little had changed since the philistine commercialism of the slave trade. The culture of civilised commerce, Ramsay Muir rued, remained restricted to a Liberal minority, a socially exclusive (predominantly Unitarian) elite, lacking in political influence and popular resonance. Debarred from political power, Liberal families turned to philanthropy and cultural benefaction as their means of "impressing themselves on the town" (Reilly 1938: 248-249). In a lecture in 1875, Philip Rathbone – revered in cultural circles as "the most original member of a family celebrated in Liverpool for their high principles, intellect and philanthropic activities" (Muspratt 1917: 255) – called for greater acknowledgement of "the political value of art to municipal life":

> It is for us, with our vast population, our enormous wealth (as a town), but without either politics or philosophy that the world will care to preserve, to decide whether we will take advantage of our almost unequalled opportunities for the cultivation of Art, or whether we shall be content to rot away, as Carthage, Antioch and Tyre have rotted away, leaving not a trace to show here a population of more than half

a million souls once lived, loved, felt and thought. Surely the home of Roscoe is worthy of a better fate? (Rathbone 1975: 45)

The failed promise of the nineteenth century, notwithstanding, Muir's *History* ended on a triumphant note of high idealism. Liverpool, the second city of empire, had at last acquired official city, diocesan and university status (although the location of the initial University College buildings in "a disused lunatic asylum in the midst of a slum district" hardly seemed appropriate).

> The city which, at the opening of a new age, is simultaneously engaged in erecting a great cathedral and a great university, is surely no mean city. It is building for itself twin citadels of the ideal, a citadel of faith and a citadel of knowledge; and from the hill which once looked down on an obscure hamlet, and which later saw ships begin to crowd the river, and streets to spread over the fields, their towers will look across the ship-thronged estuary, monuments of a new and more generous aspiration. (Muir 1907: 340)

Down in the commercial centre, the built environment was also undergoing spectacular transformation, most dramatically at the new Pier Head, land reclaimed from a redundant central dock as pressure on commercial space intensified: the domed Mersey Docks and Harbour Building (1907) applauded by Muir, was joined by the skyscraper Royal Liver Building (1911) and the Italian renaissance palazzo of the Cunard Building (1913), the photogenic sea-facing 'three graces' skyline by which Liverpool remains instantly recognisable, iconic epicentre of what is now the UNESCO Liverpool Maritime Mercantile City World Heritage Site, and the inspiration for not only US cities, but also Shanghai. Further out, new model factories, 'large, lofty and well-ventilated', were added to the tourist itinerary. Special arrangements were made for delegates to the Church Congress and Ecclesiastical Art Exhibition in 1904 to visit Bryant and May's Diamond Match Works in Litherland where "the best arrangements are made for the care and well-being of the workers, a doctor and a dentist being retained, and a matron is in constant attendance to look after the comfort of the women and the girls".[9] The prime item on display at the Exhibition was the gold trowel and mallet used by the king at the

---

[9] *The Guide to the Church Congress and Ecclesiastical Art Exhibition held in Liverpool* (1904).

laying of the foundation stone of the Cathedral – it was some time, however, before Fred Bower, the 'Rolling Stonemason' revealed 'the secret in the foundation stone'. Wrapped between copies of the *Clarion* and the *Labour Leader* (provided by his schoolboy sectarian sparring partner, Jim Larkin), Bower allegedly placed a socialist address on behalf of the 'wage slaves' building the cathedral, to remind posterity that "within a stone's throw from here, human beings are housed in slums not fit for swine" (Bower 1936: ch. 9). The Cathedral was to remain surrounded by deprivation until the 1980s.

A new arrival in Edwardian Liverpool, Charles Reilly quickly sensed the mood: "From its slums to its big houses on the outskirts, from its docks to its new University, pre-war Liverpool was throbbing with life and energy". Appointed to the Chair in the School of Architecture, Reilly was initiated into 'The New Testament', a University group enthralled by the 'Athenian' vision of Professor Mackay, Ramsay Muir's head of department: "Through its University Liverpool was to be a new Athens saving the country from its materialism by the clearness of its thought, the fineness of its work and even the beauty of its buildings". While the School of Architecture flourished under Reilly and became the world-leader in architectural education, a Faculty of Fine Arts (with chairs for Augustus John and Jacob Epstein) failed to materialise.[10] Painting and sculpture were placed under local authority control, demarcation at odds, however, with the wishes and aspirations of the local artistic community. Shortly before its demise in 1895, local artists had succeeded in infiltrating the Liverpool Art Club dominated by the Rathbone clique – "essentially a gentlemen's club for those who loved art, or who pretended to be art-lovers" (Chun 2002: 127-149) – but they bemoaned their lack of influence over municipal policy towards the arts: "It is as ridiculous in our view that the destiny of Liverpool Art should be at the mercy of 'the butcher, the baker, and candlestick maker', as it would be to place in the hands of an artist the control of the tramway system" (ibid.). There was vociferous protest when the city council, determined to eschew any suggestion of parochial provincialism on their part, awarded the commission for the frescoes in the Town Hall funded by proceeds from the 1907 Pageant to a London studio.[11] These, indeed, were sensitive times as

---

[10] See Reilly (1938: chapter 6), T. Kelly (1981) and P.E.H. Hair (1996).
[11] See *The Sport of Civic Life, or Art and the Municipality*, Liverpool, 1909.

Liverpool's pretensions as "second city of empire" were open to question, the recent failure to incorporate contiguous Bootle marking the end of plans for a 'Greater Liverpool' to keep pace with Glaswegian expansion.[12]

Seen through historical hindsight, the Edwardian years were a glorious climacteric. Given such lavish display, Edwardian civic pride required both the funds and participation of the city's merchant princes, the leading families who had built up the port and its enterprise and, as Frederic D'Aeth noted approvingly, had "thrown themselves with the same fervour into its public administration and its charitable institutions" (D'Aeth 1912: 38). Some began to display donor fatigue (as evinced by the initial poor support for the Victoria memorial, erected on the site of the medieval castle, later of St George's church) (Liverpool Review 1 June 1901), while others were drawn towards London, a seemingly unstoppable trend in part dictated by changes in business structures, practices and culture. The glory days could not last. Muir's confidence in continued commercial prosperity was disastrously misplaced. As the brief post-war boom came to an end, Harrods dropped their plans for a Liverpool store in 1920, a symbolic precursor of the city's downward spiral in the interwar decades (Daily Post 9 February 1920). A major export port, Liverpool was hit disproportionately hard by world-wide depression as trade declined more rapidly than production. Throughout the 1930s the local unemployment rate remained resolutely above 18%, double the national average (see Davies et al. 1992). Even so, Merseyside was not designated as a depressed area in the legislation of 1934. Commercial Liverpool found itself disabled within interwar discourse of unemployment and economic policy. Priority was accorded to the problems of the industrial North and other distressed manufacturing areas, while efforts to regain comparative advantage as the world's clearing house were exclusively centred on the city of London. Having to come to terms with its distinctive and accentuated structural problems, Liverpool of the depression made itself heard through humour. When asked why Merseyside produced so many comedians, Arthur Askey famously replied: "You've got to be a comic to live in Liverpool" (Shaw 1988: 25).

---

[12] In this context see also the introduction, "Let Glasgow Flourish" in Fraser and Maver (1996).

Once again, Liverpool faced an image problem. In a pioneer exercise in what is now called 'urban visioning', the Liverpool Organisation for Advancing the Trade and Commerce of Liverpool repackaged Liverpudlian culture, character and history as the city's unique selling point. Forged in early struggles against medieval overlords and surrounding gentry, Liverpool's heritage of independent, no-nonsense toughness offered a set of transferable skills, previously deployed to secure commercial pre-eminence, now ripe for industrial application. Established to attract inward investment and industrial diversification in the 1920s, Liverpool Organisation was premised on the understanding that "if we were going to meet with any success in our efforts to interest people in the possibilities of Liverpool as an industrial centre, we had first to interest them in Liverpool". As well as running extensive advertising campaigns in national and overseas newspapers, Liverpool Organisation sought to enlist local residents through the promotion of an annual Civic Week. Such was the success of the campaign that the City Council took it over and then promoted special legislation – the Liverpool Corporation Act of 1936 – by which it gained unique powers to develop outlying areas for industry. Somewhat belatedly, commercial Liverpool tried to acquire a broader economic base (including new employment opportunities for women).

There was a brief false dawn after the Second World War, extended in popular memory (and recent economic history writing) by the remarkable resonance of the Merseybeat of the early 1960s. The initial success of industrial diversification at Speke, Aintree and Kirkby, however, was not to endure, adding another 'militant' dimension to Liverpool's adverse image. With the collapse of the colonial economic system and global restructuring – the 'triple whammy' of the end of empire, the introduction of containerisation and eventual entry into the European Economic Community – Liverpool's descent appeared unstoppable. By an irony of history, Liverpool, the gateway to the west, now suffered from being ill-placed geographically, although commentators persisted in attributing its demise to self-inflicted factors of local culture and character. Liverpool, once the great 'beat city' of the 1960s, transmogrified into the 'beaten city' of the Thatcherite decades, the 'shock city' of post-industrial Britain – "a 'showcase' of everything that has gone wrong in Britain's major cities" (*Daily Mirror* 11 October 1982). Hastened by the Toxteth riots of 1981, an indictment of exclusion, deprivation and discrimination extending beyond the local black population, political concern shifted from regional development to urban regeneration. Pioneer attempts at cultural tourism, the Garden Festival and refurbishment of the Albert Dock in the mid 1980s, failed to turn the tide. Seemingly irreversible economic and demographic decline spiralled Liverpool down into European Union Objective One status in 1993, the level of GDP per head having fallen to only 73% of the European Union average.

Although at the time it seemed a badge of failure, the 'award' of Objective One funding to the Merseyside 'sub-region' may come to be seen in historical perspective as a decisive turning-point for the city. Subsequent political factors added to the impetus: under the Liberal Democrats since 1998, the city has adopted a style of urban entrepreneurialism, partnership governance and civic boosterism, anathema to the Militant politics of the 1980s, the legacy of which (budgetary and otherwise) kept Liverpool for some while behind other northern cities in urban transformation.[13] Forward-looking self-promotion, not self-pitying nostalgia, now prevails in the new 'Livercool', incipient European Capital of Culture. Population loss has been halted and employment prospects improved. Like its re-named and re-branded 'John Lennon' airport, among the fastest growing in Europe, the city has taken off, outstripping other major cities in the latest surveys of new business start-ups.[14] Once considered a hindrance, its distinctive accent is now a marketing asset, placing Liverpool at the top of the league for call centres, including the European reservations centre for US Airways.[15] From just one entry in the *Good Food Guide* in 1995, the city, picked out for special mention in the introduction to the 2005 edition, now boasts six entries. (Turvil 2004: 15; 331-334) Designer chic prevails in a city henceforth propelled by cultural and creative industries, tourism, consumption and city-centre living. In March 2003, *Tatler* dedicated 23 pages of fashion shoots to locations in what it described (quite without irony) as 'Livercool', the "jewel of the north ...

---

[13] In this context see Richard Meegan (1999: 53-79) and Gideon Ben-Tovim (1999: 227-246). And see also Peter Batey (1999: 97-111).

[14] See the website of the Liverpool Business Centre, itself part of the mission to establish Liverpool as '*the* business friendly city' of the North West: [http://www.liverpoolbusinesscentre.co.uk].

[15] There must be doubt, however, as to whether Liverpool call centres will be able to withstand competition from further afield than the United Kingdom and the European Union. (See *Guardian* 22 September 2000).

the place where tradition meets cutting edge" (*Tatler* March 2003). It was perhaps no coincidence that the leading model was Lady Eloise Anson, niece of the Duke of Westminster whose company Grosvenor Henderson were beginning work on the Paradise Project, a 42 acre city centre regeneration programme on an immense scale to provide "world-class shopping, leisure and living at the heart of a world-class city", due for completion in 2008, Capital of Culture year.[16] Although regularly handling over 30 million tonnes of cargo a year, the docks are now far distant with a workforce reduced to under 500: scrap metal has replaced manufactured goods as the main export trade, a change of greater economic and symbolic significance than the metamorphosis of Ford into Jaguar out at Halewood at the opposite outskirts of the city.

A latecomer to successful implementation of the process, Liverpool now applies state of the art regeneration procedures (as befits what the architect Will Alsop has envisaged as the western gateway to the northern 'supercity' spanning the M62 motorway corridor from Liverpool via Manchester and Leeds across to Hull). Alongside courses on social exclusion, the Department of Sociology at the University of Liverpool now offers a flagship MA programme on 'Cities, Culture and Regeneration' with Liverpool as exemplary case study, the 'ideal environment' (the brochure asserts) in which to study and contribute to key policy and academic debates about the relationship between culture and regeneration.[17] Inspired by the 1999 Rogers Report, *Towards an Urban Renaissance*, Liverpool Vision, the nation's first Urban Regeneration Company, bridges key public and private agencies in promotion of a 'Strategic Regeneration Framework' (based on seven 'action areas'), with partnership funding from English Partnerships, the North West Development Agency and the City Council. Having waited so long, Liverpool is comparatively well-placed to benefit from regeneration. While badly damaged by the Second World War blitz, the remarkable waterfront and public architecture of England's finest Victorian city (recently celebrated in a highly

---

[16] Promotional literature is available from the Paradise Project Information Centre (76-78 Lord Street, Liverpool) and the website: [http://www.liverpool psda.co.uk].

[17] For further details, see the Department's website: [http://www.liv.ac.uk/sspsw].

successful new version of Pevsner's guide) (see Sharples 2004) subsequently escaped some of the worst excesses of late twentieth-century 'planning' vandalism, perhaps the one advantage of the city's declining fortunes at the time (and an interesting parallel with Providence, Rhode Island, America's 'renaissance city') (Leazes and Motte 2004).[18] Established in 2002, HELP – the Historic Environment of Liverpool Project – brought the now obligatory partnership approach (embracing English Heritage, the North West Development Agency, Liverpool Vision, National Museums Liverpool, Liverpool Culture Company and the City Council) to the promotion of the rich architectural heritage, now valued as "a unique asset that can help provide a sustainable future for the city as it continues to change and develop" (Cossons 2003). Then in July 2004 came UNESCO inscription for the Liverpool Maritime Mercantile City World Heritage Site which covers far more than the Pier Head with its iconic 'three graces' (and new cruise liner terminal currently under construction): the site embraces the Albert Dock Conservation Area (now one of the leading visitor attractions in the North West); the Stanley Dock Conservation Area (where the sheer scale but pinched interior construction of the gargantuan Tobacco Warehouse, closed since 1980, seemingly defy any re-use or regeneration); the 'commercial' centre around Castle Street, Dale Street and Old Hall Street (now increasingly residential and 'desirable' as commercial palaces are transformed into luxury apartments); the William Brown Street 'Cultural Quarter' (where Victorian civic pride reached its acme, a heritage preserved with requisite commercial acumen by National Museums Liverpool and soon to be enhanced by major renovation schemes for the City Central Libraries); and the warehouses and merchants houses of Lower Duke Street, historic buildings which contribute much to the character of the 'Rope Walks', the parallel narrow streets which now provide the main focus of the city's thriving night life and creative industries sector. Yet another partnership scheme, the Townscape Heritage Initiative was launched in 2005, aided by Heritage Lottery Funding, to bring properties back into a good state of repair, adapt them for new uses and restore historic details.

---

[18] In June 2005, the Royal Society of Arts (RSA) in the United States organised a major international symposium at the Rhode Island School of Design, "Transforming Urban Communities: Lessons from Providence, Rhode Island, and Liverpool, England".

World Heritage Site inscription should have considerable long-term benefit for Liverpool. Will the same apply to the award of European Capital of Culture status in 2008? Announced in June 2003, this was an unexpected (but most welcome) success. The local authorities have openly acknowledged that expectations extended no further than the initial boost simply of bidding for the coveted and prestigious award, of establishing the city's credentials to be judged alongside more favoured (and less denigrated) locations. To its surprise (and delight), the Council's 'Culture Company' is now transforming its role (no easy task) from civic boosterism to major project delivery. Thanks to World Heritage inscription and Capital of Culture status, Liverpool has a brace of glittering prizes (with attendant benefits in tourism, inward investment and employment), more than adequate compensation for the end of the second round of Objective One funding in 2006. Given this impressive record, it was only fitting that Liverpool F.C. should return to European winning ways. The victory against the odds in the Champions League final in 2005 instantly served as metaphor for the city's revival and rehabilitation. Here for once was a Liverpool story with which the tabloid press wished to identify, hence headlines proclaiming "We're all scousers now". Adorned in fake wigs, breakfast television presenters somewhat guilelessly adapted Harry Enfield's 'scouse git' routine for the joyous celebration, part of a national 'freak show' in which "everybody from Natasha Kaplinsky to Tony Blair appeared to transmogrify into plastic Scousers overnight". Amidst the euphoria, only the most dyspeptic were concerned about the psychological impact on scousers themselves, so well attuned to "wallowing in mawkish laments about their defeats": success, it was feared, "could seriously damage their self-image of put-upon miserablist isolationism" (Hume 2005).

There are interesting historical ironies to observe here. In early exercises in urban promotion, culture was deployed as a counterweight to provide legitimacy and pride, to counteract the otherwise philistine, mercenary and squalid aspects of the great seaport's commercial success in the nineteenth century, "to redeem Liverpool from the reproach of an exclusive devotion to commercial pursuits and the acquisition of wealth" (*Daily Post* 22 February 1862). In the later attempts to diversify into industry, culture served as a form of proxy indicator designed to 'sell' the area, to attract manufacturing investment in Merseyside. No longer a civilising counterweight to commerce, culture was the handmaiden of manufacturing industry, providing the opportunity to display the 'new' Liverpool with its state of the art industrial estates. One of the main visitor attractions in 1951 during the Festival of Britain was the futuristic Skylon towering above the 'Daylight on Industry' exhibition, while in the 750th anniversary celebrations in 1957 the Cleveland Square-Paradise Street area was transformed from a bomb site into a 'white tent town' with 75,000 square feet of display space for the 'Industry Advances' exhibition.[19] Nowadays, by contrast, culture itself is hailed as the commercial driver, the best hope for sustained economic prosperity in the 'new Livercool'.

There are grounds to question this concentration on cultural and creative industries. Sociologists are warning of 'culture wars' between cultural policy as a tool for economic growth and cultural policy as an expression of grassroots and community-based activity – the kind of 'scouse' culture that has been so creative in dialectic reaction to recent economic adversity (Jones and Wilks-Heeg 2004: 341-60).[20] There is an important spatial dimension behind such concerns. In its official conception, cultural re-branding is reinforcing (perhaps rather too dramatically) the city-centre focus of the regeneration agenda, markedly different from interwar attempts at redefining (and reviving) Liverpool through a policy of outlying industrial diversification in Speke, Aintree and Kirkby. No longer stigmatised, Liverpool itself is the region's 'unique selling point', its cultural and 'historic' core. The rich legacy of vacated warehouses, lofts and old office buildings is being converted into stunning apartments, the latest exercise in re-cycling of city centre space – a century ago, when commercial space was at a premium, the iconic three graces, the epicentre of the World Heritage site, were built upon land reclaimed from a redundant central dock. The population of the city centre has increased some fourfold in the 1990s with bijou accommodation for affluent young professionals, miles away in every sense from the deprived outer estates. Liverpool it seems is following the pattern of Glasgow, the last British city to enjoy European city of culture status in 1990: a rapidly regenerating and

---

[19] There is a separate volume of cuttings and other material for 1957 in the Liverpool Record Office, see "Liverpool Charter Celebrations: 750th Anniversary, 1957" at [Hf394.5.SEV].

[20] See also the free magazine, *Nerve: promoting grassroots arts and culture on Merseyside*.

gentrifying urban core surrounded by a ring of intensely disadvantaged residential areas. (Garcia 2004: 312-326)

Within the city centre itself, 'official' culture is being prioritised in self-defeating manner, denying space to the alternative, diverse and challenging cultural forms of expression which have contributed so much to the city's cultural creativity and distinctive identity. As culture is commodified into corporate blandness, alternative and individual outlets cannot afford the regenerated rents, while public spaces in the city centre are being privatised and sanitised by developers (and their attendant security staff and cctv cameras), again at the expense of a diverse and vibrant street culture. For the historian there are echoes here of the 'clean-up' ahead of the 750th anniversary celebrations in 1957 with the closure of the original site of Paddy's Market, "the coloured seamen's bazaar"; the removal of Codman's Punch and Judy show from its time-honoured Lime Street location to the windswept plateau where business soon hit 'rock bottom'; and a concerted but abortive attempt to rid city centre streets of barrow boys "called a variety of things from spivs to archaic anachronisms". It was also the year when decisions were taken to abandon both the overhead railway, the 'docker's umbrella', and the tramway system.[21] With a thoroughness beyond the 1957 exercise, Liverpool city centre is currently being improved in appearance (the festival of litter, noted by Bill Bryson, however, still continues if on a less spectacular scale (Bryson 1996: 235)) but is this at the cost of its distinct identity, that 'otherness' so cherished in its past?

Although the statistics lag somewhat behind the cranes and the property developers, the census figures for 2001 should prompt concern. For a future premised on culture and consumption, these statistics fail to register any urban renaissance with the average household income throughout Liverpool just 79% of the national figure. Judged against the national average, levels of health, qualifications, home and car ownership are comparatively low in Liverpool, while those of unemployment, lone parenting and house rentals are comparatively high.[22] However, these figures fail to take account of the high levels of

---

[21] See the Town Clerk's Press Cuttings for 1957 in the Liverpool Record Office, [352CLE/CUT1/95].

[22] The figures, available from the National Statistics website [www.statistics.gov.uk], are given prominence in the *Visitor Management Plan*

disposable income of visitors attracted to the city, whether rich Dubliners visiting their weekend second apartments in Liverpool, a staggering reversal of former migrant flows (see *Guardian* 5 February 2001), or affluent 'cultural' tourists whose ever-increasing numbers are fuelling a hotel boom. Consumption aside, perhaps the most noteworthy aspect of statistics drawn from the 2001 census relates to Liverpool's ethnic composition. Once so proud of its cosmopolitanism, Liverpool is now one of the least ethnically diverse of British cities with small numbers of post-1945 'new Commonwealth' migrants. Those categorised as Asian or Asian British in the 2001 census constituted only 1.1% of the city's population against a national average of 4.6%, while the Black British registered 1.2% against a national average of 2.1%. In this respect, the strapline of the successful capital of culture bid, "The world in one city", drew upon Liverpool's historical legacy rather than its contemporary complexion. A startling historical reversal, it may indeed be open to question as to whether Liverpool, the most multi-cultural and un-English of Victorian provincial cities, now has a sufficiently cosmopolitan and bohemian complexion to attract the highly mobile 'creative classes' regarded by Richard Florida as the key drivers of economic growth in the post-industrial city (see Florida 2002).

Despite its impressive head start in accommodating migrants, 'cosmopolitan' Liverpool was not to develop into the role model or front-runner for the multi-cultural Britain which has emerged since the Second World War. Doubtless the city's rapidly declining fortunes in the twentieth century made it an unappealing destination for later generations of migrants – it was this continuing downturn which prompted an outward 'scouse diaspora' as many Liverpudlians sought better times elsewhere. But there was another factor: the growing reputation for racism, first experienced by the Chinese in the Edwardian years. In a seemingly paradoxical historical process, tensions were to persist, and at times explode into riot, despite the absence of significant new immigration and the high levels of mixed dating, marriages and parentage. For the long-established black community, the pervasive distress and deprivation were compounded by discrimination. For 'new Commonwealth' migrants, depressed and 'racialised'

---

drawn up by PLB Consulting Ltd in April 2005 for the Liverpool World Heritage Site.

Liverpool was a far from enticing proposition. The success of the city's current cultural and creative renaissance might well depend upon its ability to restore and enhance its former cosmopolitan and bohemian complexion and 'edge', that remarkable scouse blend that has contributed so much to Liverpool's culture, character and history.[23]

---

[23] For a fuller discussion, see John Belchem and Donald M. MacRaild (2006: 311-92).

Works Cited

Research Literature

Anon. (1909): *The Sport of Civic Life, or Art and the Municipality*. Liverpool.

Batey, Peter (1999): "Merseyside", in: Peter Roberts, Kevin Thomas and Gwyndaf Williams (eds.): *Metropolitan planning in Britain: a comparative study*. London: Regional Studies Association, 97-111.

Belchem, John (ed.) (2006): *Liverpool 800: culture, character and history*. Liverpool: Liverpool UP.

— (2000/2006): *Merseypride: essays in Liverpool exceptionalism*. Liverpool. Liverpool UP.

— and Donald M. MacRaild (2006): "Cosmopolitan Liverpool", in: Belchem (ed.): *Liverpool 800: culture, character and history*. Liverpool: Liverpool UP, 311-392.

Bower, Fred (1936): *Rolling Stonemason: An Autobiography*. London: Jonathan Cape.

Bryson, Bill (1992/1996): *Notes from a Small Island*. London: Black Swan.

Chun, Dongho (2002): "Collecting collectors: The Liverpool Art Club and its exhibitions 1872-1895", *THSLC* 151, 127-149.

D'Aeth, F.G. (1912): "Liverpool", in: Bernard Bosanquet (ed.): *Social Conditions in Provincial Towns*. London: Macmillan.

Davies, S. et al. (1992): *Genuinely Seeking Work: mass unemployment on Merseyside in the 1930s*. Birkenhead.

Dickens, Charles (1869): *The Uncommercial Traveller*.

Drake, B.K. (1989): "The Liverpool-African voyage c. 1790-1807: commercial problems", in: Roger Anstey and Paul Edward H. Hair (eds.): *Liverpool, the African Slave Trade and Abolition*. Liverpool: Historic Society of Lancashire and Chesshire, no page numbers.

Drescher, Seymour (1988): "The Slaving Capital of the World: Liverpool and national opinion in the age of abolition", *Slavery and Abolition* 9, 128-143.

Du Noyer, Paul (2002): *Liverpool: Wondrous Place: Music from the Cavern to the Coral*. London: Virgin.

Enfield, William (1773): *An essay towards the history of Leverpool; drawn up from the papers left by the late G. Perry*. Warrington.

Florida, Richard (2002): *The Rise of the Creative Class*. New York: Basic Books.

Francis, J. Leazes Jr. and Mark T. Motte (2004): *Providence: The Renaissance City*. Boston: Northeastern UP.

Fraser, W. Hamish and I. Maver (eds.) (1996): *Glasgow volume ii: 1830 to 1912*. Manchester: Manchester UP.

Garcia, Beatriz (2004): "Cultural policy and urban regeneration in Western European cities: lessons from experience, prospects for the future", *Local Economy* 19, 312-326.

Gideon, Ben-Tovim (2003): "Futures for Liverpool", in: Ronaldo Munck (ed.): *Reinventing the City*. Liverpool: Liverpool UP, 227-246.

Grant, Linda (2002): *Still Here*. London: Little Brown.

Hair, Paul Edward Hedley (ed.) (1996): *Arts, Letters, Society: a miscellany commemorating the centenary of the Faculty of Arts at the University of Liverpool*. Liverpool: Liverpool UP.

Henderson, W.O. (1933): "The Liverpool Office in London", *Economica* xiii, 473-479.

Hollett, D. (1988): *Merseyside and the 19th century emigrant trade to Australia*. Birkenhead.

Jones, Paul and Stuart Wilks-Heeg (2004): "Capitalising Culture: Liverpool 2008", *Local Economy* 19, 341-360.

Kearns, Gerry and Paul Laxton (2002): "Ethnic Groups as Public Health Hazards: the Famine Irish in Liverpool and Lazaretto Politics", in: Esteban Rodríguez-Ocaña (ed.): *The Politics of the Healthy Life: An International Perspective*. Sheffield: European Association for the History of Medicine and Health Publication, 13-40.

Kelly, Thomas (1981): *For Advancement of Learning: The University of Liverpool 1881-1981*. Liverpool: Liverpool UP.

Meegan, Richard (2003): "Urban Regeneration, Politics and Social Cohesion: The Liverpool Case", in: Ronaldo Munck (ed.): *Reinventing the City*. Liverpool: Liverpool UP, 227-246.

Muir, Ramsay (1907): *History of Liverpool*. London: Williams and Norgate.

— (1906): *William Roscoe: An inaugural lecture*. Liverpool.

Muspratt, Edmund Knowles (1916/1917): *My Life and Work*. London and New York: John Lane.

Powell, Frank J. (1904): *The Guide to the Church Congress and Ecclesiastical Art Exhibition held in Liverpool, October 1-7 1904*. London: Maltravers House.

Rathbone, P.H. (1875): *The Political Value of Art to the Municipal Life of a Nation: A Lecture Delivered at the Free Library Liverpool*. Liverpool.

Read, G. (1993): "The Flood-Gate of the Old World: a study in ethnic attitudes", *Journal of American Ethnic History* 13, 31-47.

Reilly, Charles Herbert (1927): "Some Liverpool Buildings", *Impressions of Liverpool*. Liverpool.

— (1938): *Scaffolding in the Sky: A Semi-architectural Autobiography*. London: Routledge.

Sharples, Joseph (2004): *Liverpool: Pevsner Architectural Guides*. New Haven and London.

Shaw, Frank (1971/1988): *My Liverpool*. Parkgate.

Stobart, Jon (2002): "Culture versus commerce: societies and spaces for elites in eighteenth-century Liverpool", *Journal of Historical Geography* 28, 471-485.

Turvil, Andrew (ed.) (2004): *The Good Food Guide 2005*. London: Which? Books.

White, Brian David (1951): *A History of the Corporation of Liverpool 1835-1914*. Liverpool: Liverpool UP.

Wilks-Heeg, Stuart (2003): "From World City to Pariah City? Liverpool and the Global Economy, 1850-2000", in: Ronaldo Munck (ed.): *Reinventing the City*. Liverpool: Liverpool UP, 36-52.

Wilson, Arline (1998): "The cultural identity of Liverpool, 1790-1850: the early learned societies", *Transactions of the Historic Society of Lancashire and Cheshire (THSLC)* 147, 55-80.

Newspaper Articles

Anon. (1850): "Emigration – Emigrants and Man-Catchers", *Morning Chronicle* 15 July.

Anon. (1862): "Festival of the Literary and Philosophical Society", *Daily Post* 22 February.

Anon. (1886): "Liverpool: Port, Docks and City", *Illustrated London News* 15 May.

Anon. (1901): "Talk in Town", *Liverpool Review* 1 June.

Anon. (1920): *Daily Post* 9 February.

Anon. (1982): *Daily Mirror* 11 October.

Anon. (2000): "Scousers put the accent on success", *The Guardian* 22 September.

Anon. (2001): "Dublin's rich add twist to tale of two cities", *The Guardian* 5 February.

Anon. (2003): "Livercool", *Tatler* March.

Cossons, Sir Neil (2003): *HELP* (newsletter October).

Grant, Linda (2003): "History broke Liverpool, and it broke my heart", *The Guardian* 5 June.

Hume, Mick (2005): "We're all Scousers now? Count me out", *The Times* 27 May.

The Lake District and Yorkshire Dales: Refuges from the Real World?

Ian Whyte

Abstract: The uplands of Northern England contain iconic landscapes which are known worldwide. The eighteenth-century movements of the Picturesque and Romanticism placed them centre-stage in terms of influencing landscape aesthetics. The fame of the Lake District in particular generated a growing tourist industry throughout the nineteenth century which placed increasing pressure on the landscape and generated a conservationism movement which again had a much wider than local influence. Out of the tensions between visitors and conservation arose the system of national parks that developed in England and Wales after the Second World War.

Key names and concepts: Daniel Defoe - Thomas Gray - Edmund Burke - Claude Lorrain - William Gilpin - William Wordsworth - John Ruskin - Beatrix Potter; Northern Uplands - Lake District - Conservation - Landscape Aesthetics - Picturesque - Claude Glasses - National Trust - 'Foot and Mouth' Disease - Windfarms - World Heritage.

1. Introduction

The uplands of Northern England encompass a wide variety of landscapes reflecting distinctive physical and human geographies. Some of these landscapes are iconic; instantly recognisable and world famous, like the Lake District. Others, such as the limestone pavements of the Yorkshire Dales, are less well known globally but are nevertheless still dramatic. This is reflected in the degree of protection given to the landscapes of these areas. This includes designations as national parks (the Lake District, Yorkshire Dales and Northumberland), Areas of Outstanding Natural Beauty (the North Pennines, Forest of Bowland and Arnside-Silverdale area) as well as many Sites of Special Scientific Interest (SSSIs) and nature reserves. Within these areas are World Heritage Sites like Hadrian's Wall and Fountains Abbey. These emphasise that the uplands of Northern England are not true wilderness areas: their landscapes represent an intricate fusion of the interactions of the physical environment and human society over several millennia, creating landscapes of great complexity and variety. The Lake District National Park Authority is currently preparing a bid for World Heritage status as a cultural landscape (Website). The roles of such landscapes in shaping the identity of Northern England and its inhabitants have changed over the last three centuries and are today multi-layered and complex. There is a good deal of truth in the suggestion that these areas act as refuges from the real world; but for whom, in what ways and under what constraints? Even today, despite the range of conservation designations which supposedly confers protection from undesirable planning developments, these landscapes are in many ways fragile and under threat. The aim of this chapter is to examine how these areas have developed their image of refuges from the real world, and the problems which this has generated for modern inhabitants and visitors alike. A good deal of the focus will be on the Lake District because it highlights particularly well many of the problems faced by such areas in the past and today.

2. The Northern Uplands and Changing Landscape Aesthetics

The ways in which the landscapes of areas like the Lake District and the Yorkshire Dales have been perceived have varied markedly since the early eighteenth century as a result of changing landscape aesthetics. Equally these areas, especially the Lake District, have affected the ways in which landscapes around the world have been viewed, described and consumed. Changing fashions in what constituted attractiveness in landscape have added elements to, and subtracted them from, the uplands of Northern England. These areas were not always as cherished as they are today. Before the mid-eighteenth century Northern England was not valued for its landscapes at all; its hills were judged to be wild and horrible, the people who inhabited them poor and backward. Travellers from the south, like Daniel Defoe, viewed the uplands in very negative terms. Defoe famously described Westmorland, the most upland county in England, as 'wild, barren and frightful' (Defoe 1971: 550). His description of crossing the Pennines between Rochdale and Leeds via Blackstone Edge sounds like an Alpine expedition (Defoe 1971: 488-489). This can be seen as part of a lowland-based mindset which valued arable farming and its landscapes, and looked down on livestock rearing (Smout 2000: 10-18; Winchester 2000: 2-4). Contemporary topographical descriptions of upland areas by writers who had been born and brought up among the fells and valleys emphasised, by contrast, the fertility of their pastures, their wealth in livestock, and the richness of their resources (Smout 2000: 10-18).

In terms of landscape aesthetics the accepted norm of beauty in the early eighteenth century was fertile, rolling lowland country. By the 1750s, however, tastes in landscape were starting to change and enthusiastic descriptions in prose and verse of the scenery of the Lake District began to attract the attention of the London literati (Andrews 1989). Even more influential were descriptions of Lake District scenery by the poet Thomas Gray, who visited the area in 1769. There are hints that the fells and valleys of the Lake District were already attracting at least some visitors by the time that Gray arrived and that there was an established tourist circuit which included Windermere, Derwentwater and Ullswater. His description of the Vale of Grasmere as 'a little unsuspected paradise [...] all is peace, rusticity and happy poverty, in its neatest, most becoming attire' (Bicknell 1984: 11) attracted much interest, although his over-dramatic and exaggerated descriptions of the scenery of valleys like Borrowdale tend to generate amusement rather than awe among modern readers. Nevertheless, his writing was an important influence in helping to make the Lake District fashionable (Bicknell 1984: 56).

By the later eighteenth-century British landscape aesthetics had developed from Burke's earlier distinction between the beautiful and the sublime to incorporate a third, intermediate category, the picturesque (Andrews 1989). A picturesque landscape was defined as a view that would look good in a picture, but specifically a picture composed by Claude Lorrain or one of his contemporaries who had worked in the Roman Campagna in the mid-seventeenth century. Lorrain's compositional structure was reminiscent of a stage set, with framing side-screens, a foreground with suitable figures, a water feature in the middle distance and a distant view of hills or mountains. From the 1770s a distinctive new activity developed, picturesque tourism, the aim of which was to decide to what degree nature fell short of art in producing ideal picturesque landscapes. Manuals such as the one by William Gilpin categorised the shape of Lake District fells, distinguishing those which had attractive, varied and rugged outlines (truly picturesque such as the Langdale Pikes) from more lumpish, rounded, unattractive forms (Gilpin 1786). Picturesque tourism was supported by guidebooks such as Thomas West's guide which took visitors to a series of viewpoints or 'stations' from which they could admire the landscape (West 1788). William Gilpin's published tours were more concerned with how to appreciate the landscape than with the practical details of where to stay and what to see. Under Gilpin's direction, visitors to the northern uplands and especially the Lake District examined particular views and then sketched or painted them or described them in prose or poetry (Gilpin 1786). Picturesque travellers came principally to see the lakes; the mountains merely served as distant backdrops. Many visitors carried with them Claude glasses, small convex mirrors which had the property of enlarging the foreground and diminishing the background. Their owners stood with their backs to the landscape and held up or suspended their glasses in order to study or sketch the views reflected in them. It was possible to overlay coloured filters on the Claude glass to give moonlit, winter or sunset effects. At Claife, above the western side of Lake Windermere opposite Bowness, a small observation house was built above the lake by a local landowner. It had windows with panes of different tinted glass which enabled visitors to view the scene under a variety of different light conditions (Bicknell 1984: 76).

After the outbreak of war with France in 1793 put much of Europe off-limits to travellers and prevented wealthy young men from undertaking the traditional Grand Tour (Black 1985), areas like the Lake District and the Pennines provided alternative, safer, venues, refuges from war, and visitor numbers increased. Gilpin's approach and the Picturesque aesthetic in general was readily satirised; crudely by Rowlandson in cartoon form and more subtly by Jane Austen in 'Northanger Abbey' (Bicknell 1984: 15). In the Lake District, however, it encouraged wealthy visitors to buy up land and build villas in styles and locations that were deemed suitably Picturesque, such as the circular classical house on Belle Isle, Lyulph's Tower above Ullswater, Wray Castle near Windermere and the rather ridiculous follies erected by a Mr. Pocklington on an island in Derwentwater (Bicknell 1984: 189-90). Picturesque tourism was also beginning to transform Lake District society by the end of the eighteenth century as inns began to cater for tourists as well as travellers while local people derived welcome additional income from hiring out horses and acting as guides. The impact of picturesque tourism on the Yorkshire Dales was more limited and more widely spread, but the Three Peaks area, especially Ingleborough, was much admired as, on a smaller scale, were individual features like waterfalls and caves.

Nevertheless, by the end of the eighteenth century, the rigid, restrictive and highly formalised approach of Picturesque tourism was starting to produce a backlash. In art this can be dated from Turner's (1798) paintings of Buttermere and Coniston which, instead of showing a clear outline of the surrounding hills depicts them vanishing imperceptibly into cloud and mist (Bragg 1990: 179-80). Wordsworth, in his 'Tintern Abbey' poem of the same year, specifically rejected the Picturesque aesthetic, though he had formerly been a disciple of Gilpin, reflecting a desire to experience nature as it was, and as it affected him personally, rather than as it was supposed to be under an arbitrary set of conventions. The Romantic Movement, of which he was a key protagonist, quite consciously represented a rejection of the increasing unattractiveness of the urbanisation and industrialisation which was starting to disfigure entire regions of Britain as the country began to move into a mature industrial economy. The Romantic Movement and its impact on Northern England is especially associated with Wordsworth (1770-1850). Indeed, although Wordsworth is comparatively little read in Britain today, it is true to say that we still view landscape through his eyes, though at several removes via the work of later writers. In 1810 Wordsworth produced the first edition of what became known as his 'Guide to the Lakes'. Like Gilpin he wrote a manual on how to appreciate and understand the Lake District landscape, in effect a model regional geography emphasising the way in which the present landscape was the result of the interaction of physical and human elements over thousands of years (Whyte 2000). If he idealised the society of the Lake District dales somewhat his observations on the landscapes they had helped to create were acute and his views on conservation are as relevant to the area today as when he first wrote them. In particular, his comment that he saw the Lake District as 'a sort of national property' in which everyone in England had an interest has been widely seen as a precursor of the national park movement (Robinson 2005: 150).

3. The Northern Uplands and the Development of the Conservation Movement

Wordsworth had been concerned about the impact of tourist developments on the Lake District landscape from as early as 1799 when he came back to his home area to live at Dove Cottage in Grasmere. In later years he was keenly aware of the classic paradox of tourism – that too many visitors will destroy what they have come to see. In his later years Wordsworth fought to prevent the opening of a branch railway line to Windermere (Bicknell 1984: 187-198). Having already seen many undesirable changes resulting from the impact of visitors arriving on foot and horseback he fully appreciated the undesirable impacts of the unregulated mass tourism that the railway would bring. His efforts were unsuccessful, however, and the line was opened in 1847 leading, as he had predicted, to a sharp rise in visitor numbers. In the second half of the nineteenth century, however, Wordsworth's writings were taken up and used as ammunition by a new generation of conservationists, both locals and incomers, among whom John Ruskin and Canon H. Rawnsley were leading figures (Berry and Beard 1980). Although unable to prevent Manchester Corporation from damming the Thirlmere valley to provide drinking water for the city's industrial population, they successfully fought off other schemes to construct branch railways and open up quarries and mineral deposits (Dowthwaite 1991). Rawnsley himself was one of the founders of the National Trust in 1895 (Bragg 1990: 163). An early policy of the Trust was to buy up lakeshore frontages around Windermere, Derwentwater and Ullswater in order to preserve public access to the lakes. By the end of the nineteenth century the development of villas as summer homes, or even as all-year-round residences for businessmen commuting by rail to work in Manchester, was having major impacts on the landscape not just in terms of the architectural style of the mansions but also in the exotic species of conifers which were planted in their grounds. Blackwell, near Windermere, built for a Manchester brewer at the end of the nineteenth century in an Arts and Crafts style, is a good example (Westall 1991). Tourism, however, was carefully regulated, particularly around the railhead at Windermere, to preserve the area's exclusive atmosphere (Walton 1991). Working-class day visitors were limited in practical terms as to where they could go. They were equally constrained in the types of entertainment which were available to them, a policy which resonates in some of the Lake District National Park Authority's recent decisions about the suitability or otherwise of certain types of recreation. Not everyone supported the conservation lobby though. In the later nineteenth century there are signs of growing tensions between them, as they tried to limit new industrial and infrastructure developments, and local people who wanted to see more employment and development in the area. Hoteliers and businessmen were concerned to expand tourism, the conservationists to control it. By the later nineteenth century the nature of Lake District tourism had changed too. There was a gradual shift in the focus of visitors' interests from a desire to see the lakes, to a growing interest in walking the fells. In the later nineteenth century the area saw the start of serious rock climbing (Bragg 1990: 169-177). Tourism in the later nineteenth century had a more modest impact in the Yorkshire Dales but nevertheless the coming of the railway brought growing numbers of visitors from the industrial towns of West Yorkshire to centres like Skipton, Ingleton and Settle. The completion of the Settle-Carlisle railway in 1876 opened up more remote parts of the area.

4. Towards National Parks

New conservation issues continued to surface after the First World War to join existing debates. Early motor vehicles brought noise and congestion. Seaplanes operating from Windermere were seen by many as a nuisance. The installation of overhead electricity lines and telephone cables was considered an eyesore (Berry and Beard 1980). In particular, opposition was directed against the activities of the Forestry Commission which, from 1919, began to purchase extensive areas of fell and moorland to create large conifer plantations (Symonds 1936). In the Lake District the afforestation of much of Ennerdale increased awareness of the extent of landscape change involved in creating conifer plantations, as well as the loss of access for walkers and cyclists. After the Forestry Commission had bought up land in Eskdale and Dunnerdale with the aim of creating new forests an agreement was reached in 1936 between the Council for the Protection of Rural England and the Forestry Commission that the central 300 square miles of the Lake District fells should not have any further plantations, an agreement that still holds good today. During the 1920s and 1930s outdoor recreation, including fell walking, rock climbing, camping and cycling, became a mass activity, centred on northern industrial towns and cities such as Manchester and Sheffield (Tebbutt 2004), encouraged by the provision of youth hostels and the active marketing of one inch to the mile Ordnance Survey maps of popular tourist areas (Daniels 1998; Matless 1998). This increase in walking in the uplands was less of a problem in the Lake District where extensive surviving areas of common pasture preserved de facto, if not de jure, public access to the fells. In the Peak District there were clashes between gamekeepers on large estates, keen to enforce the laws of trespass to prevent walkers disturbing the grouse, and groups of ramblers, culminating in the famous mass-trespass on Kinder Scout in 1932 (Shoard 1987). By the mid 1930s public and government opinion was starting to move towards creating national parks (Robinson 2005). The legislation permitting this was delayed by the Second World War and was passed as the National Parks and Access to the Countryside Act of 1949. The Lake District was designated a national park in 1951, the Yorkshire Dales in 1954 and Northumberland in 1956. At a later date further upland and semi-upland areas of high landscape quality but smaller in extent and in some cases with more limited rights of public access, were designated as Areas of Outstanding Natural Beauty (Robinson 2005: 154).

The guiding aims of the national parks were to conserve landscape and scenery, to encourage quiet enjoyment and recreation, and to promote the social and economic well-being of the populations living and working within their boundaries. Conflicts between these aims were soon apparent although the tension between development and conservation was defused by the adoption from 1995 of the 'Sandford principle' under which if there was a clash between the two then the interests of conservation should automatically prevail. A continuing problem for the national parks was a lack of adequate funding. In their early years national parks operated on tiny budgets and the original aim that their authorities should have enough money to be able to buy up a substantial proportion of the land within their boundaries as it came on to the market was never realised (MacEwen and MacEwen 1987). The powers of the national park planning boards were exercised relatively lightly during the 1950s and 1960s but thereafter with more rigour. Conservation interests could be circumvented when central government deemed it necessary though. The upgrading of the A66 road through the northern part of the Lake District in the early 1970s, to provide faster links to the new M6 motorway from the declining industrial area of west Cumbria, showed that national government could quite cynically over-ride national park objectives when it suited them (Berry and Beard 1980).

5. Mass Tourism and the Uplands

The completion of the M6 motorway to Carlisle in the early 1970s greatly increased the accessibility of areas like the Lake District and the western parts of the Yorkshire Dales for day visitors from the south. Although accurate figures are not available estimates suggest that in the 1990s as many as 16 million people visited the Lake District each year, the majority using their own vehicles rather than public transport. The increased flow of vehicles generated congestion on narrow, winding roads and parking problems at honeypot sites like Ambleside, Grasmere, Keswick and Hawkshead that have still to be resolved. Another spin off from faster road access was the demand for sites for both residential and touring caravans (Berry and Beard 1980). In terms of residential accommodation the increasing trend towards taking foreign holidays has caused a shift from people visiting the uplands of Northern England, particularly the Lake District, for extended holidays to visitors coming for weekend breaks and day trips.

The post-Second World War period has seen a further boom in outdoor recreation, including fell walking, rock climbing and mountain biking. In the towns and villages this is reflected in the proliferation of shops specialising in the sale of outdoor equipment to an extent that retailers servicing local people rather than visitors are driven out. Despite the amount of outdoor recreation available, however, many visitors focus on the honeypot sites and do not venture far from their vehicles; the Lake District, for many, has become a retail experience with an attractive backdrop of lakes and fells, something which is epitomised by the success of firms like Lakeland (formerly Lakeland Plastics) at Windermere whose operations have no real link with the region or its resources.

If the Lake District and the Yorkshire Dales do indeed serve as refuges from the real world, who do they cater for and how inclusive is their attraction? There has been recent concern that the Lake District in particular (and British national parks more generally) tend to attract visitors who are predominantly white, middle-aged and middle-class, with very limited participation from people with ethnic minority backgrounds. The Lake District has tended to cater for more discerning and well-educated visitors throughout its history as a holiday venue. Past visitors were influenced by Wordsworth. Today the white middle-class visitors may have perceptions of the area which have been shaped by different writers such as Arthur Ransome, whose children's novels, including 'Swallows and Amazons', portrayed the area as a kind adventure playground for the children of well-heeled parents. Younger children may identify the area with the Postman Pat stories, seeing it as full of quirky but inoffensive characters. The attitudes of many walkers have been shaped by the guidebooks of Alfred Wainwright. Self-consciously old fashioned and with a quirky sense of humour, Wainwright has done more to popularise walking in the Lake District, the Yorkshire Dales and intermediate areas like the Howgill Fells than any other writer. The Lake District also forms a background to many of the children's stories of Beatrix Potter. Although known worldwide these stories have a particular resonance in Japan where they are used to teach English. As a result they have a quite specific and highly distinctive view of the Lake District as 'Peter Rabbit Country' and they visit Potter's farm at Hill Top as a place of pilgrimage (Squire 1993).

6. Rural Refuges Under Pressure

These rural refuges, however cherished and idealised, are not immune from economic pressures which pose threats to the survival of their cherished landscapes. The future of farming is one of the most critical issues. In the Pennines and the Lake District hill farming fared reasonably well in the 1950s and the 1960s under a regime where grants for modernising buildings and access roads were widely available, and deficiency payments were made to support farmers when market prices for their produce were insufficient to provide adequate incomes. This support was provided for social rather than economic reasons, to maintain rural communities in being and check out-migration and decline. Following the advent of the EEC, now the EU, headage payments for each breeding ewe encouraged the over-stocking of pastures to the detriment of heather moorland and upland grasslands. During the same period hill farms increasingly lost their beef and dairying activities as these became more specialist activities. While increasingly concentrating solely on sheep farming, the amalgamation of holdings reduced numbers of farms and raised their average size, while cost-cutting led to a steady decline in numbers of hired farm workers (Reynolds 1988). The trend towards higher grazing intensities and growing pressure on the landscape, which was causing concern over loss of biodiversity and a growing problem of erosion, has been checked by the development of the Environmentally Sensitive Areas scheme covering much of the Lake District and parts of the Yorkshire Dales (see website). Under this scheme farmers receive additional payments for environmentally-friendly activities such as reducing stocking levels to allow the recovery of heather moorland, repairing drystone walls and field barns, encouraging flower-rich hay meadows and developing more sensitive management policies for farm woodlands and wetland sites. Outside the ESAs the Countryside Stewardship Scheme has brought similar benefits (see website). These developments have been seen by many people as the start of a process by which farmers may in time become part-time countryside stewards, a trend which many farmers view with mixed feelings.

Recent economic trends and particularly the direct and indirect impacts of the foot and mouth disease outbreak in 2001 have made conditions even tougher for hill farmers. Some have given up entirely. Others are diversifying into tourist activities such as running guest houses and tearooms or developing a range of small businesses. An important development has been the growing exploitation of niche markets in food, including Herdwick lamb, sold through local outlets and farmers' markets.

The foot and mouth crisis also demonstrated clearly that the income from tourism in the Lake District and upland areas of Northern England was far greater than that from agriculture. Tourism has been seen as an important engine of economic growth in rural areas. There have been efforts to encourage tourists away from traditional honey-pot areas like the central Lake District. The heritage potential of the lead mining districts of the Pennine Dales, the villages of the Eden Valley and the maritime heritage of West Cumbria has been given greater emphasis by the regional tourist board (see website).

In a situation where rural economies are so dependent on tourism, sensitive management of the landscape is essential for both local inhabitants and visitors. However, the interests of various interest groups may be difficult or even impossible to reconcile, a problem which was first evident in the late nineteenth century with the tensions between conservationists and developers. Sensitive management is needed, and the Lake District National Park Authority faces a difficult task in balancing many sets of conflicting interests. Their handling of the foot and mouth crisis is a good example of the tensions that exist today. Although it directly affected only small areas within the Lake District National Park, the threat of the disease spreading, especially the possibility that it might be carried on human feet, led to the national park officer appearing on television and virtually announcing that the area was closed to visitors. The effect on tourist-related businesses was catastrophic and there were many complaints that while farmers received much sympathy, and substantial financial compensation, tourist businesses got no assistance. Many people considered that a more sensitive message would have been to emphasise that while the footpaths were closed the towns and villages were still open for business. There were grumbles and a newspaper advertisement campaign that the Lake District National Park Authority, an unelected body, had the power to ruin the livelihoods of local people.

Similar problems have emerged with the imposition in the spring of 2005 of a 10 miles per hour speed limit for power boats in Windermere, the last of the lakes on which such craft are now permitted. The Lake District National Park Authority's aim was, quite deliberately, to make waterskiing and the use of jet-skis impossible, so removing the problem of the noise generated by power boats and the danger they posed to other lake users. This was in line with their policy of promoting 'quiet recreation' within the national park (see website). The ban, brought in with five years' warning, was seen as another example of heavy-handed management by power-boat enthusiasts who mounted a strong protest campaign claiming that the loss of income and jobs to hotels, restaurants, water-ski schools, petrol stations and boat chandlers would be substantial if the speed limit was imposed (see website). With the ban now in force for some months the National Park Authority can claim that their efforts to encourage quiet recreation have been successful. However, there has been a definite fall in tourist income in the Windermere area, some of which may be directly related to the ban. In addition the loss in income to the National Park Authority from a reduction in mooring fees and extra costs for policing the speed limit has caused a financial crisis with wider repercussions.

The national parks have also been flexing their muscles over the use of four-wheel drive vehicles on green roads such as the Garburn Pass in the Lake District and Mastiles Lane in the Dales and while restrictions are at present voluntary, the possibility of an outright ban in the future exists. Motor cyclists and mountain bikers have watched the negotiations with some concern that their own activities may be next in line for regulation. The National Park Authority's responsibility for vetting planning applications within the Lake District seems to many people unduly inflexible and heavy handed; for example in not permitting alterations to old farm buildings to allow them to be developed for the use of small businesses. The National Trust, which owns 25% of the land within the Lake District National Park, has a similar reputation among some of its tenants.

Other external pressures threaten the peace and attractiveness of these refuges. One of the most contentious contemporary issues is the location of windfarms. Although their status as protected areas has so far prevented the siting of windfarms within the Lake District or Yorkshire Dales national parks there have been high profile cases where they have been approved in locations just beyond the national park boundary but in situations where they can be readily seen from within the park. The most prominent dispute at the moment is over the proposed siting of a large windfarm at Whinash near Tebay, in a corridor between the Lake District and Yorkshire Dales national parks. The area, one of high landscape quality, was omitted from both parks when their original limits were drawn up. The windfarm, if approved, will be a very prominent feature of the landscape (see websites).

A further problem associated with tourism in the national parks is the purchase of houses by outsiders for second homes and holiday lets. This has had the effect of pushing property prices up to levels which local people cannot afford and it is now becoming extremely difficult for younger people to get a foothold on the property ladder at all. The Yorkshire Dales have started to tackle this by placing restrictions on who can buy new housing, in order to keep prices down. Such a scheme was tried briefly in the Lake District during the Thatcher era but was stopped as being an unwarrantable interference in the normal workings of a free housing market (Clark 1982). Today a challenge might be possible under European human rights legislation.

In addition tourism in these areas seems to be experiencing more general difficulties which cannot be blamed on specific issues like the Windermere speed limit though. Changes in patterns of tourism, particularly the availability of budget air fares to European cities, may be making the area less attractive for short-break holidays and it has been claimed that hoteliers and restaurant owners in the area are seeing bookings fall because their prices are unrealistically high.

The Lake District especially can be seen as a contested landscape in which some voices are dominant but other ones are ignored. This has recently been articulated by the National Park Authority which proposed cancelling their programme of free guided walks on the grounds that they did not attract people from ethnic minorities and were aimed principally at white, middle-aged, middle-class visitors. This can lead to the question whose heritage is being preserved? Other tensions, between people born and brought up in the area and off-comers, can also be identified. The Lake District and Yorkshire Dales may seem to many people to be refuges from the real world but on their visits to these areas they bring the problems of the real world with them in the form of traffic congestion, parking and housing issues.

Real world pressures also surface in wider-scale challenges to the rural landscape of Britain. If the plans of the present government for massive house building and other infrastructure developments in southern and south east England go ahead, there may be relatively little real countryside left south of the Midlands in thirty years' time. If plans for a 'supercity' stretching from Merseyside and Greater Manchester across the Pennines into Yorkshire materialise there will be pressures right on the doorstep of the Yorkshire Dales National Park.

Meanwhile, as mentioned previously, plans are being drawn up for the Lake District to be put forward for consideration as a UNESCO World Heritage cultural landscape. Such a designation, while not bringing in any extra money to the region directly, would be a great boost in terms of publicity. But will this bid, if successful, secure the best possible future for the area? There is an important distinction to be made between the preservation and conservation of landscapes. The first implies fossilisation, turning the uplands into living museums. The second involves more active and dynamic management with the acceptance of structured change. Various possible scenarios for the future have been suggested. One is to withdraw management from the uplands as farming declines, creating more 'wild' landscapes. The reintroduction of former species of animals such as lynx has even been proposed. Lack of management is not a realistic option though. The idea of leaving the fellsides, with reduced levels of grazing as hill farming collapses, to revert to scrub woodland is superficially attractive and was seriously proposed by some after the foot and mouth outbreak (Potter 2001). It might be an interesting experiment for a small enclosed upland catchment but it is not an answer for the uplands as a whole. On the other hand preserving the Lake District as something approximating to Wordsworth's Lakeland with the addition of modern conveniences and car parks is equally undesirable to most people. A suitable balance will need to be struck between over-heavy intervention which restricts the rights and activities of both residents and visitors and a free-market laissez-faire approach which would threaten to destroy the traditional character of the uplands of Northern England. There are various ways in which such a balance may be achieved. Choosing an appropriate one which will satisfy as many people as possible while maximising continuity in the landscape will be the great task of national park planning boards in the next few decades.

Works Cited

Primary References

Defoe, Daniel (1971): *A Tour Through the Whole Island of Great Britain*. London: Penguin.

Gilpin, William (1786): *Observations, Relative Chiefly to Picturesque Beauty, made in the year 1772, on Several parts of England, Particularly the Mountains and Lakes of Cumberland and Westmorland*. London.

West, Thomas (1788): *A Guide to the Lakes*. London.

Research Literature

Andrews, Malcolm (1989): *The Search for the Picturesque: Landscape Aesthetics and Tourism, in Britain, 1760-1800*. Aldershot: Scolar.

Berry, Geoffrey and Geoffrey Beard (1980): *The Lake District: a Century of Conservation*. Edinburgh: Bartholomew.

Bicknell, Peter (1984): *The Illustrated Wordsworth's Guide to the Lakes*. Exeter: Webb & Bower.

Black, Jeremy (1985): *The British and the Grand Tour*. London: Croom Helm.

Bragg, Melvyn (1990): *Land of the Lakes*. London: Hodder & Stoughton.

Clark, Gordon (1982): "Housing policy in the Lake District", *Transactions of the Institute of British Geographers* (new series) 7, 59-70.

Daniels, Stephen (1998): "Mapping national identities: the culture of cartography with particular reference to the Ordnance Survey", in: Geoffrey Cubitt (ed.): *Imagining Nations*. Manchester: Manchester UP, 112-131.

Dowthwaite, Michael (1991): "Defenders of Lakeland: the Lake District Defence Society in the late nineteenth century", in: Oliver Westall (ed.): *Windermere in the Nineteenth Century*. Lancaster: Lancaster University, 49-62.

Matless, David (1998): *Landscapes and Englishness*. London: Reaktion.

McEwen A. & M. (1987): *Greenprints for the Countryside? The Story of Britain's National Parks*. London: Allen & Unwin.

Potter, Clive (2001): "Farming on the edge, landscape in crisis?", *Landscapes* 2.2, 24-28.

Reynolds, Shelagh L. (1988): *Agriculture, landscape change and planning in the Lake District National Park since 1945*. PhD thesis, Lancaster University.

Robinson, Guy (2005): "A kind of national property?", in: Ian D. Whyte and Angus J.L. Winchester (eds.): *Society, Landscape and Environment in Upland Britain*. Society for Landscape Studies (supplementary series 2), 149-161.

Shoard, Marion (1987): *This Land is our Land: the Struggle for Britain's Countryside*. London: Paladin.

Smout, T.C. (2000): *Nature Contested. Environmental History in Scotland and Northern England since 1600*. Edinburgh: Edinburgh UP.
Squire, Shelagh (1993): "Valuing countryside: reflections on Beatrix Potter tourism", *Area* 25.1, 5-10.
Symonds, Henry Herbert (1936): *Afforestation in the Lake District*. London: Dent.
Tebbutt, Melanie (2004): "Landscapes of loss: moorlands, manliness and the First World War", *Landscapes* 5 (2), 69-90.
Walton, John. K. (1991): "The Windermere tourist trade in the age of the railway 1847-1912", in: Oliver Westall (ed.): *Windermere in the Nineteenth Century*. Lancaster: Lancaster University, 19-33.
Westall, Oliver (1991): "The retreat of Arcadia: Windermere as a select residential resort in the late nineteenth century", in: Oliver Westall (ed.): *Windermere in the Nineteenth Century*. Lancaster: Lancaster University, 34-48.
Whyte, Ian D. (2000): "Wordsworth's Guide to the Lakes and the geographical Tradition", *Area* 32 (1), 101-106.
Winchester, Angus J.L. (2000): *The Harvest of the Hills. Rural Life in Northern England and the Scottish Borders, 1400-1700*. Edinburgh: Edinburgh UP.

Websites

"Blackwell, the Arts and Crafts House", *visitcumbria* 3 November 2005. 24 November 2005 [http://www.visitcumbria.com/amb/blackwel.htm].
"Countryside Stewardship Scheme", *DEFRA (Department for Environment, Food and Rural Affairs)* 10 December 2002. 24 November 2005 [http://www.defra.gov.uk/erdp/schemes/css/default.htm].
"Environmentally Sensitive Area Scheme", *DEFRA (Department for Environnment, Food and Rural Affairs)* 10 December 2002. 24 November 2005 [http://www.defra.gov.uk/erdp/schemes/esas/default.htm].
"Lake District National Park World Heritage Site Status", *Lake District National Park Authority* (last update 2006). 24 November 2005 [http://www.lake-district.gov.uk/whs].
"Say no to the Whinash windfarm", *Committee 'Say NO To The Whinash Windfarm'* (last updated 2 March 2006). 24 November 2005 [http://www.nowhinashwindfarm.co.uk].
"Whinash windfarm public enquiry", *Whinash Enquiry* (last updated 3 March 2006). 24 November 2005 [http://www.persona.uk.com/whinash/].

Beyond the Industrial Revolution: the Transformation of Britain's Canals and their Cultural Meaning[1]

Richard Stinshoff

Abstract: This essay examines the transformation of Britain's narrow canals: Originally built as the first nationwide standardised system of transport infrastructure in the early industrial revolution, today they provide a remarkably popular post-industrial work and leisure environment. After exploring some of the historical and contemporary causes underlying this process, its cultural implications are discussed in a context of heritage and identity politics increasingly dominated by competing strategies for appropriating a much contested past.

Key names and concepts: Tom Rolt - Robert Aickman - William Morris; British Waterways Board - Industrial Past - Narrow Boat - Tow Paths - Tourism - Leisure Industry - Heritage.

1. The New Canal Age

Two hundred years after their first boom in the early 1790s, the inland waterways of Britain, namely the so-called *narrow canals*, have become remarkably popular again: this time, however, as a leisure and holiday Eldorado. Around 250,000 customers of hire boat companies every year are discovering the charm of spending a weekend or even their holidays on a cute, brightly painted and oddly shaped *narrow boat* (between 20 and 70 feet long, but only 7 feet wide). They are cruising along these seemingly inconspicuous watercourses at a leisurely maximum of two to three miles per hour. And thousands of people own a narrow boat, although this hobby doesn't come cheap at all, with costs for a fully fitted boat easily running up to £60,000 or

---

[1] This is an altered and updated version of an essay published under the title "Recycling Industrialization: The Fall and Rise of the British Canals", *Hard Times – Deutsch-Englische Zeitschrift* 75 (2003), 4-13.

even £70,000. Compared to the legions of walkers, hikers and bikers enjoying hundreds of miles of towpath the numbers of these modern 'boat-people', however, seem relatively modest. Cycling along the 87-mile Kennet-and-Avon Canal, which was reopened after complete restoration in 1990, had soon become so popular that a much protested £12.50 annual fee for cyclists was introduced in the summer of 1997 to reduce their numbers and improve peaceful coexistence with walkers, anglers and boaters (see *The Independent* 30 June 1997: 24). Today, cycling is only allowed on designated stretches of towpath and cycling permits are mandatory, but mostly free of charge.

By the beginning of our millennium the total annual number of people spending time on or along a canal in Britain was estimated at around 10 million per year – about the same number as visiting a National Trust property or site. There seems to be no limit to the ever growing number of enthusiasts indulging in "the fastest way of slowing down", according to a 1980s *British Waterways Board* promotional slogan.

Tourists taking the opportunity to explore the revitalised parts of central Manchester or central Birmingham on foot will experience the current canal-mania from yet another angle: particularly on weekends people are thronging the upscale pubs, bars, and restaurants in the restored Castlefield boat dock area in central Manchester or around Gas Street Basin in Birmingham's city centre. And on the inner city parts of the Bridgewater and Rochdale canals or the restored downtown stretches of the Birmingham Canal Network every day droves of smartly dressed crowds emerge from offices in meticulously remodelled Victorian canal-side warehouses or mills for a lunch-break stroll along the towpath. And canals are business: they account for £1.5 bn annual expenditure and 55,000 canal-related jobs.

No matter where you go, cityscape or countryside, you are never far away from a refurbished canal, especially in some of Britain's oldest industrial heartlands, namely the Midlands and the North West (i.e. in the Birmingham – Manchester – Liverpool triangle).

In fact, it seems difficult not to be fascinated by the canal environment: like a time-traveller you enter a late-eighteenth/early-nineteenth century landscape marked by towpaths, cast-iron distance markers, humpback-shaped brick bridges, hand-operated locks with oak gates and old loading cranes. Every once in a while you might pass a swing bridge carrying a country lane across the canal, or a derelict mill building about to be converted either into an industrial museum or into space for a variety of workshops, offices or small arts and crafts outfits. Exciting (and scary to some) is the passage through tunnels, some short, some over a mile or even longer. Usually, all this is backgrounded by the mild and serene beauty of what tourists tend to perceive as typically English countryside dotted with the occasional quaint old village or small town. The noises of trunk roads and railways are gracefully muffled by their distance, just far enough away to remind you that you have managed to escape from the hustle and bustle of the present. "It was possible to lose not just your sense of time, but almost to forget which century you were in", a journalist wrote, who travelled the Leeds-and-Liverpool Canal in the winter of 1994/95 (Stuart 1995: 38). And, from a canal boat perspective, even urban areas in the North of England seem to exude soothing calmness, either mixed with the solitude of grimy decay and dereliction or with the clean and beautified atmosphere of post-industrial revitalisation. Marketing such new perspectives on the industrial past have become a significant element in the attempts at creating a new image of the North. And the reuse of the remnants of its industrial past in a different socio-economic context has brought about a change in the perception of a region once dubbed the 'manufacturing heart' of the country.

Of course, you are aware that such enthusiastic perceptions of this dreamlike pastoral environment with its incredibly pastel-shaded sunsets, or the early mornings, when herons sluggishly soar up at the harsh sound of the boat's diesel not yet fully warmed up, are steeped in nostalgia and romanticism. After all, the rental boat ensures a return to the past *avec tout comfort*: central heating, hot and cold water, shower, toilets, gas stove, TV etc. none of the latest conveniences is missing. And if a water pipe is leaking, if the toilets don't flush, or if there is a short in the electric system, these are minor problems, usually quickly solved by a friendly mechanic, even if he has to drive 50 miles to get to your mooring place.

Altogether, it seems rather symptomatic that, today, old industrial canals tend to evoke sensations and moods which nineteenth and early-twentieth century travellers and observers would have associated with the Thames, the Norfolk Broads, the Lake District, or other romantic counterpoints to Victorian industrialism. Meanwhile, such perceptions (coupled with a hefty dose of sustainable development) seem to underpin even official statements of the multiple purposes that canals are supposed to fulfil:

> Today, the waterways are valued as a leisure and recreation resource for millions, are a part of our land drainage and water distribution systems whilst still providing an environmentally friendly means of transport for coal, aggregates and other materials. Where once derelict canals were an eyesore and target for vandals, they are now becoming a focus for regeneration and development schemes. These canals are an important part of our nation's past and future. The Government is committed to ensuring that they are recognised as a valuable public asset, that their full potential is secured and that as many people as possible, from all walks of life, can enjoy and benefit from what they have to offer. (DEFRA 1999a)

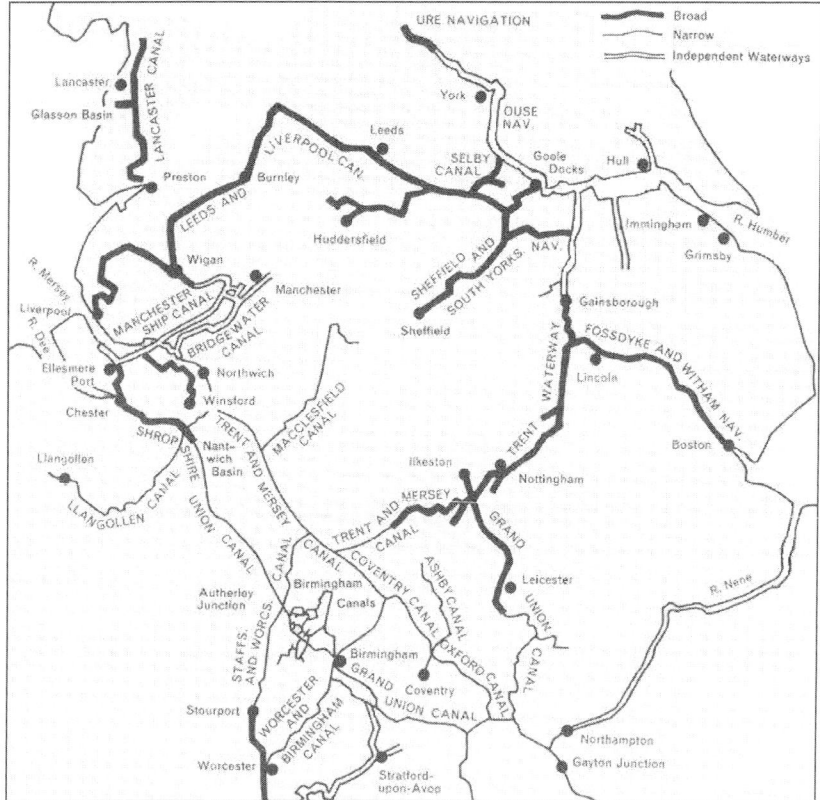

Figure 1: Detail British Waterways.

A look at an up-to-date inland waterways map will reveal the enormous extension and unique structure of the network; no other country ever managed to build artificial waterways on such a comprehensive scale:

> The waterway network includes 3,200 km of canals, 4,763 bridges, 397 aqueducts, 60 tunnels, 1,549 locks, 89 reservoirs, nearly 3,000 listed structures and ancient monuments and 66 Sites of Special Scientific Interest. Much of the network is 200 years old. (DEFRA 1999a)

This map also reveals some of the system's characteristic features:

- It has been laid out as a 'great cross', whose 'trunk' is formed by the Trent and Mersey Canal, from which other canals branch out to connect the principal river estuaries of England: Mersey, Trent, Severn, and Thames; moreover, there are two canals linking the east coast and west coast of Britain: the *Leeds and Liverpool Canal* in the north, and the *Kennet and Avon Canal* in the south.
- It includes an astounding variety of waterways: *river navigations*, i.e. rivers meeting certain standards of navigability; *broad canals*, i.e. canals considerably wider than 15 feet; *narrow canals*, i.c. canals, whose infrastructure (locks, bridges, aqueducts) measures at least 15 feet in width. The passage of goods between waterways of such different dimensions was made possible by trans-shipment ports like Gloucester, Ellesmere Port on the Mersey and others.

British Waterways (BW), formerly the *British Waterways Board* (BWB), the most important inland waterways authority, is a public corporation (not even Lady Thatcher ever cared or dared to privatise it) overseen and funded by the *Department of Environment, Food and Rural Affairs* (DEFRA)[2] in England and Wales, and the *Enterprise,*

---

[2] This department was created from the *Department of the Environment, Transport and the Regions* when the Blair government entered into its 2nd term in June 2001. In 2003/04 *British Waterways* received almost £100mio of public funding (up from less than £60m in 1999/2000); its third party funding (from the Millennium Commission, the Heritage Lottery Fund or Regional Development Agencies) has dropped from more than £50m in 1999/2000 to less

Transport and Lifelong Learning Department in Scotland. Together with other waterways authorities, as e.g. the *Broads Authority, the Environment Agency*, BW today has the statutory obligation to maintain the canal infrastructure so that it will remain suitable for traffic and leisure. This includes administration, repair, public safety, and restoration. Also, in cooperation with a number of smaller waterway authorities[3], local government authorities, local and national voluntary bodies (of which more will have to be said), and the private sector, BW (through a subsidiary public-private-partnership company called *ISIS waterside regeneration*) supports conservation and regeneration schemes, property development and the 'enhancement of amenities' along canals and canal corridors. In urban areas this may include residential, office or small business developments of all sorts and leisure facilities. All services related to the network are provided by the private sector: hundreds of boat rental companies and freight operations, thousands of commercially and privately owned boats – *British Waterways* has licensed more than 26,000 boats on the canals it owns – and everything around them – marinas, boat builders and repair yards, canal pubs and restaurants (of which there are many), shops etc.

All this sounds and mostly even looks pretty impressive, and, indeed, a lot has happened along the canals over the last forty years: hundreds of locks have been rebuilt, several major tunnels reopened, hosts of small and large canal-side structures have been refurbished and many miles of canal have been restored and reopened – in the North of England substantial work has been undertaken on the Rochdale Canal, the Huddersfield Narrow Canal including Standedge tunnel, at 3 miles the longest of them all, and one of the so-called "seven

---

than £15m in 2003/2004. Its fastest growing source of income, however, is generated from marketing its property or selling water to developers through a public private partnership subsidiary called *Watergrid*: this so-called 'trading income' has grown from less than £50m in 1999/2000 to almost £90m in 2003/2004.

3   All of them members of the *Association of Inland Waterways Authorities* (AINA), set up to facilitate the joint management of publicly and privately owned waterways. The total length of navigable inland waterways (including navigable rivers) today is a little more than 3,100 miles, of which BW owns around 2,000 miles, 75% of which are canals.

wonders" of the inland waterways[4]; Ellesmere trans-shipment port with another splendid boat museum, or the terminus of the Peak Forest Canal at Buxworth Basin near Whaley Bridge, which "is being carefully restored by the Inland Waterways Preservation Society" (Cumberlidge 1998: 46). During the 1990s the refurbishing and upgrading of canals has played a crucial role in the restoration and revitalisation of large parts of central Birmingham and inner Manchester. This includes the Central Manchester Development Corporation's inventive act of putting Castlefield as an upscale new inner city working and living quarter on the map: Britain's first urban heritage and culture park at the intersection of the Bridgewater and Rochdale Canals, where you can rent, lease or buy office space or a condominium in tastefully restored Georgian houses next to the Greater Manchester Museum of Science and Industry, the brand-new Bridgewater Concert Hall, the Greater Manchester Exhibition Centre (formerly the central railway station), and a newly created public space around the restored Castlefield boat docks.

It looks as if canals have come into their own as 'valuable assets', not only in terms of tourist attractions, but also as a much coveted environment for working, living and leisure buttressing the fundamental shift from manufacturing to services in the brave new economy of post-industrial Britain. And even what is left of the former industries along their banks, like engineering outfits in the Greater Manchester and Birmingham areas, potteries around Stoke-on-Trent, or

---

[4] It was begun by Benjamin Outram in 1795 and finished by John Rooth in 1801. The other six are: the flight of 29 locks at Devizes on the Kennet and Avon Canal, built by John Rennie and open for traffic in 1810; the 1007 feet Pontcysyllte Aqueduct rising 121 feet to carry the Ellesmere canal across the river Dee, built by Thomas Telford and opened in 1805; the Anderton Boat Lift designed by Edwin Clark, opened in 1875 as a hydraulic lift to connect the river Weaver with the Trent and Mersey Canal, closed in 1983 and reopened in 2002 after extensive restoration; Barton Swing Aqueduct designed by Edward Leader Williams and opened in 1893 to replace James Brindley's original Barton Aqueduct carrying the Bridgewater Canal across the river Irwell after the course of the Irwell was used to build Manchester Ship Canal; Bingley Five Rise Locks, a staircase flight of 5 locks on the Leeds and Liverpool Canal operating since 1774; Burnley Embankment designed by Robert Whitworth and completed in 1801 to carry the Leeds and Liverpool Canal for almost a mile above the roofs of the buildings across the centre of Burnley.

even the occasional operating steel works, seems to be there to enhance the flavour of the scenery. All of this raises the question of the canals' cultural meaning. My answer will be in two parts: first, a historic rundown of the canals' rise, decline and revitalisation; then a look at canals as part of the heritage debate.

2. The Origins, Decline, and Resurgence of the Canals

The difference between the function of the canals then and now could hardly be more striking: from the 1770s to the beginning of the railway age they quickly developed into the most important transport routes for heavy bulk commodities of the incipient industrial revolution: coal, iron ore, limestone, gravel, stones, timber, grain, but also cotton, pottery and other manufactures could be carried much faster and cheaper than would have been feasible in horse-drawn wagons on the mostly unimproved roads of the late-eighteenth century. Accordingly, the ambience of the early industrial canals was in stark contrast to today's idyllic canal environment vaguely reminiscent of an unspecified past. Life on the early canals was busy, even hectic; at the locks long queues of boats were waiting, and quarrels about who was the first to go through or about slow loading and unloading at a wharf might sometimes end in fist fights: even in those days time was money, and boatmen were deemed a rough race.

With the expansion of Britain's waterway system, which peaked around 1835 with around 3000 miles of canals and more than 1000 miles of navigable rivers, distances were getting longer, and more and more boatmen were compelled to live on their boats permanently. This often included their families crowded into a cabin at the stern which was as tiny as 4 to 6 square meters so that not too much valuable cargo space would be lost. It doesn't take a lot to imagine life on board, particularly in wind, rain and snow: there were no sanitary facilities, people used canal water for just about everything from washing to cooking and drinking, and they often had to forage for food and fuel in the neighbouring fields. Disease was rampant and life expectancy low – similar to that of many other early industrial workers. Unsurprisingly, the resident population along the canals usually considered 'boat people' to be a morally degraded lot of bullies and thieves.

The banks and towpaths, particularly in industrial towns and villages, were often strewn with garbage of all sorts. The adjacent industrial areas were marked by smoke, soot, grime, and by the absence of any planning, let alone any signs of care for the environment. From their origins to the peak of their commercial use, large stretches of the canals breathed the inhospitable atmosphere of quickly and haphazardly established industrial developments[5].

The British canal system was planned, designed, surveyed, and built between 1760, when the Act of Parliament authorising the Bridgewater Canal was passed, and the 1830s, when the railway as a new transport system arrived on the scene. In charge of canal projects and their related infrastructure were men like James Brindley (1716-1772, e.g. Bridgewater Canal, Trent & Mersey Canal, Harecastle Tunnel), William Jessop (1745-1814, e.g. Ellesmere Canal Grand Junction Canal), Thomas Telford (1757-1834, e.g. Caledonian Canal, Pontcysyllte Aqueduct), or John Rennie (1761-1821, e.g. Kennet & Avon Canal). Originally trained as millwrights, masons, or in related crafts they are among the earliest representatives of a new profession, which was only emerging in the second half of the eighteenth century: the *civil engineers*. They also built roads, bridges, ports, docks and other features of transport technology serving the gradual infrastructural integration of the country in these crucial early days of industrialisation.

These engineers, after surveying the line of the projected canal, oversaw and coordinated the process of construction and the labourers involved in it. These included carpenters, joiners, masons etc. building bridges, locks, aqueducts, tunnels and reservoirs. The actual excavating work – incredibly hard and dirty – was carried out by thousands of 'navvies', mostly with no other tools than picks, shovels and wheelbarrows. These construction workers were a rough and hardy breed (many of them Irish), who would move from site to site and literally dig the canals into the ground and then line them with puddling clay to

---

[5] Today, strangely enough, many of those who count themselves among the hard core of canal enthusiasts are specifically attracted by the bizarre contrasts between what is left of such industrial wastelands (now mostly derelict) and the pastoral beauty of quintessentially 'English' countryside, most of which was the result of the capitalist restructuring of agriculture in Britain since the beginning of the eighteenth century.

make them watertight. The result was a maze of small artificial waterways, the so-called *narrow canals*. Compared to what continental Europeans associate with the term 'canal' they look more like ditches, usually around 15 feet wide and 4 to 6 feet deep. Because of the technical difficulties involved and the initially relatively simple, yet nevertheless ingenious civil engineering techniques, eighteenth century canal projects would include only a minimal number of locks. These 'contour canals' meander across the country, and, with their many bends, are often hard to navigate. The first of them, the Bridgewater Canal, opened in 1761 and became an immediate commercial success, originally running level for some 20 miles from the coal mine of its owner, Francis Egerton, 3rd Duke of Bridgewater, in Worsley into Manchester without any locks at all, before it was later linked to other canals. But the canal had to cross the river Irwell on an aqueduct (also built by James Brindley) near the village of Barton, which was obviously perceived as an image of the progressive spirit embodied in the new transport system as a local eulogy suggested:

> Seen and acknowledg'd by stonish'd crowds,
> From underground emerging to the clouds;
> Vessels o'er vessels, water under water,
> Bridgewater triumphs – art has conquered nature.
> (from: James Ogden, *A Description of Manchester, 1783*, quoted after Hoffmann 1991: 36)

From the beginning of the nineteenth century, the new technique of 'cut-and-fill' was spreading, first in canal building and later in railway construction. It was premised on the principle of a straight line as the shortest connection between two places and often made the construction of impressively sized lock flights necessary, which needed sophisticated systems of reservoirs, side-ponds, conduits etc. An outstanding example in the North of England is the 'Bingley Five Rise', the famous 5-lock staircase on the Leeds-and-Liverpool Canal (see note 4).

The genius of James Brindley understood the advantages of uniform dimensions in canal building: when planning the Trent and Mersey Canal, which opened in 1777 as the backbone or 'trunk' of the 'great cross', whose extensions and branches connected Britain's four principal river estuaries as early as 1789, he succeeded in pushing through the first standardisation in modern industrial history. It involved all key measurements, namely of bridges, locks and the canal profile itself. These measurements were based on a standard type of boat, which came to be called *narrow-boat*, up to 70 feet in length, but only a little over 7 feet wide. Even fully loaded with 30 – 50 tons of cargo, a boat of this size could be towed by a single horse, which was an important factor at a time when wind, humans, or animals, were the only driving powers available. Small locks could easily be operated by a single person and would use limited amounts of water, just like the narrow canal itself, another important advantage, with fewer and smaller reservoirs being necessary to feed the system.

But this standardisation, namely of the narrow canals, most of which can be found in and between the former industrial conurbations of the Midlands and the North West could not prevent their decline as the dominant transport system. From the middle of the nineteenth century when the railroad was firmly established, the relatively limited payload of the boats made the survival of the canals increasingly difficult. And with the arrival of a much faster and more flexible way of transporting commodities by road and truck in the early-twentieth century the fate of the canals as commercially profitable transport routes seemed to be sealed. And profitable they had to be: from its very beginnings every part of the canal system was geared to profit making – the canal building societies, the canal companies, the boat docks, trans-shipment ports, wharves, warehouses and last but not least the boat owners large and small, companies and individuals (so-called 'number-ones'). The network had grown on the basis of private enterprise and operated without any planning or regulating intrusion by the state. Over time, the actions of thousands of entrepreneurs – small craftsmen, substantial bankers and businessmen alike – seemed to have added up to an altogether quite rational result.

But the shortcomings of a system whose origins and operation had been governed by individual cost-benefit considerations of so many competing actors became apparent when the rise of the railways as a new transport technology required that it be thoroughly modernised into something much more coherent by coordinating tariffs, routes, schedules, services etc. At the very least this would have meant cooperation, if not mergers, on a national scale, of the many canal companies, most of whom operated only locally or regionally. But in spite of the Canal Association, a nation-wide lobby group set up in 1855 "to watch railway legislation and promote canal interests"

(Paget-Tomlinson 1994: 6), they continued to compete against each other and against the ever more dominant railways, until they collapsed or were bought up, often by railway companies. Unless legally prohibited (e.g. by the 1873 Regulation of Railways Act) these would let the canals decay by a policy of non-investment, or drain them and use the canal bed for laying tracks, as in the case of the Croydon Canal providing the route for the London and Croydon Railway as early as 1831.

After 1850 only three major canal projects were completed, one of them the Manchester Ship Canal in 1886, making Manchester accessible to large sea-going vessels, while in the late-nineteenth and early-twentieth centuries, more and more canals were losing traffic, and often become dilapidated and unusable. Their closure, in turn, led to a piecemeal disintegration of the system as a whole, although some companies spent a great deal of money to upgrade their waterways and managed to retain considerable amounts of trade, e.g. the Aire and Calder Navigation, the Weaver Navigation, the Birmingham Canal Network, the Grand Junction Canal, and the Leeds and Liverpool Canal. But the recommendations of a Royal Commission in 1909 to widen and deepen the Midlands' navigations forming the 'great cross' to accommodate at least 100-ton barges were lost in the political turmoil of the day and the outbreak of World War I. Consequently, the shrinking of the system, which had begun in the middle of the nineteenth century, continued, and the total amount of goods transported by canal fell more and more. From the 1920s, increasing road transport accelerated this downward trend to less than 10 million tons annually by 1946, a mere fraction of former volumes.

It was not until after World War II that the state began to get involved in the administration and maintenance of canals and waterways: in 1948 the Attlee government nationalised them like mining and other problem-ridden industries. At this point there were some 2000 miles of canals left, with 6000 boats and 11000 people working in this sector. But nationalisation could not stanch the decline; there were never enough funds for maintenance and repair, let alone for planning or building new canals. During the severe winter of 1962/63 a 'great freeze-up' covered most waterways with ice for several months. This came as the final blow to the narrow boat carrying industry, while some transport of bulk commodities by boat has continued on large stretches of broad canals and river navigations until today, when only around 3.5 million tons of all freight moved annually are carried by canal boats or river barges.

Shortly afterwards, in 1963, the administration and management of the inland waterways was streamlined and put under the responsibility of the newly created *British Waterways Board*. In subsequent years this new authority not only embarked on a major survey of the remaining parts of the network and their condition, but by the end of the 1960s it had also redefined the function of the waterways from being a mere freight system into an important factor of amenity and recreational development (see Squires 1983: 8, 172f.; Paget-Tomlinson 1994: 12). Acknowledgement of the canals' role as a "leisure and recreation resource" has remained a consistent policy keyword from the provisions of the 1968 Transport Act down to DEFRA's 1999 policy document quoted above. Notwithstanding the merits of the BWB's work in canal administration, maintenance, and repair, however, the enormous achievements in their revitalisation made over the past 40 years are by no means owed to the efforts or loving care of the British state alone. In 1996 BW still estimated that it would need to spend £260 million "to bring all of its assets up to a fair condition or better" (DEFRA 1999b).

There had been sporadic private initiatives to preserve what was left of this unique system since the early years of the twentieth century. These efforts were intensifying from the late 1940s under the impression of a legendary travelogue *Narrow Boat* (Rolt 1978) by an engineer, who later turned into one of Britain's foremost writers on engineers and engineering history, Tom Rolt. Shortly before the outbreak of World War II he converted an old wooden narrow boat and set out on a 400-mile trip on the narrow canals of the Midlands. The austere charm of this trip (and his skilful description) encouraged a handful of canal-inspired enthusiasts led by Robert Aickman to set up the *Inland Waterways Association* (IWA), in 1946, which has developed into one of the most successful environmental lobbies in Britain after World War II. Although faced with difficulties which initially seemed almost insurmountable, this organisation eventually became enormously effective in raising public awareness of the canals and their history, and of the need to preserve or restore their crumbling infrastructure of locks, bridges, docks, wharves, warehouses etc. The IWA has also explored and used every conceivable legal and political device to push public authorities and private owners towards repairing, reopening and maintaining canals and canal-related structures.

Political and financial support by the IWA led to a mushrooming of local and regional canal societies (usually organised as charitable trusts), in which thousands of people, aptly termed *new navvies*, gave their time and skills to voluntary restoration work. From 1970 onwards these *new navvies* began to organise themselves into the *Waterways Recovery Group* (WRG), which, for financial and legal reasons, was transformed into a subsidiary company of the IWA in 1980 (see Squires 1983: 9-21). Soon, private business companies, small and large, got involved locally and nationally, donating money and equipment or setting up award schemes, like Shell UK with 'waterways restoration awards' or nationwide advertising campaigns like "Fancy helping weed a river" in 1981 (see Squires 1984: 125f., and Baldwin and Burton 1984: plate 33) – long before the greening of British parties and politics at other levels. All this helped to encourage public support for the work of the IWA, the WRG and many affiliated local canal societies, as a recent survey of the IWA's history on the occasion of its 50th anniversary has outlined in much detail (see Bolton 1996). Last but not least local authorities eventually came to realise the multiple benefits of canal restoration: not only did it make them eligible to apply for central government (and eventually, European) funds creating jobs in construction, but the spin-off has also been more long-term in generating new economic activity stimulated by the development of business, housing, and leisure facilities along refurbished canals. From a local and regional planning perspective canal restoration demonstrated the potentially beneficial effects of public-private-partnerships (PPP) long before they became a fashionable government strategy in the 1980s and 1990s. It also showed how these once neglected, unsightly ditches, often full of rubble and stagnant water, with many sections filled in to get precious space for motorways, roads and parking lots, could become crucial elements in large-scale urban renewal schemes.

On balance Tom Rolt's romanticist visions from the war-ridden early 1940s, romanticist as they were (harking back to late-nineteenth century images of a post-industrial and post-capitalist civilisation in William Morris's *News from Nowhere*), may have provided some inspiration for innumerable people involved in canal preservation and restoration: new navvies and other canal enthusiasts as well as administrators, architects, urban planners and business people.

> There are two courses open to each man in his brief lifetime: either he can seek the good life, or he can struggle for wealth and power; the former emphasises spiritual, the latter material values. After the war the choice will be ours, and if it be the good life, the land awaits our coming. If on the other hand, we continue to pursue our material obsession, the urban bureaucrats are ready to plan our lives from cradle to grave, and we shall become the slaves of a scientific 'Technocracy'. Although the war has deepened the conviction that there is something seriously wrong with our civilisation, we have become so besotted with the idea of the inevitability of scientific progress that we are contemplating plunging ever deeper into the mire of mechanised living, in the tragic belief that, despite the evidence of the past one hundred and fifty years, it is still the way to Utopia. In fact, to follow this road is to sacrifice the individuality and creative ability of man on the altar of material prosperity. ... The future of the English Canals... depends no less than that of the countryside on the order which we build after the war. ... In a society framed to cherish our national heritage the canals can play their part not only as a means of transport and employment, but as part of an efficient system of land drainage and a source of beauty and pleasure. But if the canals are left to the mercies of economists and scientific planners, before many years are past the last of them will become a weedy, stagnant ditch, and the bright boats will rot at the wharves, to live on only in old men's memories. (Rolt 1978: 193ff.)

Whatever may have happened to the 'New Jerusalem', the 'land fit for heroes' that the wartime leaders had promised to create after the war, today at least the future of the inland waterways seems secure. Over the last thirty years the properties along their banks have skyrocketed in value, now being among the choicest lots money can buy in urban areas. Canal-related leisure and tourist activities sustain throughout the year a plethora of businesses like museums, heritage centres, shops, pubs, theatre and song groups, journals, guides and guidebooks, websites etc. All this has added a lively and picturesque segment to the great new enterprise of (Cool) Britannia plc. Through millions of visitors year after year, an image of canals is projected that depicts them as steeped in the aura of authentic everyday remains[6] of

---

[6] On the use of the terms *aura* and *authenticity* see Hoffmann 2000.

Britain's past industrial grandeur. Acknowledging the canals' potential as a catalyst for economic and environmental regeneration, in February 1999 John Prescott, the Deputy Prime Minister, announced an 18% rise in the government's annual grant to the *British Waterways Board*. At the same time he expressed government backing for BWB plans in cooperation with the water industry to use the canals as a grid for pouring extra supplies of water into areas suffering from droughts and shortages (see *Guardian* 19 February 1999: 16), another example of a PPP scheme whose feasibility seemed questionable at the time, but which has become reality in the shape of *Watergrid* and, today, is generating much needed extra cash for BWB (see note 2). Truly, the canals have come into their own again!

3. The Narrow Canals and the Heritage Debate

Today, the cultural meaning of the narrow canals is constructed and transmitted on several levels:

- They provide upscale and 'lifestylish' working and living space, mainly in urban areas for service-sector professionals. Amidst the transformation of Britain's inner cities from the squalor of de-industrialisation towards the reconstruction of a viable post-industrial physical, social and economic infrastructure, their fashionably rebuilt environment recalls the vibrancy and productiveness of Britain's early industrial days;

- They constitute the most gigantic open-air industrial heritage park in the country recasting industrial history as a colourful mixture of pastoral scenery, refurbished canal-related architecture, and re-used industrial buildings with a sprinkling of industrial museums. All of this seems to provide romantic relief from a life dominated by the pressures of globalisation (an apt new metaphor for what Tom Rolt in 1944 termed "technocracy");

- Last but not least, they serve as important levers for local and regional economic revitalisation and development supporting the notion of Britain reinventing herself once again – this time as a new, service-based economy.

The question of how and why canals have come to serve these purposes cannot be answered without looking at the so-called 'heritage debate' (see Lowenthal 1985; Hewison 1987; Lowenthal 1996, 2000), which is about the uses of the past in the construction of social and cultural meaning for the present. Recently, the German Egyptologist Jan Assmann (1999) has drawn our attention to the fact that rising interest in historical features cannot simply be attributed to a general 'sense of the past' common to all civilised societies. Reminding us that the psychodynamic disposition of humans would rather make them forget what has happened instead of remembering it, he has suggested that we examine carefully those elements of the past that are appropriated for present use, and to ask why this is being done. His key point is that remembering and forgetting are socio-political phenomena which have to do with questioning or legitimising and reconciling us to present constellations of power and domination. In this context the past is put to 'prospective' uses by providing traditions as material for (re)constructing today's and tomorrow's identities. Borrowing Levi-Strauss's sociological metaphor of 'heat' created by systems of domination in structurally unequal, i.e. class societies, which in turn may fuel the engine of social and political change, Assmann goes on to explain the intimate relationship between such social 'heat' and selective remembering and forgetting and how the selective internalisation of the past in the shape of mythical or historical narrative can be used either to unsettle or to stabilise existing power structures.

Academic historiography may try to provide us with more or less objectively and disinterestedly researched facts and sober interpretations of the past. In our everyday social and cultural memories these serve a different purpose, namely to construct plausible narratives of the past that we can use, individually and collectively, to make sense of present social and political arrangements and developments. This functional process of condensing historic material into images of the past which supply meanings for today is circumscribed by the term "heritage". Analysing the politics of this process at different levels the late Raphael Samuel in his encyclopaedic last book *Theatres of Memory* (Samuel 1994) has made it clear that, by definition, the making of heritage, in the form of preserving and staging physical structures or other remains of the past, is a much contested territory, which "cannot be assigned to either Left or Right", because "it is subject to quite startling reversals over very limited periods of time" (Samuel 1994: 303).

> Politically heritage, like conservation, draws on a nexus of different interests. It is intimately bound up with competition for land use, and the struggle for urban space. Whether by attraction or repulsion it is shaped by changes in technology. It takes on quite different meanings in different national cultures, depending on the relationship between state and civil society, the openness or otherwise of the public arena to initiatives which come from below or from the periphery. In one aspect it is a residual legatee of the environmental campaigns of the 1960s, the aesthetic revolt against 'gigantism', and the rediscovery of simple lifeism. In another aspect it could be seen as the epicentre of a whole new cycle of capitalist development; the spearhead, or cutting edge of the business recolonization of the inner city, a style-setter for post-Fordist, small-batch production. ... Conservationism is a global phenomenon, and the notion of heritage as an environment under threat, and as a cultural asset to exploit, has been a feature, for some thirty years, of the advanced capitalist economies of the world. (Samuel 1994: 306f.)

This is why the transformation of the canals into heritage must be considered, both politically and ideologically, more than just (postmodernly speaking) manufacturing another metafiction. It is rather a weapon in today's complex 'culture wars' about how our work-related and political identities – our "character" as Richard Sennett has put this (see Sennett 1998) – should be reshaped after being so corrosively affected by the transition to post-Fordist structures of production and reproduction. Whoever dominates the battlegrounds of heritage teaches us which elements of the past selectively to remember or forget and thus helps us to legitimise or challenge present 'regimes of accumulation'.

But the canals are more than just a segment of the ambivalent heritage industry: by literally slowing us down, they provide opportunities for learning about the development of today's obsession with speed and universal mobility. The experience of a trip on a canal boat can help us to retrace the genesis of our perception of space and time as mere barriers to mastering and consuming more and more of our natural environments. Once we begin to see through the seemingly idyllic character of the landscape along the canals we realise how much of it is man-made, rationally constructed – an upshot of industrialised production. As James Ogden's hymnic lines on Barton aqueduct suggest, the canal builders' perception of undomesticated nature was already in stark contrast to that of eighteenth century painters and poets, for whom it represented the quintessential embodiment of the aesthetic ideal of the sublime. To the new breed of civil engineers, however, nature represented an obstacle that needed to be overcome by human art. Thus the nostalgically romantic canals turn into an ambiguous metaphor: as one of the crucial instruments of early industrialisation they represent both its progressive and destructive forces (see Stinshoff 1992: 98ff.).

And there is yet another ambiguity in the image of the narrow canals linking past and future: 800 miles of fibre optic cable have been buried under British Waterways towpaths to link London and the south east with Birmingham, Sheffield, Leeds, Manchester, Gloucester and Bristol into a network for data, picture and voice communication. In a way, canals seem to represent the 'long waves' of Britain's economic development: from the days of eighteenth century British "gentleman capitalism" (see Cain and Hopkins 1993: 17-27), when London provided merchant banking, shipping and insurance services world wide, to the beginning of the twenty-first century, when Britain is reinventing itself as a major hub of information technology based global commercial and financial services, things have turned full circle. Maybe, after industrialisation and de-industrialisation, the country is coming into its own again.

Works Cited

Research Literature

[Beyond the books that I used for quotations or references I have included a few titles that I have found useful to consult both about the history and the present state of Britain's inland waterways.]

Assman, Jan (1992/1999): *Das Kulturelle Gedächtnis. Schrift, Erinnerung und politische Identität in frühen Hochkulturen*. München: Beck.

Baldwin, Mark and Anthony Burton (eds.) (1984): *Canals, a New Look*. Chichester: Phillimore Books.

Bolton, David (1996): "Turning the Tide (part 1-5)", *Waterways World* 25 (May – September), 5-9.

British Waterways (1999): *Our Plan for the Future 2000-2004*. Watford: BWB.

Burton, Anthony (1972/1981): *The Canal Builders*. Newton Abbot: David & Charles.

— (1993): *Canal Mania, 200 Years of Britain's Waterways*. London: Aurum Press.

Cain, P.J. and Anthony G. Hopkins (1993): *British Imperialism: Innovation and Expansion 1688-1914*. London: Longman.

Cossons, Neil (1975/1993): *The BP Book of Industrial Archaeology*. Newton Abbot: David & Charles.

Cumberlidge, Jane (1998): *Inland Waterways of Great Britain*. St Ives, Cambridgeshire: Imray, Laurie, Norie & Wilson.

Department of the Environment, Food and Rural Affairs (1999a): *Unlocking the Potential – a New Future for British Waterways*. 18 February 1999. 10 February 2007 [http://www.defra.gov.uk/environment/water/iw/unlock/index.htm].

— (1999b): *Future Status: Facts and Analysis Relevant to the Government's Announcement*. 18 February 1999. 10 February 2007 [http://www.defra.gov.uk/environment/water/iw/future/index.htm]

Hadfield, Ellis Charles Raymond (1950/1984): *British Canals: An Illustrated History*. Newton Abbot: David & Charles.

Hewison, Robert (1987): *The Heritage Industry*. London: Methuen.

Hoffmann, Detlef (1991): "Art has Conquered Nature", *Kritische Berichte* 4/91, 30-37.

— (2000): "Spur. Vorstellung. Ausstellung", in: Rosemarie Beier (ed.): *Geschichtskultur in der Zweiten Moderne*. Frankfurt u.a.: Campus 2000, 167-182.

Lowenthal, David (1985): *The Past is a Foreign Country*. Cambridge: Cambridge UP.

— (1996): *The Heritage Crusade and the Spoils of History*. London and New York: Viking Penguin.

Lowenthal, David (2000): "'History' und 'Heritage': Widerstreitende und konvergente Formen der Vergangenheitsbetrachtung", in: Rosemarie Beier (ed.): *Geschichtskultur in der Zweiten Moderne*. Frankfurt u.a.: Campus 2000, 71-94.

Paget-Tomlinson, Edward (1994): *The Illustrated History of Canal and River Navigations.* Sheffield: Sheffield Academic Press.

Rolt, L.T.C. (1948/1978): *Narrow Boat* (rev. ed.). London: Eyre Methuen.

Samuel, Raphael (1994): *Theatres of Memory* — Volume 1: *Past and Present in Contemporary Culture.* London: Verso.

Sennett, Richard (1998): *The Corrosion of Character: The Personal Consequences of Work in the New Capitalism.* New York and London: W.W. Norton.

Stinshoff, Richard (1992): "'History' oder 'Heritage' – Überlegungen zur kulturellen Bedeutung der englischen Kanäle damals und heute", *Anglistik und Englischunterricht* 46/47, Heidelberg: Carl Winter, 83-105.

Stuart, Rob: "One Man in an Open Boat", *The Independent* 21 January 1995, 38.

Squires, Roger W. (1983): *The New Navvies. A History of the Modern Waterways Restoration Movement.* Chichester: Phillimore Books.

— (1984): "Waterway Restoration: Public Money, Private Muscle", in: Mark Baldwin and Anthony Burton (eds.): *Canals, a New Look.* Chichester: Phillimore Books, 110-129.

Websites

[To conclude, here is a small selection of websites useful for would-be canal buffs and waterways enthusiasts:]

[http://www.waterways.org.uk] The official Inland Waterways Association website, many links to local canal societies and, of course, to the Waterways Recovery Group;

[http://www.british-waterways.org] The official website of *British Waterways*, always useful to consult about the agency's present policy and current projects and problems on the canal network;

[http://www.canalia.com] An online magazine with news and views around canals, again with many links, one of them to *Mikron Theatre*, a group that presents canal songs and stories;

[http://www.canals.com] A commercial website with more links to boat hire companies, canal holiday packages, maps, books etc. all over the UK;

[http://www.jim-shead.co.uk/] The best of them all..., teeming with all kinds of information on hundreds of pages, over 800 links to other sites.

Speed, Steam and Nostalgia:
The Heritage Railways of Northern England

Konrad Schliephake and Keith Sutton

Abstract: In the homeland of industrialisation, railways were the indispensable instruments of mass transport. Today, northerners are well aware of the interaction between natural landscape and the man-made elements of an era so important to mankind. Here, heritage railways are not only seen as picturesque and nostalgic remainders of the past, but they attract travellers and investors. The authors give an insight into development, historic personalities and present day structure of the various lines.

Key names and concepts: Gottlieb Daimler - Timothy Hackworth - George and Robert Stephenson - Bennet Woodcraft; De-industrialisation - Industrial Heritage - Tourism - Railway Preservation - Industrial Museums - Regional Economy.

1. Introduction

When the authors met in Tunis, in 1968, they took delight in using the little TGM-train to the beaches with coaches dating from the 1910s and seen – at their age – as a living museum (see presentation of this line by Pabst 1989). As the years and the status within the universities progressed a genuine interest in railways grew, and transportation planning became a major field of research for one of them (see Schliephake and Schenk 2005). A geographical excursion to Northern England, jointly organised by the authors and one of the general editors of Spatial Practices, gave a good insight into a scene which seems so typical for this part of the country. Its past and present economic and social structures easily compare to similar developments in Germany.

When screening written material for this article, we realised that not many empirical studies have been done to present the phenomenon of heritage railways. This applies to England as well as to Germany, where Demhardt (2004) has given a structural survey and Schliephake

(2005) evaluated the economic impact of tourist railways in northern Bavaria.

The following text rather dwells on structures of present-day heritage railways in Northern England, and we may learn about the following aspects perhaps specific to all heritage railway projects but even more visible in this region:

- continuity with which individual enthusiasts have realised such projects;
- pride in the technical achievements and industrial infrastructure of earlier generations;
- awareness of the north as the cradle of world-wide industrialisation, arising from coal and steel – basic elements of earlier and current railways.

We do not know much – for the time being – about the structure of the visitors, costs, revenues, subsidies and possible direct or, respectively, indirect contributions of such railways to the regional economies; nor have we done any empirical studies concerning the evaluation and perception of such activities as being something "specifically northern". Such questions must remain open but they may point to new challenges and fields of research for human geographers who, sometimes, have to re-discover their regional settings and feelings. Nevertheless, with regard to the intensity of heritage railway activities – especially in the North of England – it is clear that these institutions cannot avoid having a part to play in the formation of a particular northern identity in post-industrial England.

2. Demise and preservation of English railways

The restructuring of regional economies, such as that of Northern England, from manufacturing to service-based economies have left abandoned many traditional industries and their transport infrastructures. Post-industrial regions have attempted to re-market themselves, at least in part, as industrial heritage regions. Furthermore, the rapid de-industrialisation of Britain in the late 1970s and 1980s "created an innate sense of loss, especially among northern communities" (Smith

2003: 95). The subsequent development of industrial heritage tourism has often aided the regeneration of areas in decline, serving to boost the local economy and recharging people's sense of identity and self-worth. Edwards and Llurdés (1996: 342) have defined industrial heritage as "man-made sites, buildings and landscapes that originated with industrial processes from earlier periods." They argue, however, that such attractions will never stimulate the level of interest among visitors that "Romanesque churches or Gothic cathedrals have done since they do not hold the same romantic or aesthetic values." Many a steam railways enthusiast would probably strongly disagree!

A major component now of Britain's industrial heritage industry, railways were equally fundamental in the nineteenth-century industrialisation of the country, adding a further transport boost to the initial contribution of eighteenth-century and early nineteenth-century canals to the Industrial Revolution. By 1870 the major part of Britain's rail network had been laid with more than 17,600 km of track constructed. Further branch lines extended the network to a maximum of 32,300 km of railway routes open to traffic in 1923. (Patmore 1983: 38) This extent had dropped only marginally to 31,160 km of track by the time of rail nationalisation in Britain in 1948, with a network then served by 8,294 stations. (Yale 2004: 8-1) Following the much criticised Beeching Report of 1963 many lines, especially branch lines, were closed and the network shrank back to 17,600 km by 1980. In England and Wales it was estimated then that 60% of the closed length of railway lines remained derelict and unused while some 4% were being used for private, usually heritage, railways, and some 9% had been converted to walking, cycling and horse-riding routes. By 2004 only 16,452 km of track remained in use, excluding the heritage railways, and 2,506 stations remained functional. Railways that originally served quarries and other industrial sites were particularly likely to have been closed as uneconomic. At the time of the 1948 nationalisation British Railways had inherited more than 20,000 steam locomotives. However, by 1968 all of them had been taken out of service, raising challenging issues of heritage loss (see the surveys at Suggitt 2003 and Welbourn 2003).

Already by the late 1960s the railway preservation movement was well established and actively saving steam engines and some branch lines across Britain. Activists were faced with but not deterred by an "essential paradox" (Simmons and Biddle 1997: 393). This comprised the contradiction that operating an old steam locomotive causes further wear and tear so that worn-out parts have to be replaced. Thus, the historic authenticity of the locomotive can be preserved, albeit in a transformed state. Railway preservation has to be a compromise between conservation and restoration to a state of active working order.

It is remarkable that the Victorians' attempts in preserving their historical environment did not stop at the objects of the industrialisation. In fact, early efforts at locomotive preservation saw them as museum pieces, however. Canterbury and Whitstable Railway's *Invicta* was preserved by the South Eastern Railway in the late 1840s. The Stockton and Darlington Railway's famous locomotive *Locomotion* was preserved at Darlington station in 1857, on a pedestal (Simmons and Biddle, 1997). Further conservation work owed much to the foresight of Bennet Woodcraft (1803-79) who established the Patent Museum which acquired, in 1862, Hedley's pioneering *Puffing Billy* of 1814, Stephenson's *Rocket* of 1829, and Timothy Hackworth's *Sans Pareil*. In 1884 these venerated engines were transferred to the South Kensington Museum which was to divide into the Science Museum and the Victoria and Albert Museum at the end of the nineteenth century (Cossons, 1993). The celebration of the centenary of the Liverpool & Manchester Railway in 1930 prompted restoration to full working order by the London Midland & Scottish Railway of the locomotive *Lion* of 1837.

The creation of full working heritage railways, rather than the conservation of museum objects, owed much to three pioneer societies in the 1950s and early 1960s. The Talyllyn Railway in Southwest Wales, the Bluebell Railway in Sussex and the Festiniog Railway in North Wales were the first of many working heritage railways. In the North of England the Middleton Railway in Leeds can also claim pioneer status. That these initial ventures blossomed into a plethora of heritage railways probably owed much to two basic stimuli: firstly, the 1960s post-Beeching closure of many branch lines and, secondly, the phasing out by British Railways of the steam locomotives, again especially in the 1960s, leading up to the cessation of steam locomotion in 1968 and its replacement by diesel and electric locomotives. Together, these two events provided both available and manageable sections of track and an abundance of steam engines to rescue, preserve and restore. Additional locomotives came from industrial users such as the

National Coal Board and from importation from abroad, often of engines originally manufactured at British locomotive works. A major source of supply was the scrap yard of Woodham Brothers of Barry in South Wales from which firm over 200 steam locomotives were purchased for preservation between 1968 and 1989 (Simmons and Biddle 1997: 394). The fact that steam engines would become the prime focus of the restoration activities by railway enthusiasts is compelling: it promotes a vision of the past that implicitly assumes a connection between early technical progress and the industrialisation of the North of England and thus serves to create a particular identity for the northern landscape. A further stimulus to the heritage railway movement was the love of nostalgia which inspired the volunteer labour of numerous railway enthusiasts who provided or acquired the necessary engineering skills together with the substantial funds required for purchase, capital, restoration work and, eventually, running costs. Only later, additional funding was generated from tourist visitors, local development authorities and, more recently, the National Lottery's heritage funds.

3. The Northern Scene

The Liverpool and Manchester Railway of 1830 was the first railway as we understand the term, with freight and passenger transport, mechanical traction, up and down roads, proper stations and signalling. It was therefore logical that the value of early rail was discovered there. The first heritage railway societies were located in Sussex and Wales, but the North of England was not far behind and participated in the rapid acceleration of the founding of new heritage railways in the 1960s and 1970s. Arguably, the North could have been anticipated to parallel its nineteenth-century role in the initial development of railways with a burgeoning of railway preservation societies, often on the same sites, such as the Stockton & Darlington line and other North-Eastern locations. Hardly anywhere else in Britain can railways with their infrastructure of viaducts and tunnels be seen as such an integral feature of the regional landscape. The Liverpool and Manchester line, the first opened for passenger traffic in 1830, has prompted a Science and Technology Museum, including transport heritage items, which is partly housed in the original Liverpool Road railway station in Manchester. The strategic location of northern rail centres, such as Crewe and York, on rail routes to Scotland have given rise to transport museums. That at York houses the National Railway Museum, created by combining collections of locomotives from the Science Museum, London and the Museum of British Transport at Clapham, also in London. Even the classic railway station film 'Brief Encounter' (1945) used a northern location at Carnforth to depict a Home Counties southern railway commuter station. Over fifty years later film nostalgia has combined with railway nostalgia to produce a touristic reconstruction of the film's atmospheric waiting room at Carnforth. Similarly, another classic film, 'The Railway Children' (1970), used a northern location, the Keighley & Worth Valley Railway. More recently the Harry Potter films have employed Goatland Station on the North Yorkshire Moors Railway. It is striking that all of these films exploit the picturesque qualities of the northern landscape which is characterised by an allusive proximity between natural and man-made topographical features. Paradoxically almost, the films assume an organic interdependence which is apt to conceal the original function of the transport infrastructure.

As the table of Heritage Railways in the appendix of this essay demonstrates, the number of heritage railways in the North has mushroomed, especially if a wider definition permits the inclusion of transport museums. There is even an academic Institute of Railway Studies, established at the University of York. As well as the preservation of old locomotives, it should be noted that the heritage of the Railway Age includes other transport and linked structures such as stations, workshops, viaducts, hotels at termini, and even railway workers' housing. Consequently, in 2003 the Railway Heritage Trust estimated that Britain has 1,570 listed railway structures, including 79 scheduled railway monuments (Yale 2004: 8-4). Network Rail is responsible for about 400 buildings of architectural or historic importance, including the Grade I Midland Grand Hotel at St. Pancras Station, London. In 2001-2002 Network Rail and the Railway Property Board received grants of £1.5 million to restore some of these monuments. Successes include Bristol Temple Meads Station and the Ribblehead Viaduct on the Settle-Carlisle railway. Elsewhere, as in Accrington and Stockport, magnificent railway viaducts are floodlit at night, reflecting civic pride in this contribution to the built environment heritage of these two towns (Burman and Stratton 1997: 62). There is even a serious suggestion by Cossons (1997) that the whole of Brunel's old Great Western main line from Bristol to Paddington be designated as a World Heritage Site. Although very much a functioning railway line, it still has intact most of its original civil engineering and architectural features. Others would extend this proposed linear heritage site as far as Plymouth along the full route of the GWR ('God's Wonderful Railway').

Many heritage railway societies devote nearly as much energy to conserving their rolling stock and stations as their locomotives. The livery of the carriages and the signage and advertising posters of the stations generally seek to recall the former heyday of steam railways, often pre-nationalisation days. The approach of the industrial open-air museum, such as Beamish in County Durham, which owes much to the European folk museum, is often taken. Some even try and involve their clientele passengers in this. The East Lancashire Railway, between Heywood, Bury and Rawtenstall, runs themed Dickensian week-ends or World War II weekends, with associated markets, mock battles, and period musical events. Numerous Santa specials at Christmas seek to attract the next generation of railway enthusiasts.

British Rail was slow to appreciate the tourist potential of some of their more scenic routes and of their now discarded array of steam locomotives. They were only narrowly prevented from closing the Settle to Carlisle line, a scenic alternative to the West Coast main line northwards to Scotland. The Settle to Carlisle Railway trust was set up to help restore the most important viaducts, such as the Ribblehead Viaduct, and to provide interpretation for tourists (Yale 2004: 8-4). Tourist Boards and local authorities collaborated to publicise the line which was built between 1869 and 1876 by the Midland Railway Company as one of the last great building projects of the Victorian Railway Age. As a heritage railway on what is still an existing section of the main railway system the Settle-Carlisle Railway now sees its daily passenger services from Leeds to Carlisle augmented by steam and diesel charter services. Eight stations along the line have been reopened. It is now a major heritage tourist attraction in the Yorkshire Dales National Park.

4. The Current Situation – Railways

As the tables in the appendix illustrate, there are now around 20 heritage railways functioning in Northern England and the Isle of Man plus eight railway/transport museums. The Settle-Carlisle Railway, Carnforth Station, the Manx Electric Railway and an industrial locomotives site add to the transport heritage ensemble. It is worth highlighting a few of these railway societies to illustrate the variety and richness of this industrial heritage in the North of England. The Middleton Railway at Leeds claims to be the world's oldest working railway. "Never having closed since 1758 the railway still operates under its original Act of Parliament" (Butcher 2004). It also claims to be the first standard gauge railway to be taken over by a preservation society in 1960. Its 15 steam locomotives and 11 diesels make up the "Leeds Collection" which comprises a representative collection of locomotives built by the Hunslet Engine Company of Leeds between 1812 and 1995. The Tanfield Railway in County Durham also claims to be the "oldest railway in the world" with its 1725 Sunniside to Causey section of track. Its oldest section of wagon way dates back to 1647 and used to move coal down to the River Tyne. Its 58 locomotives and its significant architectural feature, namely the 1727 Causey Arch viaduct, serve to attract about 40,000 visitors a year. Nearly three times as many passengers (117,600 in 2005) visit the Keighley & Worth Valley Railway, which passes through Haworth and the literary 'Brontë Country' as well as having film associations with the 'Railway Children' link. This branch line was closed by British Railways in 1962 and then re-opened by the society in 1968, just over a century after its original opening back in 1867. Visitor numbers total about 150,000 a year. The most popular heritage railway in the North is the North Yorks Moors Railway with about 280,000 visitors a year travelling all or part of its 18 miles of track from Grosmont to Pickering through the geomorphologically significant Newtondale Gorge, a glacial overspill channel. Its collection of steam locomotives includes the *George Stephenson* (LMS – 1947) and the elegant *Sir Nigel Gresley* (LNER – 1937). Other well-known engines have also been preserved by the East Lancashire Railway whose claim to fame is that the line of the 8 miles of track between Bury and Rawtenstall is owned by the local authorities of Bury M.B.C. and Rossendale Borough Council. They then lease it to the trust which makes it available to the Society.

Originally opened in 1846 the branch line was closed to passengers in 1972 and for freight in 1980. The Society re-opened the East Lancashire Railway in 1991 and has recently extended services to Heywood which links the heritage line into the national rail network. The railway has 47 locomotives plus 6 industrial locomotives and over 50 coaches. Its star engines are *Princess Elizabeth*, the *Duke of Gloucester*, *Morning Star* and the *Western Prince*.

By way of contrast with these well-established heritage railway societies, a couple of more recently opened railway societies can be instanced. The Wensleydale Railway started passenger services in 2003 along part of the line between the East Coast main line and the Settle-Carlisle line at Garsdale. Indeed it was the reprieve in 1989 for the Settle-Carlisle line which triggered the formation of this Wensleydale Railway Association with the ambition eventually of restoring rail services to a lengthy 40 miles of track. Another recently opened heritage railway, the Weardale Railway Project in County Durham, started up services in 2004. This moth-balled branch line running westwards from Bishop Auckland was originally built in 1847 and extended in 1862. Indeed, a section of the 'new' heritage railway runs on part of the historic Stockton & Darlington Railway. The most recent addition to this set of heritage railways was re-opened to passenger services in 2006, namely the Eden Valley Railway based at Appleby. However, the loss of viaducts will pose problems for its extension.

According to the tables in the appendix six of the North's heritage railways are narrow-gauge. These are often former industrial or mineral lines as in the case of the Ravenglass and Eskdale Railway on the western side of the Lake District (see section 6). Seen from a regional perspective, these lines are even more significant for the formation of regional identities: strictly tied into the history of the industrial activities of the particular region they can demonstrate history as a local denominator rather than the grand railway lines connecting Britain's major urban centres.

5. Railway and Transport Museums

It should be kept in mind that Northern England was also home to some of the most important locomotive works. Vulcan Foundry at Newton-le-Willows, Merseyside, produced its first engines in 1832, designed by Robert Stephenson, took its name in 1847 and finally closed in 2000. Perhaps more significant for railway enthusiasts is the souvenir of the Beyer-Peacock locomotive works founded in 1854 at Gorton, Manchester. Engineer Beyer migrated from the German state of Saxony, and his fame attracted Gottlieb Daimler (1834-1900) to work in Gorton from 1861 to 1863, certainly bringing much English experience to his later automobile factory at Stuttgart. Beyer-Peacock produced the articulated Beyer-Garratt locomotives from 1909 up to 1958, a type much in favour in Southern Africa and still present in South Africa. One specimen is displayed today at the Manchester Museum for Science and Technology.

With such a tradition, railway or transport museums, often with a limited length of demonstration rail track, are of specific importance, as given in the tables in the appendix. Together they preserve a large number of often significant heritage steam locomotives and attract many visitors. The Timothy Hackworth Victorian & Railway Museum is built on the original Stockton & Darlington Railway's Shildon Works site and is obviously named after the illustrious railway engineer. He competed in the 1829 Rainhill Trials on the Manchester & Liverpool Railway with *Sans Pareil*; a replica of which is in this museum. Shildon is one of the world's oldest railway towns and its museum houses what amounts to the 'reserve collection' of the National Railway Museum, York consisting of some 60 items. The main collection of the NRM York consists of over 100 locomotives and nearly 200 other items of rolling stock. It houses a wide range of railway icons such as *Mallard*, the 1923 *Flying Scotsman*, and the 1903 *City of Truro* as well as the early classics, *Puffing Billy, Sans Pareil, Novelty* and *Rocket*. As a branch of London's Science Museum, the NRM also stores over 1 million engineering drawings of locomotives, carriages, etc. dating from 1820 to the present. Open since 1975, this is essentially a static collection of engines but there is an active programme of loans to heritage railways around the country. About 900,000 people annually visit this heritage centre which was 'European Museum of the Year' in 2001. One such long-term loan from the NRM is *Locomotion No. 1* to the Darlington Railway Centre and Museum which is located appropriately on the original 1825 route of the pioneering Stockton & Darlington Railway. In addition to housing the 1825 *Locomotion* and the 1845 *Derwent*, an associated trust is building the first new steam locomotive in Britain for over 40 years called *Tor-*

nado. Locomotion and the year 1825 also feature at the Beamish North of England Open Air Museum which covers some 300 acres in County Durham. Established in 1970 Beamish aims to demonstrate the living, working experience of life as it was in the Great North in the early 1800s and early 1900s, more specifically 1825 and 1913. Buildings are transferred and re-erected on the site, following the 'folk museum' approach. Beamish 'town' now includes a 1913 branch-line railway station, moved from Rowley, near Consett. On the 1825 railway, the Pockerley Waggonway, runs a replica of *Locomotion No. 1* with replica 1825 carriages. There are plans to create a working replica of *Puffing Billy*, built by William Hedley in 1814 to run on the 1825 railway. The 1913 section also has an operational fleet of restored trams dating from the early twentieth century.

6. Some Case Studies

Our tables in the appendix of this essay give a good insight into the various heritage railways and museums. Just one specific area and one specific railway are presented in the following paragraphs. They perhaps are not more or less typical of the scene than the others, but, for the foreign visitor, they present a specific and most folkloristic aspect.

6.1 Isle of Man

Specific mention must be made of the four working heritage railways on the Isle of Man which has some 65 miles of Victorian railways and tramways. The Manx Electric railway, founded 1893, runs 17.75 miles from Douglas to Ramsey. Two of its tramcars are claimed to be the oldest working examples in the world. The Snaefell Mountain Railway has since 1895 ascended the 2,036 feet summit of Snaefell from Laxey on its 3'6" narrow gauge. Thirdly, the Manx Steam Railway, dating from 1874, runs on a 3 foot gauge the 15.5 miles from Douglas to Port Erin. A Beyer-Peacock locomotive dates back to 1874. Finally, another steam railway, the Groudle Glen Narrow Gauge Railway was opened in 1896 and closed in 1962. The Isle of Man Steam Railway Supporters Association managed to re-open it in 1986 with diesel, and later steam locomotives. The restoration of its track was completed in

1992-93. Thus the Isle of Man is not just a Mecca for motorcyclists during its TT races; it is also a paradise for heritage railway enthusiasts.

6.2 Ravenglass and Eskdale Railway

This is probably one of the most impressive – and most incredible – pieces of railway a continental visitor can encounter in this part of the world, probably only possible in Northern England. In 1876 a 0.91-metre gauge track was laid from the mainline station of Ravenglass (on the Carnforth-Carlisle main line) to Dalegarth in Eskdale where iron ore was being mined from haematite deposits. Due to the poor quality of the ore and to limited prospects of passenger traffic in a sparsely populated mountain valley the line went bankrupt and finally closed altogether in 1913 (according to Jenner 2002). However, miniature railways engineer and toy designer Wenman Joseph Bassett-Lowke (1877 to 1953) from Northampton detected, during a visit in 1915, the charms of the line and its setting. He decided to change the track to 15" (= 0.38 metres), in order to test and present miniature steam locomotives produced according to his design by toy railway factories. Granite for road and railway construction was taken from the railway's quarries, crushed and transported to the main line. This generated, together with general freight, a solid income. When quarrying stopped in 1953 the line was offered for sale and the 1960 passenger train season thought to be the last. But instead of being scrapped, the railway was taken over by a local landowner, who, together with a successful stockbroker, provided the necessary funds for the new Ravenglass and Eskdale Railway Preservation Society. Voluntary work remains essential for the existence of the railway which annually carries ¼ of a million of passengers on its seven miles of track. The perfect condition of its operating seven steam and nine combustion locomotives as well as the passenger cars present a success story. It brings a continuous flow of visitors to this remote valley. Continental visitors rather feel that the little puffing engine, with its four-wheeled, double-seating carriages behind, would jump the rails and end in disaster. They may also have in mind all those "specialists", again from the continent, who declare such a railway in such a remote area to be economic nonsense and a waste of public and private funds. Obviously, such feelings and declarations are erroneous. The railway in its present form has been operating for more than 90 years.

7. Economic prospects and outlook

Enthusiasts looking for the cradle of industrialisation and the various signs and elements remaining from this historical period are being attracted more and more to Northern England. Its industrial and transportation heritage, which also encompasses restored canals[1], textile mills, coal mines, aircraft and maritime museums, now form a major tourist attraction in their own right to be set beside the Gothic cathedrals, Roman frontier walls, castles and stately homes. In fact, the reminders of the oldest and once most dense railway network of the world, together with other elements of industrial archaeology, seem to be the most important intrinsic attraction to the region, bringing an increasing number of tourists. Together with the National Railway Museum in York and the Museum of Science and Industry in Manchester (with one of the famous Beyer-Garratt articulated steam locomotives on display) heritage railways form a grid of attractions covering most of the north. The re-privatisation of the British railways has given them more freedom and flexibility, but also more technical and economic responsibility. And these railways have grown, from an enthusiast's event, into elements of importance for the regional economy.

The 83 miles or approx. 135kms of individual lines in operation in 2005 carried a total of 1.2 million passengers in that year. This is relatively a much higher intensity than in Germany where, on 1,400kms of track, museum and tourist railways counted 2.5 million passengers in 2003 (according to Schliephake 2005: 133).

Our empirical findings from a survey of about 800 users of two heritage railways in northern Bavaria, in 2003 and 2004, give a picture differing from prejudices often held about railway enthusiasts. Where a heavy dominance of male pensioners was supposed, in fact the gender and age groups were quite balanced with only 20% pensioners and only 59% male customers.

---

[1] See the essay by Richard Stinshoff in this volume.

And visitors often come from far away: 46% of our sample came from outside the region and ⅓ of the total had exclusively or mainly come because of the heritage railway. The visitors from outside had spent an average of €49 or £33 per day in the area served by the railway, mostly on food, lodging and souvenirs.

In Great Britain, according to our knowledge, things are not much different. If we transfer the German findings to Northern England the 1.2 million annual visitors, ⅓ of them perhaps from outside the area, would contribute a sum of 1.2 x 0.33 x £33 = £13.1 million or 19.5 million Euros to the local economy.

The additional 1.3 million visitors to railway and transport museums certainly create similar effects. Incidentally, our figures directly correlate with findings from the National Railway Museum at York. Although entrance to the premises is free, the 997,000 visitors (in 2004) bring £30 million annually or £30 per person and visit into Yorkshire's economy (from NRM Review 2004-05). Such calculations may look hypothetical, but they point to the growing importance of heritage railways and technical and transportation museums in the region.

Perhaps, this is the message from the north and to the north. It forms the cradle of industry and technology and northerners are proud of it. They know what they have contributed to the modern world. Despite preserving and valorising a sensitive part of its heritage, the north has not turned into a museum; but it makes visible the rules of our global economy in an area which intensely profits from today's globalisation.

Works Cited

Research Literature

Biddle Gordon and O.S. Nock (1983): *The Railway Heritage of Britain*. London: Michael Joseph.

Burman, Peter and Michael Stratton (eds.) (1997): *Conserving the Railway Heritage*. London: Spon.

Butcher, Alan C. (2004): *Railways Restored 2004*. Hersham/Surrey: Ian Allan Publishing.

Cossons, Neil (1993): "Landscapes of the Industrial Revolution: Myths and Realities", in: S. Glyptis (ed.): *Leisure and the Environment: essays in honour of Professor J.A. Patmore*. London and New York: Belhaven, 33-52.

— (1997): "An agenda for the railway heritage", in: P. Burman and M. Stratton (eds.): *Conserving the Railway Heritage*. London: Spon, 3-17.

Demhardt, I. J. (2004): "Verkehrslinien als touristische Attraktionen", in: C. Becker and H. Job (eds.): *Freizeit und Tourismus (Nationalatlas Bundesrepublik Deutschland)*. Heidelberg and Berlin: Spektrum, 64-66.

Edwards, J.A. and J.C. Llurdés (1996): "Mines and quarries: industrial heritage tourism", *Annals of Tourism Research* 23, 341-363.

Jenner, David (2002): *The visitor's guide. Ravenglass and Eskdale railway*.

Pabst, M. (1989): *Tram & trolley in Africa*. Krefeld: Röhr.

Patmore, J.Allan (1983): *Recreation and Resources. Leisure Patterns and Leisure Places*. Oxford: Blackwell.

Schliephake, Konrad (2005): "Museumsbahnen im Raum. Die 'Mainschleifenbahn' Seligenstadt-Volkach und ihre Benutzer", in: Winfried Schenk and Konrad Schliephake (eds.): *Würzburger Geographische Manuskripte vol. 70*, 123-146. Würzburg: Universität Würzburg.

Schliephake, Konrad and T.A. Schenk (2005): "Verkehr und Mobilität", in: Winfried Schenk and Konrad Schliephake (eds.): *Allgemeine Anthropogeographie*. Gotha and Stuttgart: Klett-Perthes, 531-580.

Simmons, Jack and Gordon Biddle (eds.) (1997): *The Oxford Companion to British Railway History*. Oxford: Oxford UP.

Smith, M.K. (2003): *Issues in Cultural Tourism Studies*. London: Routledge.

Suggitt, Gordon (2003): *Lost railways of Lancashire*. Newbury: Countryside Books.

Timothy, Dallen J. and Stephen W. Boyd (2003): *Heritage Tourism*. New York: Pearson.

Welbourn, Nigel (2003): *Lost lines north-eastern*. Hersham/Surrey: Ian Allan Publishing.

Yale, Pat (2004): *From Tourist Attraction to Heritage Tourism*. Huntingdon: Elm.

Websites (see also tables below):

<http://www.heritagerailways.com/>
<http://www.uksteam.info/links.htm>

Appendix: Heritage Railways, Museums and Collections in Northern England

Table 1: Standard Gauge/Branch Lines

Aln Valley Railway Society, Alnwick

Date of Opening:	In future
Length:	3 miles
Visitor Nos:	n.d.
Significant Features:	Seeking to re-instate branch line Alnwick to Alnmouth.
Website: <http://www.avrs.co.uk/>	

Bowes Railway, Gateshead

Date of Opening:	1976
Length:	1.5 miles
Visitor Nos:	c. 3000 a year
Significant Features:	A scheduled ancient monument. Only working standard gauge rope-hauled railway in the world. Also 1.25 miles of rope haulage incline railway.
Website: <http://www.bowesrailway.co.uk/>	

Derwent Valley Light Railway (East of York)

Date of Opening:	1993
Length:	n.d.
Visitor Nos:	c. 10,000 a year
Significant Features:	Original railway was private and never nationalised. Works in partnership with the Yorkshire Museum of Farming.
Website: <http://www.dvlr.org.uk/>	

East Lancashire Railway, Bury

Date of Opening:	1991
Length:	8 miles
Visitor Nos:	c. 110,000 a year
Significant Features:	Line owned by local councils. Leased to trust. Heywood link will connect to main line. 47 locos include *Princess Elizabeth*, *Duke of Gloucester*, *Morning Star*, *Western Prince*.

Website: <http://east-lancs-rly.co.uk/>

Eden Valley Railway Trust, Appleby

Date of Opening:	2006
Length:	6 miles
Visitor Nos:	n.d.
Significant Features:	Demolished viaducts pose problems for extension.

Website: <http://www.evr.org.uk/>

Elsecar Railway, Barnsley

Date of Opening:	n.d.
Length:	1 mile
Visitor Nos:	n.d.
Significant Features:	Original closed in 1984 when Cortonwood Colliery was closed down.

Website: <http://www.elsecarrailway.cjb.net>

Embsay & Bolton Abbey Steam Railway

Date of Opening:	1979
Length:	4.5 miles
Visitor Nos:	c.103,000 a year
Significant Features:	Also known as 'Yorkshire Dales Railway'; serves Bolton Abbey, a major visitor attraction in the region.

Website: <http://www.pogo.org.uk/railway/>

Keighley & Worth Valley Railway

Date of Opening:	1968

Length:	4.75 miles
Visitor Nos:	c. 150,000 a year
Significant Features:	Serves Haworth and 'Brontë Country'. Community-orientated with residents' railcard discounts. Features in 1970 film *The Railway Children*.

Website: <http://www.kwvr.co.uk/>

Lakeside & Haverthwaite Railway (Newby Bridge)

Date of Opening:	n.d.
Length:	3.5 miles
Visitor Nos:	c. 170,000 a year
Significant Features:	Branch of line to Barrow-in-Furness in S. Lakes District. Furness Railway Trust owns Britain's oldest working standard gauge steam locomotive, *Furness Railway Number 20*.

Website: <http://www.lakesiderailway.co.uk/>

Middleton Railway, Leeds

Date of Opening:	1960
Length:	1.25 miles
Visitor Nos:	c. 20,000 a year
Significant Features:	Still operates under its original Act of Parliament, 1758 – "never closed". Its "Leeds Collection" specialises in locomotives built by the Hunslet Engine Corporation. 5 regular locos and 24 industrial locos.

Website: <http://www.middletonrailway.org.uk/>

North Yorkshire Moors Railway, Pickering

Date of Opening:	1974
Length:	18 miles
Visitor Nos:	c.280,000 a year
Significant Features:	Its 22 steam locos and 10 diesel locos include *George Stephenson* (LMS, 1947) and *Sir Nigel Gresley* (LNER, 1937).

Website: <http://www.nymr.demon.co.uk/>

Tanfield Railway, County Durham

Date of Opening:	n.d.

Length:	3 miles
Visitor Nos:	c. 40,000 a year
Significant Features:	Oldest railway in the world with its 1725 route and 1727 Causey Arch viaduct. 58 locos including 17 narrow gauge.
Website: <http://www.tanfield-railway.co.uk/>	

Weardale Railway Project, County Durham

Date of Opening:	2004
Length:	18.7 miles
Visitor Nos:	n.d.
Significant Features:	On part of Stockton & Darlington Railway. Original line built in 1847.
Website: <http://www.weardale-railway.org.uk/>	

Wensleydale Railway, North Yorkshire

Date of Opening:	2003
Length:	22 miles
Visitor Nos:	n.d.
Significant Features:	Links East Coast main line with Settle-Carlisle railway. Only 12 miles operating in 2003. More opened since.
Website: <http://www.wensleydalerailway.com/>	

Table 2: Narrow Gauge Railways

Kirklees Light Railway (near Huddersfield)

Date of Opening:	n.d.
Length:	4 miles
Visitor Nos:	n.d.
Significant Features:	15 inch gauge. 6 locos (4 steam, 2 diesel)
Website: <http://www.kirkleeslightrailway.com>	

Ravenglass & Eskdale Railway, Lakes District

Date of Opening:	1876/1915
Length:	7 miles
Visitor Nos:	250,000 a year

Significant Features: 2' 9" gauge. 13 locos, steam and diesel. Privately owned.
Website: <http://www.ravenglass-railway.co.uk/>

South Tynedale Railway, Alston

Date of Opening:	1983
Length:	2.25 miles
Visitor Nos:	c.22,000 a year
Singificant Features:	2 foot gauge. 14 locos. On track of earlier standard gauge Haltwhistle to Alston branchline.

Website: <http://www.strps.org.uk/>

West Lancashire Light Railway

Date of Opening:	1967
Length:	n.d.
Visitor Nos:	c.13,500 a year
Significant Features:	2 foot gauge. Approximately 30 locos. On track at a local brickworks, not on a branch line.

Website: <http://www.westlancs.org>

Snaefell Mountain Railway, Isle of Man

Date of Opening:	1895
Length:	4 miles
Visitor Nos:	n.d.
Significant features:	3' 6" gauge. Ascends to summit of Snaefell at 2,036 feet altitude.

Website: <http://www.isle-of-man.com/heritage/transport/index.shtml>

Manx Steam Railway, Isle of Man

Date of Opening:	1874
Length:	15.5 miles
Visitor Nos:	n.d.
Significant Features:	3 foot gauge. Douglas to Port Erin.

Website: <http://www.iomguide.com/steamrailway.php>

Table 3: Railway/Transport Museums

Beamish North of England Open Air Museum, County Durham

Date of Opening:	1970
Visitor Nos:	c. 320,000 a year
Significant Features:	Focuses on 1825 and 1913. Replica of *Locomotion No.1*. Re-created a 1913 railway station. Fleet of trams on tramway.

Website: <http://www.beamishmuseum.co.uk/>

Darlington Railway Centre and Museum.

Date of Opening:	1980
Visitor Nos:	c. 22,000 a year
Significant Features:	0.25 miles of track on line of 1825 Stockton & Darlington railway. *Locomotion No.1* (1829) and *Derwent* (1845).

Website: <http://www.drcm.org.uk/default.htm>

Armley Mills: Leeds Industrial Museum

Date of Opening:	1982
Visitor Nos:	n.d.
Significant Features:	33 locos, of which 9 are standard gauge.

Website: <http://www.leeds.gov.uk/armleymills/>

Museum of Science and Industry in Manchester

Date of Opening:	1983
Visitor Nos:	n.d.
Significant Features:	Partly housed in Liverpool Road Station – world's oldest passenger station. Replicas of *Novelty* (1829), *Lion* (1838).

Website: <http://www.msim.org.uk>

National Railway Museum York

Date of Opening:	1975
Visitor Nos:	c. 700,000 a year
Significant Features:	100 locos & nearly 200 other rolling stock. *Puffing Billy*, *Sans Pareil*, *Novelty*, *Rocket*. Railway icons such as 1923 *Flying Scotsman*, 1938 *Duchess of Hamilton*, 1903 *City of Truro*, 1960 *Evening Star*.

Website: <http://www.nrm.ork.uk/>

The Railway Age, Crewe

Date of Opening:	n.d.
Visitor Nos;	n.d.
Significant Features:	15 locos plus 1 industrial loco. In Crewe Heritage Centre.

Website: <http://www.therailwayage.co.uk>

Stephenson Railway Museum, Wallsend/North Shields

Date of Opening:	1986
Visitor Nos:	n.d.
Significant Features:	Exhibits relocated here from Tyne & Wear Museums and former Museum of Science and Industry in Newcastle. Stephenson's *Puffing Billy* (1813) features as a stationary exhibit. Steam and diesel locomotives used on Tyneside from the 1880s to 1980s.

Website: <http://www.twmuseums.org.uk/stephenson/>

Timothy Hackworth Victorian & Railway Museum, Shildon

Date of Opening:	1975
Visitor Nos	n.d.
Significant Features:	On Shildon Works site on Stockton & Darlington Railway. Replica of *Sans Pareil*. Houses reserve collection of NRM York.

Website: <http://www.railcentre.co.uk/museum/museum.htm>

Table 4: Industrial Locomotives and Other Heritage Sites

Carnforth Station

Date of Opening:	2003
Visitor Nos:	n.d.
Significant Features:	Location for 1945 film *Brief Encounter*. Brief Encounter Café and Visitor/Heritage Centre in restored waiting room. Steamtown Railway Museum operated from Carnforth Railway Sheds, 1968-1997. Now closed.

Website: <http://travel.to/carnforth#>

Manx Electric Railway

Date of Opening:	1893
Visitor Nos:	n.d.
Significant Features:	Douglas to Ramsey for 17.75 miles. Two of its tramcars are the oldest working examples in the world.

Website: <http://www.isle-of-man.com/heritage/transport/index.shtml>

Ribble Steam Railway

Date of Opening:	2005
Visitor Nos:	n.d.
Significant Features:	1.5 mile of track in Preston Dock/Marina location. Newly built workshop.

Website: <http://www.ribblesteam.org.uk/>

Settle-Carlisle Railway

Date of Opening:	1989
Visitor Nos:	n.d.
Significant Features:	Part of national rail network. Pressure group kept it open when threatened. Ribblehead Viaduct restored and 8 stations re-opened. Steam and diesel charter services.

Website: <http://www.settle-carlisle.co.uk/>

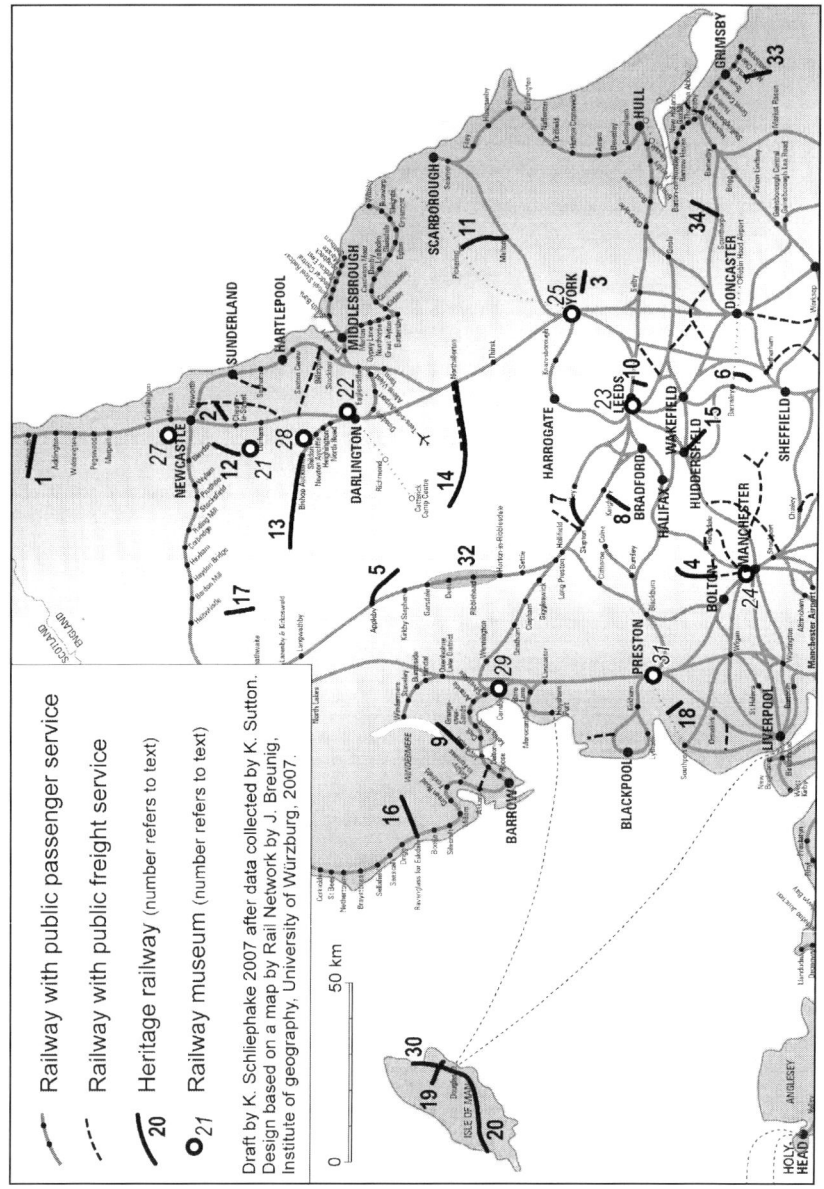

CHAPTER IV
MEDIASCAPES

Constructing an Emblematic Northern Space under Thatcherism: The New Brighton Photographs of Martin Parr and Tom Wood

Merle Tönnies

Abstract: In the 1980s the English photographers Martin Parr and Tom Wood each started to document the decline of the northern seaside resort New Brighton. The essay discusses the individual representational strategies of the two artists and illustrates how their photographic surveys functioned as a radical comment on the ideology of the Thatcher years and at the same time as a statement of northern English identity.

Key Names and Concepts: Martin Parr - Tom Wood; New Brighton - Thatcherism - North-South Divide - Representational Spaces - Spatial Practices - De-industrialisation.

1. Introduction

Traditionally, the North of England was stereotyped from outside (i.e. mainly Southern) perspectives as a highly industrialised, but lively and productive area – one need only think of George Orwell's "clatter of clogs in the Lancashire mill towns" and "to-and-fro of the lorries on the Great North Road" (1956 [1941], 250).[1] In the last decades of the twentieth century, however, the region acquired a new set of far more negative connotations that were quoted and requoted in diverse representations such as newspaper articles, novels and pop songs. The decline of heavy industry meant that it increasingly came to stand for unemployment, social problems and a lack of hope. Due to New Brighton's specific history, this coastal resort on the north-east corner

---

[1] See the combination of bleakness with energy that Dave Russell observes in English heterostereotypes of Northernness (2004: 37, 268). Fowler, Robinson and Boniface (2001: 126) focus more on the negative side of the North as "a foreign country".

of the Wirral Peninsula can be made to embody such associations in a very graphic form. It was conceived as a rival of the Southern town Brighton in 1830 when with the advance of the Industrial Revolution, the North looked ready to embark on a bright and successful economic future (see e.g. Musgrove 1990: 265, 267). A retired Liverpool merchant and builder purchased heathland and sand hills in this area to develop an upmarket residential and watering place. For the first 30 years of its existence, New Brighton did indeed work as a rather genteel spa. A pier was built for a steam ferry to Liverpool, and in 1867 the Promenade Pier was added with a number of entertainments for tourists.

However, with the growing popularity of trains and especially after the Bank Holiday Act of 1871,[2] visitors' social status dropped, as working-class residents from the larger Liverpool area and Lancashire mill workers started to come to New Brighton on day trips. The 1920s then saw the beginnings of decline, when the 1900 observation tower fell into disrepair and had to be taken down. Its height, which had made it the tallest building in the country at that time (even surpassing the Blackpool Tower) could be taken to symbolise the former high hopes of the region. The brick basis of the tower was later destroyed by fire in 1969. Even more symbolically, the New Brighton ferry closed in 1971 for lack of passengers, and the Promenade Pier was dismantled in 1978. The beginning of the Thatcher years brought the most dramatic deterioration to the town, as tourists increasingly preferred low-cost package holidays on the continent. The failing businesses, run-down amusement arcades and declining population figures of New Brighton could be (and were) seen as pinpointing the disastrous effects of Thatcherism on British society in general (see e.g. Walker 1986) and the growing North South divide of this period in particular.[3]

This was exactly the time when two photographers, Martin Parr and Tom Wood, started to work in New Brighton.[4] They had met in

---

[2] For the consequences see also Walton (1983: 33-35).

[3] See the statistics collected in Hudson and Williams (1995: 220-225, 246); Martin (2004: 24-27).

[4] It should be noted that photography is curiously absent in Russell's otherwise very comprehensive study of representations of the North in different media (2004).

1981 and were thinking of publishing a book together – a project which ultimately never materialised. Although they went together on photographic excursions to the resort in the mid-eighties and sometimes photographed quite similar motifs, each of them has his own special viewpoint. Thus, the ways in which their pictures construct impressions of New Brighton, and of the North in general, differ in content and form (despite the same medium). The present paper will analyse how each photographer turns New Brighton as a geographical place into a particular space (in de Certeau's sense of "*practiced place*"),[5] both by showing how his subjects use it and by making his own visual use of the seaside resort. As a result, New Brighton comes to stand for a specific social landscape in the North of Thatcherist England. In Henri Lefebvre's (1994: 39) terminology, one can therefore say that the photographs construct 'representational spaces' which overlay the actual physical space.

For Martin Parr, the book that emerged from the New Brighton photographs, *The Last Resort* of 1986, was the beginning of his professional success which not only made him a member of the photographic agency Magnum but in addition very famous outside Britain. Ironically, this happened through works that pointedly focus on endings rather than new beginnings. As the literal meaning of the title stresses, there is a sense in most of the pictures that they show the last stages in New Brighton's life or possibly in the existence of any northern seaside resort. Emblematically, the very last Parr photograph in the book (Parr 1986: 40)[6] shows a woman sunbathing face-down on a spotlessly white towel next to a little girl and an old rusty machine. Together with their belongings, the woman and the girl are the only spots of colour in a scene that is otherwise dominated by different shades of grey and brown. These 'non-colours' also characterise an older man walking by. In contrast to the traditional structures that are no longer 'working' (in a very literal sense), the two colourful tourists might thus at first sight constitute a new beginning (especially when one takes into account that Parr moved into colour photography with the *Last Resort* pictures). If one looks more closely, however, there is no foundation for such optimism. The 'spatial practices' (cf. Lefebvre

---

[5]   Cf. de Certeau 1984: 117 (his emphasis).
[6]   There is no pagination in the book, but the numbers mark the (untitled) photographs.

1994: 33, 38) adopted by the two are fitting for a beach but not for the patch of concrete on which they find themselves.[7] We would expect the mother's posture to become extremely uncomfortable on the hard ground and the towel to be soiled by the grimy surroundings before

Figure 1: Martin Parr *The Last Resort*

long (with the purity of its present colour already being mocked by the equally white discarded plastic bag next to it). Similarly, there is no use for the daughter's plastic beach toys which lie scattered around her. Not only have the greater industrial processes come to an end (symbolised by the disused machine) but tourism, too, no longer 'works' in New Brighton. Significantly, the sunbathing woman is lying at a right angle to the dominant direction of the other lines in the picture, i.e. she sticks out from the overall course of events and cannot be accommodated. The grey man walking along the promenade, on

---

[7] For an analysis of characteristic beach practices see Fiske (1989: 46). He points out how these activities mediate between nature and culture, which is impossible here for the lack of genuine nature.

the other hand, is completely in tune with New Brighton's 'future'. In contrast to the woman's static posture, he is moving – but is going straight towards the impasse of the seashore. It can thus be considered a case of scathing irony that the very last picture of the collection reproduces an old postcard from the resort which cheerfully announces "Cheerio & lots of luck". While it proudly flaunts all the sights of the traditional New Brighton as a successful tourist town, its sepia colours unavoidably recall the representation of decline on the previous plate. The optimism with which the resort was founded is thereby undermined most effectively.

Situated in a very prominent position in a book that carries the word 'last' in the title, the picture of the woman and the girl condenses most of the elements of Northernness as constructed by Parr. First of all, there is a pervasive sense that people have stopped caring about their surroundings. Discarded waste forms a recurrent motif in the book, and its impact is heightened by the fact that Parr usually portrays families going about their daily business directly next to it. Two very similar photos (Parr 1986: 25, 28) show different generations (from young children with their parents to an older couple and a baby) eating stoically right next to an overflowing rubbish bin. Any changes in the different subjects' behaviour are far less conspicuous than the variations in the actual nature of the rubbish. Rather private family affairs appear to be transferred into the public sphere, i.e. the protection that used to go with the smaller units of society is no longer present. At the same time, the public space itself has become as repugnant as it can be. Although Thatcher won the 1979 election by blaming Labour for the decline in public spirit in the preceding 'winter of discontent', the pictures suggest quite pointedly that this development was aggravated during her time in office. Not only do public services seem dysfunctional, but the public itself has lost any interest in a working society. As in the pictures that the British photographer Paul Graham took in public buildings like unemployment offices in roughly the same period and published in his collection *Beyond Caring* (1986), 'caring' about anything at all has become a completely foreign concept – in spite of the Prime Minister's understanding of 'charity' as an essential element of Britishness (see Thatcher 1989a: 85; 1989b: 269-270).

Indeed, a good number of pictures suggest that a feeling for the needs of others is a luxury that one can no longer afford in the eighties New Brighton; in a perverted version of Thatcher's own view, there can no longer be such a thing as 'society', only individuals. Just as the two related photographs discussed above link different generations with regard to the rubbish in public spaces, two further pictures express the scarcity of resources (Parr 1986: 23, 24). In the first one, a group of kids is crowding around the counter of an improvised ice-cream parlour. While they jostle for the desired refreshment, the shop assistant looks in the opposite direction, directly at the camera, betraying an unfathomable degree of boredom in her look and posture. While she could not care less for the children's needs, they cannot afford to care for each other, as it seems by no means certain that she will continue to serve them. The emotional coldness of the image is intensified by the appearance of the ice-cream itself, which has a garishly artificial green colour. Even if the 'customers' obtain what they are queuing for at all, it will only be a very low-quality product. The situation is still worse in the following picture, which also includes members of the parent generation. They are struggling for drinks in plastic cups and cheap-looking hotdogs, with the name of the fast-food item itself potentially drawing attention to the 'dog-eat-dog society' that is portrayed. Moreover, the equally grave expression of the people in the queue and those who have already obtained their food suggests that ultimately no satisfaction is possible. In the context of the book with 'New Brighton' in the subtitle this hopelessness is tied directly to the North of England; it seems to condense a more general national mood in the most graphic form. Referring to the figurative sense of Parr's title, one can say that the 'last resort' is shown to be none after all; although it still offers hope for the bright holidays with which it was associated in the past, this promise can no longer be fulfilled in times of Thatcherist decline.

The topic of vain illusions runs through the photographs on a far more general level as well, affecting the very creation of space they are engaged in. Throughout the book, Parr deliberately omits the conventional seaside views that his subtitle seems to promise and that can be found in the old postcard at the end. Many pictures indeed seem to quote such scenes in a perverted form: instead of the combination of sand and sea for which New Brighton used to be famous, they construct the resort as consisting of dirty concrete strips and equally polluted water basins. Thus, nature itself seems to have been conquered by its harsh, artificial opposite where nothing grows any longer and no comfort can be found. Implicitly, Parr thereby not only opposes stereotypical touristic images,[8] but also the representations of Southern English seaside towns by an older generation of British photographers. Works like Tony Ray-Jones's "Hotel, Newquay" (1967) or "Eastbourne" (1968) depict traditional beach practices in the 'correct' setting.[9] By contrast, the people who use the very different places in Parr's pictures do not seem to realise that a paradigmatically 'English' landscape has degenerated into a squalid urbanised location. In a number of related pictures, groups of women look after little children in or near pools of dirty water (see especially Parr 1986: 12, 13, 17, 32). Like the woman and the girl already analysed, they behave exactly as one would usually expect them to do on a beach, i.e. their spatial practices are relics of better times, as if they refuse to realise that the place itself has changed beyond recognition. This impression of people living in a dream-world and ignoring the actual state of society is already pinpointed very early on in the book in a picture of a woman with a baby on a merry-go-round (Parr 1986: 6). She is sitting in an aeroplane, and her pensive expression suggests that she is on a mental journey taking her far away from New Brighton. The picture shatters this illusion almost brutally. Not only is the pretend plane never going to take her very far, but it is not even 'flying' as part of the entertainment. The merry-go-round is standing still; perhaps it has even already closed for the night. There is no way in which Parr's subjects can transcend the impasse in which they are caught and move on into a better future.

The impossibility of keeping up illusions based on the past also figures in the relationships depicted in the photographs. As one would assume in a seaside town, young families make up the great majority of the communities shown by Parr. However, even their composition already diverges sharply from traditional expectations. Women and children make up by far the greatest percentage of the people photographed, with men only rarely part of the family circle. This is all the more striking as the North of England is traditionally coded as masculine (see Russell 2004: 38). The women physically gather together

---

[8] See also the collections of traditional postcards at <http://www.newbrightonpostcards.org.uk> accessed on 20 March 2007 and <http://www.newbrightononline.org.uk/history/index.htm> accessed on 20 March 2007.

[9] For the two pictures see <http://www.ssplprints.com> accessed on 1 March 2007.

around the children, as if to protect them in the harsh climate in which they themselves have been left by their husbands. (The real reason for the scarcity of men in the photographs is probably that they have less leisure-time or no inclination to go on family outings. However, the construction of the pictures, especially those with the concrete-rimmed water pools, pointedly suggests abandonment. The viewer can moreover be expected to be familiar with the particularly high percentage of single mothers in Britain and to make a connection here.) Just as prominently, however, the women's protective posture towards the children is undermined again by their facial expressions and by the direction of their gaze. Eye contact between mother and child and even among the women in the pictures is extremely rare and the number of cases in which it is shown roughly equals that of pictures where people pat dogs and forget about their children. The women either look directly at the photographer (and thus the viewer of the picture) or – more frequently – gaze vacantly into space with their faces marked by exhaustion. The apparently coherent groups are thus fragmented and shown to constitute no real community. Parr emphasises this sense of isolation by the photographic focus, which is usually on the children. In one example (Parr 1986: 14), a crying baby in a buggy is sitting exactly in the centre of the picture, with a pink umbrella and a pink toy drawing the viewer's gaze directly to its face, to which the effort of crying has given a similar colour. However, the young woman lying in front of the buggy (probably the mother) shows no reaction; she is shading her eyes with her hand and looking nowhere. Another woman behind the baby appears to be looking vaguely in its direction but betrays no interest in it.

The uncaring adults are sometimes even cut up by the focus of the pictures to show that they are not really present as human beings at all. Most strikingly, an early photograph in the book (Parr 1986: 4) shows two children (again surrounded by rubbish), one of whom seems to be crying. The woman standing in front of them is shown only from the back, and additionally the picture cuts off her figure from the shoulders upwards. At the same time, her reflection in the window in front of which she is standing is situated directly above the unhappy boy and seems to be bending over him like a guardian angel. The optical illusion thus reveals what is missing in the real relationships, or perhaps shows genuine family relations to have become an illusion. Not only has care for public spaces and society at large become impossible, but also a loving attitude to family members. With regard to the Thatcherist ideology of the period, the pictures can thus be said to parody the proclaimed return to Victorian values with derisive irony. The only return that is taking place is one to Dickensian images of lonely children for whom no-one can afford to care in a world where everyone is (and perhaps even has to be) interested in his or her own benefit. This parallel becomes most striking in another early picture in the book (Parr 1986: 5), which shows a run-down amusement arcade. A row of older tired-looking women is slumped before the slot machines in completely frozen postures. Only their arms move quickly (as indicated by their blurred impression in the

Figure 2: Martin Parr *The Last Resort*

photograph) to respond to the requirements of the machines. Instead of productive work, they operate machines for an imagined pecuniary benefit. This 'entertainment' yields no enjoyment for them and is carried out as mechanically as work on a conveyor belt. On the opposite side of the room, rushing along another row of slot machines, is a small child, whose face remains hidden from the viewer. With her white dress and the intense movement expressed by her blurred shape in the photo, she seems to constitute the exact opposite of the static women. However, a conventional reading of the younger generation as providing a sense of a new beginning is as much out of the question here as in the other New Brighton photographs. Instead the surroundings draw attention to the abandonment of the strangely depersonalised child; it is not even clear to which woman she belongs since they are all equally oblivious to her presence. This drastic picture suggests that one can read the frequent images of crying children in the book as their response to the horror of the situation to which the members of the older generation have already become numb and against which they can no longer fight.

Although Parr's photographs seem to have started off as documentary pictures of a particular northern resort in a specific period and he himself described them as documentary at the time,[10] it has thus become obvious that they ultimately go much further. Instead of simply documenting place, they construct emblematic spaces that convey social criticism about Thatcherist Britain as a whole. The inescapable downward movement depicted and highlighted in the title is connected especially graphically with the North of England, a region that is shown to have been very vulnerable to the effects of Thatcherism due to de-industrialisation and the social problems it entails.

While Parr – despite going beyond documentation – does not seem to be bothered by this label, Tom Wood has often insisted that he is not interested in contributing to a social discussion through documentary photos[11] and has also expressed his exasperation that his work is discussed almost exclusively in these terms.[12] In reading his photographs, one thus has to pay even more attention to the ways in which they construct spaces, especially as in contrast to Parr, Wood was much more intimately familiar with New Brighton (he lived in Liverpool from 1978 to 2003). It is also important to note in this con-

---

[10] Jürgen Kisters quotes Parr (without giving a source) as having said about his New Brighton work: "I'm a documentary photographer, and if I take a 'good' photograph in the process, that's a bonus." (1999: 90)

[11] See e.g. Wood's statement "It's not enough to document" quoted in Kisters (1999: 92); cf. Böhmer (2001: 9).

[12] Interview with Tom Wood, Cologne (Galerie Zander), 3 December 2005; Dikkers (2004: 43).

text that Wood himself stresses the local rather than the regional (or even national) aspects of his pictures. His work, the photographer explains, "could be [set] anywhere, but it obviously is very specific to Liverpool. They are a particular type of people – mixture of races – Lancastrian (in your face), Welsh, Irish, and all the other nationalities a seaport brings to a city, and a long history of 'moral disorder' and an extreme sense of humor!" (Dikkers 2004: 38) Compared with Parr's tendency to generalise, Wood thus stays much more involved in the particular situation of his subjects, many of whom are known to him personally. He even expresses a certain wariness about seeing Liverpool as a northern English location: "it is more Irish".[13] At the same time, he stresses that, in contrast to Parr, he has no agenda. Thus, although the Liverpool area was home to the greatest opponents of Thatcher for him, he claims that there are no conscious references to that context in any of his works.[14]

When one surveys Wood's New Brighton pictures from the 1980s (as collected in his latest publication *Photie Man* of 2005) with that background in mind, it is first of all striking that one can find quite a few examples where the overall set-up echoes Parr – perhaps products of their joint excursions. In particular "Pregnant women" of 1984 (Wood 2005: 102-103)[15] recalls Parr's groups of women with children, as the two women and a child are sitting on dirty concrete steps, all of them looking straight ahead. Behind them, there is an extremely crowded scene with sunbathers sitting in various attitudes or moving in different directions. The diffuse energy of these surroundings is emphasised by the mix of very diverse bright colours in the people's clothing and gadgets, reminiscent of Wood's statement that because of his training as a painter, "there has to be a lot in [his] pictures".[16] Against this backdrop, the three people in the foreground seem to exude an atmosphere of calm contemplation, in contrast to the stasis and resignation expressed by equivalent Parr pictures. Each of the three protagonists shows only one dominant colour, and apart from the child's yellow bucket, these are rather subdued. The photographic

---

[13] Interview 3 December 2005.
[14] Interview 3 December 2005.
[15] The pictures in *Photie Man* are provided with titles (and usually years as well) in a list at the back of the book.
[16] Interview 3 December 2005.

focus on the three is very close, so that they make up much of the picture and allow only glimpses of the activities in the background. Together with their balanced distribution in the picture, each taking up roughly one third, this conveys a sense of confidently using the necessary space and thereby physically blocking out the less agreeable characteristics of the setting like the concrete ground. Indeed, when discussing blown-up versions of his work used in exhibitions, the photographer himself has emphasised that he enjoys it when his characters (e.g. women waiting in a bus queue) "start taking up real space".[17] The three people here seem to rest contentedly in themselves, so that communication is not needed at the moment.

The use of intense activity and equally pronounced calm is also characteristic of other pictures with Parr-like settings. "Alsation [sic] beach" of 1989 is tellingly not set on a real beach but on yet another strip of soiled concrete (Wood 2005: 16). The picture is almost bursting with energy, as people dressed in colourful clothes quickly move in different directions. The Alsatian of the title forms the centre of the picture and possibly contributes to the movement, as some groups of people seem to want to get away from the dog. Even it, however, is walking along the promenade, and the children who have stopped to watch it will have to move in a second to let it pass. In contrast to this apparent perpetuum mobile, "Girl at slot machine" from 1992 (i.e. from a slightly later period than the other New Brighton pictures analysed here) shows almost reverent contemplation (Wood 2005: 29). The angelic 'girl' with long shining blond hair is quietly looking up at the machine full of sparkling coins, her hands brought together in front of her. There is nothing of the dead postures and mechanised movements of Parr's older women in the arcade, nor of the loneliness of the child rambling in that

Figure 3: Tom Wood "Girl at a slot machine"

---

[17] Interview 3 December 2005.

picture. The girl (older than Parr's child and therefore more capable of looking after herself) seems to belong where she stands. Conspicuously, the combination of intense pink with a darker colour that can be found both on her jumper and in the contrast between her lipstick and her brown eyes is echoed by parts of the machine. Moreover, due to the photographic angle, all of its edges seem to lead straight to the point where her figure touches one of the machine's corners. The peacefulness of the picture is still heightened by the semi-darkness of the arcade, in which (again in contrast to Parr's photo) one cannot see the potentially run-down details and where the lights of the machines glow like the stained-glass windows in a church. It is obviously easy to read social criticism into this image of youth enthralled by the attraction of money, but whereas in Parr's photographs the overall atmosphere pushes the viewer directly towards critical interpretations, Wood's pictures primarily express his subjects' dignity as human beings. Whether active or still, they seem to be in control of the situation and refuse to let the circumstances dominate them.

The differences from Parr are highlighted by Wood's central New Brighton publication of the 1980s, *Looking for Love* of 1989. This is a collection of pictures taken at the now defunct Chelsea Reach nightclub over a longer period of time (mostly between 1984 and 1987), so Wood was already known to many of the people there and could get quite close to them. Here he picked a topic that Parr (judging by *The Last Resort*) did not associate very much with New Brighton. For Wood on the other hand "football and music along with drinking and socializing" are among the "cultural elements" for which Liverpool is most famous (Dikkers 2004: 37). Quite apart from the topic, merely the titles of the two collections emphasise their different perspectives: in contrast to the downward movements and broken illusions depicted by Parr, Wood is interested in people's hopes and desires in their own right. Fittingly for this aim, his subjects in *Looking for Love* are mainly adolescents – somewhere in between the numbed adults and the lonely children on whom Parr focuses, they seem capable of standing for both a certain degree of independence and (possibly naïve) dreams about the future. Wood's negotiations between activity and calm can also be found in these pictures, as scenes of intense dancing alternate with more tranquil ones. *Photie Man* for instance juxtaposes an obliquely photographed row of girls from the *Looking for Love* series, who sit in front of a mirror, with a picture of two young women actively pushing their way through the crowd. The slightly overexposed faces, on the far right and left respectively, almost make the two photographs look like mirror images (an extension of the mirror in the left picture), or like two sides of the same coin ("Pleated skirt", 1990 and "Pink hair swing girl", 1985; Wood 2005: 52-53).[18] The pictures indeed seem like two readings of the title: the first group 'looks' for love in the literal sense, whereas the second pair actively embarks on the search. These two sides can also be combined in one picture. In an inversion of standard gender stereotypes, shots of passive men watching women actively enjoying themselves and trying to attract a partner are especially frequent, and the two poles of such pictures are even allocated to separate pages in two subsequent double spreads reprinted in *Photie Man* ("Bloke looking cheeky girl", 1986 and "Red haired girl", 1986; Wood 2005: 54-55, 56-57).

The present participle in the phrase *Looking for Love* stresses the ongoing character of the search, and this is also expressed by the pictures where couples have already been formed. Two people deeply engrossed with each other are often accompanied by a third left on his/her own. Another double spread ("Chelsea intro", 1985) is especially graphic here, with a man left out in the picture on the left and a woman on the right – but a dividing wall makes the potential third couple unaware of each other (Wood 2005: 44-45). Through the urgency with which the couples press their bodies against each other, one even gets a sense that the search for love is still going on for them as well. They seem to be trying to extract 'love' or at least emotional contact from their extreme physical closeness. These rather private activities take place in the (half-)public sphere of the club, but in contrast to Parr's families going about their business in the street, one has to keep in mind that the semi-darkness of the club would normally preserve the couples' privacy to a certain extent and is only broken by the photographer's flash. Moreover, the private/public mixture in Wood's pictures points less to a dysfunctional private realm than to a shared search for love, where the different stages of the quest are more or less proudly displayed before others pursuing the same aim.

---

[18] As *Looking for Love* is out of print and almost inaccessible, the present paper will refer to the photographs as reprinted in *Photie Man*.

This sense of a Chelsea Reach community which even includes the 'losers' of the night is strengthened by the parallels between the

Figure 4: Tom Wood "Double grope/legover"

couples' behaviour patterns. As its title highlights, the photograph "Double grope/legover" (1985, Wood 2005: 141) shows two couples touching each other up in very similar ways. They are positioned on the far left and the far right of the picture, leaving a conspicuous empty part of the red couch between them. The viewer is thus invited to hold up the two individual scenes for comparison and to discover links between them despite their physical isolation from each other.[19] Exactly the same effect is produced by "Tongue out" (1985) and "Cupsnog" (1986) on two facing pages of *Photie Man* (Wood 2005: 150, 151). Through the distribution of the partners and the assertively active role that the women play in both couples, the two kisses achieve a high degree of symmetry. Whether the couples actually manage to find 'love' or not, there is a sense of all of them being part of a larger group acting according to the same rules. Tellingly, Wood

---

[19] See also the almost symmetrical distribution of the couples in the fittingly entitled picture "3 Chatups" of 1984 (Wood 2005: 147) as well as in "Last Dance" of 1985, where in addition all the men have one hand on their partner's behind (reprinted in Dikkers 2004: 40).

himself has judged *Photie Man* (where many pictures from *Looking for Love* are reprinted) to be concerned with two topics: 'boy and girl' on the one hand and the passage of time,[20] i.e. the developments that the individual couples share, on the other. The Chelsea Reach visitors even seem to be conscious of this community to some extent and able to play with its rules. "Two touches (Chris Curry)" of 1984 for instance does not show two comparable couples, as one might have expected against the background of the other pictures discussed here, but only one. The man puts his hand on the woman's behind and is himself touched in the same place by another man (Wood 2005: 59). This seems to be less a homosexual advance than a joking reference to shared codes of behaviour.

Strikingly, these patterns can even be seen to go beyond the boundaries of the Chelsea Reach. *Photie Man* contains yet another photograph where a couple is joined by a third party who has not managed to 'score' in the game in which they are all engaged. In "Tired drink picture" (1986), an isolated woman is sitting on one side of the table and an intertwined couple on the other with an arrangement of glasses between them (Wood 2005: 152). The reprint of this photograph in *Issue*, no. 8, which tellingly spreads it out over two pages and thus highlights its internal equilibrium, gives the location as Grand Hotel, New Brighton, i.e. as a rather more refined venue (Dikkers 2004: 54-55). The forms of behaviour, however, seem to transcend any such class differences to create a shared community of young people in New Brighton and potentially in the North of England more generally. These patterns seem to operate for both men and women, and this apparently allows the women much more calm self-assurance than Parr's female subjects can ever have. Even when they are tired at the end of the evening and seem to have been unable to find 'love', Wood's women still seem to retain a degree of control. This is expressed by a sense of balance and symmetry in the pictures,[21] often accentuated by the use of double spreads; the basic order of life is still intact for the characters.

---

[20] Interview 3 December 2005.

[21] David Chandler has fittingly described the arrangement of the subjects in *Looking for Love* as a "frieze-like formation across the picture plane" (1989: n. pag.).

As in the "Pregnant women" photo, Wood's subjects generally take up a lot of space in *Looking for Love*, which adds to the impression that they are given adequate importance in the picture; the distribution of space supports their claim on the viewer's attention. Although Wood's physical closeness to the depicted scenes can have a voyeuristic touch when his subjects' activities are of a very private nature, the photographs always convey that he feels close to them in an emotional way as well.[22] Not only do the people in the pictures seem much more linked to each other than Parr's lonely individuals, but the photographer, too, is integrated into their community. His subjects often seem to be looking directly at him. Tellingly, the title of the *Photie Man* collection uses the nickname that Wood was given by his Liverpool neighbourhood. Through this basic proximity, his pictures generally look far less intrusive and brutal than Parr's works, which seem to burst in upon their subjects from the outside and to present them to an audience of outsiders at the same time. It is thus probably no coincidence that Parr has been much more successful abroad than Wood, who seems to presuppose the viewer's willingness to share the characters' circumstances, at least emotionally. After all, the camera takes him/her right into the middle of their lives.[23]

All in all, Martin Parr and Tom Wood thus show a very similar situation in New Brighton – economic and social decline and the impossibility of finding a real way out in the Thatcher years. However, whereas Parr constructs a hopeless space populated by isolated individuals, Wood allows his subjects' unattainable dreams to give them a degree of shared resilience. Although they cannot get out of the dead end in the North either, they at least seem able to find a common identity and thereby handle their fates with greater confidence. The pictures by Tom Wood analysed here are confined to the 1980s and the early 1990s, i.e. they cannot yet refer to the sense of a new beginning which one can now discover in this region (cf. also Russell 2004: 285-288) and which includes a number of regeneration projects in New

---

[22] Wood has been said to use the interplay between distance and proximity in his pictures of bus journeys (especially in *All Zones Off Peak* of 1998; see also Böhmer 2001: 9), and this is just as essential for the *Looking for Love* photographs.

[23] For the camera as the audience's stand-in in the *Looking for Love* pictures see Chandler 1989: n. pag.

Brighton itself. Nevertheless, in taking people's dreams seriously, Wood's photographs seem to look towards these more hopeful developments at least potentially – although the Chelsea Reach club itself is tellingly no longer in business.[24] As Wood entitled a picture of a lone teenage mother with her baby (who appears uncharacteristically small in front of a run-down housing estate): "Maybe baby" (1990; Wood 2005: 208). Even if the situation seems desperate, there is still a chance, and the ambiguous term 'baby' relates this to both mother and child. Perhaps it is no coincidence that this photograph is among the last ones included in the unchronological *Photie Man* sequence; it may point towards a future where – maybe – the name New Brighton will have more positive connotations again.

---

[24] General visitor statistics for the twenty-first century by no means look unequivocally positive for the North West either, with numbers especially for seaside holidays in the region declining from 2000 to 2003 see <http://www.staruk.org.uk//webcode/contents.asp?id=715&parentid=469&bg=white> accessed on 20 March 2007.

Works Cited

Primary References

Parr, Martin (1986): *The Last Resort: Photographs of New Brighton*. Stockport: Dewi Lewis.

Orwell, George (1941/1956): "The Lion and the Unicorn", in: Richard H. Rovere (ed.): *The Orwell Reader*. New York: Harcourt, Brace & World: 249-270.

Thatcher, Margaret (1979/1989a): "The Swinton Lecture at the Conservative Political Centre Summer School", in: id.: *The Revival of Britain. Speeches on Home and European Affairs 1975-1988*. London: Aurum Press, 83-95.

— (1988/1989b): "To the Conservative Party Conference", in: id.: *The Revival of Britain. Speeches on Home and European Affairs 1975-1988*. London: Aurum Press, 267-280.

Wood, Tom (1989): Looking for Love. Manchester: Cornerhouse.

— (1998): *All Zones Off Peak*. Stockport: Dewi Lewis.

— (2005): *Photie Man*. Göttingen: Steidel.

Research Literature

Böhmer, Sylvia (2001): "Bus Odyssey", in: Tom Wood: *Bus Odyssey*. Ostfildern-Ruit: Hatje Cantz, 8-12.

Chandler, David (1989): "Foreword", in: Tom Wood: *Looking for Love: Chelsea Reach Photographs*. Manchester: Cornerhouse Publications, n.pag.

de Certeau, Michel (1984). *The Practice of Everyday Life*. Berkeley: University of California Press.

Dikkers, Jan-Willem (2004): "Interview with Tom Wood", *Issue* 8, 37-55.

Fiske, John (1989): *Reading the Popular*. London and New York: Routledge.

Fowler, Peter, Mike Robinson and Priscilla Boniface (2001): "Pride and Prejudice: Two Cultures and the North East's Transition", in: John Tomaney and Neil Ward (eds.): *A Region in Transition. North East England at the Millennium*. Aldershot et al.: Ashgate, 120-135.

Graham, Paul (1986): *Beyond Caring*. London: Grey Editions.

Hudson, Ray and Allan M. Williams (1989/1995): *Divided Britain*. Chister et al.: John Wiley.

Kisters, Jürgen (1999): "Sad Beautiful Life", in: Tom Wood: *People*. Cologne: Wienand, 89-93.

Lefebvre, Henri (1994): *The Production of Space*. Oxford and Cambridge, Mass.: Blackwell.

Martin, Ronald L. (2004): "The Contemporary Debate over the North-South Divide: Images and Realities of Regional Inequality in Late-Twentieth-Century Britain", in: Alan R.H. Baker and Mark Billinge (eds.): *The North-South Divide, Material and Imagined.* Cambridge: Cambridge UP, 15-43.

Musgrove, Frank (1990): *The North of England. A History from Roman Times to the Present.* Oxford: Basil Blackwell.

Ray-Jones, Tony (1967): "Hotel, Newquay", *Science and Society Picture Library* (no date). <http://nmpft.memoryprints.com>, accessed on 1 May 2006.

— (1968): "Eastbourne", *Science and Society Picture Library* (no date). <http://www.ssplprints.com> accessed on 1 March 2007.

Russell, Dave (2004): *Looking North: Northern England and the National Imagination.* Manchester: Manchester UP.

Walker, Ian (1986): "The Last Resort", in: Martin Parr: *The Last Resort: Photographs of New Brighton.* Stockport: Dewi Lewis. n. pag.

Walton, John K. (1983): *The English Seaside Resort. A Social History 1750-1914.* Leicester: Leicester UP.

Illustrations: The editor unsuccessfully tried to trace copyright holders for pictures of Tom Wood, and would be grateful for any information.

Of Popular Spaces: Northern Heterotopias, Morrissey and the Manchester Britpop Scene

Ralph Pordzik

Abstract: This essay traces the development of a northern sub-cultural scene in Great Britain since the late 1970s, proceeding on the assumption that it formed to punctuate the influence of the London-based music industry and that it sought to make an ideological statement about regional forms of identity. The 'Northern' as represented in musical history will be regarded as a *heterotopia* of culturally interrelated sites, i.e. a space in which divergent attitudes interact across a wide range of different meaning-systems. The discussion focuses mainly on the lyrics of former *Smiths* front man Morrissey, one of the most widely reviewed sub-cultural icons in the history of Britpop. Some of his work as a writer will be analysed with special respect to the influence of Shelagh Delaney's kitchen-sink drama *A Taste of Honey* (1958) and other literary pre-texts, showing how the writing epitomises the overlaying of individual messages with a broad variety of meaning-bearing patterns adapted from different realms of creative thought. Also, what comes in for inquiry in these media is the formative influence of a distinct type of 'northern female' as represented in British TV soaps such as *Coronation Street*. In the course of the essay, the deconstruction of gendered identities with respect to a particularly northern 'way of life' will thus be elucidated, along with the routines of local populations and the post-punk refashioning of the industrial and factory image in poetry, film and music.

Key names and concepts: Michel Foucault - Smiths - Morrissey - Shelagh Delaney - Oscar Wilde; Britpop - Coronation Street - Heterotopia - Subculture - Music Scene - Northern Iconography - Gender - Northern Female - Punk Movement - Thatcherism.

1. Going Down in (Northern) Musical History

> *I decree today that life is simply taking and not giving*
> *England is mine and it owes me a living.*[1]

In this essay, I am tracing the emergence and development of a northern sub-cultural scene in Great Britain since the late 1970s, proceeding on the assumption that it originally formed to challenge and punctuate the economic influence of the London-based music industry and that it sought to make a valid ideological statement about regional forms of northern identity. Since then different bands and musicians have formed a loose, informal network of like-minded artists in order to mark themselves off from the 'dominant centre' of British national culture, their main objective being that of challenging accepted forms of media representation and reformulating the position and future role of the North in contemporary England.

To assess the significance of the North as a distinct region within the increasingly widening boundaries of a national musical culture (see Viol 2000: 81) is to set oneself no easy task. In fact, it means to focus on the question of how different music genres, youth cultures and life-styles have impinged upon attitudes towards the North and its place within already existing notions of 'Englishness'.[2] Recent work in the area of British Cultural Studies has shown that the postulation of fixed and self-centred cultural or regional identities is not acceptable any longer; therefore, I shall use as a point of departure for further discussion French philosopher Michel Foucault's notion of heterotopias as culturally and socially related spaces in which local sites mix with wider political patterns or modes of life and ideological positions are placed or delineated in a way which makes them "irreducible to one another and absolutely not superimposable on one another" (Foucault 1998: 239). The 'Northern' as represented in musical history will be regarded as such a heterotopia of culturally interrelated sites, as an ideologically flexible and undesignated space in which the most widely divergent attitudes interact across a wide range of differ-

---

[1] "Still Ill" (Smiths 1984b).

[2] For notions of the term in the context of recent cultural and national debates see Lunn (1996), Bennett (1998), Hall (1996), Rawnsley (2000) and Russell (2004).

ent systems of meaning. Northern subcultures are discursive 'formations' in the sense laid out by Foucault in that they include larger units of analysis – that is, narratives, statements, clusters of interlinked images and idiomatic forms of speech operating across a whole variety of texts.

Historically divergent ideas about northern identity and life have shaped the texts under scrutiny; differences between 'high' and 'low', English and British culture have been blurred; text, image and music have been rearranged in a heterot(r)opical fashion so as to express an exciting overlay of distinct ideas. Especially with regard to the history of popular music, life in the North, seen ultimately as 'other' by many (Rawnsley 2000: 5f), has shown itself capable of stimulating the creative imagination of writers and musicians and invigorating English culture in sometimes surprising ways. Unfortunately, this relationship – which is one between a growing variety of subcultures and a fixed or 'classical' understanding of regional identity – has received only limited consideration in the past; in order to throw light upon recent developments, it is therefore necessary to draw a preliminary map for future work in the field.[3]

The discussion will focus in particular on the lyrics of former *Smiths* front man Stephen Patrick alias Morrissey, one of the most widely reviewed sub-cultural icons in the history of Britpop. Some of his work as a singer and writer will be analysed here with special respect to the influence of Shelagh Delaney's 'angry' kitchen-sink drama *A Taste of Honey* (1958) and other literary pre-texts, showing how the writing epitomises the overlaying of individual messages with a broad variety of divergent bits of texts and meaning-bearing patterns adapted from different realms of creative thought. Of special importance will be the mediatory interaction between the generically different texts, the way in which they work together to erode but also to re-

---

[3] Some recent works that deserve recognition for their assessing the merits of popular music in the context of the formation of youth cultures and identities are the studies by Negus (1992, 1996), Bennett (1998, 2000) and Brackett (1995). A general survey of popular music has been offered by Shuker (2000). As opposed to the view promoted in this essay, Claus-Ulrich Viol (2000) holds that a good deal of British pop music is "permeated with national discourse(s) [...] particular songs make use of symbols and myths that are nation-specific – activating an automatic response from members of the national community." (2000: 82)

align formerly distinct positions and how they arrive at a new form of expression indicating a 'mixed' but autonomous view of northern identity – one which depends for its identity on the implied spaces (London, 'Southern', upper class, etc.) it appears to deny.

Also, what comes in for inquiry in these media is the formative influence of a distinct type of 'northern female' as represented, for instance, in British TV soaps such as *Coronation Street* and adopted to serve an entirely different purpose in the vernacular lyrics of Morrissey. In the course of the essay, the deconstruction of gendered identities with respect to a particularly northern 'way of life' will thus be elucidated, along with the habitual routines of local populations (the world-view and supposedly 'dry' humour of the 'average' Mancunian, for example) and the post-punk refashioning of the industrial and factory image in poetry, film and music.

2. 'Who put the 'M' in Manchester?' Britpop and the 'Staging' of the North as a Distinct Region Within Musical Discourse

> *Farewell to this land's cheerless marches*
> *hemmed in like a boar between arches...*[4]

In one of his most widely remembered lyrical pieces, "Suffer Little Children", English pop icon Morrissey refers his listeners to the 'Moors Murderers' Ian Brady and Myra Hindley who, in the mid-Sixties, kidnapped several children, tortured them to death and dumped their mutilated bodies into unmarked graves in the Manchester moors: "Over the moors, take me to the moors / dig a shallow grave and I'll lay me down / Lesley-Anne, with your pretty white beads / Oh John, you'll never be a man / And you'll never see your home again" (Smiths 1984a). The powerful and embarrassingly direct identification presented in the lyrics cannot gloss over the fact that, apart from Morrissey giving the undiscovered victims a chance to rise and speak from their graves, the "sullen misty moor", these lines also help reclaim for modern industrial and urban Manchester the 'uncultured' and emptied moor landscape as presented in the song.

---

[4] "The Queen is Dead" (Smiths 1986).

Left to themselves, as a piece of undifferentiated northern landscape, the moors would be entirely featureless, a wild and gloomy area subjected to the levelling effects of wind and water, a rain-soaked form of nothingness. Restored to serve as a historical background for a literary staging of the horrible murders, however, they seem to turn into an emblem of northern society itself, blurring the line between Brady and Hindley in particular and adult (Mancunian) society in general. The location itself, the 'values' it represents, the education it affords and the life it offers, is now held responsible for the fact that so many children could be killed in the midst of a society regarded, especially in the South, as 'stubborn', 'barbarous' and 'superstitious' (Rawnsley 2000: 5). "Oh Manchester, so much to answer for / over the moor, I'm on the moor / the child is on the moor..." the song aptly if somewhat eerily ends, challenging the twin Victorian myths of childhood innocence and the seemingly unalterable positive centrality of the middle-class family.

It seems as if Morrissey, lacking a 'natural' image in which to cast Mancunian ways of life, needed to try his hand at writing about the "most glamorous thing that had ever happened to Manchester" (Simpson 2004: 44), ambiguously reinterpreting the brutal events in terms of a culturally viable if drastic image of regional 'belonging'. The delinquents themselves, Ian Brady and Myra Hindley, can be seen to represent, in this particular context, the most fashionable couple popular culture in the mid-Sixties had to offer. According to the public, they were cold-blooded and unrepentant murderers but also passionate and hedonistic rebels engaged in a war against society, an estranged couple standing up to fight the accepted class conventions and sexual role models; already in the Sixties, Myra Hindley's media image stared at people not like a grotesque outsider but like a very up-to-date woman wearing modern clothes and listening to contemporary Beat music. In the eyes of the tabloids, she always seems to have represented the strong and emasculating type of unruly English female that many 'respectable' women feared might lurk inside them.[5]

---

[5] Her popularity and local 'cult' status is reflected in the fact that she achieved national fame during the famous Brit Art exhibition of the late 1990s when a controversial giant reproduction of her face, composed of the handprints of children, was shown in public.

Morrissey's "Suffer Little Children" can be seen to tie in with a distinctly northern tradition of imposing upon the region's unmarked rural territory a body of more or less arbitrarily selected sub-cultural meanings. As a melodious pop song composed in the vein of 'jangly' folk-inspired 1960s guitar music, it seeks to restore a local history and imagination to a place thoroughly transformed by an uninterrupted series of shockwaves of social change and economic drainage.

Manchester itself, the region's capital, was at its lowest ebb in the late Seventies when Britpop started out as a new phenomenon; a vicious economic recession had hit the North harder than anywhere else. The city centre was a destitute site disfigured by boarded-up warehouses and abandoned office buildings when the Smiths released their famous first album in 1984, offering their listeners a bleak view of the real life behind the facades of glazed redbrick edifices that had once teemed with people at work but whose sightless windows now bore testament to a society that had given up on the future.

The former hub of the nation's industry and enterprise was badly in need of a new cultural input in order to look forward to the future. The Smiths and other local pop and punk bands contributed to this revival by re-mapping the place according to their own, highly idiosyncratic and polyphonic understanding. As writer Chris Bohn has put it, local bands managed to turn into a creative advantage the

> corrosive effects on the individual of a time squeezed between the collapse into impotence of traditional Labour humanism and the impending cynical victory of Conservatism (quoted in Savage 1995: xii).[6]

The emerging local music scene self-confidently reanimated the inherited image of the North as an 'uncultured' place devoid of any specific interest and surrounded by a provincial wasteland of uninhabited and underdeveloped moors. At the same time, they put Manchester at the centre of what was happening in the music business for the first time, slating Londoners "for their smug complacency" (Curtis 1995: 47) while providing a self-confident and instinctive musical energy of their own. In the late 1970s, according to Deborah Curtis,

---

[6] A critical view of Savage's teleological interpretation of punk has been offered recently by Susanne Rupp. According to Rupp, Savage seeks to align the varied subcultures of punk with other 'elitist' art movements by ascribing to them the reductive "pattern of rise and fall" (Rupp 2006: 81).

no one waited to have their talents recognized. Instead, they decided
what they wanted to do and did it, be it pop photographer, producer,
journalist, or musician. It was a deliberate snub of the London scene
and, as far as music was concerned, Manchester was set to become the
new capital. (Curtis 1995: 46)

It was Morrissey, more than any of the other local 'bards' or pop and
punk celebrities, who showed how to really transform the drab Mancunian landscape into something more fertile in art, something more
earnestly given to creative reinvigoration.[7] British Pop, according to
many critics, has always been "essentially Northern" (Simpson 2004:
28), but now Manchester and the North were 'really' given the chance
to turn into the capital of the British music scene, especially in an economic and strategic sense. In musical terms, the region no longer sub-
mitted to the image of a fluid, uncharted existence afforded it by London and the 'South' but opened itself up to the re-mapping made possible by the sub-cultural iconography of the North.

3. The 'Northern Woman', Delaney's *A Taste of Honey* and the Transcultural Mission of Britpop

*I'm spellbound but a woman divides
and the hills are alive with celibate cries.*[8]

From the very beginning, the strategic interlacing of different cultural
spaces or, in the current 'globalising' terminology of Arjun Appadurai, "cultural flows" (Appadurai 2000: 33) played an important role
in this process of translating an 'unmarked' and undifferentiated landscape into a legible piece of text. Various forms of established literature and writing came in alongside the cruder manifestations of urban
pop fandom and the rough energy spread by Manchester punk rock
bands in the 1970s, such as The Buzzcocks (Howard Devoto), Joy Division and Mark Smith's The Fall, or the infrastructure supplied by
Tony Wilson's influential record label *Factory* (see Simpson 2004:

---

[7] Another formative influence of the late 1970s who deserves more recognition than he has yet achieved is the 'Salford Bard', Mancunian local poet John Cooper Clarke.

[8] "These Things Take Time" (Smiths 1984b).

28; Curtis 1995: 47). Some of the effects of this regional creative input are reflected in the richly orchestrated aesthetic structure and allusiveness of Morrissey's lyrics written shortly after he formed The Smiths with guitarist Johnny Marr in 1982.

Among the major influences to be mentioned here is Shelagh Delaney's new realist or kitchen-sink play *A Taste of Honey* which is not only one of the most widely read plays about Mancunian life in the 1950s but also a striking example of the heterogeneous cultural spaces arranged in Morrissey's subtly 'Northern' code of writing. The text, made into a film in 1961 by Tony Richardson, has influenced a whole generation of disenchanted writers and artists struggling against the constraints of provincial life.[9] For Morrissey, certainly a rather protective artist when it comes to assessing the cultural legacy of the North, *A Taste of Honey* seems to have represented all the virtues of 'stubborn' Mancunian realism as a locally produced form of art – before the commercial success of American movies sidelined this form of popular drama to the small-screen cinemas (see Simpson 2004: 55). References to the play run through his entire work, often mixed with other quotations from contemporary writing, film and music adapted to suit his particular aesthetic purpose. Among those writers and actors whose words have been 'taken on loan' by Morrissey are Keith Waterhouse, Dorothy Parker, Joe Orton, Edith Sitwell, Leonard Cohen, Noel Coward and Richard Allen – to name just a few. As in Delaney's play, technique, in Morrissey's pop lyrics, mainly appears to be "justified by the material at hand" (Oberg 1983: 136).

Pop journalist Johnny Rogan has drawn attention to the fact that large parts of the earliest Morrissey lyrics are made up of references to *A Taste of Honey*, suggesting a symbolically rich landscape of local life and habit in these songs (Rogan 1992: 172). The adaptation of this particular play calls to mind Morrissey's instructive technique of creating layer upon layer of text within the restricted space of a short pop lyric that helps reconfigure this 'genre' as a testing-ground for the exploration of local registers and forms of life. In the hands of Morrissey, the English pop lyric of the 1980s has thus turned from a rather insipid form of expressing 'spontaneous' feeling to a glamorous open stage of self-referential personal analysis laying bare the cultural and

---

[9] For a critical account of the play, especially with regard to its indebtedness to the British music-hall tradition, see Taylor (1962: 109–14) and Oberg 1983.

habitual techniques that sustain the idea of pop stardom. Indeed, *understanding* Morrissey means to achieve a fairly adequate idea of the deliberation with which contradictions and tensions are erased in commercial pop culture, how fragmentations are concealed and differences bypassed or compromised through the formal device of the media-hyped pop song and its accompanying lyric.

It is easy to see why *A Taste of Honey* could have made such a wide-ranging impact on Morrissey, an emerging vocalist and "Angst-filled" (Frith 1996: 151) pop poet still looking, at that time, for his supposedly 'true' Mancunian identity. Written by a female (of Anglo-Irish descent like Morrissey and the other band members) at the age of eighteen and set in her home town Manchester, the play recounts the flirtatious 'affair' between teenage girl Jo and homosexual art student Geoff. At the time the play starts, Jo has already undergone her first traumatic experience: she was left pregnant by her former boy friend, a coloured Navy sailor who had wanted to marry her once but didn't return in the end to avoid being "trapped into a barbaric cult [...] Matrimony" (Delaney 1982: 25). The destitution generated in the protagonist by this shock is reproduced in some of the most memorable lines ever written in a pop lyric, magnifying the limited 'Northern' experience addressed in Delaney's play:

> In a river the colour of lead
> Immerse the baby's head
> Wrap her up in the *News Of The World*
> Dump her on a doorstep, girl
> This night has opened my eyes
> And I will never sleep again
> You kicked and cried like a bullied child
> A grown man of twenty-five
> He said he'd cure your ills
> But he didn't and he never will
> So, save your life
> Because you've only got one[10]

Talent borrows, genius steals, as Oscar Wilde once put it. This passage is peculiar not for its supposedly authentic voice but for its unacknowledged use of material from Delaney's play and its re-ordering it in such a way as to produce a strangely twisted and 'cross-gendered'

---

[10] "This Night Has Opened My Eyes" (Smiths 1984b).

form of lyrical utterance.[11] The boundary lines between the fictive character Jo from the original play and the lyric's persona are deliberately blurred, thus making space for a curious mixture of two mutually transgressive voices, the one male, the other female. The lyric's meaning wholly depends on the narrator's assumed sex – which it is impossible to determine from listening to the text alone, however. Modern-day passivity and disillusionment are mapped onto differently gendered subjects, calling to mind Geoff and Jo from the play *and* at the same time the mysterious persona hidden behind the singer's longing, dramatic voice. The appeal of this arrangement is, above all, its cross-gender quality: as Mark Simpson has put it, rather pointedly, Morrissey's voice here is not only 'Northern' in its use of "native black humour" and mocking self-deprecation but also in that it is the 'true' voice of the "Northern Woman" (Simpson 2004: 57).

This needs some elaboration. In the play, main character Jo (played in the film by Rita Tushingham) is shown as struggling not to end up a victim of modern urban life, whether in the form of her sex, her class or her Anglo-Irish origins. She is the neurotic product of her mother's passionate love affair with a man "that lasted five minutes" (Delaney 1982: 43) and thus above all a symbol of lower class circumstances in the early fifties. But her cheerful manner of dealing with her problems also presents a vigorously new outlook on long-established forms of local life, one that appears to have been particularly attractive for Morrissey during the early stages of his career. In an interview transmitted on Australian Radio in 1985, he said:

> I gaze upon them [the British sixties new realism films] fondly because it was the first time in the entire history of film where regional dialects were allowed to come to the fore and people were allowed to talk about squalor and general depression and it wasn't necessarily a shameful thing. (Quoted in Simpson 2004: 58)

This may only be a pop celebrity's personal creed, to be taken with a grain of salt like everything else produced in the media. At the same time, however, it does point towards the keen sense of survival connected to modes of existence that had been regarded as unwelcome in

---

[11] For a complete list of Morrissey's borrowings from Delaney's work and other British new realist writers see Simpson 2004, 56f. Further details about Morrissey's intertextual practice can be found in Goddard (2003).

England in the 1950s and were still embarrassing in the glossy world of 1980s commercial Britpop. Having turned into an outsider within her own community on account of her love affair with a black sailor, Jo finally reconciles herself to a single life under reduced circumstances and embarks on a platonic romance with Geoff, a penniless art student and effeminate homosexual trying to mother her. Without any prospect of a professional career, she tries to scrape a living, refusing, like Hardy's Sue Bridehead, the gender conformity imposed on her by respectable British society: "I don't want this baby, Geoff. I don't want to be a mother. I don't want to be a woman" (Delaney 1982: 75). Almost imperceptibly, Geoff and Jo have amalgamated into a single 'character' at this point, presenting an extraordinary northern couple unified by their unhappiness in life and their striving to eradicate all visible gender demarcations.

A similar kind of social estrangement and transgressive fusion in gender or character can be detected in the wry humour and the introspective mood of various Smiths lyrics written during the Eighties, all of them deliciously vague in terms of the gender of the speaking subject and submerging sexual attitudes behind a smokescreen of private insinuations:

> Mine eyes have seen the glory of the sacred *wunderkind*
> you took me behind a disused railway line
> and said "I know a place where we can go
> where we are not known"
> and then you gave me something that I won't forget too soon[12]

This is arrestingly realist and matter-of-fact, calling to mind the nostalgic image of a disappearing Manchester memorable for its black-and-white cinematography of cobbled streets, narrow houses and factory chimneys of the 1950s. It brings to attention the lonely life of social outsiders and misfits forced to undergo unpleasant physical experiences in backyards and side-alleys 'teaching them' about sexuality in ways their own prudish social expectations would never allow them to articulate. Again, male and female points of view are interlaced in a textual pattern indicative of Morrissey's overriding 'cross-gender' purpose; by playing down and even denying the importance of sexual differences, the lyric evokes the constructivity of gender roles and lays

---

[12] "These Things Take Time" (Smiths 1984b).

bare the absurdity of privileging masculinity and a pompous "cock rock" (Frith 1996: 150) or exclusively male sexual message in pop music. As in Delaney's play, sexual identity is highlighted in a way that shows it to reside 'outside' all the institutions through which society tries to civilise it and to speak in an estranged and disillusioned idiom attributable to both male and female.

Given the vagueness and subtlety of presentation, it is certainly no coincidence that Morrissey, the most self-conscious vocalist ever to emerge from the ruthless fashion industry of Britpop, has frequently been identified with the two destitute characters Jo and Geoff and the underprivileged life they are made to lead in *A Taste of Honey* (see Rogan 1992: 174) – especially with Jo, who struggles to liberate herself from restrictive definitions of femininity or, in a larger social context, from notions of gender as a preconceived and fixed mode of identity. In many cases, it is almost impossible for the listener to decide whether Morrissey sings about himself or whether he addresses the hardships of a 'simple' northern woman as filtered through the views and reflections of a male speaker's angle of vision.

But how 'simple', how natural and ingenuous, is this kind of female, actually? Gender definitions are notoriously hard to grasp. By constantly coming back, throughout his career, to Delaney's *A Taste of Honey* and the specular mood of northern solitude and "magnified realism" (Oberg 1983: 140) it vibrates, Morrissey appears to have taken his 'identification' with the northern female to its ultimate conclusion, deliberately *transcending* the gendered identity of the various speakers he employs and providing both male and female listener with multiple points of identification. This knack of identifying with the northern female in many of his lyrics has long been regarded as one of the most characteristic features of his work, showing above all his ambition to invest new cultural ideas in a worn-out local stereotype[13]:

---

[13] See also the lyrics of "Girl Afraid" and "Reel Around the Fountain" from the 1984 Smiths album *Hatful of Hollow*. "Reel Around the Fountain" is another song for which Morrissey borrowed heavily from Delaney's play. Both songs deal with the essential absurdity of gender and the problem of having to find one's own sexual identity – symbolised, e.g., in the suggestion of genitalia and sexual desire in the lines "in the *room downstairs* / he sat and stared" and "Boy afraid / prudence never pays / [...] I'll never make that mistake again" ("Girl Afraid").

However common the Northern woman might be, she is still a very special creature, thriving only in damp, cool, slightly backward climes where people actually talk to one another at bus stops and check-out queues, and where you're never more than a ten-minute walk from a good fish and chips shop. She has a certain intensity mixed with a certain breeziness, a certain desperation mixed with a lot of self-irony – perhaps the product of her awareness of her contradictions. [...] She is direct, but frequently overdone. She is a survivor, but strangely tragic. She is strong, but touchingly vulnerable. She is all woman, but sometimes there seems to be more than a little man in her. She's a bit of a queer fish is the Northern Woman, and she is Morrissey. (Simpson 2004: 49)

The comic as well as aesthetic potential of the northern female has always been acknowledged in British film, but it was in the 1980s in particular that it drew a strong response from well-known writers and dramatists such as Alan Bennett and Victoria Wood – from the northern counties of Yorkshire and Lancashire, respectively. Fostered by the media, the new image was soon appropriated as a regional statement about the North, showing the place and its inhabitants to lead an 'essentially' unique life of their own (as opposed to that of the city of London under the Iron Lady's long and troublesome reign). Simpson, by self-consciously posing as a lukewarm parodist of gender clichés, turns the same image on its head in the above passage, foregrounding its almost unlimited cultural transferability and pointing to the degree of cultural and national idealism imposed upon all gender stereotyping.

Morrissey's achievement, in this context, is to have incorporated the inherited voice of the northern female into his own lyrics, introducing her to new listeners in the United Kingdom and elsewhere who had never heard of her before, and thus to set up a monument to this notion of a subversive and rebellious local English type. However, this would not have been possible without the discreet media collaboration between the enormous success of the first Smiths records and the growing tendency within British television of the 1980s to represent northern life as 'hip' or affectionately weird in productions such as *Coronation Street* or the later *Mrs Merton*. Uncoordinated individual efforts within popular culture first made possible and then helped spread the multifarious image of the North which had been derided and pitied for so long in the South. Viv Nicholson, e.g., a young woman from Yorkshire whose spectacular football pools win in 1961 came to stand for the first 'global' success making the 'North' known to the rest of the world, was afforded the prestigious honour of gracing three Smiths record sleeves, thus inaugurating the vital connection of word and picture, text and icon, innovation and nostalgia, so important for the emergence and survival of the 'mood-enhancing' machinery of Britpop.[14] Popular enough to find her way frequently onto the front pages of the national tabloids, Viv Nicholson had even turned into a living sign for the self-assertive and coarse 'new' northern woman shortly before Julie Christie made her appearance as 'Scruffy Lizzie' in the play *Billy Liar* (1963), based on Keith Waterhouse's successful comic novel about regional life. In many respects, her story had taken on the proportions of a real-life soap opera that not even the BBC around that time would have dared to write and produce.

In a cultural sense, then, the image of the northern woman came to define the protest of the northern provinces against the alleged 'conceitedness' of the Southern bourgeoisie. It found its way into pop culture in a myriad ways because it represented, more than anything else, common life and the values of the northern working classes who, in the 1960s, were slowly beginning to have their share in the new spending power and well-being of an economically successful Great Britain. Generally, the 1960s in Great Britain was an era of upward social mobility and, along with it, one of tentative longing for a more 'permissive' form of private life; the emerging but still modest consumer culture was fuelled by wage increases, the musical industry burst into life in Liverpool, Manchester and other locations, and along with this came a new sense of working-class consciousness and fashionability soon to be exploited in a growing number of records and musical styles – a sense that re-emerged in the wake of the British punk movement (Fowler 1996: 172ff) and has survived, albeit in a transformed and domesticated way, in many Smiths lyrics, where it was made to fuse with a parody of the neo-liberal and market-economy ethos of the Thatcher government, itself regarded as a further instance of the imperial and preposterous South set on besieging and secluding the 'ordinary folk' of the English North Country:

---

[14] For a critical and resourceful analysis of modern pop and rock culture as a 'mood-enhancing' device, see Lawrence Grossberg 1995: 371.

> All the streets are crammed with things
> eager to be held
> I know what hands are for
> And I'd like to help myself
> you ask me the time
> but I sense something more
> and I would like to give you
> what I think you're asking for[15]

The commercial success of Britpop in the 1980s made it possible for artists like Morrissey – northern, working class and Irish – to become a vital part of the successful music scene and to introduce a 'genuinely' northern accent itself made up of fragments, texts and divergent sociolects. This is where the heterotopian dimension of the Britpop phenomenon comes in: as writer and lead singer of a pop band struck by sudden and unexpected success, Morrissey never really had in mind the tactic of hinting at some kind of psychological complexity behind the apparent spuriousness of the images now beginning to circulate. Indeed, the 'Northern' as a style or fashion in British Pop, distinct as it may seem, has always been a conglomerate of ideas themselves produced by the 'postmodern' counter-culture of the late 1960s with its ambition to oppose all notions of universality in life, politics and literature. Providing a wide range of competing lyrical or narrative forms and structures, Morrissey has only tried to put into perspective the submerged presences of northern life and history, seeking to replace the (Southern, 'British', economic) supremacy with a new, multiply affiliated identity that pleases him and his listeners alike. The lyrics themselves, through their combined use of interpolated bits of tales and anecdotes, their constant recounting of different but also strangely repetitive autobiographical stories, their use of snippets from literary works that obstruct the fluency of the individual song, enact this recuperative project of writing the North as a 'puzzle' of as-yet-unrealised possibilities and modes of cultural self-empowerment while at the same time reinforcing the *laissez-faire* ideology and hard commercial realities of Thatcher's liberal revolution they so appear to reject.[16] There is a prevailing sense of unity here to be discovered, para-

---

[15] "Handsome Devil" (Smiths 1984b).

[16] Morrissey's complex relationship with former Prime Minister Margaret Thatcher has never been expressed in a more thorough and weird fashion than in the lyrics of his "Margaret on the Guillotine": "The kind people have a

doxically, in dissent, conflict and difference. Unconsciously, maybe, the 'rebirth' of England under Thatcher's conservative regime was seen by Morrissey to coincide with his own reinvention of the North as a distinct scene and location of regional life and value.[17]

This 'unity in diversity' is borne out in the gorgeous lyrics of the later "Piccadilly Palare" (Morrissey 1990) where Morrissey addresses the problem of sexual ambiguity once again, this time with regard to the repressed tradition of homosexuality in Great Britain. The song reviews, in a superbly ironical and humorous fashion, the 'attractions' of being a teenage rent boy[18] 'on the game', carefully rearranging snippets of homosexual slang as widely employed in the nineteenth century: "on the rack I was / 'easy meat' / but a reasonably good buy [...] / so bona to vada, Oh you / your lovely eek and / your lovely riah / We plied an ancient trade / where we threw all life's instructions away." The text frankly reveals its intertextual sources, referring the reader in particular to Oscar Wilde as the most prominent of the mundane Anglo-Saxon heroes in Morrissey's pop pantheon. The thinly disguised, sexually charged idiom turns the text into a subjective mirror for the singer's heartfelt affiliation with a domestic culture of the downtrodden, the multitudes of lost and disoriented youth or immigrants, and thus into another cleverly understated document of the North's alternative history set out to challenge the supremacy of self-sufficient (Southern) cultural space – a space fairly ambiguously 'championed' as a monolithic power exploiting the passivity and youthful innocence of northern migrants.[19]

---

wonderful dream / Margaret on the Guillotine". The harshness of the words is superbly balanced by the moody, softened notes of the ballad-like composition (Morrissey 1997).

[17] The far-reaching effects of Thatcher's economic reforms on the North have been explored by Osmond 1988: 44–50.

[18] 'Rent boys' were young working-class males who worked as street prostitutes in London in the late nineteenth century. They usually met their 'lovers' around Piccadilly Circus, in a pick-up area unofficially called the 'meat rack'. For further details see Simpson 2004, 140.

[19] It should not go unnoticed that musical definitions of Northern identity are inextricably wedded to the invention of 'Northern Soul' – a distinctive style imported to the North in the early 1960s. It began when 'Motown mania' swept the country and Soul was favourably received by Mod youth culture. Especially in the UK, listening to music has always been connected to the different consumers' regional orientations; e.g., when by the late seventies Funk

4. Conclusion: The Heterotopian Spaces of Britpop and the 'New' Sense of Place in England

> *Irish blood, English heart / this I'm made of*
> *there is no one on Earth / I am afraid of*[20]

Does the North as a dialogic cultural space and musical community really point towards something new in the history of British pop culture, then? Does it really manage to undercut fixed notions of coherence and identity as still widely promoted in the British media? In a way, Morrissey's work does provide a striking example of an imaginative space not yet fully corroded by the strictures of commercial practice. In the lyrical space he offers, alternative versions of life are drawn up not so much to serve the interests of the North as a self-enclosed cultural space; rather, as Michel Foucault puts it, they are brought to life as sites so "different from one another that it is impossible to find a place of residence for them, to define a *common locus* beneath them all" (Foucault 1998: 239).

This strategic diversity must be seen as one of the most powerful traits of the Mancunian singer's work in general, calling attention not to Britpop's allegedly conservative tendencies (see Viol 2000: 82) but to its de-totalising power and hybrid reconfiguration of contemporary culture. In the lyrics of "Cemetery Gates", written back in the mid-1980s, Morrissey has set up his own cultural programme in support of this idea, demonstrating that his main interest lies not so much in separating but in rearranging the different conceptions of art that make up the whole of the English tradition, holding a mirror to the English public that "is necessarily a broken mirror [...] reflecting the points of reality, but distorting the distances which separate them" (Crumey 1994: 234). Set to a self-confident and rhythmic folk tune, the song unsettles the widespread notion of cultural homogeneity in

---

became the dominant genre in London, the North remained loyal to a style influenced by Rhythm'n'Blues. The type of venue often differed as well, with the South adopting smaller and more intimate clubs while the North continued to prefer larger venues such as dilapidated Victorian dance halls, working men's clubs and seaside piers. For the history of Northern Soul see Ritson and Russel 1999 or Nowell 2001.

[20] "Irish Blood, English Heart" (Morrissey 2004).

England by calling to witness some of its most widely celebrated literary heroes:

> A dreaded sunny day
> so I meet you at the cemetery gates
> Keats and Yeats are on your side
> while Wilde is on mine
>
> So we go inside and we gravely read the stones
> all those *people* all those *lives*
> *where are they now?* [...]
>
> If you must write prose / poems
> the words you use should be your own
> don't plagiarise or take "on loan" [...]
>
> You say: "ere long done do does did"
> words which could only be your own
> you then produce the text
> from whence was ripped
> (some dizzy whore, 1804)
>
> A dreaded sunny day
> so let's go where we're happy
> and I meet you at the cemetery gates [...]
> Keats and Yeats are on your side
> *but you lose*
> because weird lover Wilde is on mine[21]

The allusion to the pre-Romantic genre of graveyard poetry and especially Thomas Gray's famous "Elegy written in a Country Churchyard" (1751) is too patent to be overlooked. Frankly revealing his indebtedness to the Romantic movement, Morrissey establishes himself as the latest heir to a native tradition and forcefully writes back against all those critics who, in the past, have charged him with undermining pop's authenticist ethos by plagiarising or 'taking on loan'. "Cemetery Gates", juxtaposing nonsense and 'highbrow' literature, fully-fledged poetry and impromptu pop lyric, demonstrates that in order to create 'new' art one simply has to continue writing, blending the old texts with the new, and, in the process, transforming the already given forms into a richer version of their own possibilities.

---

[21] "Cemetery Gates" (Smiths 1986).

Also, by taking sides with Oscar Wilde, the tragic victim of middle-class conformity, Morrissey manages to enrich the symbolic space of the classical pop lyric, moving beyond the formal patterns of musical expression trapped in their repetition of self-righteous and redundant phrases inherited from mainstream rock and pop. Like Oscar Wilde who ended up in Reading gaol merging his uncompromising art in life, Morrissey in "Cemetery Gates" transcends the territorial and ideological boundaries of the regionalist debate haunting the world of Britpop: laying bare the techniques of writing and composition, his lyric metamorphoses into an allegory of the cultural process that reimagines existing relations among texts and pre-texts and thus confronts some of the doctrines associated with the claim to ultimate 'authenticity' or spontaneous genius as propagated in popular music.

The realities of northern working-class life in the late Seventies, along with the frustrated creativity and urban boredom of a new generation, called for a new cultural space providing an identity for those who refused to persist according to the mono-cultural modes of life developed back in the 1950s and partly sustained throughout the turbulent Sixties. The growing diversity in British pop culture surfacing since at least the early 1980s has not only been reflected in the realm of aesthetic utterances, e.g. in the pop lyric, but also involves the concretely lived practices of musicians, their actual spaces of everyday existence.

In *A Taste of Honey*, it is Jo and Geoff who forge their own identity in the midst of the conventionalised routines of British middle-class urbanity. In the world of 1980s northern pop, it was the band name *The Smiths* which struck a sensitive chord in many listeners, offering them an entirely different notion of regional 'family' life that extended beyond the constraints of the average person's idea of social and individual existence. As Irish immigrants and representatives of post-industrial Manchester, the four musicians involved in the band project seemed to insist on setting up their own 'alternative' way of communal life, suggesting a popular concept of heterotopia which not only deliberately parodied English normality; in fact, it staked out an entirely new imaginative terrain where conflictive notions about national and local life and family values could be put to a test against the background of the coercive cultural formations they were interdependent with and complementary to. This 'family' emerged from the derelict, condemned spaces of early Eighties Manchester to manifest a new and uncommon ideal of existence widened to include, first, the listeners and fans and, later, all the consumers of Smiths pop in the whole wide world who could identify with the charismatic singer and 'bastard' child Morrissey – the 'fatherless' son who even went so far as to change his name and identity (Stephen Patrick Morrissey) until there was only the non-gender-specific but strongly suggestive 'Morrissey'. The Smiths, during the 1980s, put on a stage the divergent fantasies of their frustrated fans, opening new figural territory for those passed over by the scribes of a monochrome national history and suggesting pop culture as the only remaining area connected with a positive notion of the heterotopian, a common yet multi-faceted northern space harbouring those whose imagination had brought them into conflict with the mind-set of respectable English society.

Works Cited

Discography

Morrissey (1990): "Piccadilly Palare". *Bona Drag*, EMI Records Ltd. 7942982.
— (1997): "Every Day is like Sunday". *Viva Hate*, EMI Records Ltd. 724385632525.
— (1997): "Margaret on the Guillotine". *Viva Hate*, EMI Records Ltd. 724385632525.
— (2004): "Irish Blood, English Heart". *You are the Quarry*, Sanctuary / Attack ATKDD013 / 5050759301390.
The Smiths (1984a): "Suffer Little Children". *The Smiths*, Rough Trade.
— (1984b): "Still Ill". *Hatful of Hollow*, WEA / Warner Music UK 4509918932.
— (1984b): "These Things Take Time". *Hatful of Hollow*, WEA / Warner Music UK 4509918932.
— (1984b): "Handsome Devil". *Hatful of Hollow*, WEA / Warner Music UK 4509918932.
— (1984b): "This Night Has Opened My Eyes". *Hatful of Hollow*, WEA / Warner Music UK 4509918932.
— (1984b): "Girl Afraid". *Hatful of Hollow*, WEA / Warner Music 4509918932.
— (1984b): "Reel Around the Fountain". *Hatful of Hollow*, WEA / Warner Music UK 4509918932.
— (1986): "The Queen is Dead". *The Queen is Dead*, WEA / Warner Music UK 4509918962.
— (1986): "Cemetery Gates". *The Queen is Dead*, WEA / Warner Music UK 4509918962.

Research Literature

Appadurai, Arjun (1996/2000): *Modernity at Large: Cultural Dimensions of Globalization*. Minneapolis and London: U of Minnesota Press.
Bennett, Peter (1998): "Britpop and National Identity", *Journal for the Study of British Cultures* 5, 13–25.
— (2000): *Popular Music and Youth Culture: Music, Identity and Place*. London: Macmillan.
Blake, Andrew (1997): *The Land without Music: Music, Culture and Society in Twentieth-Century Britain*. Manchester: Manchester UP.
Brackett, David (1995): *Interpreting Popular Music*. Cambridge: Cambridge UP.
Crumey, Andrew (1994): *Music, in a Foreign Language*. Sawtry: Daedalus.
Curtis, Deborah (1995): *Touching from a Distance: Ian Curtis and Joy Division*. London: Faber & Faber.
Delaney, Shelagh (1958/1982): *A Taste of Honey*. London: Methuen.
Foucault, Michel (1998): "Of Other Spaces", in: Nicholas Mirzoeff (ed.): *The Visual Culture Reader*. London and New York: Routledge, 237–244.

Fowler, Pete (1996): "Afterword: The Shadow of Our Night", in: Charlie Gillett and Simon Frith (eds.): *The Beat Goes on: The Rock File Reader*. London: Pluto Press, 168–185.
Frith, Simon (1996): "Youth Culture/Youth Cults: A Decade of Rock Consumption", in: Charlie Gillett and Simon Frith (eds.): *The Beat Goes on: The Rock File Reader*. London: Pluto Press, 143–152.
Goddard, Simon (2003): *The Smiths: Songs that Saved Your Life*. Richmond, Surrey: Reynolds and Hearn.
Grossberg, Lawrence (1995): "MTV: swinging on the postmodern star", in: Jessica Munus and Gita Rajan (eds.): *A Cultural Studies Reader*. London: Longman, 367–379.
Hall, Stuart (1996): *Questions of Cultural Identity*. London: Sage Publications.
Lunn, Kenneth (1996): "Reconsidering 'Britishness'. The Construction and Significance of National Identity in Twentieth-Century Britain", in: Brian Jenkins and Spyros A. Sofos (eds.): *Nation and Identity in Contemporary Europe*. London and New York: Routledge, 83–100.
Negus, Keith (1992): *Producing Pop: Culture and Conflict in the Popular Music Industry*. London: Edward Arnold.
— (1996): *Popular Music in Theory*. Cambridge: Polity Press.
Nowell, David (2001): *Too Darn Soulful: The Story of Northern Soul*. London: Robson Books/Chrysalis.
Oberg, Arthur K. (1966): "*A Taste of Honey* and the Popular Play", in: Klaus Peter Steiger (ed.): *Das englische Drama nach 1945*. Darmstadt: Wissenschaftliche Buchgesellschaft, 135–142.
Osmond, John (1988): *The Divided Kingdom*. London: Constable.
Rawnsley, Stuart (2000): "Constructing 'The North': space and a sense of place", in: Neville Kirk (ed.): *Northern Identities*. Aldershot: Ashgate, 3–22.
Ritson, Mike and Stuart Russel (1999): *In Crowd: The Story of the Northern and Rare Soul Scene*. London: Bee Cool Publishing.
Rogan, Johnny (1992): *Morrissey and Marr: The Severed Alliance*. London: Omnibus Press.
Rupp, Susanne (2006): "Writing Punk: Punk Narratives in the 1990s and John King's Novel 'Human Punk'", *Zeitschrift für Anglistik und Amerikanistik*. Special Issue: The Cultural Validity of Music in Contemporary Fiction. 54.1, 79–91.
Russell, Dave (2004): *Looking North: Northern England and the National Imagination*. Manchester: Manchester UP.
Savage, Jon (1995): "Foreword", in: Deborah Curtis: *Touching from a Distance: Ian Curtis and Joy Division*. London: Faber & Faber, xi–xiii.
Shuker, Roy (1994/2000): *Understanding Popular Music*. London and New York: Routledge.
Simpson, Mark (2004): *Saint Morrissey*. London: SAF Publishing.
Taylor, John Russell (1962): *The Angry British Theatre: New British Drama*. New York: Hill and Wang.
Viol, Claus-Ulrich (2000): "A Crack in the Union Jack? National Identity in British Popular Music", in: Hans-Jürgen Diller et al. (eds.): *Youth Identities: Teens and Twens in British Culture*. Heidelberg: Universitätsverlag Winter, 81–106.

Between L.S. Lowry and *Coronation Street*: Salford Cultural Identities

Susanne Schmid

Abstract: Salford, "the classic slum", according to Robert Roberts's study, has had a distinct cultural identity of its own, which is centred on the communal ideal of working-class solidarity, best exemplified in the geographical space of "our street". In the wake of de-industrialisation, Roberts's study, lyrics by Ewan MacColl, L.S. Lowry's paintings, and the soap opera *Coronation Street* all nostalgically celebrate imagined northern working-class communities, imbued with solidarity and human warmth. Thereby they contribute to constructing both English and northern identities.

Key names and concepts: Friedrich Engels - Robert Roberts - Ewan MacColl - L.S. Lowry - Charles Dickens - Richard Hoggart - George Orwell; Slums - Escaper Fiction - Working-class Culture - Nostalgia - De-industrialisation - Rambling - *Coronation Street*.

1. Salford as an Imagined Northern Community

For a long time, Salford, situated right next to the heart of Manchester, has been known as a place that underwent rapid and painful industrialisation in the nineteenth century and an equally difficult and agonising process of de-industrialisation in the twentieth. If Manchester, the former flag-ship of the cotton industry, has been renowned for its beautiful industrial architecture, its museums, and its economic success, Salford has been hailed as "the classic slum", as in the title of Robert Roberts's seminal study about Salford slum life in the first quarter of the twentieth century (Roberts 1990, first published in 1971). The equation of "Salford" and "slum", however, dates back further than that. Friedrich Engels's *The Condition of the Working Class in England*, written in 1844/45, casts a gloomy light on a city made up of dwellings hardly fit for humans:

> If we cross the Irwell to Salford, we find on a peninsula formed by the river, a town of eighty thousand inhabitants […]. All Salford is built in courts or narrow lanes, so narrow, that they remind me of the narrowest I have ever seen […]. If, in Manchester, the police, from time to time, every six or ten years, makes a raid upon the working-people's districts, closes the worst dwellings, and causes the filthiest spots in these Augean stables to be cleansed, in Salford it seems to have done absolutely nothing. (Engels 1973: 92).

Salford was a problem zone during much of the twentieth century, too. The 1930s economic slump hit the city badly, and from the 1970s onwards, the remaining mills began to close down rapidly. A high petty crime rate, a high teenage pregnancy rate, the notoriously poor quality of housing as well as insufficient health care facilities contributed to making Salford stand out as one of Britain's worst blackspots. If Manchester has repeatedly hit the headlines in the last 15 years as the youthful centre of northern nightlife, as the newly emerging tycoon of cultural events (Cass 1996), Salford, unable to muster up a similarly glamorous setting, lies in the shadow of its neighbour. Nevertheless, Salford is much more than a Manchester without clubs: it has its own cultural history, much informed by the working-class people, although the agents of Salford's history were by no means blue-collar workers only. My contribution aims to show how Salford cultural identities have been forged by resorting to (a) Roberts's study *The Classic Slum*, one of the first widely circulated academic texts that constructed, the ideal of a close-knit northern English working-class community as seen from within, (b) folk-singer and activist Ewan MacColl's lyrics, (c) L.S. Lowry's paintings, and (d) one of Britain's most famous and long-running soap operas, *Coronation Street*.

Salford cultural identities need to be seen in the larger framework of constructions of "the North", a fascinating yet strangely under-researched field.[1] A recent study by Dave Russell, *Looking North* (2004), maps out the large number of differing, even contradictory images of the North and the mechanisms that lead to the view that the South is perpetually central, whereas the North is marginal. Although

---

[1] Russell provides a comprehensive survey of images of the North and the different media/fields through which these are transported (travel writing, literature, speech, drama, film, TV, music, sports). The wealth of material he offers is a good starting point for further explorations of an area situated off the academic's beaten tracks.

some northern regions (the Lake District in particular) have been appropriated for the myth of rural England, of a pastoral, green, and true England (Russell 2004: 7), the predominant image of the North contains the following elements: bleakness, coldness, industry, decay, social problems, working class, exploitation, lack of serious culture. The northerners are seen as devoid of social graces at worst, as "humorous if crude" at best (Russell 2004: 37). Russell convincingly argues that this "North" is a product of the national imagination, no precisely demarcated geographical location. So – where is the North? The simple answer "North of the Watford Gap", which, if spelt out, means "To the North of the South", does not suffice and shows how little conceptual clarity about the North we have. Many prevailing images of the North focus on one county (the Lancashire of George Orwell's *Road to Wigan Pier*), one city (the post-industrial Sheffield of the film *The Full Monty*), or one area ("our street" as in *Coronation Street*). Our prevailing images of the North are "imagined communities" as proposed by Benedict Anderson:

> In fact, all communities larger than primordial villages of face-to-face contact (and perhaps even these) are imagined. Communities are to be distinguished, not by their falsity/genuineness, but by the style in which they are imagined. (Anderson 1983: 15)[2]

One striking example of an imagined northern community is Charles Dickens's mid-nineteenth-century novel *Hard Times*, set in Coketown (i.e. Manchester), which has been immensely successful in conveying the stereotype of the North as a corrupted paradise, as hell on earth. Dickens, born in Portsmouth, a Southerner, determined the reception of the "North" in the larger framework of texts demarcating "Englishness".

Any analysis of cultural representations of the North needs to consider the point of view of the writer, singer, painter, or producer. The North may be seen from without or from within. A surprisingly large number of cultural products depicting Salford have been or are being produced in the region, like *Coronation Street*, filmed in the Granada Studios, yet some of them constitute what Philip Dodd (1990: 22) has ironically termed "escaper fiction": this escape can be regional, through a geographical move away from the region, or social

---

[2] See also Russell (2004: 8).

through climbing up the ladder. Despite his upbringing in the Salford slums, Roberts wrote from the position of one "who made it". The painter Lowry, who chose many of his motives from Salford's industrial spaces, worked as a rent-collector and thus in fact held a white-collar job. Folk singer Ewan MacColl performed and recorded many of his most emotional songs about Salford working-class life when he had effectively moved beyond his old background. This move away, the look back with nostalgia, influences the way in which the Salford community is imagined. My contribution aims to show that the cultural products I have chosen all present a more or less nostalgic view of tight-knit communities, of days and places gone by forever: working class life before the advent of American popular culture, a neo-Romantic belief in nature and community, the longing for the limited area of "our street" as it existed in the good old days before de-industrialisation.

2. The Classic Slum

Roberts is sometimes counted among the intellectual founding fathers of the Birmingham Centre for Contemporary Cultural Studies. Like Richard Hoggart's *The Uses of Literacy* (1958), Roberts's *Classic Slum* (first published in 1971) evokes the author's very own experience of northern English working-class life. If descriptions like Engels's are written from the outsider's point of view, Roberts recounts his own first-hand experience of growing up in the slums. Like Hoggart, Roberts, who was born in 1905, describes the idyll of a pre-Americanised working-class culture, of days irrevocably gone by. If Engels speaks about a community without letting Manchester's or Salford's inhabitants have a say, Roberts shows their interaction. He describes the hierarchical structure within the working class, people's awareness of their own rank, status symbols (furniture, bedding, cleanliness), food, morals, the ideology of the home as a safe haven, schools, work, and finally the release and the changes brought about by World War I. If Engels – as in the above-quoted passage – is interested in slum architecture and the hazards to which inhabitants are exposed, Roberts, whose report is set about 60 years later, mainly focuses on people's interaction and communication. For example:

> In our community, as in every other of its kind, each street had the usual social rating; one side or one end of that street might be classed higher than another. Weekly rents varied from 2*s* 6*d* for the back-to-back to 4*s* 6*d* for a 'two up and two down'. End house often had special status. Every family, too, had a tacit ranking, and even individual members within it; neighbours would consider a daughter in one household as 'dead common' while registering her sister as 'refined', a word much in vogue. (Young women with incipient consumption were often thought 'refined'.) (Roberts 1990: 17)

This passage is typical of Roberts's style: it brims with factual information (rents, types of houses) but also conveys the spirit of Salford community life in its smallest communal unit, the street. By using the people's own language ("dead common", "refined"), Roberts lets the inhabitants of the street have a voice, too, which they are denied throughout Engels's text. Yet at the same time, Roberts speaks from the lofty position of the successful "escaper", mocking his own background, for example through his use of "refined". In a working-class context, a "refined" young woman would be one who aspires to the middle-class ideal of the passive angel in the house, who maybe cultivates some accomplishments, possesses different tastes, or is of a pale appearance. Yet by stating that "refined" also connotes the looks of women about to fall seriously ill from consumption, Roberts ironically comments on his working-class background and desirable constructions of "otherness".

Numerous texts about northern English working-class life take cleanliness as opposed to dirt into account. Both Engels's *Condition of the Working Class in England* and Orwell's *Road to Wigan Pier* present the members of the working class they encounter as deficient in hygiene. Engels wrote about Salford in 1844/45:

> In this district I found a man, apparently about sixty years old, living in a cow-stable. He had constructed a sort of chimney for his square pen, which had neither windows, floor, nor ceiling, had obtained a bedstead and lived there, though the rain dripped through his rotten roof. This man was too old and weak for regular work, and supported himself by removing manure with a hand-cart; the dung-heaps lay next door to his palace! (Engels 1973: 93)

Living close to manure is probably the most extreme way of departing from standards of hygiene and situates the poor old man close to the animals whose pen he already inhabits. The boundary between human civilisation and a nature that stands only for decay, never for growth, has broken down. Engels's text brims with examples of such human misery, yet his fellow-men, into whose eloquent spokesman he turns, never have a say; they are the objects of description but not the subjects of speech. Like Engels, Orwell, who, as a Southerner, writes from outside, defined the northern English working class, whose accommodation he shared, as appallingly dirty: "Hanging from the ceiling there was a heavy glass chandelier on which the dust was so thick that it was like fur" (Orwell 1989: 3). Yet accounts of working-class life written from within emphasise cleanliness as an essential status symbol, and the rituals involved in producing it as the very core of women's power in the house:

> Some houses sparkled. Few who were young then will forget the great Friday night scouring ritual in which all the females of a house took part. (Dance halls closed on Friday evenings for lack of girls.) Women wore their lives away washing clothes in heavy, iron-hooped tubs, scrubbing wood and stone, polishing furniture and fire-irons […]. Two of these compulsives left us for the 'lunatic asylum', one of them, I remember vividly, passing with a man in uniform through a group of us watching children to a van, still washing her hands like poor Lady Macbeth. (Roberts 1990: 37)

In Roberts's description, cleaning is synonymous with protecting one's status. If Orwell's and Engels's accounts of working class housing tell stories of unbelievable bleakness, Roberts's "slum" possesses the aura of a charming little village, whose inhabitants run their lives according to their own traditional rules. Roberts's individual agents constantly interact through communal activities, through gossip, through competing displays of their modest prosperity.

When Roberts's nostalgic account was published in 1971, much of Salford's typical working-class architecture, the rows of terraced houses, had already been demolished, while the Lancashire mills were closing down at the rate of one per week. The end of the "classic slum" had already arrived with World War I. Roberts's final chapter "The Great Release" describes a new openness to ways of life and ideas beyond one's street. Written in retrospect, *The Classic Slum* contributes to the creation of an Englishness no longer existent. American culture, which came to influence European popular culture more and more, is relegated to the margin, and only at the end of his study does Roberts deal with phenomena like the jazz age or what he terms "Noel

Cowardism" (Roberts 1990: 229). In this respect, he resembles Hoggart, whose immensely influential account of English working-class life also nostalgically focuses on a pre-Americanised, "pure" English popular culture.

3. MacColl and the Mass Trespass on Kinder Scout

Ewan MacColl, folk singer, dramatist, actor, political activist, known as Jimmie Miller until 1945, was born in Salford in 1915.[3] His father was an active member of a union, involved in organising strikes, and after being unemployed for long periods of time, eventually found out that he had been blacklisted because of his political views. MacColl, much concerned with workers' rights, devoted one song to his father, "My Old Man", describing his struggle for his rights. Like Roberts, MacColl attempted to convey a sense of a genuine English working-class culture, in which the fight for one's rights counted as a worthy cause. In the 1930s, MacColl got involved with the Lancashire British Workers' Sports Federation (BWSF), which was under the influence of the Young Communist League. Among the sports activities promoted was rambling, particularly in the surroundings of northern industrial towns, at a time when archaic legislation seriously impeded free access to the open country and to public footpaths. Rambling or walking had turned into a mass sport especially for working-class youngsters in the 1930s (Harker 2005). Partly because of its declared political aim – freedom of way for everybody – rambling was regarded as a quasi-revolutionary activity. Particularly in the North, the demand for access to the open countryside was a radical demand because the land belonged to the aristocracy, who wanted to keep it for hunting and shooting and did not wish the game to be disturbed by crowds of noisy walkers from the cities. On 21st June 1932, the famous mass trespass on Kinder Scout in the Peak District took place, a deliberately staged breach of law, when about 8000 ramblers walked up to the peak of Kinder, where they encountered a handful of armed gamekeepers. Among the ramblers, the police identified several ringleaders, who received severe sentences ranging from two to six

---

[3] I am grateful to Ian Foster (Salford University), who pointed out the relevance of MacColl's autobiography (1990) and of the mass trespass.

months of hard labour. Only in 2006 it became known that MacColl, the publicity officer of the mass trespass on Kinder Scout, had ended up on MI5's files in 1932 because of his political activities (Taylor 2006).

The struggle for free walking was closely linked to folk music. As outdoor singing was banned, the right to sing while walking became a political aim, too. MacColl's famous song "The Manchester Rambler", which was written in 1932 and has remained popular until today, celebrates the mass trespass. The lyrics mention various popular locations for ramblers:

> I've been over Snowdon, I've slept up on Crowden
> I've camped by the Wain Stones as well
> I've sunbathed on Kinder, been burnt to a cinder
> And many more things I can tell
> My rucksack has oft been my pillow
> The heather has oft been my bed
> And sooner than part from the mountains
> I think I would rather be dead.
> (MacColl 2001: 370)

"The Manchester Rambler" celebrates the emergence of a "neo-Romanticism" in the early twentieth century that went hand in hand with a revival of folk culture and fed into constructions of Englishness (Trentmann 1994: 583). The new turn to a benevolent, rejuvenating nature ("bed") as opposed to the dirty, corrupt, and unjust industrial city was a reaction to modernity. Rambling and nature meant liberty not available elsewhere, a view captured in the refrain "I may be a wage slave on Monday/But I am a free man on Sunday". MacColl's song glorifies individual agency in combination with the liberty to roam. An encounter with a gamekeeper, the guardian of aristocratic as opposed to working-class interests ("the worst face that ever I saw"), not only fails to make him leave his beloved moorland but confirms his view that he has the same natural right to stay in his favourite habitat as the grouse.

If walking and singing in the open air were suspicious activities in 1932 and could land one on MI5's files, MacColl's famous song was gradually depoliticised during its reception and, in the public consciousness, turned from a radical demand into a nostalgic celebration of rural Englishness. In 2002, on the 70th anniversary of the mass trespass, the Duke of Devonshire, the Peak District's largest landowner, apologised to the walkers for what his grandfather had done in 1932. The event was accompanied by "a rousing rendition of Ewan MacColl's 1932 walkers' anthem" (Anon. 2006). This hazard-free communal singing of "The Manchester Rambler" emphasised the values of solidarity and community while celebrating a supposedly classless Englishness.

4. Lowryscapes

Among Salford's most famous cultural export articles are L.S. Lowry's paintings and the numerous popular and affordable reprints in circulation. Lowry, who was born in 1887 and spent all his life in or around Manchester, worked as a rent collector and clerk and thus held a white-collar job. Influenced by Adolphe Valette, he studied art at the Municipal College of Art, Manchester, and at Salford Art School. For nearly forty years (1909 to 1948), he lived a quiet and sedate life in Pendlebury (Salford) and did most of his painting in the evening (see Rohde 1999). Among his subjects are industrial landscapes and urban pastoral idylls, made up from typically northern architectural features such as railway viaducts, terraced houses, factories, rows of chimneys, adorned with heaps of coal, anonymous crowds of workers, trains, and machines, which he jumbled together. Even though he used some of the sombre colours prevailing in industrial Manchester and Salford, he added white as a background to many of his paintings, thus literally highlighting everyday experiences and giving special glow to what others might regard as dreary lives. In addition, some of his bleakest landscapes sport shades of reddish pink and pale blue, which add heavenly lightness to heavy industry. Lowry's art achieved such fame that it set standards for an "iconography of 'the North'" (Dodd 1990: 22). Not only have his popular paintings, gloomy yet touching, been used for book covers (for example Hoggart's *Uses of Literacy*), posters, and postcards, but even Prime Minister Harold Wilson selected Lowry's paintings for his official Christmas cards in 1964 and in 1965, namely "The Skaters" and "The Pond" (1950) (Waters 1999: 127).

Like Roberts and MacColl, Lowry was concerned with representations of a genuine English working-class culture, which he saw gradually disappearing as a result of de-industrialisation. One of his paintings of Salford, "Francis Street" (1957), which depicts a set of terraced houses on the East side of River Irwell (Sandling, Leber 2000: 42-43), was produced when the post-war slum clearance projects were already well under way and derelict terraced houses, notorious for being damp and unhealthy, were demolished while the former inhabitants were moved to new housing estates. "Francis Street" is full of playing children and their caring mothers. The very short street is framed by a fence, behind which two huge smoking chimneys appear, and as the houses are Lowry-white, the street scene exudes brightness and light. The few square meters of space, on which the children are playing, resemble a huge living room, open only on one side, that of the spectator. Human warmth coincides with an idyllic and nostalgic domesticity. In this as in many other Lowry paintings, the chimneys have taken the place of trees. On the one hand, they function as signifiers of working-class culture, on the other hand, their towering shapes seem to offer shelter, a shelter from a grim, post-World War II modernity which no longer needs factory work or workers. "Francis Street" is an "urban pastoral" viewed from outside (Waters 1999: 139).

If many Lowrys seem to be entirely lacking in natural flora and fauna but group elements of industrial settings in a way that produces idyllic, sheltered places, others are more apocalyptic mixtures of paradise and hell, like "The Lake" (1937) (Sandling, Leber 2000: 36-37), a painting that was inspired by the frequent flooding of the River Irwell in Salford. The whitish and glaring surface of the lake is framed by black and dark green land at the bottom, on the left and on the right side. At the top, a kind of heavenly industrial city appears, more colourful than the rest of the painting. Some spires, accompanied by chimneys, Christian and secular symbols of transcendence, are towering above the buildings. Attempting to cross over is dangerous, as some half-sunk boats on the lake, close to the spectator, show. On the shoreline closest to the spectator, several telegraph poles and other industrial leftovers appear like crosses and headstones marking a graveyard, reminding the observer of those who dared to cross, who dared to aspire to the heavenly city, where access is granted only to the few. Heaven and hell are often closely linked in Lowry's paintings. "The Lake" was painted at a time of economic depression, when work in the mills and foundries would have been heaven, not hell. Unlike the domesticity of "Francis Street", the apocalyptic dimension of "The Lake" imbues English working-class culture with a transcendent significance beyond the everyday.

From the end of World War II onwards, Lowry's paintings, which depicted a world that no longer existed, became increasingly popular in Britain. Both celebrations of the old community spirit of "our street" and existentialist visions of overpowering industrial might helped to invent a northern type of Englishness which was on the verge of disappearing forever. While cheap reproductions of his paintings were circulated (Waters 1999: 133), Lowry both partook in the new mass culture and seemingly stayed aloof from it, as the lonely observer of his landscapes. "The Lowry", a cultural centre situated in the rebuilt docklands of Salford Quays, opened in 2000 and has a Lowry gallery with the paintings that had been collected by the Salford Art Gallery, paying a nostalgic homage to a Salford that no longer exists.

5. Coronation Street

Coronation Street, one of Britain's most successful soap operas, began to run in 1960 while the old living quarters were being demolished. In 1963, Manchester and Salford seriously planned to tear down all that was left of terraced houses within eight years. This slum clearance project, which aimed to move inhabitants from derelict housing to more modern estates, destroyed an established way of life cherished by Roberts, MacColl, and Lowry. *Coronation Street* began as yet another nostalgic celebration of a typical northern English community threatened by modernity. Set in fictitious Weatherfield, which stands for Salford, the series is produced in the Granada studios in Manchester, and can thus be called a truly local product (Little 1995, Frey-Vor 1991, Dyer et al. 1981, Shields 1991: 207-51). Originally planned as a twice-weekly serial for thirteen weeks, *Coronation Street* soon came to enjoy an extended run and has been broadcast for over 45 years, while the number of episodes transmitted per week has gradually increased to five on four evenings. Despite its national and international audience, the series has always presented itself as a local programme, a celebration of English Northernness, which is distinctly tied to an urban environment and far removed from the Lake District's call of nature. Most actors are from Greater Manchester and sport the essential signifier (Gillett 2003: 19) of a northern English identity, namely the accent, which is so strong that the subtitling on offer is needed not merely by those whose hearing is impaired. The street consists of a few houses only, kept in the typical "two-down, two-up" architectural style, a pub (the Rovers Return), two shops, a café, to which, over the years, several additional places of interaction have been added. Some of those are geographically distant from Coronation Street, such as Reg Holdsworth's supermarket Bettabuy, which symbolises the advent of modern habits of consumption. The post-industrial urban ambience is signified by the backdrop of "our street", which could be found anywhere in Salford, Manchester, or any other northern city. The terraced houses, a railway viaduct, the backyards all function as the adequate backdrop of northern English street life. The opening shot presents elements of local architecture: roofs, chimneys, cobbles; for some years, a brief view of the blocks of flats near Salford Precinct was shown. In recent years, locations in Manchester have been introduced. The series includes occasional trips to the countryside, which, however, run contrary to the aesthetic of the sublime associated with the Lake District because such excursions tend to go wrong in a comic way. In 1983, for example, Betty Turpin and Bet Lynch, the barmaids who pulled pints at the Rovers Return for years, went to Tatton Park for an outing and, while sitting in the car, accidentally rolled backwards into a shallow lake.

Coronation Street is a microcosm of ordinary northern English city life in a de-industrialised age and adheres to a strict agenda of realism. Up to 1969, the programme was recorded live. The characters appearing in it are supposed to represent the type of people who live in "our street". One of the reasons for the success of *Coronation Street* is its mix of characters: several generations, different social background (working class, middle class, those aspiring to be middle class, the occasional capitalist such as Mike Baldwin), skillfully cast types.[4] The characters are "created" with a view to the locals. Bet Lynch, barmaid and later manageress at the Rovers Return, was researched on the streets of Salford by actress Julie Goodyear and the street's creator, Tony Warren:

---

[4] For the complete storyline see Hardy (2004).

"Everytime we went out, we would see a Bet at the bus stop or a Bet at the market shopping, and Tony or I would say "Look at that silver mac/hairdo/earrings etc." [...] When Bet first appeared, her hair was ironed flat and she wore tight black dresses. After observing the Salford characters, Bet instructed make-up to pile her hair up in a beehive and steered the character from black to leopard skin. (Little 1995: 153-54).

The realism of *Coronation Street* is intensified through the contact between actors and audience. Bet Lynch, the tarty barmaid, wore earrings on TV which had been sent to her by her fans, particularly by children, who had bought these items with their pocket money. The actors receive numerous letters from the audience advising them on issues ranging from make-up to the marriage problems of the characters they embody. The Granada studios used to operate popular tours both for locals and for tourists, who could for example have a pint at the Rovers Return and thus slip into the "reality" of a northern English street life that pretends to be more authentic than the interaction available on housing estates built after World War II.

Over the years, *Coronation Street* has undergone several face-lifts and has been repeatedly modernised. For example, the opening shot has changed several times and now incorporates more greenery. Metrolink, a light railway system introduced in 1992, is occasionally visible on the viaduct towering above the street. Adjacent streets have been made more prominent, thereby extending this imagined northern community. Topics have changed, too: if an episode in 1965 was concerned with the dramatic collapse of house No. 7, it reflected both the authorities' and the population's growing concern with the safety standards in former slum areas. The more recent controversial story lines have dealt with child abuse, teenage pregnancy, over-ambitious parents, gay coming out. If sex was virtually no issue until 1985 when the first bedroom scene was shown, later episodes have been more open about the inner life of relationships. The street has also changed in terms of class: With the disappearance of industry and of the old working class, the characters in "our street" have taken up work in the service sector (e.g. as a hairdresser). This modernisation has enabled the street to keep its place in the popular imagination.

Salford cultural identities all centre on the nostalgic vision of a community that is imbued with solidarity and human warmth, represented by signifiers of northern working-class culture: cobbles, terraced houses, chimneys. Within the boundaries of this imagined community, a northern type of Englishness can be construed, which is retrospective in its outlook. If industrialisation once was a threat to human health and well-being, its leftovers now serve as a backdrop for visions of a social cohesion no longer readily available in a post-industrial age.

Works Cited

Anderson, Benedict (1983): *Imagined Communities: Reflections on the Origin and Spread of Nationalism*. London: Verso.

Anon. (2006): 'Duke Apologises for Unjust Treatment of Trespassers [29 April 2002]'. Online at http://www.ramblers.org.uk/news/archive/2002/Kinder29 Apr02.html (consulted 15.09.2006).

Cass, Eddie (1996): "Manchester, a New City? The Role of Urban Heritage and the Arts in a City Revival", *Journal of the Study of British Cultures* 3, 45-58.

Dickens, Charles (1995): *Hard Times for These Times*. Kate Flint (ed.). London: Penguin.

Dodd, Philip (1990): "Lowryscapes: Recent Writings about 'The North'", *Critical Quarterly* 32, 17-28.

Dyer, Richard, Christine Geraghty, Marion Jordan, Terry Lovell, Richard Paterson, and John Stewart (1981): *Coronation Street*. London: British Film Institute.

Engels, Friedrich (1973): *The Condition of the Working Class in England: From Personal Observation and Authentic Sources*. Moscow: Progress Publishers.

Frey-Vor, Gerlinde (1991): *Coronation Street: Infinite Drama and British Reality. An Analysis of Soap Opera as Narrative and Dramatic Continuum*. Trier: WVT.

Geraghty, Christine (2005): "The Study of Soap Opera", in: Janet Wasko (ed.): *A Companion to Television*. Oxford: Blackwell, 308-323.

Gillett, Philip (2003): *The British Working Class in Postwar Film*. Manchester: Manchester UP.

Hardy, Katherine (2004): *Coronation Street: The Complete Saga*. London: Granada.

Harker, Ben (2005): "'The Manchester Rambler': Ewan MacColl and the 1932 Mass Trespass", *History Workshop Journal* 59, 219-228.

Hoggart, Richard (1958): *The Uses of Literacy: Aspects of Working-Class Life with Special Reference to Publications and Entertainments*. Harmondsworth: Pelican.

Little, Daran (1995): *The Coronation Street Story: Celebrating Thirty-Five Years of the Street*. London: Boxtree.

MacColl, Ewan (1990): *Journeyman: An Autobiography*. London: Sidgwick & Jackson.

— (2001): *The Essential Ewan MacColl Songbook: Sixty Years of Songmaking*. Peggy Seeger (ed.). New York: Music Sales.

Orwell, George (1989): *The Road to Wigan Pier*. London: Penguin.

Roberts, Robert (1990): *The Classic Slum: Salford Life in the First Quarter of the Century*. London: Penguin.

Rohde, Shelly (1987/1999): *L.S. Lowry. A Bibliography* (formerly publ. as *Private View of L.S. Lowry*). Salford: Lowry Press.

Russell, Dave (2004): *Looking North: Northern England and the National Imagination*. Manchester: Manchester UP.

Sandling, Judith and Mike Leber (2000): *Lowry's City: A Painter and His Locale*. Salford: Lowry Press.

Schmid, Susanne (1997): "Exploring Multiculturalism: Bradford Jews and Bradford Pakistanis", *Journal for the Study of British Cultures* 4, 163-179.

Shields, Rob (1991): *Places on the Margin: Alternative Geographies of Modernity*. Routledge: London.

Taylor, Paul (2006): "Ewan MacColl and the MI5 Files", *Manchester Evening News* 6 March.

Trentmann, Frank (1994): "Civilization and Its Discontents: English Neo-Romanticism and the Transformation of Anti-Modernism in Twentieth-Century Western Culture", *Journal of Contemporary History* 29, 583-625.

Waters, Chris (1999): "Representations of Everyday Life: L.S. Lowry and the Landscape of Memory in Postwar Britain", *Representations* 65, 121-150.

Classy Northerners: Class, Space and the Wonderful Illusion

Christoph Ehland

Abstract: The clichéd ideas about the North of England have been characterised by an extreme polarisation between images of the deprived industrial cities and the beauty of the rural northern landscapes. This essay traces the development of these stereotypes and their ideological undertones and relates them to the ways in which the writer's house as a literary institution actively utilises and recreates established conceptions of landscapes. It is argued that the literary site becomes an instrument of class identity that grants access to a landscape as an imagined possession.

Key Names and Concepts: H.V. Morton - Hugh Miller - Elizabeth Gaskell - William Wordsworth - Ian Ousby - Raymond Williams - John Urry; Lake District - Dove Cottage - The World of James Herriot - Middle-class Identity - Landscape - Tourism - Romantic Gaze - Aesthetic Concepts - Nostalgia - Literary Site - Writer's House - Hyper-reality - Authenticity.

1. Even here! An Introduction

It comes as no surprise that the constructions of identity which frame and organise our experience of life and society are class specific. But how do these constructions reflect or rather absorb regional identities, or, to put it differently, how are these identities mutually constructed and experienced in a region of Britain which – historically – represents a battleground of class identities, as many of the essays in this volume show?

In Northern England, the heartland of the historical development which would eventually be called the Industrial Revolution, the associations that come most readily to mind are those of the industrial landscapes. During his first "search" for England in 1927 H.V. Morton gives a paradigmatic insight into the clichéd image of the region:

> I looked at the map. I was passing between Liverpool on the left and Manchester on the right, and about sixteen miles from both cities. Far off to the left I could see the Mersey estuary, with red smoke-stacks rising above the flat lands by the sandy shore. To the right there was an ominous grey haze in the sky which meant Manchester. For months I have been motoring through a green England which might never have known the Industrial Revolution. Round Bristol, it is true, I saw factories. I left Birmingham on my right, and saw no trace of that monster as I went on into Old England. Here was New England: an England of crowded towns, of tall chimneys, of great mill walls, of canals of slow, black water; an England of grey, hard-looking little houses in interminable rows; the England of coal and chemicals; of cotton, glass and iron. (Morton 1933: 185-186)

As Michael Bartholomew observes, Morton approached his subject matter as if he were writing a 'motoring pastoral' (cf. Bartholomew 2004: 90) so that it seems half in keeping with the book's theme that on his first tour of England the writer avoided the urban North. Only on his second journey in 1928 would he fill the gap in his account of England and dare to venture into the "giants of the north". In the passage quoted he is only passing, almost slipping, through the stretch of land which lies between Liverpool and Manchester. But the little he sees suffices to provoke a compelling image. The passage quoted cannot be interpreted as other than stigmatising: two large cities are reduced to two smoke screens: "red smoke-stacks" in the case of Liverpool and "an ominous grey haze" in the case of Manchester. The tone of the narrative is one of suspicion, of disgust, of escape. But even Morton acknowledges the fact that quite different images in the North can occur side by side: "Yet how difficult it is to kill an English field, to stamp out the English grass, and to deform an English lane! Even here, within sixteen miles of the two great giants of the north, men were raking hay in a field within a gunshot of factory chimneys." (Morton 1933: 186) However, the contrast between the two aspects of the landscape only heightens the intensity of the opposing images. In their confrontation with the features of what Morton defines as "Old England", green fields and men raking hay, the industrial cities are branded as something in essence un-English. The characterisation is as sweeping as it is reductive, and given that Morton's literary objectives were always conservative rather than radical the contrasts his text ceaselessly constructs narrow down the image of the North to an accessible stereotype: smoking chimneys, canals and railway lines, blackened back-to-back houses, etc. But what do these images communicate? Undoubtedly, it would create an objectionable series of ontological fallacies if one were to ask how real Morton's picture of Northern England actually is. In postmodern times the 'real' is not a trustworthy concept any more. But even if one cannot expect to find the 'real' mimetically incorporated in textual representations one may still identify something *real* in the purpose of a text: the dominant argument, that is to say, the ideological taint of the text.

Morton's vision of England derives from the imagery of a long line of travelogues on Northern England. Travel writers were apt to look at the industrial cities of the North as a phenomenon rather than as real places because they evidently had difficulties in relating their experience to traditional notions of England. From the astonished reports of eighteenth-century travellers on the industrial sublime to the more ambiguous accounts of travellers during the nineteenth century, much of the reception of the North has depended on the success of the economic model it represented. In 1851 on his journey from York to Manchester the Scottish writer Hugh Miller remarks on the paradigmatic contrast between the two places: "I had seen two of the ecclesiastical cities of *Old* England, and I was now desirous to visit two of the great trading towns of the modern country, so famous for supplying with its manufactures half the economic wants of the world." (Miller 1851, 55) On approaching Manchester the traveller's earlier enthusiasm is somewhat moderated and Miller not only notices the "innumerable chimneys" and the "lurid gloom of the atmosphere" (60) but also comments on the contrast between the magnificence of the public buildings and the environmental deprivation in the town.[1] Despite this, the economic justification for the existence of the industrial city remains in the background of his mind. Miller's narrative may not shy away from the downside of the industrial modernity he finds in

---

[1] Miller's description of the river Irwell may indeed represent an early attempt to raise environmental awareness: "The hapless river – a pretty enough stream a few miles higher up, with trees overhanging its banks, and fringes of green sedge set thick along its edges – loses caste as it gets among the mills and the print-works. There are myriads of dirty things given it to wash, and whole wagonloads of poisons from the dye-houses and bleach-yards thrown into it to carry away. [...] till at length it rolls on [...] considerably less a river than a flood of liquid manure, in which all life dies, whether animal or vegetable, and which resembles nothing in nature, except perhaps the stream thrown out in eruption by some mud volcano." (Miller 1851, 62)

Manchester but throughout his account his observations remain more acute and balanced than those recorded by the stigmatising gaze of Morton.

If one keeps in mind their economic circumstances, Morton's evident dislike of the industrial northern cities is understandable: they are an inescapable reminder of the fact that Victorian Britain with its pompous pride in its achievements and its seemingly unlimited opportunities to capitalise on the economic spirit of the *laissez-faire* was inevitably gone. By the late 1920s economic success could no longer counterbalance the deprivation of the industrial cities. The outlook in Morton's writing therefore represents a flight from the critical condition of British society during the interwar years. The author, as the critical reader may infer, shies away from the economic and social crisis of the postwar depression. Instead he and his readership escape into a kind of nostalgic fantasy-land haunted by a phantom, as it were, of Englishness. The judgemental implications of Morton's ever-present distinction between the 'old' England and the 'new' industrial England are a distortion of Miller's differentiation between the ecclesiastical cities of 'old' England and the "great trading towns of the modern country" (Miller 1851, 55).

With regard to Morton's travelogues there can be no doubt that their author is bashfully selective and shamelessly manipulative in his representations of the North; so what does he want to show to his readers? Rather than giving an answer straight away it seems sensible to look at Morton's second journey through England in 1928. Although the writer's return to the North is more comprehensive than his first journey, his entry into the urban centres of the region is only a half-hearted attempt at rehabilitating its industrial character. It soon becomes clear that Morton's effort to look for those other places which present a divergent image from that of the smoke-stained industrial city only means that he finds the odd traditional English pub in Manchester's Market Square or the Gothic building of the John Rylands Library in the same city. Places like these remind him of a better, more *English,* England, and he readily implants them into the same model of differentiation between an 'old' England and a 'new' England which governs all his writing on Britain. As previously noted, the depiction of places which offer an aesthetic aura of tranquillity amidst the commercial buzz of their urban setting serves predominantly to emphasise and generalise the negative connotations of that setting. Although one must assume that the contrastive arrangements in the text primarily contribute to the overall rhetorical strategy, it cannot be doubted that they are ideologically charged. In Manchester Morton symptomatically plays with feelings of loss when he represents the city as a "labyrinth" (Morton 1949: 116) or a "maze" (124).[2]

The effect Morton creates with his representation of the labyrinthine character of the urban environment becomes clearer in those instances where he notes how "warehouses swarm with their varied workers" (121), or how "thousands of men and women [are] passing by" (123). He paints the picture of a crowded place, an artificial conglomerate in "the full blaze of electric lights" (113), which is apt to remove the distinctive features of the people who appear in faceless swarms in its streets. In Morton's tone and in the way he develops his associations one can perceive the old image of the masses "als Schreckgespenst des Zerfalls und des Untergangs" [transl.: as the bogeyman of dissolution and decay] (König 1992, 15). In the lurking shadow of the indistinguishable masses urbanity and industrial activity are combined as threatening forces which potentially aim to kill the real, the old, the rural England.[3] In the end the feeling prevails that for Morton "Manchester [...] offers no escape from itself" (Morton 1949: 118). The image of a decentred place, robbed of its soul, is established: "Manchester is an elusive city; one is always searching for its centre and never finding it." (114)

Admittedly, the concentration on the urban side of the North is apt to produce a forced and one-sided image, a provocative and very common stereotype of the northern regions in which problematic associations dominate. Overshadowed by negative connotations, the image of the industrial North may for many become synonymous with Northern England.

For this essay it seems sensible to restrict the discussion at this point to the illustrations found in Morton's travelogues, not only because he is arguably the most successful and widely read travel writer of the interwar years but predominantly because the conservative stance of his vision of England ideally reveals a particularly "classy"

---

[2] This image of the Northern city is also visible in J.B. Priestley's travelogue of 1933: "It [Manchester] is an Amazonian jungle of blackened bricks." (Priestley 1979: 239)

[3] In this context see the essay by Stephan Kohl in this volume.

perceptive model of Northern England. Morton writes with the quintessential outlook of the educated, middle-class tourist[4] and constantly displays an attitude which Orvar Löfgren has shown to be the typical "middle-class resentment against collectivity" (Löfgren 1999: 103). Ben Knights has pointed out to what extent Morton's literary technique depends upon a mode of solitary travelling: Morton, the motorist traveller, is on his own with his impressions and reflections. In a Wordsworthian sense he finds renewal of his imaginative approach to his environment in the dissociation from his social self (see Knights 2006: 172-173). This becomes most obvious when Morton pays a brief visit to Blackpool during his second journey and sees nothing more than "England's greatest experiment in organized pleasure." (Morton 1949: 141) Again, phrases like "organized pleasure" function to channel the contempt of the writer for the dehumanising uniformity of organised mass tourism. One can perceive something more than just the subliminal dislike of the middle-class protestant for the lower classes and their unashamed pursuit of pleasure.[5] For Morton Blackpool is the same as it is for the masses: "It is the logical result of Lancashire." (142)

The pleasure-seeking working-class crowd is the cream on a cake which he finds difficult to swallow. Morton's disparaging gaze at the seaside resort is stigmatising in the extreme:

> It [Blackpool] is the silver lining to all the smoke-clouds. It is as eloquent of Lancashire as the smoke-stacks of Bolton and Oldham: it is Lancashire's idea of the earthly paradise.
>
> There are millions of people all over the north of England who have been saving up for the past twelve months for a glorious week's 'fling' at Blackpool." (142)

Hastily almost, Morton reassures his reader that the 'wakes', those pleasure-seeking workers from the urban sprawl of Lancashire, have

---

[4] For a detailed sociogram of the middle-class holiday maker, see Orvar Löfgren's study of vacationing (Löfgren 1999: 102-103).

[5] Morton stands perplexed in the face of what he presents as the utter senselessness of the typical working-class amusements at Blackpool: "He [the average working-class northerner] arrives in Blackpool with his holiday money, and he spends every penny, and goes home 'broke' to start all over again. But he carries back with him the memory of a week free from the nagging humiliation of slender means." (Morton 1949: 142).

nothing to do with the traditional northerner. But, looking closely, the idealised image of the hardy, hay-raking rural characters that should instead people the dales and moors of the North in Morton's England is granted as little individuality by the nostalgic gaze of the travel writer as is the herded swarm of weekend-trippers he watches at the pleasure pier in Blackpool. The distinctions and classifications Morton constantly applies to the things he sees inevitably expose the writer's own conceptions and prejudices. He is seeking for the "genuine"[6] people of the North, a species that is decorative at its best and that may never have existed outside guidebooks and travelogues.

In general it can be said that Morton's approach to the things he sees and experiences in the North of England is nostalgic. He is apt to paint clichéd landscapes of the North in which the traces of the industrial appear as unreal and unnatural, in which the "ominous" smell of the working classes won't fade away. He thereby confirms that his gaze is a radicalised romantic one, in many respects a politicised distortion in which the remnants of a romantic sensitivity are transformed into an instrument either of idolisation or of stigmatisation. His gaze thereby not only confirms deep-rooted sensitivities and affinities of middle-class society, but also reveals its inherent taboos and anxieties.

Nonetheless, this perspective is characterised by a perceptive paradox: by ceaselessly lamenting the desecration of the northern landscape the idea of the industrial North defines the writer's dominant axis of perception which becomes indispensable as it is elevated to be the argumentative cornerstone of the travel narrative. Symptomatically, Morton expands his vision of Northern England by using the contrastive power of the available imagery:

> In the south of England we suffer from a false idea of the manufacturing north. It is almost within the times of our grandfathers that the coal-fields of the north became more important than the cornfields of the south, and we, having perhaps seen Sheffield from the train – one of England's saddest sights – imagine that a northern city must, in the nature of things, be an ugly one. The commercial prominence of those recent giants, Liverpool, Manchester, Leeds, Sheffield, Bradford, and

---

[6] Löfgren explains in *On Holiday* how the typical urban middle-class holidaymaker is looking at the local people as a genuine part of the scenery; e.g. quoting from a 1903 guidebook he writes: "'these simple but healthy and worthy people of the lower classes,' a population not yet harmed by the diseases resulting from civilisation." (Löfgren 1999: 125)

> Halifax, blinds us to the real north, which apart from these areas of dense populations, remains, as it always has been, one of the most historically romantic and naturally beautiful divisions of England. (Morton 1933: 207)

As this shows, there are at a second glance quite different images available which also provoke a different idea of Northernness. For Morton it is, as he puts it, "the real north": the Yorkshire dales and moors, the Lake District, the cathedral cities of York, Durham or Ripon, the coastal villages of Scarborough and Whitby. It seems less than a coincidence that these places – or, more strictly speaking their image – have been built into a different map of the North: a middle-class map. It will be the aim of this essay to show how literary culture contributes a significant aspect to this allusive and elusive perspective on the landscape of Northern England. The following pages will discuss how the idea of the 'literary' landscape becomes an affirmative tessera in the mosaic of activities which establish and maintain middle-class identity in Northern England.

2. Temporal Diversity

As Raymond Williams has made clear in *The Country and the City*, the contrastive presentation, the inescapable mutuality of urban and rural imagined places is deeply enshrined in the cultural consciousness of the western world.[7] Though the relationship between the two "has been astonishingly varied" (Williams 1973: 1), the following extract seems to summarise the background of the nostalgic vision seen in Morton:

> [...] the English experience remains exceptionally important: not only symptomatic but in some ways diagnostic; in its intensity still memorable, whatever may succeed. For it is a critical fact that in and through these transforming experiences [those of the so-called agrarian and industrial revolutions of the eighteenth and early nineteenth centuries] English attitudes to the country, and to ideas of rural life, persisted with extraordinary power, so that even after the society was predominantly urban its literature, for a generation, was still predominantly rural; and even in the twentieth century, in an urban and indus-

---

[7] In this context see also Aitchison, MacLeod and Shaw 2000: 51-71.

trial land, forms of the older ideas and experiences still remarkably persist. (2)

It is striking that the polarisation between the country and the city is still defining the difference between an English dream and its nightmarish opposite. On the one hand, the rural ideal: the country churchyards, the small villages, the weather beaten faces of 'ye good olde' stock of healthy country people. On the other, the urban deprivation of all that Englishness should stand for: the destitute landscapes of the Northern cities with their forests of smoking chimneys and blackened warehouses, the crowded treeless dens of cheap brick houses, the bowed backs of a faceless, crowded population of unhealthy workers. Morton's concept of the distinction between an 'old' and a 'new' England exemplifies the more popular and nostalgic side of this particularly English experience. At the same time the travelogue hints at the essential temporality of the landscape images. In this context Elizabeth Gaskell's novel *North and South*[8] may be of help in gaining a better understanding of this paradigm of perception. As in the case of Morton, Gaskell constructs in her novel an indigenous opposition between the 'old' England of the agrarian south and the 'new' England of the newly defined classes of the industrial North. The novel depicts the experiences of the uprooted family of a dissenting minister from the hamlet of Helstone in the South of England in their new environment, the northern industrial town of Milton. The set of oppositions Gaskell introduces in her text reminds one of the tendentious contrasts used by Morton but her approach is notably more subtle and balanced. Seen through the inner eye of Margaret Hale the idealised image of the southern village represents the ever-present contrastive background to the heroine's excursions into the grim reality of the northern industrial town. Gaskell shows the extent to which her initial nostalgic longings stand for a negotiation between the inevitable progression into an industrial future and a past – nostalgically and often stubbornly – glorified by many, mostly by comparison. In the novel Gaskell al-

---

[8] The geographical polarisation in the title was not initially intended by Gaskell. She would have preferred the name of her heroine but Charles Dickens, who serialised the novel in *Household Words*, did not like the idea. It remains unclear by whom this particular title was adopted. In this context see Sally Shuttleworth's introduction to the 1998 Oxford World's Classics edition of the novel (Gaskell 1998: xi).

lows her protagonist to experience a gradual process of understanding of the new classes formed by the necessities of an industrial society in Northern England. Andrew Sanders writes about Gaskell's concern in *North and South*: "Its highly perceptive heroine [...] may at first be shocked by the market economy which works 'as if commerce were everything and humanity nothing' but she is later impressed by a dinner at which Manchester men 'talked in desperate earnest, - not in the used-up style that wearied her so in the old London parties'." (Sanders 1994: 410)

Despite the allusive geographical polarisation in the title of the novel the distinction between the North and the South, between the country and the city, is a spatial construction for a temporal differentiation: Helstone stands for the past just as Milton represents a turbulent present and an uncertain future. Gaskell emphasises this point when she removes the rural idyll into the mere memory of her characters. As reminiscence, the image is kept in perspective: remote, unreal and inaccessible. If Morton presents the differences between rural and urban England as an aesthetic dichotomy Gaskell recognises the space between them as the product of the historical process. From this vantage point *North and South* is not about regional differences, it is about the experience of time and change. In turn, however, time is a space to be claimed and in many respects the hegemonic struggle for the collective memory of a nation represents itself as a territorial conflict. As Gaskell presents it, the different temporal zones represented by the idea of the South and the North also demarcate different societies.

Turning now from the realm of literature to the material side of literary culture it is clear that the images that govern creative minds also influence the formation and reception of those landscapes which shape regional identity. Looking at the image of the North of England it is evident that the conflict between the country as the nostalgic haven of an allegedly golden past and the city as the representative of the challenges of the present is not restricted to travelogues and novels. The oppositions which have structured the argument of Gaskell's novel also materialise in the manifold institutions which mould a stretch of land into a landscape. In the context of this essay the focus is on the application, as it were, of the one literary element for the creation of the other, the literary landscapes of the North of England. Potentially, these places may be designed as touristic abodes of a nostalgic sentimentality for the rural past. In terms of the class distinctions enshrined in these landscapes of aesthetic idealisation and touristic sites, it is evident that they are generally endowed with the propensity to serve escapist projections, a fact that highlights their broad egalitarian appeal[9]; despite this qualification the traditional images of the 'old' North of England which come readily to mind tend predominantly to present the country as a repository of middle-class values whereas the image of the urban space in the region often remains tainted by proletarian associations, depending of course on the beholder. From this it follows that it is important to realise that the construction as well as the reception of landscape as a historical space is inescapably charged by social concerns: in the landscapes of its spatial environment society not only materialises its own social structures – e.g. in the distribution of space to the habitats of the different social stratifications and their individual figuration – but in landscapes society imagines its preconceived ideas about itself. Landscape is nothing aesthetically fixed or static, it "works," as W.J.T. Mitchell has made clear, "as a cultural practice [...] it is an instrument of cultural power that is (or frequently represents itself as) independent of human intentions." (Mitchell 2002, 1-2) One should therefore read and understand landscape as a historical discourse, a narrative of the hegemonic processes within society.

With regard to literary discourse as a "landscaping" practice the situation becomes particularly complex: ever since English Literature was first introduced as a university discipline in the late eighteenth century in the University of Edinburgh it has been closely connected with middle-class identity (see Court 1992: 18-21). When Adam Smith compiled his lectures on Rhetoric and Belles Lettres on behalf of Lord Kames vernacular literature served as an element in an educational programme designed for the professional classes. It seems fair enough to assume that the rise of capitalism and the ascent of the middle classes during the eighteenth century fostered their identification with the immaterial values of literary culture. In *Die protestantische Ethik*, Max Weber deduces that the Protestant preference for the liter-

---

[9] This is an aspect which David Dimbleby illustrates in his book *A Picture of Britain*: with regard to the war efforts in Britain during 1940/41 Dimbleby points out in the chapter "The Art of Defence" that the images of idealised English landscapes allowed the nation to identify with itself. (see Dimbleby 2005: 77-83)

ary realm is no coincidence but a logical consequence of the combined forces of the Protestant loathing for the unnecessary and the search for the didactically sensible:

> Aber am Gesamtbild ändert das insofern nichts als die mächtige *Verinnerlichung* der Persönlichkeit, welche die weitere Fortbildung der puritanischen Lebensluft mit sich bringen konnte und tatsächlich mitbestimmt hat, doch vorwiegend der Literatur und auch da erst späteren Geschlechtern zugute gekommen ist. (Weber 1965: 178)

Ever since literature was thus acquired as a constituent of middle-class identity it has remained a domain of this particular class and has become a building block of a widespread and varied literary culture, reaching from the various facets of the book market (such as reading events, antiquarian book fairs, book-launch parties etc.) to institutions like writers' houses and literary museums.

3. Imagined Places

The discussion so far has served to shed light upon the subtle literary system of spatial and temporal differentiation that underlies the image of Northern England. The next part of this essay will focus on the cultural practices by which institutions like writers' houses and literary museums actively utilise and create this particular set of landscape associations and thus introduce literary culture as a significant element in the spatial identity of the North of England. In this context it will be necessary to seek an answer to the question how a real place is turned into an imagined place.

The scope of the problem comprised by the notion of the 'imagined place' becomes clearer when one looks at Elizabeth Helsinger's discussion of Turner's landscape paintings of England. In respect of the function of the picturesque guidebooks of the early nineteenth century she writes:

> Two problematic concepts underlie such books: circulation and possession. The purchaser is offered visual possession of an England whose images have been placed in circulation. For their largely middle-class intended audience, this might be construed as a gesture toward inclusion within the ranks of the landowners, who still retained primary political and social authority in England in the years preced-

ing the enactment of the Reform Bill in 1832. Purchase these books and you too may gain at least visual access to the land. (Helsinger 2002: 105)

The idea of 'access' as it is raised by Helsinger is particularly helpful in approaching the literary landscapes of the North of England in the context of this essay: this does not mean that one must ask for whom access is granted, or to which stretch of land this access will lead, but one has to tackle the problem of how the layers of the bio-literary discourse define and limit the access to an imagined landscape. Naturally, this requires a broader concept of what 'access' in the context of literary landscapes really means. It must of course be clear that one is only speaking about an imagined access or, more precisely, access to the imagination: just as the picturesque guidebooks of the early nineteenth century were a substitute for material possession, so the idea of the literary landscape highlights an access route to the land as a specific landscape. Marxists would undoubtedly expose these literary landscapes as societal pacifiers.

Without abandoning in any way a critical attitude towards the enquiry into the institutions of literary culture, it seems that one must first deal with the phenomenon that the very existence of these places alters the appearance of the imaginary map of Northern England which – in most cases unintentionally yet inevitably – sustains rather than subverts the stereotypical images of the North. Or, to rephrase this observation as a question, does the particular ontology of the writer's house as a touristic site help to create an escapist idea of an 'old' England as opposed to an industrial 'new' England, as popularised by writers like Morton? Do literary institutions and their activities, by inversion of thought, stigmatise that part of the North of England which is not regarded as literary?

Obviously, one must lift the blanket of cultural reverence from a literary map which often seems to consist of an ephemeral landscape scattered with literary sites and fuelled by literary associations, at least in the eyes of the proprietors and beholders of the places it contains. The cultural processes and practices, however, which contribute to the creation of this remote, sheltered hinterland of the imagination are characterised by selective, sometimes manipulative stage-management. They stand for an often sentimental clinging to an historical perspective that is an illusion of a status quo set against the ever-changing realities that encompass society.

The first literary memorial houses[10] were acquired and opened to the public through the self-confident esteem of the educated Victorian middle classes as quasi-religious shrines for their cultural and societal self-assurance. Although these places have survived into the present day society has changed: the move into modernity has created manifold challenges not only for the individual writer's house but also for the concept of the literary memorial house as such. Whether the proprietors of a literary house attempt stubbornly to maintain their original mission or to adapt themselves to the transformation of society their property has been transformed by the fact that it is inevitably perceived in the context of a touristic experience. Despite the remnants of Victorian ardour in the foundation stories of the majority of the literary houses discussed in this essay, one can see that these institutions are more recently making an effort to open the exclusive literary world they stand for to a broader audience. But does this necessarily change the fact that these places are often seen as an excuse to dream the timeless dream of an 'old' England of thatched cottages, men raking hay and an unspoiled natural habitat?[11]

In fact, the houses which are preserved as writers' memorials in England today prove[12] that the literary imagination has an affinity for

---

[10] Shakespeare's Birthplace in Stratford-upon-Avon was acquired in 1847, Milton's Cottage in Chalfont St. Giles in 1887, Dove Cottage in Grasmere in 1891 and the Brontë Museum in Haworth in 1893.

[11] In fact, as one flips through the pages of *The Oxford Illustrated Literary Guide to Great Britain and Ireland* it becomes clear how dominant this view is in places of literary memory. After a glance at the pictures the reader may come to the conclusion that the overwhelming bulk of English literature was written on the lawns and in the orchards of country vicarages. A further critical remark may be permitted here: looking at the abodes even of the literary avant-garde of the interwar years, those writers who set out in their literature to shake the established conventions, one may be astounded by the fact that the most conventional preferences governed the aesthetics of their living environment: whether one thinks of Virginia Woolf's Monk House or of Rita Sackville-West's Sissinghurst Castle, the majority of the Bloomsbury writers had a strong affinity to the picturesque settings commonly found in the illustrated coffee-table books intended to feed the imagination of a bourgeois audience.

[12] With the exception of London: on closer analysis, however, it is clear that in contrast to the other urban centres of England London is primarily perceived

rural and small town environments. Only slowly and hesitatingly have places in urban environments been added to the list of literary memorial houses in Britain in recent decades. The rule seems to be that the more picturesque and touristic a region is the more likely it is that a writer's house is preserved as a literary memorial; at the same time the reverse holds true for the urban element in literary culture: the more industrial an environment the less likely it is that a former writer's house is turned into a memorial. It is therefore no coincidence that the big cities of the North have for long been omitted from its literary map: Bradford, the birthplace of J.B. Priestley, is not even mentioned in *The Oxford Illustrated Literary Guide to Great Britain and Ireland* although in 1986 a statue of the writer by Ian Judd was unveiled in the city in front of the National Museum of Film, Photography and Television. Nor is Salford listed as the native city of Walter Greenwood, the author of *Love on the Dole*. With the sole exception of the Gaskell House at 84 Plymouth Grove in Manchester – and this is only a recent acquisition – the industrial North has not been fully recognised as a literary space. It is true that the same could be argued for most other urban spaces in Britain. But in the North of England with its preconceived associations of a moral conflict[13] between industrial cityscapes and rural landscapes this omission is of particular significance: although the Priestley statue in Bradford and the Gaskell House in Manchester indicate that things are about to change, for more than a century the overall picture painted by the existing literary sites in the North has been dominated by the images of rural idylls as found in the Lake District and at Haworth.

More than in any other region of England the examination of literary places in the North shows the extent to which the collective memory of Britain is firmly hooked on a rural ideal. Although the rest of this essay will look at literary places in the North the paradigmatic example for the forces of this particular aesthetic preference is provided by Shakespeare's Birthplace. The changes that were made to the

---

as the cultural and political capital and less so as an urban or industrial conglomerate. The fact that London is seen through a different lens from other urban centres in England also becomes visible in Morton's characterisation of the city in his numerous books on the capital: *The Heart of London*, *The Spell of London*, *The Nights of London*, *H.V. Morton's London*, *Ghosts of London*, *A London Year* and *Guide to London*.

[13] See Stephan Kohl's essay in this volume.

Birthplace during the Victorian period show how deeply this particular aesthetic inclination guides representational strategies: the house in a side-street of Stratford-upon-Avon's town centre originally stood amidst a row of houses; in Victorian times these neighbouring buildings were removed one after another, and since then the house has been fully-detached, enclosed in an English flower garden:

> Thus embedded in a garden, the house becomes eminently reminiscent of a countryside cottage. The [...] townhouse is re-contextualized in the discourses of Englishness and its expectations and clichés of rural England. (Ehland 2006: 17)

Evidently, there is a general propensity towards the belief that the project of the 'personality house' fosters the creation of a hyper-reality: the effort to preserve the 'aura' of a place may lead curators and proprietors of historic houses to the point where they carefully restore and arrange a setting that emulates a historical reality that in truth serves a preconceived aesthetic concept. At this point one must ask what aesthetic sensibilities are, other than an acquired way of seeing things?

In the North, where an aesthetic outlook delineated by romantic sensibilities defines a dichotomy between the industrial and the rural aspects of the region, it becomes clear that one needs to discuss how the traces of literary lives preserved in the region integrate into the particular aesthetic concept of the landscape. In other words, one has to deal with the question how the objects of literary culture serve to structure a region as a specific cultural landscape and at the same time function as screens for the projection of class identities.

Two literary places in Northern England have been chosen to illustrate the role of the literary world in the creation of particular images for the North of England: the discussion will first look at memorial houses in the Lake District and will then compare the findings from that area with the so-called James Herriot Country in Yorkshire.

4. Safe Small World: The Wonderful Illusion of the Lake District

One cannot escape the suspicion that there is a subtle system of differentiation between 'good' landscapes that deserve special conservation and 'bad' areas not worthy of attention and protection.[14] That these distinctions somehow concur with class structures is more than suspicious and may lead one to think that class is indeed the decisive issue where landscapes are concerned.

In a conversation with a British friend I once happened to circumscribe the North of England and when I included Cumbria in my geographical musings he interrupted politely and corrected what he saw as my mistaken association of the Lake District with Northern England. He may be eccentric in his understanding of Britain's geography but his views on the relationship between the two geographical terms are not as isolated as one might expect: a glance at the maps included in *The Oxford Illustrated Literary Guide* shows that there is indeed a map of "Northern England and the Lake District". But why should there be a distinction? The Lake District is in the North of England; it is south of England's border with Scotland but north of the Midlands. Why shouldn't it feature as part of Northern England? In terms of geography its inclusion seems to make sense, at least for a foreigner; in terms of its social profile, however, the case seems to be more difficult.

Admittedly, the task of circumscribing 'Northern England proper' is as difficult as that of giving a reliable definition of England's regional identities. Its margins of differentiation, of inclusion and exclusion, change with the perspective of the beholder. With regard to the literary element in conceptions of northern identity a class-sensitive point of view offers interesting insights: if one looks at the social profiles of tourists visiting the regions of the UK Cumbria's middle-class image is confirmed: 76% of the tourists visiting the Lake District have a middle-class background, a figure which is 8% higher

---

[14] Of course, it is true that the notorious nuclear power station at Sellafield has been built on the coastline of Cumbria; however, the Lake District proper, as it were, never included the coast as an indigenous part of its landscape. Margins, or rather spaces that fail to be claimed by a specific conceptual landscape, are more readily available for industrial purposes.

than the average for the UK as a whole (68%).[15] Conversely, the number of working-class holiday makers in the region is 14% below the UK average. There are a number of factors which may contribute to these trends: first of all, according to the statistical data holidays in the Lake District require a private vehicle; despite the fact that the region is marketed as the ideal territory for environmentally friendly hill-walking, 87% of visitors in the region prefer to travel by car to their environmentally friendly exercise, while only 7% use public transport. Secondly, landscape preservation[16] in the region imposes a number of limitations on the range of attractions and activities that can be offered to the holiday makers. If in earlier years the range of tourist activities was still sufficient to satisfy the recreational needs of a broader social stratification of tourists, today the statistical figures paint a different picture: British holiday destinations face strong competition from around the globe since affordable package holidays have become available in more sunny climes and in areas where there are fewer restrictions in terms of preservation. But while once popular seaside resorts in England experience a decline the Lake District is still going strong. Its unique profile as a holiday destination is reflected by the fact that 80% of the trips in the region take place to the countryside and small towns. Given that the national average for England is only 36% (30% visiting large cities, 33% holidaying at the seaside) the question may be asked to what extent this sort of inland-tourism reflects the social stratification of tourists in the region.

The statistics show that Lakeland tourism is characterised by a sort of social segregation: working-class holidaymakers avoid the Lake District whereas middle-class tourists continue to come in great numbers. Evidently, the bone of contention is not mass tourism as such but rather the question of who constitutes the mass. Holiday destinations are chosen with class distinctions in mind: the educated middle-class tourist is apt to avoid places of *mass* tourism, that is to say places where the mass goes on holiday; the Lake District offers a counter-programme, as it were, to the "deluge of free men and women who will [...] descend on Blackpool like a riot migrating to the seaside." (Morton 1949: 141) Bourdieu has given close attention to the

---

[15] All statistical data refer to the year 2004 and are taken from *StarUK: Statistics on Tourism and Research.*

[16] In this context see Ian Whyte's essay in this volume.

aesthetic disposition that defines the cultural practices of different classes and comes to the conclusion that the emphatic postulation of the democratisation of art and culture is in fact a highly ambiguous, even hypocritical issue: the attempts of museums and galleries to make high art accessible for everybody is in fact a kind of didactic packaging for societal processes by which classes are kept apart and class identities remain distinct (see Bourdieu 1987: 360-361): the relationship mirrors that of teachers and pupils or, more provocatively, that of priests and laymen. It is clear that these differences also influence the class-specific perception of places. With regard to the aesthetic programmes it is evident that Morton's biting sarcasm is once more stigmatising, highlighting an implicit social differentiation. As a subtext to this, however, the social profile of the place is closely linked to an aesthetic concept of touristic space. John Urry observes:

> differences in social tone of resorts (the 'resort hierarchy') seem to be explicable in terms of the intersection between landownership and scenic attractiveness. Those places which ended up as working-class resorts, or what might be described as 'manufacturing resorts' linked into a particular industrial city, were those which generally had had [...] a relatively undesired scenic landscape. (Urry 2002: 23)

The implied noise, as it were, of the working-class "riot" at Blackpool[17] is an inversion of the *other* place for which Cumbria's touristic heartland stands. The irony here clearly is that the "riots" at Blackpool and the tours of the middle-class tourist in the Lake District may seem a world apart but in fact they share the same inspirational source: both are conceived by the romantic idealisation of the relationship between man and his natural habitat and both are firmly rooted in a cultural concept that distinguishes between the necessity of an urban lifestyle and the need to counter its emotional deprivations by the recreational pleasures of being out in the country or by the sea (see Urry 2002: 44-45). Despite this common origin the distinctions between these two forms of 'pleasure' are the more vehemently asserted. J.A. Walter has pointed out that the

---

[17] Interestingly enough, Blackpool is the epitome of mass tourism in Britain even in statistical terms: among the country's admission-free attractions Blackpool's Pleasure Beach was the most visited place in Britain with 6.2 million visitors in 2002 (data only available up to the year 2002).

> [...] professional opinion formers (brochure writers, teachers, Countryside Commission staff, etc.) are largely middle-class and it is within the middle class that the romantic desire for positional goods is largely based. Romantic solitude thus has influential sponsors and gets good advertising. By contrast the largely working-class enjoyment of conviviality, sociability and being part of a crowd is often looked down upon by those concerned to conserve the environment. (Walter 1982: 303)

Although the romantic ideology has been more or less the essential trigger for the invention of mass tourism and has left its trace on both touristic practice and expectations, to this day the middle-class character of the romantic gaze cannot be doubted. The romantic as a particular way of relating to the environment has predominantly been claimed, internalised and reproduced by the middle classes.

In this sense the Lake District is necessarily represented as the landscape where the real free men – these are of course those who can properly appreciate the scenery – can spend the night "an den ruhigen, klaren Gewässern von Buttermere in der so völlig anderen Welt der Lake District's Western Fells." (Botting 1990: 62) One should take note of the fact that Douglas Botting, in his hill walking guide to the British Isles, is really using the phrase "entirely different world" to describe his experience of the Lake District, where in the solitude of the landscapes he rediscovered his essential humanity: "In der Einsamkeit und Schönheit dieser Hügel- und Seenlandschaft wurde ich langsam wieder zum Menschen." (Botting 1990: 62)

In the North of England – which after all was the birthplace of two of the four Victorian foundations of writers' memorial houses in Britain – literary sites have been prone to reproduce this one-sided vision. Haworth is an ideal and at the same time a radical model for the implications of the romantic gaze, when it is directed at the literary landscapes of the North: the vista prescribed by the idea of the Brontë Country has for long been apt to ignore the fact that the Brontës lived in a place which was in very close proximity to the industrial transformation of England. The typical guidebook rhetoric, however, conceives "the Brontë country from Thornton to Haworth" as "a stretch of wild hills and rocks and yawning quarries; of harshly outlined fields, with relentless moors creeping up their black walls" (Southwart 1923: 3). This is a literary image fished from *Wuthering Heights* rather than any real place. But even today, the industrial Haworth has not really been included in the touristic map of activities. Leaflets and guidebooks suggest walks "amidst the moorland made famous by the Brontës" (Bradford District Council 2003) but even the maps which are included ignore the existence of any other part of Haworth beyond the Parsonage and the local churchyard.[18]

In the Lake District, which for various reasons has seen little direct industrialisation, the imagination finds an even easier territory for this sort of literary elusion. Landscape preservation has ensured that this 'entirely different world' remains fairly unmolested by the harsh contrast which is to be discovered at Haworth. It is fair to say that the otherworldly quality of the region is an aesthetic concept long in the making. In *The Englishman's England* Ian Ousby gives a detailed history of the development and effect of tourism in the Lake District (see Ousby 2002: 106-115).[19] The region is among the oldest destinations for the polite, that is to say educated, tourist. Whether he came or comes in search of the sublime, the picturesque or the literary associations of the region, his preconceived gaze, trained by guidebooks, travelogues and poetry, creates the landscape.[20]

Although this essay will concentrate on the concept of the writer's house one has to take note of the fact that in the Lake District these memorial houses represent only one type of literary place: there is a countless number of literary trails, markers indicating particular literary spots, and other features of literary interest in this slow-moving, crowded landscape. The complex grid of literary associations is in fact so tightly knit that the question arises whether it is possible to visit the region without soaking up at least the more obvious of the literary sites. But even if the actual sites are avoidable, the literary element in general has become so deeply enshrined in the concept of the Lake District's particular scenery that it has become inescapable. In fact, the precise relationship between landscape aesthetics and the

---

[18] The official guidebook to the Parsonage Museum, however, makes an effort to be more politically correct by pointing out some aspects of the social history of Haworth. (Brontë Society 1998: 9)

[19] In addition see Ian Whyte's essay in this volume.

[20] In this context Ousby writes: "the Lake District [...] can be characterized as predominantly the object of the romantic gaze, it is historical and it is apparently authentic." (Ousby 2002: 94)

role of the writers' houses in this context has been the subject of an ongoing discussion among scholars:

> The literary shrine is joined, and soon overshadowed, by the newer and more potent concept of the literary landscape. Seeing the landscape – we might now say almost literally 'reading' the landscape – in terms of the poems describing it became the nineteenth-century equivalent of the earlier systems that the cults of the Sublime and the Picturesque had established for teaching visitors what to look at, what to see and what to feel. The cultivated tourist convinced himself that he had experienced the distinctive atmosphere of the places he visited, or even come to know their essential character, by opening his volume of Wordsworth. (Ousby 2002: 140)

Ousby is undoubtedly right in his assumption that the idea of the landscape itself has become the more "potent" literary discourse in the Lake District. Nevertheless, the relationship between the literary landscape and the writers' houses in the region has always been a particularly close one. There is no other region in Britain outside of London and Edinburgh which features a higher density of literary sites open to visitors than the Lake District: three houses connected with William Wordsworth alone are open to the public and these are accompanied by the former farmhouse of Beatrix Potter and John Ruskin's house at Coniston.[21] The dates when these houses were established as memorial sites – Dove Cottage (1891), Ruskin's Brantwood (1934), the Wordsworth House in Cockermouth (1938), Beatrix Potter's Hill Top (1944) and Rydal Mount (1969) – show that the effort to give material substance to the imaginary forces of literature has been a permanent concern in the region.

In this context it seems important to point out that the desire to acquire and institutionalise the houses of poets and writers was preceded by the literary associations of the landscape of the Lake District. The eighteenth-century concept of picturesque landscape was easily translated into the expectations of the literary tourist with a volume of romantic verse in his hands. But as early as the 1870s William

---

[21] There is no doubt that this list could easily be extended if the regional tourist authorities or groups of literary enthusiasts chose to do so: to name just some of the properties in Cumbria still waiting to be turned into memorials, there is Greta Hall above Keswick, where Coleridge and Southey lived in succession, or Fox Howe, the Arnold family retreat, or The Knoll, the house of the Victorian novelist and abolitionist Harriet Martineau.

Knight[22] complained that "[m]any of Wordsworth's allusions to Place are obscure; and the exact localities, as well as individual objects, are difficult to identify." (Knight 1878: viii) The fact that in 1891 a group of enthusiasts acquired Wordsworth's first domicile in the Lake District, Dove Cottage, for "the eternal possession of all those who love English poetry all over the world" (Wordsworth Trust 1998: no pag.) shows that the general aura of the landscape was not enough: the imagination required and requires fixed locations.

Like the literary anecdotes cited in guidebooks, the literary houses serve to create a biographical trail through the Lake District and thus to add to the topography of the region a layer of meaning whose interpretation oscillates between an extemporal aesthetic sphere and an encapsulated version of the past. As with Morton's idea of 'old' England, the effect of the aesthetic concept is to 'de-temporalise' the immediate present and re-contextualise it in an historical and often nostalgic perspective. One can observe that the more captivating the idea of the literary landscape becomes the more does it reflect back upon the memorial houses. The evidence given below shows that it does indeed become prescriptive for the representational strategies of the proprietors of writers' houses. It follows that the memorial house needs to be placed within the prevalent aesthetic discourse; this means that its exhibits need to be appropriated and re-contextualised according to the dominant theme of the way the landscape is perceived.

It is not necessary to deal with all of the literary houses open to the public in the Lake District because the limitations of this essay dictate that the argument should concentrate at this point on the paradigmatic case rather than the comprehensive picture. In this regard, the most compelling example for the practice of re-contextualisation can be found in the recently restored and re-themed Wordsworth House in Cockermouth. The National Trust has highlighted the following "set of key themes" for the house:

---

22   William Angus Knight (1836-1916) was professor of moral philosophy at the University of St Andrews but is mainly remembered for his enthusiasm for English literature and his manifold personal contacts with writers throughout Britain. He became one of the most influential protagonists in the movement for the foundation of writers' houses such as Wordsworth's Dove Cottage in Grasmere or Coleridge's Cottage in Nether Stowey.

1. Wordsworth's life and works were shaped by his childhood in Cockermouth
2. Wordsworth House was, and remains, an integral part of the community of Cockermouth
3. The life of the Wordsworth family was very different to [*sic*] family life today
4. Wordsworth House is a fine example of a mid-18th century, north country town house. (NT 2002: 4)

In the context of the discussion in this essay the most striking of these four themes is the idea that not only Wordsworth's life was influenced by the experience of his childhood in Cockermouth but also his literary work. Admittedly, in *The Prelude* Wordsworth draws this connection himself; but looking closely one can see that he describes childhood as an integral stage in human development, involving both the maturation of the emotional and intellectual capacities of the child's mind and his exposure to and experience of his natural and man-made environment.[23] Given the complexity of Wordsworth's train of thought in this context, one must come to ask how it is possible to compress this complex period of childhood into the static environment of the memorial house?

In Cockermouth one can observe that the house in all its spatial variety – that is to say, the several available rooms and the garden – has to be turned into a set of metonymical signifiers in order to represent this process. Therefore the static setting has to be opened up to a wider range of interpretations. In fact, it is at this point that the reference to the literary work gains its function in the epistemology of the house because it allows the romantic conception of landscape to be related to its static environment. In compliance with the themes imposed upon the house and its exhibits, the National Trust has set up a number of learning, behavioural and emotional objectives that guide its efforts at Cockermouth. For example, one of the learning objectives aims to communicate how "rooted in his childhood years, Wordsworth's passion for the Cumbrian countryside lead [*sic*] to his role as a pioneer of countryside conservation and appropriate tourism" (NT 2002: 4). This objective sheds light on a paradigmatic argument that underlies the

---

[23] See Wordsworth's description of his childhood in the various versions of *The Prelude* (Wordsworth 1995).

commemorative practice. In the context of the discussion in this essay the inference of "appropriate tourism" sounds rather problematic. By the back door a differentiation has slipped in that may readily remind one of the dichotomy between good and bad landscapes, as explained earlier. Here, however, with reference to tourism the differentiation is amplified even in a moral sense. How prescriptive, or as the National Trust proprietors would put it, how suggestive these objectives are meant to be, becomes even clearer with regard to the anticipated emotional impact of the house: "Visitors will share in the young Wordsworth's enthusiasm for the natural environment of the garden and surrounding area." (NT 2002: 5)

But how can a house, a built structure, inspire "passion" and "enthusiasm" for the countryside in its visitors? In the case of the Wordsworth House the garden has to become a metonymy for the nature of the Lake District as such. This means that the garden itself has to be 'naturalised' and thus turned into a repository of the natural environment. The concepts which are communicated in the environment of the house have to be reintegrated into the broader aesthetic concepts that structure the regional landscape.

If the case of Shakespeare's Birthplace has shown that the memorial house is likely to be appropriated according to the prevalent theme of an idealised vision of the past, the example of the Wordsworth House in Cockermouth reveals the subtle strategies of a programming of a space in terms of the broader aesthetic concept of landscape perception. The impression of the front garden – set out as a formal courtyard garden – is subdued by its function as the approach to the property: visitors are not really expected to stop and look at it – it is omitted from the official leaflet to the house – but to use it as a waiting area before entering the house. In contrast the rear garden's function in the layout of the memorial house has been emphasised to allude to a garden culture that has become almost proverbial in discourses on Englishness, as the following statement illustrates: "the garden has been re-planted to reflect the needs of the Wordsworth household for a productive garden and to provide an attractive view from the 'family' rooms at the rear of the house." (NT *Wordsworth House* 2005) The reference to the productive garden is of course a rhetorical smoke-screen that hides what tourists perceive as the prevalent decorative meaning of the setting behind the assumed utility of the place.[24] The decorative aspect, however, is the Trojan horse whose sole function is to link the house with the "surrounding area". It is the strategy by which the static settings of the memorial house become contextualised in the broad vision of the romantic conception of the Lake District. This becomes most obvious when one looks at the pictures of the back of the Wordsworth House below.

Figure 1: Back door, Wordsworth House, Cockermouth © C.E.

The small patch of green which is visible at the threshold of the door is a picturesque detail, a charming piece of décor. The photograph shows the contrast between the neatly paved entrance area at the back door and the small, insignificant plant growing out of the wall. Just like the recreated period-toys scattered decoratively about the house in order to sustain the childhood theme of the setting, the little weed is a functional element in the creation of the authentic atmosphere for the

---

[24] One might argue, of course, that the Wordsworth family might already have laid out the gardens according to this dual purpose; but the leaflet's argument is clearly aimed at the modern visitor: nor does one know either the exact historical function of the rooms inside the house or the layout of the original garden. The setting as it has been *re*-created is to a large extent imaginary and aimed at emotional impact.

house in which William Wordsworth spent his early years. It is the only natural touch amongst the cleanliness and orderliness of the National Trust's typical and much-appreciated perfectionism. And despite the obvious effort to create an 'authentic' environment, the arrangement creates essentially the same kind of hyper-reality as was noted before in the context of Shakespeare's Birthplace. One might be inclined therefore to dismiss it as sentimental, unreal and artificial. Nevertheless, the production of the hyper-reality that has been noted at Cockermouth exemplifies the crucial ideological implementation of the idea of the writer's house in an aesthetically preconceived environment like the Lake District. Its assumed authenticity is a material resonance of the effort to integrate literary discourses into a preconceived perceptive model of a landscape.

Outside Dove Cottage in Grasmere there is a notice board which quotes the first six lines of Wordsworth's poem "Daffodils" and issues an invitation to visit the cottage. One paragraph of the text which promises the visitor the main highlight of his visit to the building deserves special attention: "To see how one of the world's greatest writers and his family lived, visit Dove Cottage, including the beautiful natural garden where Wordsworth composed the daffodils poem (and many other great works) and the room upstairs where it was first written down."

One can trace a paradigmatic line of associations by means of which the house is first turned into a biographical space which then becomes a creative space which finally is projected back on to an assumed natural habitat. The reference to the "natural garden" emphasises particular affinities of the romantic creative mind and functions once more as a metonymical marker for the particular sensibilities of landscape perception which have been developed for interpreting the Lake District. But at Grasmere the rhetoric of the notice board is only the foreplay to a complex system of stages and projection screens for the commemoration of Wordsworth and his work. The Wordsworth Trust, proprietor not only of Dove Cottage but also of the Wordsworth Museum and the Jerwood Centre, makes an effort to offer more than just a guided tour through the more or less atmospheric cottage of the poet. The existence of the on-site research facilities which grant access to the extensive collections of the Wordsworth Trust and a lively exhibitions programme as well as educational activities show that at Grasmere the writer's house is but a tessera in a large mosaic of all sorts of aspects and incarnations of literary culture. In the end, however, when broken down to their broadest and most general common denominator all the activities which take place in and around the writer's house are designed to confirm a preconceived vision of this region of Northern England. Of course, this is an oversimplification but it helps to make one point clear: walks with children into the landscape which inspired Wordsworth and exhibitions of paintings of the Lake District and of the lives of writers and artists in the region sustain the romantic image of the place because they appear under the implied label 'Wordsworth' and must therefore refer to the regional topography as a concept, as a *scape*. The picture below shows a worksheet designed for the educational programme offered to schoolchildren at the Wordsworth Trust (see figure 2).

The task of the pupils is to link the landscape features with the words and phrases from Wordsworth's poem "Influence of Natural Objects in Calling Forth and Strengthening the Imagination in Boyhood and Early Youth" (1809). The question here is not whether this didactic concept is good or bad – bringing children into contact with nature must be seen as an important task of modern education – but the point is that in the context of the Wordsworth Trust – which calls itself "a living memorial to the life and poetry of William Wordsworth" – activities like this implicitly subscribe to and promote a specific view of landscape. An important factor here is that the visitor is told and taught how to see the surrounding environment. However, one should not overestimate the prescriptive powers of the site managers. Even with the help of guided walks, audio tours, leaflets, and information boards no literary site is able to mastermind and programme the complexities of the perception processes that take effect in the place being visited. In the end every visitor will see and experience the place in the light of his own system of signification.[25] The product of the literary site is the experience itself, whatever it might in

---

[25] In this context Urry refers to the research undertaken by Sharon MacDonald: "Indeed sites are not uniformly read and passively accepted by visitors. MacDonald shows in the case of an exhibition at the Science Museum that visitors frame and interpret the visit in ways not expected or planned by its designers. They connect exhibits that were not meant to be linked, they read the exhibits as prescriptive when they are not intended to be, and they mostly do not describe the exhibition in ways that the designers had intended." (Urry 2002: 101)

the end represent for the individual tourist. What remains to be analysed, however, even if the outcome and effect of visits to literary sites cannot be standardised, is the implicit or explicit intention of the exhibition designers and the associations conjured up by their displays. In

Figure 2: Worksheet © Wordsworth Trust

this respect the most significant strategy of the writer's house can be identified in the effort to relate the static environment of the literary site to the practice of a particular touristic gaze.

Morton's travelogues perceive the North of England as being on an imagined borderline between two different Englands. It is clear that an institution like a writer's house, which represents the spatial extension of the bio-literary discourses on a writer, is barred from such a contrastive perspective. Even at Haworth, where the disparity between the image of the wild moorlands and the traces of industrialism almost imposes itself on the beholder, the memorial house is apt to ignore possible contrasts and single-mindedly pursues a preconceived aesthetic stance. The case of Haworth exemplifies the fact that the spatial integration of a literary site is deceptive: although the place seems to be presented as a part of its surroundings it is actually only integrated into a particular concept of landscape perception. The cultural practices which are discernible in the bio-literary space of a memorial house are therefore governed by the processes of selection and by the emphases on specific elements in this conceptual landscape. The eighteenth century had discovered the Lake District as a place that could be perceived as not being part of the real world. Whether at Rydal Mount, Cockermouth or Grasmere the literary memorial houses assert the set of romantic landscape values which are commonly associated with the Lake District. If the limited space of this essay allowed discussion of the other writer's houses in the region, similar strategies of contextualisation would become visible.

This leaves the question of the relationship between the literary site and class identity in the North of England: clearly, class-consciousness, landscape preservation and literary associations relate to each other. But wouldn't it be too easy to identify the sort of 'otherworldliness' represented in and by literary sites as a mere fig-leaf to conceal social inequalities? (see Urry 2002: 99) Does the supply of society with the right quantity of nostalgia serve as opium of the people in the Marxist sense of the phrase?

In the wake of the economic opportunities granted by mass tourism one can notice an egalitarian tone in the self-positioning of the literary sites in the North of England. In their attempt to broaden the societal contexts of the cultural institution of the writer's house heritage organisations have particularly drawn on the connection between the literary site and the preservation movement in Britain. The fundraising rhetoric makes use of the specifically close association of the literary sites with the scenery of the Lake District. For example, the Wordsworth Trust woos potential donors by pointing out that "[a] gift in your will would enable us to continue to conserve and protect the unspoilt appearance of the landscape that Wordsworth loved [...]." (WT legacy leaflet) The same point is made by the National Trust which states in a pamphlet for the Wordsworth House in Cockermouth: "The National Trust looks after around a quarter of Wordsworth's beloved Lake District. Why not become a member and support this important work." (NT leaflet)

These excerpts serve to show how close is the bond between landscape protection and the literary site. It is no coincidence that William Wordsworth, John Ruskin and Beatrix Potter are presented and remembered in the Lake District as important environmentalists. In the context of the National Trust and its historic mission to save England's 'historic sites and natural scenery' for future generations this link has been programmatic from the very beginning. One might comment extensively and critically on the Trust's initial statement "to act as a Corporation for the holding of lands of natural beauty and sites and houses of historic interest to be preserved intact for the nation's use and enjoyment" (Waterson 1994: 14). What, one might rightly ask, defines 'beauty' and whose historic interest is to be saved?[26] A certain amount of healthy distrust seems appropriate. However, in recent decades the Trust has shown that its interpretation of 'beauty' and 'historic interest' has become more far-reaching and democratic – political correctness is evidently an issue diffusing through every aspect of societal activities. To view the National Trust as "a gigantic system of outdoor relief for the old upper classes" (see Urry 2002: 100) is therefore certainly unfair when one takes into consideration how widespread the support for and the activities of the Trust are today. Nonetheless, the bond between literary sites and the preservation movement represents a noteworthy alliance because it

---

[26] Philip Lowe writes about the National Trust's preferences in terms of land acquisitions: "Some landscapes and regions, though, are much more strongly represented than others. [...] This reflects a number of factors. One has been the Romantic predilection of the Trust's founders and its subsequent leaders for the wilder landscapes, epitomised above all in the scenery of Wordsworth's Lake District." (Lowe 1995: 95)

puts the emphasis on the relationship between the literary and a specific conception of the landscape. With the aesthetic associations reinforced, the literary site remains a fortress to protect a specific vision of England.

In this respect Lowe, Murdoch and Norton have shown in their detailed study of the work and influence of the CPRE (Council for the Protection of Rural England) that organisations for landscape preservation increasingly find their supporters among the new residents in the countryside: "The new rural residents were mostly 'counterurbanisers' who were moving out of towns and cities to the countryside to be close to 'green and pleasant' environments." Asked for their main reasons for their move into the countryside they pointed to their desire "to live within 'real' communities and to develop closer relationships with 'nature'." (Lowe, Murdoch and Norton 2001: 12) Accordingly, they readily identify themselves with the credo of the CPRE of "beautiful, tranquil and diverse countryside that everyone can value and enjoy" (see http://www.cpre.org.uk/about/vision) and have become the influential "bedrock of the CPRE support" (Lowe, Murdoch and Norton 2001: 57). It does not need lengthy explanations to understand that the expressed wish to live in a 'real' environment in close relationship to 'nature' is the commuter's version of the romantic ideology.

One can note here a compelling concurrence between the new residents' political activism in organisations like the CPRE to promote their vision of a 'preserved' countryside and the missionary zeal which fostered the foundation of literary memorial houses in England. Looking at the spirit of the educational programmes, the marketing activities and the self-imposed didactic tasks of the modern literary site one may indeed ask whether it is wrong to entertain the suspicion that writers' houses represent places created to separate the educated classes from the plebeian mass. Admittedly, they do not actively pursue this separation. The question, however, must be put forward whether the literary element *per se* defines and limits the social range of an undertaking such as the literary memorial house. One must at least come to terms with the fact that it still holds true statistically that "the proportion of the service class[27] visiting museums and heritage

---

[27] Urry has replaced the term 'middle class' by the idea of the service class: a group within society which consists mainly of the white-collar representatives

centres in any year is about three times that of manual workers." (Urry 2002: 96)

The romantic gaze has come down to modern and postmodern society basically in the form of a desire and a demand for the otherworldly qualities of a landscape. As such it is part of an ideology of perception that is – though subject to the subtle shifts in the hegemony of society[28] – an instrument of social differentiation because "nostalgic memory is quite different from total recall; it is socially organised construction." (Urry 2002: 99)

In the North of England the integration of the institutions of literary culture into the contexts of landscape preservation tends to serve the purpose of asserting a conservative aesthetic attitude. As the discussion of literary sites illustrates, the literary element becomes integrated as a statement in the particular construction of a landscape.

5. The Popular Zone of James Herriot Country: Rather than a Conclusion

Evidently, sites in a region that is perceived and marketed as "Wordsworth's Lake District" are particularly prone to be constantly adapted according to the pre-visualisations of a romantic gaze. But the case of Haworth shows that this gaze is easily transferable to any other part of the country – as long as the literary radiance of the commemorated writer is close enough to a popular image of Romanticism and the site itself remains at least peripherally rural. Especially in the wake of the preservation movement such aesthetic predilections become self-affirmative processes of signification. And although mass tourism potentially means a democratisation of the access to the 'sacred' landscapes of the literary imagination it must fail to open up the aesthetic concepts through which these landscapes are perceived. For the touristic discourse is derivative and compensatory. It stages otherness and by the experiences it trades, it paradoxically pronounces the customary and the habitual. Dean MacCannell states in this respect that "[…]

---

[28] of the working population who "enjoy superior work and market situations" but "do not own capital or land to any substantial degree". (Urry 2002: 80)
See Bourdieu's analysis of the sociological changes in the 'cultural capital establishment' (Bourdieu 1987: 355-367).

mass tourism produces in the mind of the tourists juxtapositions of elements from historically separated cultures and thereby speeds up the differentiation and modernization of middle-class consciousness." (MacCannell 1999: 27) The practice of literary tourism in places like the Lake District is based on the consumption of such juxtapositions: the historically removed and aesthetically elusive realm of the literary past constantly contrasted by the tourist with the threat of an urban and industrial modernity. In this respect tourism and the literary sites serving the touristic needs function in a similar way to Morton's travelogues: each in its particular way pronounces the dialectic relationship in which the romantic gaze inevitably stands. Ralph Pordzik states that

> travelling as a cultural commodity made the new middle classes adopt the sentiments and ideals of Romanticism, turning tourism into an effective opportunity for self-staging and reviving the childlike sense of wonder at the world inherited from the early romantics. (Pordzik 2005: 16)

In this regard tourism and the touristic site offer a territory of experience that not only organises attitudes and predilections but also affirms and reaffirms class identities.[29] The issue at stake clearly is that the reason for this omnipresence of the popularised nostalgia of the romantic gaze in the case of the literary site depends on the particular sociological demarcations of the writer's house as a cultural institution. The institution is defined by the cultural practice which it both stands for and facilitates. The writers' houses in Britain have invariably been the brainchild of the literary culture initially established by the Victorian middle classes (see Ehland 2004: 443-448). It follows that irrespective of whether the literary house is donated to a heritage organisation or acquired by a group of literary enthusiasts it is still set up to function within the ideological contexts of the culture, class and society in which it is conceived. In other words, the writer's house is an institution defined and delineated by the fact that it itself is a practice of literary culture. As a place that acquires the right to exist from its capacity to communicate a sense of 'otherworldliness' access to it

---

[29] One should not overlook the fact that "cultural productions [...] are not merely repositories of models for social life; they organise the attitudes we have towards the models and life". (MacCannell 1999: 27)

depends on being included in the 'reading' community, sharing the means of decoding the message.

When one compares the different concepts for museums and their appeal to particular types of clientele it becomes obvious that *The World of James Herriot* in Thirsk provides a markedly more inclusive and egalitarian approach to the traditional model of the literary house. The material it contains of course lends itself to an interpretation that is accessible to a wider social stratification, just as the appeal of the name James Herriot rests on the wide circulation of his novels as well as on the immensely popular BBC series *All Creatures Great and Small* (1978). Opened only in 1998 on the initiative of Hambleton District Council and funded by the same body, the museum marks a diversion from the institutional paradigm. Public money is not a rare thing in cultural institutions. The Lottery Fund and other organisations have become a major source of funding for the cultural scene. But a museum run by a public body like the Hambleton District Council is an atypical phenomenon: the only other literary museum in Britain that falls into this category is the Edinburgh Writers' Museum. Public funding does not make the idea of the literary version of the personality museum any less hagiographical but public money and public initiative may potentially provide the opportunity to change the sociological profile of the institution and its target groups.

The fact that the museum in Thirsk has acquired the original set and props of the BBC series shows that it evades the traditional approach to exhibiting a literary life. It creates a different media reality for the museum so that the typical picture-book atmosphere of the "happy towns" and "earthy farmers" (Herriot 1982: 116, 57) is pushed into the background. One might infer that the material reference to the image of James Herriot in the BBC series feeds the very expectations of the popular image of the rural North of England, and naturally popular imagination is escapist and tends to romanticise its objects. One has only to think about the trailer of the BBC production in which James Herriot's little car roams the rolling hills of Yorkshire to the accompaniment of Johnny Pearson's memorable theme music to see clearly that its popularity rests on the fact that it produces an apparently intact rural image of Northern England. The threats of industrialisation are carefully kept out of the picture. This is also the image local tourist authorities like to emphasise in their publications: "it was from this quiet corner of North Yorkshire that he [James Herriot alias

Alf Wight] drew inspiration for his tales of veterinary life." (*Herriot Country* 2006: 1)

However, in the end one must ask whether the museum itself fits into this image? It is not the popular TV image of the Yorkshire moors and dales that the museum presents to its visitors but the means of producing it in the first place. The visitor on his tour through the house is first shown the 'authentic' 1940s interior of the house and veterinary consultancy before he enters the studio set of the BBC production. The exhibition is set up so that the visitor is not only able to see the items on display but is also encouraged to interact with them and become part of the display himself (see figure 3).

The display of the historical interior is thus juxtaposed with its media image. In this way the fictitious setting of the TV studio sustains and authenticates the staged reality of the 'real' house interior. But one can observe here an unusual postmodern wink of the eye: the presence of the other media level in the museum generally questions the authenticity inherent in any of the exhibited settings. The reality of fiction, as it were, is exposed and thus the imagery it represents is also called into doubt. The productive and consumptive processes of the culture industries come into focus as the museum creates different layers of media presence for the image of James Herriot and his world. In contrast to the Lake District or Haworth where the literary site is contextualised within a vision of the romantic landscape the museum dissolves its imagery in the inauthenticity of the staged reality.

Evidently, new forms of funding and new organisational bodies have instigated changes to the socially exclusive associations of the writer's house: they communicate differently and they communicate a different set of values. To be honest, the vision of England offered by Morton and his like is – in its way – an attractive, even a seductive one. But it is an illusion, a coffee-table fantasy that belongs on the coffee-table and nowhere else. Canonisation is not so much about the choice of who is remembered at a literary site but about a way of seeing and organising the experience of the world. Landscape projections, as in the case of the deep-rooted dichotomy that structures one of the most readily available stereotypes about the North of England, are potential means for sustaining class identities. In a way one may ask whether the differences visible in Thirsk fulfil Guillory's request

Figure 3: BBC Studio set of *All Creatures Great and Small, The World of James Herriot* © C.E.

for the reformation of the practices of canon formation: "[t]he point is not to make judgment disappear but to reform the conditions of its practice" (Guillory 1994: 340).

At *The World of James Herriot* one can see that the new institutional patterns of the writer's museum, in particular the new sources of funding and the new body of proprietors, change its approach to the business of communication. To a certain extent the broadening of the media basis of the writer's house starts with the utopian dream of "socializing the means of production and consumption" (Guillory 1994: 340). The margins are narrow: it remains a museum, more precisely a personality museum, and therefore it must retain the approach of a middle-class institution. It is impressionistic and slightly didactic. But it is also playful, ironic and accessible. In contrast Wordsworth's Lake District seems an entirely different story. So, where can one locate it then? In the North of England or in a world apart?

Works Cited

Primary References

Gaskell, Elizabeth (1998): *North and South*. Oxford: Oxford UP.

Herriot, James (1979/1982): *James Herriot's Yorkshire*. London: Mermaid.

Knight, William Angus (1878): *The English Lake District as interpreted in the poems by Wordsworth*. Edinburgh: David Douglas.

Miller, Hugh (1851): *First Impressions of England and Its People*. Boston: Gould and Lincoln.

Morton, Henry Vollam (1927/1933): *In Search of England*. London: Methuen.

— (1928/1949): *The Call of England*. London: Methuen.

Priestley, John Boynton (1934/1979): *English Journey: Being a Rambling but Truthful Account of What One Man Saw and Heard and Felt and Thought During a Journey Through England During The Autumn of the Year 1933*. Harmondsworth: Penguin.

Southwart, Elizabeth (1923): *Brontë Moors & Villages: From Thornton to Haworth*. London: John Lane and Bodley Head.

Wordsworth, William (1995): *The Prelude. The Four Texts (1798, 1799, 1805, 1850)*. Harmondsworth: Penguin.

Research Literature

Aitchison, Cara, Nicola E. MacLeod and Stephen J. Shaw (2000): *Leisure and tourism landscapes: Social and cultural geographies*. London and New York: Routledge.

Bartholomew, Michael (2004): *In Search of H.V. Morton*. London: Methuen.

Botting, Douglas (1988/1990): *Großbritannien: Wege in die Wildnis*. Braunschweig: Westermann.

Bourdieu, Pierre (1979/1987): *Die feinen Unterschiede: Kritik der gesellschaftlichen Urteilskraft*. Frankfurt/Main: Suhrkamp.

Burden, Robert and Stephan Kohl (eds.) (2006): *Landscape and Englishness*. Amsterdam and New York: Rodopi.

Court, Franklin (1992): *Institutionalizing English Literature: The Culture and Politics of Literary Study, 1750-1900*. Stanford: Stanford UP.

Dimbleby, David (2005): *A Picture of Britain*. London: Tate Publishing.

Eagle, Dorothy, Hillary Carnell and Meic Stephens (eds.) (1992): *The Oxford Illustrated Literary Guide to Great Britain and Ireland*. Oxford: Oxford UP.

Ehland, Christoph (2004): "Literary Commodities: Writers' Museums and the Tourist's Imagination", in: Christoph Bode et al. (eds.): *Anglistentag 2003 München: Proceedings*. Trier: WVT, 439-450.

— (2006): "Stratford's Shakespeare Industries. A Study in Corruption?", in: Jürgen Kamm (ed.): *Medialised Britain: Essays on Media, Culture and Society*. Passau: Stutz, 11- 27.

Guillory, John (1993/1994): *Cultural Capital: The Problem of the Literary Canon Formation*. Chicago: University of Chicago Press.

Helsinger, Elizabeth (1994/2002): "Turner and the Representation of England", in: W. J. T. Mitchell (ed.): *Landscape and Power*. Chicago: Chicago UP, 103-125.

Knights, Ben (2006): "In Search of England: Travelogue and Nation Between the Wars", in: Robert Burden and Stephan Kohl (eds.): *Landscape and Englishness*. Amsterdam and New York: Rodopi, 2006. 165-184.

König, Helmut (1992): *Zivilisation und Leidenschaften: Die Masse im bürgerlichen Zeitalter*. Reinbek: Rowohlt.

Löfgren, Orvar (1999): *On Holiday: A History of Vacationing*. Berkeley: University of California Press.

Lowe, Philip (1995): "The Countryside", in: Howard Newby (ed.): *The National Trust: The Next Hundred Years*. London: National Trust, 87-103.

—, Jonathan Murdoch and Andrew Norton (eds.) (2001): *Professionals and Volunteers in the Environmental Process*. [www.ncl.ac.uk/cre/publish/Books/-CPREfinal.pdf].

MacCannell, Dean (1976/1999): *The Tourist: A New Theory of the Leisure Class*. Berkeley and Los Angeles: University of California Press.

Mitchell, W. J. T. (1994/2002): "Introduction", in: id. (ed.): *Landscape and Power*. Chicago: Chicago UP, 1-4.

Ousby, Ian (1990/2002): *The Englishman's England: Taste, Travel and the Rise of Tourism*. London: Pimlico.

Pordzik, Ralph (2005): *The Wonder of Travel: Fiction, Tourism and the Social Construction of the Nostalgic*. Heidelberg: Winter.

Sanders, Andrew (1994): *The Short Oxford History of English Literature*. Oxford: Oxford UP.

Urry, John (1990/2002): *The Tourist Gaze*. London: Sage.

Walter, J.A. (1982): "Social Limits to Tourism", *Leisure Studies* 1.3, 295-304.

Waterson, Merlin (1994): *The National Trust: The First Hundred Years*. London: National Trust.

Weber, Max (1920/1965): *Die protestantische Ethik*. München and Hamburg: Siebenstern.

Williams, Raymond (1973): *The Country and the City*. London: Chatto and Windus.

Guidebooks, Leaflets, etc.

The Brontë Society (1998): *Brontë Parsonage Museum: A Souvenir Guide*.

The City of Bradford Metropolitan District Council (2003): *Four Walks from Haworth Village* [leaflet].

Hambleton District Council (2006): *Herriot Country: Short Breaks & Visitor Guide 2006* [brochure].

Hambleton District Council (no date): *Herriot: Museum – Attraction – Historic Site* [guide book].

The National Trust (2005): *Wordsworth House* [house guide].

The National Trust (2002): *Wordsworth House, Cockermouth: Interpretation Plan*.

The National Trust (no date): *Wordsworth House: Bringing the Past to Life* [leaflet].

The Wordsworth Trust (1996/1998): *Dove Cottage*. Andover: Pitkin Guides, 1998 (1996).

The Wordsworth Trust (no date): *Leaving a Legacy* [leaflet].

Websites

StarUK: Statistics on Tourism and Research. Star UK (no date). 20 January 2007 [http://www.staruk.org.uk].

Campaign to Protect Rural England. CPRE website (no date). 18 January 2007 [http://www.cpre.org.uk/about/vision].

APPENDIX

Northern England in Facts and Figures

Christoph Singer

There are three kinds of lies: lies, damned lies and statistics.
attributed to Benjamin Disraeli

1. Introduction

"Language is a sinister simplification of reality" (Eagleton 2006: 9) and so are statistics. Or, to put it differently, one might feel inclined to ask whether empirical sciences can really offer a more accurate image of reality than any other way of representation?

Looking at the recent statistics relating to Great Britain presented here, one will realise how the majority of the tables confirm well-established stereotypes about the North of England. The picture emerges of a region which, compared with the rest of England, is (still) characterised by higher unemployment and lower wages, by a higher crime rate and a lower economic activity rate (also GVA Gross Value Added).

But before accepting as reliable the image that results from this empirical typecasting, it is important to challenge the general assumption that numbers provide a more trustworthy account of social and cultural reality than other means of representation. In fact looking at the potential manipulability of empirical accounts of the world, Winston Churchill's saying that "the only statistics you can trust are those you falsified yourself" still seems to hold true. It is therefore only at first sight that empirical and artistic methods of signification, such as visible in the fine arts or literature, form a dichotomy. When their findings are compared they show striking similarities: whatever strategy of representation is used, whatever aspect of reality is covered, however intense their comments, and by whatever method they finally choose to present their findings, both are inevitably limited to the representation of only one particular part of reality. It does not matter how extensively the information is collected, presented and examined. At no moment does there exist the possibility of illuminating the picture as a whole. Even if one were able to collect all the available information for empirical or e.g. narrative signification, ranging from data on society to data on the individual, one will always be limited to the presentation of only one part of reality, for the perfect mimesis, that is to say the possibility of depicting the totality of reality, requires a complete indication of how the information given is interrelated. For example a statistical account of the comparatively high amount of money spent on the public lottery in Northern England may instantaneously feed deep-rooted prejudices but for a proper understanding of this figure one would have to take into account people's wages, their social and economic background, the history and the roots of the local economy and so on. And even if it were possible to do this, would this kind of presentation not absolutely contradict the goal of empirical studies which is to simplify the perception of reality and to make it more accessible?

But if this is the case, then empirical studies cannot be the ever-objective collection of information which they are widely regarded to be. Indeed, the assumed binary opposition between the objectivity of empirical studies and the subjectivity of art is highly questionable: is a Dickensian presentation of a specific local and temporal social reality really less reliable than a presentation of the same reality with the help of charts and digits?

Both systems put a specific frame on reality, and both infuse this frame with meaning by differentiating it from the reality outside the chosen perspective. Whether with the help of words or numbers, the effect is the same: to change the points of reference for the differentiation is constantly to change the meaning of what is presented.

This signification of the information presented leads to another noteworthy similarity between the interpretative openness of empirical and artistic forms of representation. Both, intentionally or not, may be swallowed up in the creation and the confirmation of stereotypes. Every attempt at representing social reality in 'realistic' terms is bound to fail once the differentiation previously mentioned has taken place, for from this moment on the information provided is biased. In any case, one must realise that statistics have a tendency to level reality as they must accumulate and relate their data to an average figure; but does an average figure necessarily represent the experience of life in a region? Is there such a thing as the average northerner? Can we deduce identity by looking at tables full of digits? Of course, as has been said by others before, if one puts one's feet in an ice-bucket and one's head in the oven one's *average* body temperature may well be 37°C but it may be asked whether this *average* still makes sense. That is why statistics and their interpretation are not necessarily more trustworthy and reliable than other ways of communication.

If the reliability of assumptions based on statistical data can be questioned, how can one deal with those stereotypes which are apparently confirmed by statistical accounts? One has to reject stereotypes that are based on mere assumptions, "[b]ut some derogatory stereotypes are perfectly justified" because, for example, "[r]efusing to acknowledge that the Scots have not been famed for their cuisine is to suppress the history of poverty which underlies this fact" (Eagleton 2006: 9). To refuse to acknowledge that the social standards of Northern England are among the lowest in England is to ignore the economic and social history they are based upon. Thus the following selection of statistics relating to the North of England is already an interpretation in itself and hence has to be approached like one: not as an empirical add-on, but as a second-level reading of the social reality of the North of England; not as a mere confirmation of the stereotypical deficits of the region, but as an implicit reminder of the historical developments which have moulded the image as well as the reality of life in Northern England.

The following tables, figures and percentages and their statistical 'facts' may paint a picture of the situation in the North of England that confirms the prejudice against a region dominated by working-class problems: despite Britain's booming economy the northern regions in many respects still represent what the opposition tends to call a 'deprived region'. But this is only the statistically levelled image of the northern regions of the UK. An awareness of the possible pitfalls of statistical reckoning may prevent one from confusing this picture with the reality of life in the North.

2. Selected Facts in Focus

Population – Ethnicity – Housing – Homelessness. As every set of statistics must take account of population it must be noted that the documented increases/decreases of population in the individual regions of the UK, when considered against their national comparators, may illustrate not so much the specific attractiveness of a region as its economic ability to sustain its population. In this context the statistics show that while the UK as a whole experienced an increase in its population by 4.2% during the period between 1991 and 2004, the North East (-1.6%) and the North West (-0.2%) stand out as the only regions in the UK which saw a decrease of population (see Table 1b). Only as the regional economy picks up does this trend become stoppable or even reversible; the more promising data for the years between 2001 and 2004 show that the population decline in the North East and the North West has been reversed and that the population in these two regions is now slowly increasing (see Table 1a). Interestingly, not only has the population grown in the past few years but household numbers have also steadily increased all over Britain since 1981 (see Table 2). Nonetheless, the comparatively slower economic development in the North is documented by the fact that over a period of ten years between 1994 and 2004 the North East showed the lowest rate of growth in its housing stock with a marginal increase of only 3.7%, whereas over the same period the South West experienced a rise of more than 10% (see Table 3).

Although figures relating to the mere increase and decrease of population are as neutral as statistical data can get, time and again they also reveal that there is indeed a deep socio-economic gulf between life in England's prosperous and middle-class South and the deprived and working-class North. A good example of such data in the context of population figures is the rate of conceptions and teenage pregnancies: the North East had the highest rate of conceptions by women aged under 18 (52.1 per 1,000 population in 2003). The South East had the lowest rate of conceptions by under 18 year-olds (33.1 in 2003) (see Table 18). It is hardly possible to read these figures without interpreting them in a somewhat stigmatising way. If these figures reveal a gulf between England's South and North, another statistic exposes a rare similarity between these areas: in terms of the ethnic configuration of the population there is a striking concurrence between northern and southern regions which are otherwise economically so far apart: the North East and the North West, just like the South East and the South West, have an ethnically more homogeneous population than the national average of 91.3%.[1] This, however, is a good example of how difficult it is to draw conclusions from statistical data: if in the South the homogeneity of population might be due to the relative lack of urban centres, in the North this homogeneity is observed despite the great number of large cities in most of the northern regions (see Table 1c).

Ethnicity, as Amir Saeed shows in his study of minority groups in Sunderland, is part of the experience of one's immediate living environment. Another is housing: if the deficit in the size of the housing stock already points to a different social stratification in the North, a glance at the types of dwellings further adds to this picture: in 2002/03 the North East had the highest proportion of terraced houses (36%) and the lowest proportion of detached housing units for any region outside London. The North West and Yorkshire and the Humber also had figures above 30% for terraced houses (see Table 4). In recent years, however, (between 2001/02 and 2002/03) the North East showed a considerable increase of 11% in the percentage of semi-detached houses, with a corresponding reduction in the proportion of terraced houses.

Taking into consideration the property boom in the last few years and the effort of an ever higher percentage of British society to get their foot on the "property ladder", one can understand why across the UK only about one quarter of all households had been at their current address for 20 years or more in 2002/03. In comparison, in the North East residential stability has been markedly more pronounced with a proportion as high as 31%. Correspondingly, at the other end of the table, the number of households that had been living at their current address for less than 5 years was 5% below the national average. It must remain an open question whether these remarkable "staying powers" in the North are generally connected with the population's deeper local roots and are thus evidence for a strong local identity (see Table 5).

---

[1] For the problematic implications of this phenomenon see Amir Saeed's essay in this volume.

The situation might change when the property market in the North catches up, as the more recent figures indicate: between 2003 and 2004 the northern regions (North East, North West and Yorkshire and the Humber) each experienced increases in property value between 17% and 18% compared with only 6.1% in London or 9.0% in the South East. This disparity, of course, has to do with the higher level of property prices in the areas in and around London. But it also adds a further piece of evidence for the economic catching-up process that is currently taking place in the North of England (see Table 6a and 6b).

The downside of Britain's economic prosperity during the last decade becomes visible in the statistical account of homelessness: the only region in the country where the total number of statistically recognised homeless households was reduced between 2002 and 2003 and then again between 2003 and 2004 was the South West where the figure went down by 12% to a total of 11,230 households. In contrast the North West had the largest growth of homelessness by 3,010 households. This represents a rise of 20% from 2003 to 2004, and gave the North West the second highest number of homeless households in England after London (18,030 and 30,080 respectively) (see Table 7).

Social Profile – Education – Workforce. Looking in detail at the social profile of the northern regions, more pronounced disadvantages become visible in such areas as education, qualification, gender-specific employment rates, etc.

In comparison to London and the South East, which had the highest proportion of people engaged in higher managerial and professional occupations with 14.2% each, the North East showed the lowest proportion at 7.1% for this group of employees (see Table 9). The same picture is shown by the data for the general qualifications of the population of working age: in 2005, as expected, London as an urban society had the highest proportion of any population of working age with a qualification at degree level or equivalent (26.1%). The UK average was 17.6%. The North East had the lowest proportion at 12.4% (see Table 9).

In general, the employment rate for the population of working age was the highest in the South West with 79% in 2005; that is 4.5%

above the UK average. Northern Ireland, London and the North East had the lowest employment rates with 68, 69 and 70% respectively.

Between 2001 and 2005, the size of the labour force increased in the UK, rising by 516,000 to 27.1 million people (see Tables 8a and 8b). While this increase can sufficiently be explained by the demand for workers in a prospering economy, a gender-specific analysis reveals more long-term developments: in every region of the UK there were more male persons employed than female, ranging from a disparity of 11% in the North East to 25% in London. Over the last five years male employment in the whole of the UK peaked in 2001 with a rate of 79% of the male population of working age in jobs, whereas for females the highest overall employment rate was 70% in 2005. The largest regional increase in female employment between 2001 and 2002 was in the North East, rising by 2.5% to 66%. The North West was the only region where the number of self-employed female persons had continued to grow in the last three years (see Tables 8c and 8d).

If these increases signal a general modernisation of the attitudes in the North towards female employment the more traditional, blue-collar image of the North of England is sustained by data that show the number of working days lost to labour disputes: in England the regions with the highest rate were Yorkshire and the Humber and the North East. Within the UK, however, Scotland proved most inclined to participate in industrial action and had by far the highest rate of lost working days: 160 (in contrast, the highest number of days lost in any English region was a tame 37 days) (see Table 11). Whether the relative tendency to strike also influences the low average income level in the northern regions can only be conjectured; it is, however, a statistical fact that, while the average gross weekly household income in the UK was £554 during the period 2001 to 2004, households in the North East had the lowest average income of £458 per week, just over three-fifths of the figure for London, £740. With regard to the figure for London it may be added here that the total household expenditure in the capital was almost 20% above the UK average of £406 per week for the period 2001 to 2004, whereas the figure for the North East was the lowest of all regions at £336 per week (see Table 12).

Further evidence of the lower general income level in the north is given by Table 14: both before and after taking account of the different levels of expenditure for housing the North East had the lowest percentages of individuals with an annual net income ranked in the top 20%. As is to be expected, in the UK London had the highest percentage of individuals with an income liable to tax assessment of £20,000 or over (46.6%). In the three northern regions, the number of income tax payers who fall into this group ranges from 30.4% in the North West to 31.8% in the North East, somewhat less than the national figure of 36%. In fact, the differences here seem to bespeak a general income gap between rural and urban areas in the UK. An interesting observation is that at the bottom of the income ladder the regional differences are far smaller than at the top end (see Table 13). Poverty, obviously, is a phenomenon which is far less dependent on the region where one lives: provocatively, one may even come to the conclusion that for being poor it does not matter where you live in Britain whereas for being rich the region seems to be an all-important matter.

Alcohol and Drug Consumption – Criminal Offences. Although statistics show that "binge drinking" is not an exclusively British phenomenon[2] the problem has predominantly been linked with Britain[3] and here particularly with the industrial cities of the North (see Table 21). In fact, a comparison with London shows that the problem is more pronounced in the urban spaces of the UK than in the rural areas. Nonetheless, with the exception of London there is a clear North-South divide. Like the consumption of alcohol the use of illegal drugs has generally increased in the UK: ecstasy is used by approximately 5% of 16- to 29-year-olds and between 2002/03 and 2003/04 the proportions of young drug-users have increased in many areas but particularly in the North East, Yorkshire and the Humber and the West Midlands (see Table 22).

Schott's Almanac 2007 lists the "Worst UK Areas for Crime": whether it is murder, rape, burglary, gun crime or assault the industrial cities of the North and the Midlands rank regularly among the top five. In fact, the official government statistics show that people's experiences of criminal offences were higher in the North West than in any other region of the country, with almost 3,500 crimes per 10,000 households in 2004/05. The lowest rate was in the North East with

---

[2] See *Schott's Almanac 2007*, 109.

[3] E.g. see article "Neue englische Krankheit heißt ‚binge drinking'" (*Ärzte Zeitung*, 24.09.2004).

2,560 crimes per 10,000 households. More promising data show that Yorkshire and the Humber had the largest drop in household offences from 4,300 (per 10,000 households) in 2003/04 to 3,100 in 2004/05, a reduction of more than 25% (see Table 20).

3. Statistics[4]

Population
Resident Population
Table 1a

				Population (thousands)
All people	1981	1991	2001	2004
United Kingdom	56,357.5	57,438.7	59,113.5	59,834.9
England	46,820.8	47,875.0	49,449.7	50,093.8
North East	2,636.2	2,587.0	2,540.1	2,545.1
North West	6,940.3	6,843.0	6,773.0	6,827.2
Yorkshire/Humber	4,918.5	4,936.1	4,976.6	5,038.8
East Midlands	3,852.7	4,011.4	4,189.6	4,279.7
West Midlands	5,186.6	5,229.7	5,280.7	5,334.0
London	6,805.0	6,829.3	7,322.4	7,429.2
South East	7,243.1	7,629.2	8,023.4	8,110.2
South West	4,383.4	4,688.2	4,943.4	5,038.2

Table 1b

		Total population growth in percentages	
	1981- 1991	1991- 2001	1991- 2004
United Kingdom	1.9	2.8	4.2
England	2.3	3.2	4.6
North East	-1.9	-1.8	-1.6
North West	-1.4	-1.0	-0.2
Yorkshire/Humber	0.4	0.7	2.1
East Midlands	4.1	4.3	6.7
West Midlands	0.8	1.0	2.0
London	0.4	7.0	8.8
South East	5.3	5.1	6.3
South West	7.0	5.3	7.5

---

[4] In order to allow comparisons to be made, figures for the East Midlands, the West Midlands, London, the South West and the South East are quoted in the following tables alongside the data for the northern regions. (Note: not all regions are included in all tables.)

Table 1c

	Eng-land and Wales	North East	North West	York-shire and the Humber	London	South East	South West
					Resident population: by ethnic group, 2001		
						Percentages and thousands	
All People	52,042	2,515	6,730	4,965	7,172	8,001	4,928
White	91.3	97.6	94.4	93.5	71.2	95.1	97.7
Non-White	8.7	2.4	5.6	6.5	28.8	4.9	2.3

Housing
Household numbers
Table 2

	1981	1991	2001	2002	2003
				Household numbers	
					Millions
Great Britain	20.18	22.39	24.17	24.36	--
North East	0.98	1.05	1.08	1.09	1.09
North West	2.55	2.72	2.83	2.85	2.87
Yorkshire/Humber	1.83	1.99	2.09	2.10	2.12
East Midlands	1.41	1.60	1.74	1.76	1.78
West Midlands	1.86	2.04	2.16	2.17	2.19
London	2.64	2.84	3.18	3.21	3.24
South East	2.64	3.03	3.35	3.37	3.40
South West	1.64	1.90	2.10	2.12	2.14

Housing stock
Table 3

	Thousands			Housing stock Percentage increase
	1994	1999	2004	1994-2004
UK	24,135	25,097	25,953	7.5
England	20,139	20,927	21,613	7.3
North East	1,086	1,108	1,126	3.7
North West	2,838	2,920	2,989	5.3
Yorkshire/Humber	2,060	2,132	2,190	6.3
East Midlands	1,682	1,764	1,843	9.6
West Midlands	2,124	2,197	2,259	6.4
London	2,972	3,059	3,146	5.9
South East	3,188	3,338	3,466	8.7
South West	2,029	2,139	2,236	10.2

Type of dwelling
Table 4

	Households: by type of dwelling, 2002/2003				
					Percentages
	Detached house	Semi-detached house	Terraced house	Purpose-built flat or maisonette	Other
UK	22	31	27	16	4
England	22	34	28	12	4
North East	13	40	36	9	2
North West	19	40	32	7	2
Yorkshire/Humber	20	39	32	7	2
East Midlands	30	39	23	6	2
West Midlands	22	43	22	10	2
London	5	21	31	30	13
South East	30	29	26	11	4
South West	28	29	28	10	5

Length of time at current address
Table 5

	Less than 12 months	12 months, less than 5 years	5 years, less than 10 years	10 years, less than 20 years	20 years or more
					Households: by length of time at current address, 2002/03 Percentages
UK	11	25	17	21	26
England	11	26	16	21	26
North East	10	21	15	23	31
North West	9	25	16	21	29
Yorkshire/ Humber	11	26	16	22	25
East Midlands	10	27	18	21	23
West Midlands	9	23	16	21	30
London	13	28	16	20	23
South East	10	27	17	22	24
South West	11	27	18	21	23

Average dwelling prices
Table 6a

	Detached houses	Semi-detached houses	Terraced houses	Flats/ maisonettes
			Average dwelling prices, 2004 Average sale price (£ thousands)	
England	287	171	143	172
North East	215	121	89	104
North West	248	138	87	129
Yorkshire/ Humber	230	128	95	127
East Midlands	223	130	109	115
West Midlands	258	144	116	121
London	561	318	279	241
South East	371	215	179	152
South West	294	183	160	145

Table 6b

Average dwelling prices, 2004
£ thousands and percentages

	Average price (£ thousands) 2003	Average price (£ thousands) 2004	All dwellings Percentage increase 2003- 2004
England	167	186	11.2
North East	103	122	17.9
North West	113	133	17.5
Yorkshire/ Humber	114	134	17.0
East Midlands	134	152	13.4
West Midlands	140	157	12.5
London	259	275	6.1
South East	209	228	9.0
South West	176	199	13.0

Homelessness
Table 7

Households accepted as homeless: by reason, 2003/ 2004
Percentages and numbers

	No longer willing or able to remain with parents, relatives or friends	Breakdown of relationship with partner	Reasons for homelessness Rent arrears or other reason for loss of rented or tied accommo- dation	Total (=100%) (numbers)
England	37	20	20	135,430
North East	35	29	17	8,350
North West	27	26	18	18,030
Yorkshire/Humber	30	24	16	16,190
East Midlands	33	26	20	9,590
West Midlands	36	23	19	15,600
London	51	10	18	30,080
South East	41	17	26	15,150
South West	33	19	27	11,230

Socio-economic Classification
Employment
Table 8a

Employment percentages

All people	2001	2002	2003	2004	2005
UK	74.3	74.1	74.4	74.5	74.4
England	75.1	74.8	74.8	74.9	74.8
North East	68.1	68.2	67.8	68.9	69.7
North West	72.7	71.7	73.3	73.1	72.9
Yorkshire/Humber	73.0	72.5	73.7	74.3	73.8
East Midlands	75.4	76.2	75.7	76.7	76.0
West Midlands	73.9	73.9	73.8	73.7	74.6
London	70.9	70.6	69.8	70.2	69.3
South East	80.1	79.8	79.2	78.2	78.6
South West	78.6	78.7	78.2	78.3	78.9

Labour Force Total Population
Table 8b

					Labour force thousands
All people	2001	2002	2003	2004	2005
UK	26,590	26,671	26,891	27,016	27,106
England	22,452	22,518	22,595	22,739	22,823
North East	1,038	1,040	1,034	1,051	1,063
North West	2,948	2,919	2,993	2,992	2,987
Yorkshire/Humber	2,187	2,185	2,232	2,256	2,246
East Midlands	1,912	1,951	1,945	1,977	1,965
West Midlands	2.342	2,356	2,353	2,354	2,383
London	3,288	3,323	3,304	3,347	3,334
South East	3,876	3,876	3,869	3,848	3,892
South West	2,278	2,293	2,291	2,308	2,341

Labour Force Male Population
Table 8c

					Labour force thousands
Males	2001	2002	2003	2004	2005
UK	14,524	14,502	14,635	14,700	14,702
England	12,285	12,267	12,238	12,400	12,418
North East	565	547	560	554	560
North West	1,584	1,558	1,617	1,611	1,601
Yorkshire/Humber	1,182	1,196	1,218	1,232	1,222
East Midlands	1,065	1,069	1,069	1,073	1,068
West Midlands	1,298	1,307	1,293	1,287	1,318
London	1,800	1,814	1,836	1,879	1,875
South East	2,133	2,121	2,091	2,104	2,111
South West	1,239	1,234	1,234	1,248	1,260

Labour Force Female Population
Table 8d

	2001	2002	2003	2004	Labour force thousands 2005
Females					
UK	12,605	12,170	12,256	12,315	12,405
England	10,167	10,250	10,267	10,339	10,405
North East	473	493	474	497	504
North West	1,363	1,361	1,376	1,381	1,386
Yorkshire/ Humber	1,004	989	1,014	1,024	1,024
East Midlands	856	881	876	905	898
West Midlands	1,044	1,049	1,060	1,067	1,065
London	1,487	1,509	1,468	1,467	1,477
South East	1,743	1,755	1,777	1,744	1,782
South West	1,039	1,059	1,057	1,060	1,081

Education and Qualifications
Table 9

Population of working age: by highest qualification, spring 2005

	Degree or equivalent	Higher education qualification	Other qualification	Percentages No qualification
UK	17.6	8.4	12.5	14.1
North East	12.4	8.2	13.0	15.2
North West	14.8	8.9	10.5	15.5
Yorkshire/Humber	14.5	7.2	14.1	15.3
East Midlands	14.9	8.1	13.3	14.8
West Midlands	14.8	8.2	11.9	16.6
London	26.1	5.9	18.5	14.2
South East	20.5	8.7	11.8	10.0
South West	16.6	9.6	12.2	10.5

Graduate destinations
Table 10

Destination of full-time first degree graduates, 2004
Employment in percentages and thousands

Area of Study	UK employment only	Combination of employ-ment and study	Further study only	Believed unemployed	Total of known destina-tions (thousands)
UK	60.3	8.7	16.1	6.5	187.9
England	60.8	8.7	15.6	6.6	153.0
North East	56.7	9.5	19.3	6.0	10.0
North West	65.3	8.4	13.6	5.9	21.4
Yorkshire/ Humber	61.7	7.8	15.7	5.7	19.0
East Midlands	63.1	7.8	14.2	6.6	16.7
West Midlands	60.5	10.1	14.5	6.8	14.0
London	59.7	8.9	15.4	7.8	25.1
South East	60.0	8.9	15.7	6.9	22.0
South West	60.6	9.0	14.3	6.6	15.2

Labour Market Disputes
Table 11

Working days lost due to labour disputes
Days lost per 1000 employees

	2000	2001	2002	2003	2004
UK	20	20	51	19	34
North East	6	12	119	2	33
North West	20	32	76	10	19
Yorkshire/Humber	4	24	44	8	37
East Midlands	5	8	50	6	20
West Midlands	20	33	41	8	23
London	7	24	60	51	18
South East	4	4	36	6	16
South West	1	8	32	7	13
Scotland	136	29	54	39	160

Household Income
Table 12

	Household income: by source, 2001/02- 2003/04				
	Percentage of average gross weekly household income				Percentages and £ Average gross household income in £ per week (=100%)
	Wages and salaries	Self-employment	Annuities, pensions, investments	Social security benefits	
UK	68	8	10	12	554
England	68	9	11	12	568
North East	68	4	8	18	458
North West	67	7	10	15	489
Yorkshire/Humber	66	6	11	15	474
East Midlands	69	8	???	12	532
West Midlands	68	8	???	14	505
London	71	12	8	8	740
South East	68	10	12	9	658
South West	62	9	14	14	517

Income and tax assessment
Table 13

	Distribution of income liable to assessment for tax, 2002/03					
	Percentage of taxpayers in each annual income range					
	£4,615 to £4,999	£5,000 to £9,999	£10,000 to £19,999	£20,000 to £29,999	£30,000 to £49,999	£50,000 and over
UK	1.5	23.4	39.0	19.7	11.4	4.9
England	1.5	22.9	41.5	19.9	11.8	5.2
North East	1.7	26.4	41.5	19.6	8.5	2.3
North West	1.6	25.4	41.3	18.4	9.9	3.5
Yorkshire/Humber	1.8	26.0	41.1	18.5	9.4	3.2
East Midlands	1.5	23.8	41.5	19.1	10.4	3.8
West Midlands	1.6	24.2	41.1	19.8	9.7	3.6
London	1.4	19.3	32.6	22.4	15.6	8.6
South East	1.3	20.3	36.2	20.2	14.1	7.8
South West	1.5	24.6	40.4	19.2	10.3	3.9

Income distribution
Table 14

Income distribution of individuals, 2003/04
Quintile groups of individuals ranked by
net equalised household income (percentages)

	Before housing costs				
	Bottom fifth	Next fifth	Middle fifth	Next fifth	Top fifth
Great Britain	20	20	20	20	20
North East	23	25	21	20	11
North West	21	23	20	20	16
Yorkshire/Humber	23	23	21	19	14
East Midlands	20	21	21	20	17
West Midlands	24	22	20	19	16
London	22	14	15	18	31
South East	13	16	20	23	28
South West	18	22	23	20	17
	After housing costs				
	Bottom fifth	Next fifth	Middle fifth	Next fifth	Top fifth
Great Britain	20	20	20	20	20
North East	20	24	24	20	12
North West	20	22	21	21	17
Yorkshire/Humber	21	24	20	20	15
East Midlands	19	21	22	21	18
West Midlands	21	22	21	20	16
London	27	15	14	17	28
South East	16	16	19	22	28
South West	18	23	22	20	17

Expenditure
Table 15

Total household expenditure in relation to the UK average, 2001/02 to 2003/4	
UK	
North East	-17
North West	-6
Yorkshire/Humber	-11
East Midlands	-3
West Midlands	-8
London	+19
South East	+17
South West	-4

National Lottery
Table 16

	Participation in National Lottery, 2001/02 – 2003/04	
	Percentages and £ per household per week	
	Percentages of households participating	Average household expenditure (£)
UK	51	4.40
England	50	4.50
North East	63	4.70
North West	57	4.20
Yorkshire/Humber	55	4.60
East Midlands	54	4.30
West Midlands	53	4.60
London	39	4.60
South East	47	4.30
South West	45	4.20

Regional Productivity
Regional Accounts (GVA per capita)
Table 17a

	\multicolumn{6}{c}{Gross value added (GVA) at current basic prices £ million}					
	1991	1996	2001	2002	2003	2004
UK	9,119	11,699	14,944	15,691	16,485	17,258
North East	7,560	9,396	11,552	12,136	12,805	13,433
North West	8,139	10,286	12,980	13,586	14,269	14,940
Yorkshire/Humber	8,097	10,263	12,806	13,510	14,284	14,928
East Midlands	8,507	10,776	13,325	13,950	14,682	15,368
West Midlands	8,231	10,605	13,361	13,944	14,624	15,325
London	11,620	14,633	19,169	20,438	21,582	22,204
South East	9,843	12,836	17,128	17,933	18,788	19,505
South West	8,314	10,669	13,621	14,312	15,019	15,611

Table 17b

	Gross value added (GVA) in billion £ and deviance per capita (2004)	
	GVA Total £ billion	GVA per capita (deviance from UK average in %)
UK	1005.4	0
North East	34.2	-21.1
North West	102.0	- 11.1
Yorkshire/Humber	75.2	- 11.2
London	165.0	+ 32.2
South East	158.1	+ 16.1
South West	78.7	- 7.1

Societal Data
Conceptions and birth rates
Table 18

	Conceptions by women aged under 18: by outcome			
	Percentage and totals for 2003 (changes from 1994)			
	Leading to maternities	Leading to abortions	Total number	Rate per 1,000 population
England and Wales	54.3 (-2.7)	45.7 (+2.7)	42,162 (+134)	42.3 (-2.8)
North East	58.5 (-4.6)	41.5 (+4.6)	2,613 (-53)	52.1 (-3.2)
North West	58.1 (-2.0)	41.9 (+2.0)	6,159 (-124)	45.0 (-3.8)
Yorkshire/Humber	61.1 (+0.2)	38.9 (-0.2)	4,589 (-28)	46.8 (-4.2)
London	41.3 (-5.4)	58.7 (+5.4)	6,467 (+492)	50.8 (+0.3)
South East	51.7 (-2.7)	48.3 (+2.7)	4,932 (-126)	33.1 (-2.8)
South West	53.4 (-0.5)	46.6 (+0.5)	3,139 (-32)	34.1 (-3.4)

Anti-social-behaviour-orders (ASBO)
Table 19

	Number of anti-social behaviour orders issued by all courts			
				Numbers
	2001	2002	2003	2004
England and Wales	323	404	1,040	2,643
North East	22	29	43	85
North West	43	139	339	612
Yorkshire/Humber	32	34	124	402
East Midlands	25	6	33	177
West Midlands	90	80	129	296
East	31	26	85	210
London	13	19	95	293
South East	33	49	85	287
South West	29	10	48	193

Crime and Justice (recorded crimes)
Offences committed against households
Table 20

	Offences committed against households, 2004/05			
	Offences per 10,000 households			
	Vandalism	Burglary	Vehicle thefts	All household offences
England and Wales	1,125	331	1,068	2,978
North East	900	317	928	2,560
North West	1,400	404	1,263	3,481
Yorkshire/Humber	820	404	1,313	3,120
East Midlands	1,166	332	906	2,863
West Midlands	1,185	336	1,061	2,971
London	1,007	426	1,691	3,184
South East	1,306	283	842	3,015
South West	1,099	278	871	2,830
	Percentage of households victimised at least once			
	Vandalism	Burglary	Vehicle thefts	All household offences
England and Wales	7.1	2.7	8.2	18.4
North East	6.5	2.2	7.2	16.5
North West	8.8	3.3	9.6	20.6
Yorkshire/Humber	5.9	3.5	9.7	20.2
East Midlands	6.6	2.6	7.1	16.9
West Midlands	7.1	2.5	8.0	18.0
London	6.4	3.7	12.3	20.2
South East	8.4	2.3	7.0	19.0
South West	6.9	2.1	6.8	17.1

Alcohol consumption
Table 21

Alcohol consumption among people aged 16 and over: by sex, 2003/04

Percentages

Maximum daily amount

	Males			
	Drank nothing last week	Drank up to 4 units	Drank more than 4 up to 8 units	Drank more than 8 units
UK	26	34	17	23
North East	26	27	22	25
North West	26	29	17	28
Yorkshire/Humber	23	30	19	28
East Midlands	22	33	18	27
West Midlands	23	35	19	23
London	33	35	15	28
South East	23	42	17	18
South West	22	41	15	22

	Females			
	Drank nothing last week	Drank up to 3 units	Drank more than 3 units and up to 6 units	Drank more than 6 units
UK	41	37	13	9
North East	39	36	17	9
North West	38	36	13	13
Yorkshire/Humber	37	38	13	13
East Midlands	38	36	16	9
West Midlands	45	34	12	9
London	50	35	10	5
South East	36	42	14	9
South West	32	44	15	9

Drug consumption
Table 22

Drug use among 16-29 year olds, 2003/04

Percentages

	Used any illegal drug	Used any hallucinants	Used cannabis	Used ecstasy	Used any 'opiates+' substances
England and Wales	25.9	8.7	22.8	5.1	5.9
North East	28.5	12.3	25.0	7.3	5.7
North West	27.8	11.6	23.2	6.5	7.7
Yorkshire/Humber	24.9	9.1	20.5	4.7	4.4
East Midlands	22.7	6.4	20.7	2.6	2.9
West Midlands	24.1	7.8	21.2	4.1	4.1
London	25.3	7.7	22.5	5.3	9.3
South East	27.2	8.4	25.1	5.5	5.4
South West	28.3	9.4	24.6	5.2	4.7

Tourism
Table 23

Tourism, 2004

Millions and (£ million)

	UK residents		Overseas residents	
Area visited	Number of trips (millions)	Expenditure (£ million)	Number of visits (millions)	Expenditure (£ million)
UK	126.6	24,357	27.8	12,930
England	101.4	18,960	23.6	11,343
North East	3.8	700	0.5	194
North West	12.9	2,337	1.8	558
Yorkshire/Humber	10.0	1,584	1.1	346
East Midlands	8.0	1,201	1.0	440
West Midlands	8.6	1,447	1.7	552
London	12.8	2,759	13.4	6,439
South East	16.6	3,006	3.9	1,467
South West	20.5	4,103	2.0	714

Works Cited

Eagleton, Terry. Review of *Typecasting: On the Arts and Sciences of Human Inequality* by Elizabeth Ewen and Stephen Ewen (New York: Seven Stories Press, 2006) in *London Review of Books* 28 (23): 9-10.

'Regional Trends 2006'. Online at: http://www.statistics.gov.uk/StatBase/Product.asp?vlnk=14356 (consulted 18.12.2006)

Schott, Ben (ed.). *Schott's Almanac 2007*. London: Bloomsbury, 2006.

Index

abolitionism 220, 222, 384
Ackers, James 208
Adams, Annmarie 206
aesthetics 22, 88, 96, 127, 129, 204, 239-243, 274-275, 281, 337, 358, 366, 372-373, 376, 385, 396
    aesthetic concept 25-26, 358, 363, 378, 381, 383, 385-389, 392
    aesthetic experience 107, 394-395
Ahmed, Akbar 170
Aickman, Robert 257, 269
Albion 220
Allen, Richard 332
Alsop, Will 229
Althusser, Louis 156
Altick, Richard D. 144-145, 147-148, 151
Anderson, Benedict 167-168, 208, 349
Andrews, Malcolm 241
Andy Capp 83
anecdote 339, 385
Appadurai, Arjun 193, 197-198, 204, 209, 331
Areas of Outstanding Natural Beauty 239, 246
Arnold, Matthew 139, 146, 384
Arnside-Silverdale 239
Arts and Crafts 244, 255, 259
Askey, Arthur 226
Assmann, Jan 273
asylum 165, 175, 182, 184
    asylum seekers 163-164, 166, 171-174, 176, 181, 183
asymmetry 21, 40, 44, 47, 50, 67
aura 271, 352, 366, 378, 385
Austen, Jane 17, 242

Northanger Abbey 242
authenticity 193, 203, 271, 282, 343, 363, 389, 398
    inauthenticity 398

Bainbridge, Beryl 93, 94, 101, 105, 111
    English Journey 94
Balibar, Etienne 146, 150, 167
Barnickel, Klaus-Dieter 76, 85
Barthes, Roland 150
Bartholomew, Michael 99, 107, 364
Basque Country 37, 42
Bassett-Lowke, Wenman Joseph 290
Batey, Peter 228
Baugh, Albert C. 76
Bavaria 280, 291
BBC 33, 52, 62, 338, 397-399
Beal, Joan C. 75-76, 78-80
Beamish 285, 289, 299
Beard, Geoffrey 244-245, 247
Beatles, The 85
Beatlemania 20
Beaufoy, Simon 85
    The Full Monty 73, 83, 85, 349
    (see also Cattaneo)
Beetham, Margaret 145
Belchem, John 25, 217-218, 235
Bennett, Alan 326-327
Benjamin, Walter 204
Bentley, Phyllis 82
Ben-Tovim, Gideon 228
Berry, Geoffrey 245, 247
Beyer-Peacock 288-289, 291
Bhamani, Payman 163
Bicknell, Peter 241-242, 244
Biddle, Gordon 281-283
Billig, Michael 168-169
Birkenhead 76, 221

Birmingham 33-34, 36, 74, 76-77, 96, 104, 151, 212, 258, 263, 268, 275, 350, 364
Black and White 205
black population 164, 166, 169-170, 173-174, 179, 181-183, 228, 234
Black, Jeremy 242
Blackpool 306, 368-369, 380-381
Blair, Tony 19, 33, 35, 41-42, 48, 58, 60, 63, 66, 176, 231, 261
Blake, Norman F. 81-83
Blunkett, David 172-173
Bogdanor, Vernon 41-42, 44-46, 50-51, 65
Böhmer, Sylvia 314, 321
Bohn, Chris 330
Bolton Abbey 295
Bolton, David 270, 276
Bond, Ross 61, 68
Boniface, Priscilla 305
Botting, Douglas 382
Bourdieu, Pierre 380-381, 395
Bower, Fred 225
    Rolling Stonemason 225
Bowness 242
Brackett, David 327
Bradbury, Malcolm 149
Bradford 76, 101-102, 105, 136, 370, 377, 383
Bradley, A.W. 45
Brady, Ian 328-329
Bragg, Melvyn 243-245
Brantwood 384
Break-up of Britain 35, 52
Brecht, Arnold 51
Briggs, Asa 193, 196
Brindley, James 263, 265-266
British National Party (BNP) 175-176, 178, 182
British Waterways (BW) 258, 260-262, 269, 272, 275
Britishness 18, 48, 54, 171, 309
Britpop 28, 325-331, 335-343
Brontës 382-383
    Brontë Country 286, 296
    Brontë, Emily 80-81
    Wuthering Heights 80-81

Brook, George Lesley 77, 79, 82-83, 87
Brothers, Alfred 202
Brown, Ford Madox 193, 197-198
Brown, Fred 82
Brown, Gordon 33, 60
Brummell, Beau 151
Bryson, Bill 73, 86, 102, 105, 233
    Notes from a Small Island 102
Bulpitt, Jim 39-40
Bunce, Michael 98, 112
Burke, Edmund 25, 241
Burke, Peter 119
Burke, Thomas 96, 99-100, 106, 109-110
    The Beauty of England 99
Burman, Peter 284
Burt, Thomas 140-144, 157-158, 160
Burton, Anthony 270
Butcher, A.C. 286
Buttermere 243, 382
Buzzcocks, The 331

Cable, Thomas 76
Cain, P.J. 275
Calder, Angus 43
Callaghan, James 45
Campagna 241
Campbell, Beatrix 95, 108
canals 19, 26, 257-275, 281, 291, 364
    Bridgewater Canal 198, 263, 265-266
    Ellesmere Canal 263, 265
    Leeds-Liverpool-Canal 259, 263, 266, 268
    Manchester Ship Canal 201, 203, 263
    Rochdale Canal 258, 262-263
    Trent & Mersey Canal 261, 263, 265-266
canonisation 398-399
Cardiff 41, 43, 45-46, 51
Carlisle 76, 247, 285-286
Carls, Uwe 78
Cass, Eddie 348
Cassell, John 140, 144-145, 153
    Cassell's Family Paper 140, 142, 144-145, 152-158

Catalonia 42
Cattaneo, Peter 83
　The Full Monty 73, 83, 85, 349
　　(see also Beaufoy)
Ceausescu, Nicolae 65
Certeau, Michel de 307
Chalaby, Jean K. 145
Chandler, David 320-321
Chaucer, Geoffrey 77
Chesshyre, Robert 103, 105, 112
　The Return of a Native Reporter 103
childhood 329, 386, 388
Christianity 122
　Christian 24, 120, 125, 144, 164-165, 356
Christie, Julie 338
Chun, Dongho 225
Churchill, Winston 407
City News 202, 204
civil service 43-46, 56
civilisation 22, 25, 33-34, 56, 100, 108-109, 222, 270-271, 352, 369
Clark, Edwin 263
Clark, Gordon 252
Clark, John Cooper 331
class 23, 29, 48, 57, 80, 125, 131, 146, 160, 273, 329, 355, 363, 396, 398
　class distinctions 57, 121, 131-132, 320
　middle class 83, 108, 120, 122, 127, 129, 145, 148, 150, 176, 194, 198, 212, 248, 252, 329, 343, 351, 358, 368-399
　working class 28, 83, 86-87, 112, 127, 142, 144, 148, 194-195, 244, 306, 338-340, 343, 347-359, 368-399
Claude glasses 242
coast 22, 124, 126, 305, 370, 379
coastline 123, 379
Cobbett, William 157
Cochrane, Alan 35
Cockermouth 386-389, 392-393
Codell, Julie F. 197-198
Cohen, Leonard 332

Cole, Alistair 47
Coleridge, Samuel Taylor 384-385
collective memory 26, 29, 34, 38, 372, 377
Collier, John 83
Collins, Wilkie 149
'Colonial and Indian' Exhibition 205
colonialism 23, 78, 140-141, 154, 158, 205, 227
Commonwealth 234
commerce 24-25, 135-136, 152-153, 193, 195, 197-198, 204, 206, 208, 213, 217, 222-223, 227, 231, 372
Coniston 243, 384
conservation 239-240, 243-246, 250, 252, 262, 274, 282, 379, 386
Conservative Party 35, 41, 52, 55-56, 59, 61, 63, 65, 170
consumers 22, 24, 135, 204, 338, 340
Cornhill Magazine, The 139, 144, 153-156
Coronation Street 28, 83, 325, 328, 337, 347-361
Cossons, Sir Neil 230, 282, 285
Cottle, Simon 173
Council for the Protection of Rural England (CPRE) 245, 394
countryside 100-101, 249, 252, 258-259, 265, 353, 358, 378, 380, 386-387, 394
Coupland, Reginald 67
Coventry 96
Coward, Noel 332
Crinson, Mark 24, 196
Crumey, Andrew 341
culture 16, 20, 25, 28, 38, 56, 59, 61, 63, 112, 119, 121-122, 126, 134, 145-146, 153, 158, 166, 172, 198-199, 203, 220, 231-235, 308, 327, 349, 353-359, 381, 387
　folk culture 126, 354
　leisure culture 26, 263
　literary culture 153, 370-375, 377, 389, 395-396
　cultural identity 218, 227
　cultural power 154, 194, 398

pop culture 341, 343
popular culture 337-338, 344, 350, 352-353
sub-culture 326-327, 330, 339-340
Cumbria 247, 249, 379-395
Curtice, John 49
Curtis, Deborah 330-332

D'Aeth, Frederic G. 226
daffodils 20, 389
Daily Mirror 227
Daily Post 226, 231
Daimler, Gottlieb 288
Daldry, Stephen 83
  Billy Elliot 73, 83, 86 (see also Hall)
Daniels, Stephen 246
Darbyshire, Alfred 193, 196, 201-205
Davies, S. 226
De Toqueville 194
Defoe, Daniel 240
  Journey Through Britain 101
decentralisation 37-40, 42, 48
de-industrialisation (see industry)
Delaney, Shelagh 325, 327, 331-336
  A Taste of Honey 325, 327, 331-336, 343
Dellheim, Charles 198
Demhardt, I.J. 279
Derwent (locomotive) 288, 299
Derwentwater 241-242, 244
Devine, Tom 67
Devoto, Howard 331
dialect 21-22, 73-88, 108-109, 129, 154-155
Dicken, Peter 213
Dickens, Charles 146, 154, 221, 285, 313, 349, 371, 408
  Hard Times 146, 349
  The Uncommercial Traveller 221
Dikkers, Jan-Willem 314-315, 317, 319-320
Dimbleby, David 113, 373
Disraeli, Benjamin 407
Dodd, Philip 119, 349, 355
Dove Cottage 244, 376, 384-385, 389
Dowthwaite, Michael 244

Drescher, Seymour 220
Du Gay, Paul 144
Du Maurier, George 127-130, 133
  At the Fountain-Head 133-134
  The Viqueens of Whitby 127-128
Du Noyer, Paul 219
Dublin 45, 234
Durham 60, 76, 86, 99, 121, 140, 285-287, 289, 296-299, 370
Dyer, Richard 357

Eagleton, Terry 407, 409
Eastern Eye 172
Easthope, Antony 94
Ebbatson, Roger 111-112
Economist, The 63
Eden Valley 249, 287, 295
Edinburgh 41, 43-44, 46, 51, 373, 384, 397
Edinburgh Evening News 41
Edinburgh Guardian 144
Edwardian period 25, 225-226, 234
Edwards, J.A. 281
Egerton, Francis (3rd Duke of Bridgewater) 266
Ehland, Christoph 29, 378, 396
Elazar, Daniel 42
Ellesmere 261, 263, 265
Emigration 67, 169, 221
Enfield, Harry 231
Enfield, William 220
Engels, Friedrich 193-195, 208, 213, 347-352
  The Condition of the Working Class in England 347, 351
English character 99
English identity 15-19
English Question 15, 33, 47, 49, 53-55, 66-67
English culture 16, 20, 112, 166, 199, 327, 387
English Heritage 230
English Parliament 16, 44, 50-52, 54
Englishness 16-19, 22-24, 28, 57, 93-94, 97, 99, 106, 108, 110-113, 117, 203, 326, 349, 352, 354-355, 357, 360, 366, 371, 387
Epstein, Jacob 225

Esterbauer, Fried 38-39
ethnicity 38, 166, 170, 176-177, 410-411
European Union (EU) 52, 61, 64, 228, 248
Ewing, Winifred 47

Fabian Society 54
Fairfax-Blakeborough, J. 101
Fanon, Frantz 185
Fekete, Liz 172-173
financescape 197
Finney, Nissa 165, 182-183
Fiske, John 308
Florida, Richard 234
Flying Scotsman (locomotive) 288, 299
folklore 126, 285, 289, 354
Foot and Mouth disease 249-250, 253
Ford Cars 229
Ford, Boris 149-150
Forestry Commission 245
Forman, Nigel 40
Forest of Bowland 239
Foster, Ian 353
Foucault, Michel 135, 326-327, 341
Fountains Abbey 239
Fowler, Pete 338
Fowler, Peter 305
Fraser, W. Hamish 226
Frey-Vor, Gerlinde 357
Frith, Simon 333, 336

Gamble, Andrew 49
Gandy, Oscar H. 166
Garcia, Beatriz 233
Gaskell, Elizabeth 15, 57, 82-83, 89, 371-372, 377
    North and South 15, 57, 73, 82, 371-372
gaze 312, 366, 368-369
    imperial gaze 23
    male gaze 130
    romantic gaze 382-383, 395-396
    touristic gaze 121, 129, 369, 383, 392
gender 125, 135, 160, 318, 325, 328, 334-337, 344, 412-413

gender construction 22, 119
Gerdts, Abigail 128
Germany 51, 279, 291
Giddens, Anthony 159
Gillett, Philip 358
Gillies, A. A. 202
Gilpin, William 241-243
Gilroy, Paul 165-167
Gimson, Alfred C. 77
globalisation 213, 218, 272, 292
Goddard, Simon 334
Graham, Paul 309
    Beyond Caring 309
Granada Studios 349, 357, 359
Grand Tour 242
Grant, Linda 221
    Still Here 221
Graphic 124, 127
Grasmere 241, 244, 247, 376, 385, 389, 392
Gray, Thomas 241, 342
    Elegy written in a Country Churchyard 342
Great Exhibition 201
Greenslade, R. 165, 170, 183
Greenwood, Walter 377
    Love on the Dole 377
Grimwade, Peter
    All Creatures Great and Small 397, 399
Grossberg, Lawrence 338
Guardian, The 35, 42, 176, 221, 228, 234
guidebooks 94, 242, 248, 271, 369, 374-375, 383, 385
Guillory, John 398-400

Hadrian's Wall 239
Hain, Peter 172
Hair, Paul Edward H. 225
Halewood 229
Halifax 108, 370
Hall, Lee 86
    Billy Elliot 73, 83, 86 (see also Daldry)
Hall, Stuart 141, 144, 166, 169-170, 326
Hansen, Klaus 78

Hardy, Katherine 358
Hardy, Thomas 120, 335
Harker, Ben 353
Harrison, Frederic 146
Harrison, M. F. 202
Hartley, John 82
Hartmann, Paul 166
Harvie, Christopher 36
Haworth 286, 296, 376-377, 382-383, 392, 395, 398
Hayes, Louis 203
Hazell, Robert 49-55
Hechter, Michael 37-38
Hedley, William 282, 289
Heffer, Simon 52, 54
hegemony 60, 373, 395
    hegemonic struggle 15, 372
Held, D. 166
Helsinger, Elizabeth 374-375
HELP 230
Henderson, W.O. 218, 229
heritage 26, 48, 227, 230, 239, 249, 252, 257, 261, 264, 273-274, 392, 394, 396
    heritage industry 20, 26, 209, 263, 271, 274, 279-292
    industrial heritage 208-209, 249, 272, 280-292
    World Heritage 224, 230-232, 234, 239-240, 252, 285
Herman, Mark 83-84
    Brassed Off 73, 83, 86
Herriot Country 398
Herriot, James (James Wight) 378, 397-400
heterostereotype 305
Hetherington, Peter 62, 65
Hewison, Robert 273
Hewitt, Jan 22
Hiley, Michael 128
Hill Top 248, 384
Hillaby, John 96, 101-102, 105, 108-110
    Journey Through Britain 101
Hillier, Caroline 95-96, 104, 106
Hindley, Myra 328-329
Hoffmann, Detlef 266, 271

Hoggart, Richard 149-150, 350, 353, 355
Holden, Adam 209
holidays 247, 252, 257, 306, 310, 322, 380
Hollett, D. 221
Home, Henry (Lord Kames) 373
Home Counties 22, 34, 57, 93, 284
Hopkins, A.G. 275
Hopkins, John W. 45
Household Words 144, 146, 152, 156, 371
Howard, Michael 41
Howkins, Alan 118
Huddersfield 106, 108, 262, 297
Hudson, George 121
Hudson, Ray 306
Hughes, Arthur 88
Hugill, John 121
Hull 76, 95, 229
Humberside 18, 76
Hume, Mike 231
Husband, Charles 166
hygiene 351
hyper-reality 378, 389

iconography 331, 355
Icons Project 16-18
idealisation 104, 373, 381
identity 15, 20, 34, 111, 142, 220, 233, 281, 343, 347, 363, 409
    class identity 29, 363, 370, 373-374, 392
    English identity 15-19, 27, 305
    Ethnic identity 167
    gender identity 336
    linguistic identity
    national identity 139, 158, 163-169, 172, 183, 185
    regional identity 21-29, 38, 42, 58-64, 73-88, 111-113, 136, 158, 204, 240, 280, 321, 327-328, 333, 340, 358, 372, 379, 411
    spatial identity 25, 37, 140, 194-197, 283, 328, 374
Illustrated London News 125, 127, 218

imagined communities 28, 168, 349
immigration 165, 169-170, 182, 184-185, 234
imperialism 154, 197
industry 23-24, 103, 194, 196, 203, 213, 217, 227, 231-232, 268, 292, 305, 347-349, 355, 359
    de-industrialisation 19, 59, 135, 193, 195, 206, 272, 280, 314, 347, 350, 356
    industrial England 280, 366
    industrial heritage 208-209, 272, 280-281, 286
    industrial landscape 22, 26, 193, 355, 363
    industrial North 27-28, 85, 135, 226, 367, 369, 371, 377
    industrial spirit 118
    industrial sublime 24, 193, 365
    industrialisation 19, 26, 73, 100, 118, 140, 152, 243, 265, 275, 280-283, 291, 360, 383, 397
    post-industrial 135, 194-195, 212, 214, 227, 259, 263, 270, 280, 343, 349, 358
    pre-industrial 24, 193, 195-196, 202-203, 208, 211-212
Industrial Revolution 97-98, 158, 193, 219, 264, 281, 306, 363-364
Inland Waterways Association (IWA) 269-270
inter-war years 93-94, 103-104, 108-111
Irish Famine 223
Irishness 223
Islamophobia 173, 179

Jaguar Cars 229
Jalland, Pat 125
James Herriot Country 378
Jamieson, Bill 35
Jay, Anthony 33, 56
jazz age 352
Jeffery, Charlie 49, 55
Jenner, David 290
Jerwood Centre 389
Jessop, William 265

Jewell, Helen M. 95, 151
John, Augustus 225
Jones, Paul 232
Jones, Peter 36
Joy Division 331
Joyce, Patrick 198
Judd, Ian 377

Kames, Lord (see Home)
Kaplinsky, Natasha 231
Kearns, Gerry 223
Keating, Michael 47-48, 55
Kelly, Thomas 225
Kendle, John 42
Kidd, Alan 201, 203, 206
Kinder Scout 246, 353-354
Kisters, Jürgen 314
Knights, Ben 368
Knight, William Angus 385
Knock, Katy 62-63
Kohl, Stephan 22, 367, 377
König, Helmut 367
Krosigk, Friedrich von 37, 40
Kundnani, A. 163, 171

Labour Government 35, 40-41, 43-44, 59, 62, 173
Labour Party 18, 35, 38, 47-48, 52, 59-60, 63-64, 66, 309, 330
laissez-faire 253, 339, 366
Lake District 25-26, 29, 239-253, 259, 287, 349, 357-358, 370, 377, 379-396, 398, 400
Lake Windermere 242
Lancashire 76, 78-80, 82-83, 88, 95-96, 99, 107-108, 136, 140, 219, 285-287, 305-306, 337, 349, 352-353, 368-369
landscape
    aesthetics 239-243
    literary 149, 370, 372, 375, 382-385
    pastoral 98, 105-106, 258, 265, 272, 349, 355-356, 364
    picturesque 120, 134, 241, 384
    romantic 392, 398
Lang of Monkton, Lord 48
Lanigan, Chris 58-59

Lark Hill Place 24, 195, 206-208, 211
Larkin, Jim 225
Laurenson, Diana 148, 151
Lawrence, Stephen 173
Laxton, Paul 223
Leazes Jr, Francis J. 230
Leber, Mike 356
Ledger, Sally 125
Leeds 19, 24, 76, 106, 151, 154, 156, 229, 240, 259, 261, 263, 275, 282, 285-286, 296, 299, 370
Lefebvre, Henri 307
Leighton, Frederic 202-204
Leisi, Ernst 77
leisure 19, 26, 120-121, 128, 135, 148-149, 194, 212, 229, 257, 260-263, 270-271, 312
Leuerer, Thomas 21
Lewis, M. 183
Lijphart, Arend 41-42, 49
Lindisfarne Gospels 17
Linskill, Mary 22-23, 117-136
   Between the Heather and the Northern Sea 117-119, 123
   The Haven under the Hill 119, 125-126
   In and About Whitby 132
   In Exchange for a Soul 119, 128-132
literary site 29, 363, 375, 382-384, 390-398
Little, Daran 357, 359
Liverpool 24-25, 73, 88, 97, 105, 136, 149, 151, 217-235, 258, 283, 288, 299, 306, 314-315, 321, 338, 364
Llurdés, J.C. 281
Locomotion No. 1 (locomotive) 288-289, 299
Lodge, Guy 55
Löfgren, Orvar 368-369
Lorrain, Claude 241
Lowe, Philip 393
Lowenthal, David 273
Lowry, L. S. 28, 194, 347-357
   Francis Street 356-357
   The Lake 356-357
   The Pond 355

The Skaters 355
Lübbe, Hermann 38
Lübbren, Nina 124
Lucko, Peter 78
Lunn, Kenneth 326
Lynn, Jonathan 33, 56

MacCannell, Dean 395-396
MacColl, Ewan 28, 347-357
   My Old Man 353
   The Manchester Rambler 354-355
McCrone, David 61
MacDonald, Sharon 390
Mace, Renate 82-83, 87
Macherey, P. 146, 150
MacRaild, Donald M. 235
Mair, Christian 77
Mais, S.P.B. 96, 99, 106, 110
   England's Character 110
Manchester 19-20, 24-25, 28, 62, 136, 146, 149, 151-152, 193-214, 217-218, 222, 229, 258, 263, 266, 268, 275, 288, 291, 299, 325-344, 347-360, 364-367, 370, 377
Manchester railway 282-283
Manchester Weekly Times 204
Marquard, Odo 27
Marcus, Steven 194-195
Marr, Johnny 332
Martineau, Harriet 384
Marwick, Arthur 49
Mason, David 166-167, 180
mass trespass 246, 353-354
Massey, Andrew 44
Massie, Allan 66
Matless, David 246
Mawson, John 55
McAllister, Laura 48
McArthur, Tom 74, 82-83
McGregor, Ewan 84
McGrew, T. 166
McMillan, Janice 44
mediascape 27
Meegan, Richard 228
Mellor, Rosemary 213

memorial house (see writer's house) 377-394
mentality 170, 218
Mersey 25, 76, 219, 221-224, 261, 265-266, 364
Merseyside 74, 76, 218, 226-228, 231-232, 287
metropolitan 119-120, 126-127, 132-135, 156
middle class (see class)
MI5 354
Milburn, Alan 63
Miles, R. 167-168
Miles, Steven 59
Miller, Hugh 365-366
Miller, Jamie (see MacColl)
Mitchell, Austin 54-59
Mitchell, Don 160
Mitchell, James 60
Mitchell, W.J.T. 373
Modood, Tariq 166, 171-172, 176
Moore, Charles 165
morphology 73, 78-79
Morris, William 270
  News from Nowhere 270
Morrissey (Stephen Patrick) 28, 325-344
  Piccadilly Palare 340
  Margaret on the Guillotine 339-340
  Irish Blood, English Heart 341
Morton, H.V. 94-99, 107-109, 363-372, 375, 377, 380-381, 385, 392, 396, 398
  In Search of England 94, 97, 107-109
  The Call of England 95, 98-99, 107
motorways 229, 247, 270
Motte, Mark T. 230
Morrow, Albert 130
Münter, Michael 65
Muir, Ramsay 219-220, 222-226
Mullholland, Hélène 52, 65
Mullin, Chris 174
multi-racial 23
Murdoch, Jonathan 394
museology 24, 206, 208, 211

Musgrove, Frank 306
music scene 20, 28, 330-331, 339
Muslim community 23, 166, 171-173, 177, 183
Muspratt, E.K. 223

National Lottery 230, 261, 283, 397, 408, 427
national park 26, 239-240, 243-248, 250-253
National Park Authority 240, 245, 250-252
National Trust, The 244, 251, 258, 385-389, 393
nationalisation 268, 281, 285
nationalism 52, 165-168
nationalists 46, 48-49
Negus, Keith 327
Network Rail 284
New Brighton 27, 305-322
Newcastle 19, 24, 59, 74, 76, 107, 121, 136, 140, 174, 180, 300
Newton, Laura 128
Nicholson, Viv 337
Nidderdale 99
"9/11" 23
North East 18, 21, 35-36, 39, 45, 49-50, 54, 56-66, 163, 174-175, 179-180, 184-186, 410-414
North-East Constitutional Convention 60
North Pennines 239
North Riding 120
North-South divide 15, 22, 27, 57-58, 95, 97, 111, 150-156, 414
North West 18, 64, 174, 229, 258, 267, 410-414
North West Development Agency 229-230
Northampton 290
northern
  northern character 110
  northern identity 20, 24, 27-29, 34, 57-58, 61, 64, 83, 111-113, 236, 280, 327-328, 379
  northern speech 74, 78-80, 87
Northern Echo 60, 64

Northern Ireland 19, 35, 39, 44-46, 62, 413
Northernness 86, 88, 111, 135, 142, 305, 309, 357, 370
Northumberland 239, 246
Norton, Andrew 394
nostalgia 24, 26-28, 34, 37, 118, 165, 204, 228, 259, 275, 279, 283-284, 335, 338, 347, 350, 352-359, 366, 369-373, 385, 392, 395-396
Novelty (locomotive) 288, 299
Nowell, David 341
Nowell-Smith, Simon 144-145
Nseir, Tarek 35

Oberg, Arthur K. 332, 336
O'Brien, Peter 60
O'Donnell, W.R. 81
Ogden, James 266
'Old Manchester and Salford' Exhibition 24, 195, 200-206, 208, 211
Ordnance Survey 246
Orient 107, 154
Orton, Joe 332
Orwell, George 96, 103-104, 111-112, 146, 305, 349, 351-352
 The Road to Wigan Pier 103, 349, 351
Osmond, John 34, 39, 58, 95, 340
Ousby, Ian 383-384
Outram, Benjamin 263

Paasi, Anssi 38
Pabst, M. 279
Page, Norman 81-82
Paget-Tomlinson, Edward 268-269
paradise 97, 100, 102, 110, 349
Paradise Project 229
Park, Nick 83
Parker, Dorothy 332
Parker, Geoffrey 151
Parr, Martin 27, 305-321
 The Last Resort 307, 317
Parry, Richard 43
Patmore, J.A. 281
Patrick, Stephen (see 'Morrissey')

Peach, Esme 165, 182-183
Peak District 246, 353, 355
Pearson, Johnny 397
Philanthropy 197, 223
Phillipson, N.T. 43
Photie Man (see Wood)
Picturesque 241-243, 374-377, 383-384
Pilkington, Andrew 169
Plaid Cymru 59
Pocklington, Joseph 242
popular music 219, 327
Pordzik, Ralph 28, 396
postcolonial 19, 23, 39, 165, 173
postmodern identity 19-20
Potter, Beatrix 248, 384, 393
Potter, Clive 253
Powell, David 57
Powell, Enoch 170
Pratt, Marie Louise 119
Prescott, John 65, 172
preservation movement 281, 393, 395
Preston, P.W. 54
Prettejohn, Elizabeth 204
Priestley, J.B. 96-97, 100-102, 105, 108, 367, 377
 English Journey 100, 105
Prussia 51
public footpath 353
public transport 247, 380
Puffing Billy (locomotive) 282, 288-289, 299
Punch 127, 133
Pykett, Lyn 125

Queen, The 45

racism 23, 163-186, 234
Radway, Janice 124
Railway Heritage Trust 284
Railway Property Board 284
railways 26, 210, 244, 259, 267-268, 279-301
Rallings, Colin 60, 62
Ralston, J. 203
rambler 246, 353-354
Ramblers Association 122
Ramisch, Heinrich 78, 80

Ransome, Arthur 248
  Swallows and Amazons 248
Rathbone, Philip H. 223-225
Ravenglass 287, 290-291
Rawnsley, Canon H. 244
Rawnsley, Stuart 95, 108, 326-327, 329
Ray-Jones, Tony 311
  Hotel, Newquay 311
  Eastbourne 311
Read, Donald 140, 146, 151, 158
Read, G. 221
Received Pronunciation (RP) 77-78, 95
reconstruction 24, 51, 203-204, 206, 208, 211, 272, 284
referendum 21, 35-36, 39, 45, 54, 57, 60-66
Regional Development Agencies 55, 60-61, 228, 261
regionalism 33, 35-39, 53-61, 64, 197, 213
Reilly, Charles Herbert 222-223, 225
Rennie, John 263
Reynolds, Shelagh L. 249
Ribblehead 284-285, 301
Richardson, Tony 332
Ritson, Mike 341
Roberts, Robert 28, 347-348, 350-353, 355, 357
Robinson, Fred 61
Robinson, Guy 243, 246
Robinson, Mike 305
Rochdale 240, 258
Rocket (locomotive) 282, 288, 299
Rodriguez-Ocana, E. 237
Roebuck, John Arthur 139, 152-154
Rogan, Johnny 332, 336
Rolls Royce 18
Rolt, L.T.C. 269-272
Romanticism 25, 239, 259, 354, 395-396
  romantic gaze (see gaze)
  romantic ideology 123, 394
  Romantic Movement 243, 342
Rooth, John 263
Roscoe, William 222-224
Rowlandson, Thomas 242

Royal Jubilee Exhibition 24, 195, 200-201, 205, 208
Royle, Edward 151, 158
Rupp, Susanne 330
rural England 94-98, 104-106, 112, 245, 349, 367, 378, 394
Rushdie, Salman 171
Rushton, Edward 222
Ruskin, John 244, 384, 393
Russell, Dave 58, 67, 305-306, 311, 321, 326, 348-349
Russel, Stuart 341
Rydal Mount 384, 392

Sackville-West, Rita 376
Saeed, Amir 23, 166, 170-172, 182, 184, 411
Said, Edward 153-154, 156
Sanders, Andrew 372
Sandford, Mark 49, 55, 60, 62, 65
Sandling, Judith 356
Sans Pareil (locomotive) 282, 288, 299-300
Samuel, Raphael 205, 273-274
Schenk, T.A. 279
Schliephake, Konrad 26, 279, 291
Schmid, Susanne 28
Schmitt-Egner, Peter 37
Schubert, Christoph 21
Scotland 15, 18-19, 21, 35-49, 52, 54-55, 57-60, 62, 65-66, 100, 157, 262, 284-285, 379, 413
Scotland Act 1998 41, 45
Scottish National Party (SNP) 35, 59
Scottish Parliament 21, 35, 41-42, 44-47, 50
Sebald, W.G. 206-207
  The Emigrants 206
Sellafield Nuclear Powerstation 379
Sennett, Richard 274
Settle 245, 285
Shakespeare, William 15
  Richard II 15
  Shakespeare's Birthplace 376-377, 387, 389
Sharples, Joseph 230
Shaw, Eric 48
Shaw, Frank 226

Shaw, Keith 61
Shaw Stephen J. 370
Sheffield 76, 85, 100, 104, 139, 149, 151-153, 246, 275, 349, 369, 370
Sherlock Holmes 17
Shields, Rob 95-96, 107, 357
Shoard, Marion 246
shopping 24, 193-195, 206-207, 209-213, 229, 359
Shuker, Roy 327
Shuttleworth, Sally 371
Simmons, Jack 281-283
Simpson, Mark 329, 331-332, 334, 337, 340
Singer, Christoph 29
Sitwell, Edith 332
Sivanandan, A. 170
Skipton 122, 245
slang 83, 155, 340
slum 24, 194-196, 218, 224-225, 347-348, 350, 352, 356-357, 359
Smith, Adam 373
Smith, M.K. 280
Smiths, (The) 28, 325-344
   Cemetery Gates 341-343
   Girl Afraid 336
   Handsome Devil 339
   Hatful of Hollow 336
   Reel Around the Fountain 336
   Still Ill 326
   Suffer Little Children 328, 330
   The Queen is Dead 328
   These Things Take Time 331, 335
   This Night Has Opened My Eyes 333
Smout, T.C. 241
Snell, K.D.M. 126
soap opera 28, 83, 325, 328, 338, 347-348, 357-360
South East 49, 54, 410-412
South West 410-412
Southey, Robert 384
Southwart, Elizabeth 382
space 24, 43, 96, 98, 101, 109-112, 118, 123, 156, 159-160, 195, 211, 218, 233, 274, 307, 310, 312, 314, 321, 325-328, 334, 372-373, 381, 387, 414
   biographical space 29, 389, 392
   commercial space 224, 232
   cultural space 28-29, 331-332, 340-341, 343
   emblematic 27, 314
   English space 105-106
   feminine space 118
   literary space 377
   representational space 27, 307
spatial practices 307, 311
Spectator, The 165
Spitfire 17
Squire, Shelagh 248
Squires, Roger W. 269-270
Staffordshire 219
Standard English 78-80, 84-85, 87-88
Steed, Michael 40
Stephenson, Robert and George 282, 286, 288
stigmatisation 173, 369
Stinshoff, Richard 26, 275, 291
Stobart, Jon 222
Stonehenge 17
Stratford-upon-Avon 376, 378
Stratton, Michael 284
Sturm, Roland 41
sublime 24-25, 124, 193, 241, 275, 358, 365, 383, 384
Suggitt, Gordon 281
Suliman, Annisa 23
Sun, The 173, 175
Sunday Magazine 130-132
Sutcliff, Frank Meadow 128-129
Sutton, Keith 26
Sutton, Mike 93
Symonds, Henry Herbert 245
syntax 73, 78-79

Tatler 228
Taylor, John Russell 332
Taylor, Paul 354
Taylor, Peter J. 34-35
Tebbutt, Melanie 246
technoscape 197, 213
Teesside 121
television (TV) 212, 328, 337, 398

Telford, Thomas 263
temporal zones 372
Thatcher, Margaret 86, 170, 176, 261, 338-340
  Thatcherism 15, 27, 58, 227, 251, 305-322
Theroux, Paul 102, 105
Thirsk 397-398
Thompson, John B. 159
Thrasher, Michael 60, 62
Three Peaks 243
Tickell, Adam 60, 63-64
Times, The 139, 153, 165
Todd, Loreto 81
Tomaney, John 38, 50, 58, 60-61, 67
Tönnies, Merle 27
topography 22, 385, 390
tourism 22, 26, 29, 132, 228, 231, 241-245, 249-252, 281, 308, 368, 380-383, 386-387, 392, 395-396
  tourist destination 22, 134
  tourist industry 135, 239
  touristic experience 376
tradition 24, 28, 37, 43-44, 47, 108-112, 133, 151, 198, 203, 211, 273, 309, 311, 330, 340-342, 365, 369
transculturation 119, 331
  transcultural communities 20
travelogue 22, 94-95, 104, 106, 112, 154, 269, 365-367, 369, 371-372, 383, 392
Treaty of Union of 1707 44, 47
Trench, Alan 43
Trentmann, Frank 354
Trudgill, Peter 73-80, 88
Turner, Graham 34
Turner, Joseph Mallord William 243, 374
Tushingham, Rita 334

Ullswater 241-242, 244
un-English 24, 67, 94, 98, 105, 107-109, 217-218, 234, 364
UNESCO 217, 224, 230, 252
Umpleby, Stanley 82
Upton, Clive 79, 82

urbanisation 121, 156, 243
Urry, John 121, 123, 381, 390, 392-395

Valette, Adolphe 355
Van Dijk, Teun A. 166, 170
vernacular 22, 73, 82-87, 328, 373
Victorian period 23, 141, 151, 282, 378
Viereck, Wolfgang and Karin 78, 80
Viol, Claus-Ulrich 326-327, 341
Vulcan Foundry 287

Wahab, I. 171
Wainwright, Alfred 248
Wakelin, Martyn F. 84
Wales 15, 18-19, 21, 33, 35-44, 46-49, 54, 58-60, 62, 65-66, 239, 261, 281-283
Wales, Katie 74, 77, 82-83, 85-88
Walker, Ian 306
Waller, Philip 142, 149
Wallerstein, Immanuel 167
Walter, J.A. 381-382
Walters, Edward 196
Walton, John K. 244, 306
Ward, Paul 48
Warren, Tony 358
Wars of the Roses 15, 151
Waser, Georges 52
Waterhouse, Keith 332, 338
  Billy Liar 338
Waters, Chris 355-357
Waterson, Merlin 393
Watt, Dominic 88
Waugh, Edwin 83
Waugh, Patricia 156
Weber, Max 374
Weight, Richard 58
Weiner, Martin J. 118, 199
Welbourn, Nigel 281
Wells, John C. 74, 76-77
Welsh Assembly 21, 45-47
West, Thomas 242
Westall, Oliver 244
Westminster 21, 37-38, 40-48, 50-51
White, Andrew 121
White, B.D. 222

Whitby 22, 99, 117-136
Whitby Gazette 121, 132
white elephant 61, 63
White Paper 38, 45, 54, 62
Whitehall 35, 43-44, 55-56
Whitworth, Robert 263
Whyte, Ian D. 25-26, 243, 380, 383
Widdowson, J.D.A. 79, 82
Wigan 108-109
Wilde, Oscar 343
Wilks-Heeg, Stuart 47, 218, 232
Williams, Allan M. 306
Williams, Edward Leader 263
Williams, Richard 210, 212
Williams, Raymond 146, 149, 370
Wilson, Arline 222
Wilson, Harold 355
Wilson, Tony 331
Winchester, Angus J.L. 241
Wincott, Daniel 49
Windermere 244-245, 247, 250
windfarm 251
woman writers 126
Wood, Tom 27-28, 305-306, 314-322
   All Zones Off Peak 321
   Alsation beach 316
   Bloke looking cheeky girl 318
   Chelsea intro 318
   Cupsnog 319
   Double grope/ legover 319
   Girl at a slot machine 316
   Looking for Love 317-318, 320-321
   Last Dance 319
   Maybe baby 322
   Photie Man 28, 315, 317-322
   Pink hair swing girl 318
   Pleated skirt 318
   Pregnant women 315, 320
   Red haired girl 318
   3 Chatups 319
   Tired drink picture 320
   Tongue out 319
   Two touches (Chris Curry) 320
Woodcraft, Bennet 282
Woolf, Virginia 376
Wood, Victoria 337

Wordsworth, William 20, 25, 243-244, 248, 253, 368, 384-395, 400
   Composed A Few Miles Above Tintern Abbey 243
   Guide to the Lakes 243
   Influence of Natural Objects in Calling Forth and Strengthening the Imagination in Boyhood and Early Youth 390
   The Prelude 386
Wordsworth House 384-388, 393
Wordsworth Trust, The 389-391, 393
working class (see class)
World Heritage (see heritage)
World of James Herriot, The 397, 399-400
World War I 245, 268, 350, 352
World War II 26, 206, 213, 227, 229, 234, 239, 246-247, 268-269, 285, 356-357, 359
writer's house 375-377, 383, 389-390, 392, 396, 398, 400

Yale, P. 281, 284-285
Yes, Prime Minister 33, 56
York 76, 156, 300, 365, 370
Yorkshire 240-253, 284-285, 292, 296, 337, 370, 378, 397-398, 411-414
Yorkshire Dales National Park 251-252, 285
Youth Hostel Association 122